KU-267-359

LEARNING LEGAL RULES

A Students' Guide to Legal Method and Reasoning

Fifth Edition

James A Holland LLB, PhD, Barrister
Professor of Law, Associate Dean (School of Law),
Faculty of Law, University of the West of England, Bristol

Julian S Webb BA, LLM, FRSA
Professor of Law, School of Law,
University of Westminster

GRIFFITH COLLEGE LIBRARY
South Circular Road, Dublin 8
Tel: 4150490/1/2 Fax: 4549265

OXFORD
UNIVERSITY PRESS

340.1
HOL

OXFORD

UNIVERSITY PRESS

Great Clarendon Street, Oxford OX2 6DP

Oxford University Press is a department of the University of Oxford.
It furthers the University's objective of excellence in research, scholarship,
and education by publishing worldwide in

Oxford New York

Auckland Bangkok Buenos Aires Cape Town Chennai
Dar es Salaam Delhi Hong Kong Istanbul Karachi Kolkata
Kuala Lumpur Madrid Melbourne Mexico City Mumbai Nairobi
São Paulo Shanghai Taipei Tokyo Toronto

Oxford is a registered trade mark of Oxford University Press
in the UK and in certain other countries

Published in the United States
by Oxford University Press Inc., New York

© J.A. Holland and J.S. Webb 2003

First published by Blackstone Press Limited

All rights reserved. No part of this publication may be reproduced,
stored in a retrieval system, or transmitted, in any form or by any means,
without the prior permission in writing of Oxford University Press,
or as expressly permitted by law, or under terms agreed with the appropriate
reprographics rights organization. Enquiries concerning reproduction
outside the scope of the above should be sent to the Rights Department,
Oxford University Press, at the address above

You must not circulate this book in any other binding or cover
and you must impose this same condition on any acquirer

British Library Cataloguing in Publication Data

Data available

Library of Congress Cataloging in Publication Data

Data available

ISBN 0199254826

Typeset by Newgen Imaging Systems (P) Ltd., Chennai, India
Printed in Great Britain
on acid-free paper by
T.J. International Ltd.,
Padstow, Cornwall

*This book is dedicated to our respective parents and
particularly to the memories of Jim Holland and Sidney Webb*

Contents

Foreword to the First Edition

The Rt Hon Lord Templeman MBE,
Lord of Appeal in Ordinary

This book answers all the questions which a student of the law ought to ask and propounds answers to questions which every lawyer and every judge should ask himself from time to time.

The lawyer is a manipulator of words; this is an assertion and not a criticism. Language is the means of disclosing facts, expressing ideas, and applying principles. The ultimate solution of any legal problem is to be found in the application of basic principles to ascertained facts. The difficulties which obstruct the ultimate solution lie in the selection of appropriate principles and the rejection of irrelevant facts. The practice of the law is an art and not a science because the applicability of principle and the analysis of complicated facts depend on the language employed. The judge resembles a conductor of a nineteenth-century symphony. The conductor and the judge must establish the main themes, eliminate discordant sounds, and present an harmonious whole. Modern litigation, like a twentieth-century symphony, suffers from the obscurity of themes and the tyranny of discordant sounds. In this book the authors set out to teach the art of conducting the law.

For the student the first task is to become well acquainted with the instruments of English law and Community law, namely, primary legislation, delegated legislation, judicial authorities, and textbooks. The first three chapters introduce all these sources of the law. The fourth chapter deals with the interplay of law, fact, and language. The authors illustrate the fact that the flexibility of words affords a danger to logic as well as an effective aid to explanation. Rhetoric and jargon may disguise principle and obscure uncomfortable fact. The fifth and sixth chapters are invaluable guides to the dissection and application of precedents—those themes which enable the lawyer and the judge to determine the presence or absence of compatible variations. The seventh and eighth chapters manfully grapple with the different problems of construing English and Community legislation. The differences are substantial; Articles 30 and 35 of the Treaty of Rome, prohibiting quantitative restrictions on imports and exports, enabled the European Court of Justice to establish a free trade regime which could only have been established by about four English statutes containing 500 sections and 15 Schedules and hundreds of statutory instruments. The interplay of United Kingdom law and Community law is explored, not always in agreement with the House of Lords. Finally, in Chapters 9 and 10 [now 10 and 11 in this edition] the art of reconciling fact, principle and language in English law and in Community law is explained and illustrated.

The book is aimed at law students but is valuable to the citizen who knows no law, the lawyer who has forgotten some law and a judge who fears that a just result may be buried under torrents of oral and written words. The book should enable all its readers to guard against asking a silly question and thus provoking a silly answer. The language of the book is clear and the style interesting and thought-provoking.

The authors make a new contribution to legal literature and, at the same time, illuminate and recognise old controversies.

Templeman
House of Lords

Preface to the Fifth Edition

Our aim in this edition remains the same as with the first edition in 1991, where we said: 'research, both here and in the United States, has shown that for many students, learning to "think like a lawyer" is the most important of legal skills; however, many also feel that it is not always sufficiently emphasised in the curriculum (see, e.g., Sherr & Webb, 1989:239–40). We have written this book in an attempt to fill the gap which we feel exists for a practical, but critical, introduction to legal method.'

Since that time we are pleased to say that 'Legal Method' has become an established part of most law courses in one form or another. As regards this book, we have been extremely grateful for all the comments we have received from academics, students, and practitioners and in this edition we have tried to incorporate these into the text wherever possible without losing sight of the most frequently occurring comment we have received: that the book is readable and user-friendly.

We have made three structural changes from previous editions. The first comes from views received from our own and other students: to use numbered headings within the chapters for ease of reference. The second change emanates from comments received from many academics who asked us to alter the focus of Chapter 7 so that now we have reduced the amount of material on how statutes are *drafted* and added in more detail on how statutes are *structured* and how a student new to law can approach reading them. The final change is that we have re-ordered the old Chapters 10 and 11 so that the chapter on 'Exploiting Legal Reasoning' now comes at the end of the book.

This book is now supported by a companion web site, which can be accessed at http://www.oup.com/uk/booksites/law. The web site will be regularly updated, and contains a variety of resources for both students and lecturers. These include: updates on recent cases and legislation; guidance on answering legal problems; guidance on essay writing; self-test questions for students; ideas for seminars for lecturers; and Web links.

Within these pages we hope you will find an attempt to demystify Legal Method; to show that, in fact, it probably is not so very different from (for example) thinking like a doctor, an accountant, or a systems analyst. This book takes a step-by-step approach to the mechanics of reasoning, precedent, and interpretation, with the support of practical exercises which are designed to enable the student to gain experience in, as well as knowledge of, the area. In the first edition to this book we set out some guidance on how to use the text, and we repeat that here.

Extracts from the First Edition Preface

Why Read a Book on Legal Method?

If you are new to studying law as an undergraduate or postgraduate student, the chances are that you are finding it (or will find it) a distinctly different experience from any previous education you have had; if not a disconcerting one!

This book is intended to help you develop both the learning and reasoning skills appropriate to the study of law. The most common problem a law student faces is not '*what are the rules?*' but rather '*how do I make use of the rules?*' Our text aims to arm you with the techniques required to support your studies of the substantive law subjects.

What this Book is About

This book is not about learning specific laws, it is about learning to study the use and construction of legal rules. Studying law at any level, whether as a specialist lawyer or not, is not just a matter of acquiring legal knowledge about 'substantive' law subjects, such as Contract Law, or Crime. It is also fundamentally about developing 'Legal Method', or what is sometimes called the technique of 'thinking like a lawyer'.

A great deal of mystique has built up around the idea of 'thinking like a lawyer'. We would suggest that, in essence, it is concerned with the way lawyers reason and analyse, and, in particular, the adoption of the rules and principles that they use in legal reasoning.

In law, reasoning is based on three things explored in this book:

First, it is dependent upon an ability to **find** and make sense of a wide variety of legal material including documents such as *statutes, law reports,* and textbooks (see Chapters 1 to 3).

Secondly, it is built upon the **interpretation** of *authorities*; and by the term 'authorities' we mean primarily *statutes* and reported *cases* that can be found in a law library (see Chapters 5 to 8, and 10).

Thirdly, it is also based upon an ability to **construct** arguments both about the *facts* of a case, and as to *how* and *why* a particular authority should or should not be applied in that case. Inevitably, this overlaps substantially with our second point. As the Oxford jurist (i.e. legal philosopher) Ronald Dworkin has said: **'legal reasoning is an exercise in constructive interpretation'** (1986: p.vii). That is probably as good a definition as any to send us on our way.

'Thinking like a lawyer' largely requires techniques of information-gathering and reasoning that are of general application. Indeed, we would suggest that much of what passes for 'thinking' is in reality a matter of style—of talking and writing like a lawyer.

How to Use this Book

This book can be used either to support a course of study in Legal Method, or as a self-teaching guide to the subject. We are aware that more and more people are now studying law by independent or distance-learning methods, and have tried to anticipate their needs, in addition to those of students on traditional full- or part-time courses. We would, however, say that the course of study laid down in this book cannot be wholly followed without access to, at least, a basic library containing some primary sources (law reports and statutes).

Unlike many legal texts, which are made up of largely self-contained chapters, this book adopts a narrative structure, which is intended to build your knowledge sequentially from Chapter 1 to Chapter 11. You are advised not to read the later chapters until you have worked through the earlier material. Having said that, there are two chapters which are more heavily theoretical than the rest (Chapters 4 and 11). These may not be appropriate material for all courses at either first degree or postgraduate level, and so we have tried to ensure that the material in them may be disregarded (or taken far more selectively) without destroying the sense of the rest of the text.

In order to make the text easier to follow, we have avoided the use of footnotes. All case references appear in the text. References to books and articles in the text are cited using what is called the Harvard reference system. This gives the name of the author followed by date of publication and (if appropriate) the page number, thus, 'Smith (1986:123)'. The full citation of references is listed at the end of each chapter. Some of those references are marked with an asterisk (*). This indicates a text which we consider particularly suitable for further reading; though you should (where possible) be guided by your teachers with regard to what additional reading is required for your course.

Before we begin, a final word of advice: learning legal rules is *not* like the substantive law subjects you will study as a student. Contract and Crime (etc.) are concerned with the rules and policies which govern specific areas of human behaviour. Legal Method, on the other hand, is about developing skills that you should apply to those substantive topics. It follows that because Legal Method is not a substantive subject, it does not consist of hard-and-fast rules and cannot be 'learnt' in the same way. Courses on Legal Method do not produce 'notes' that can be memorised. 'Thinking like a lawyer' is a technique that you must develop by practice. It is for that reason that most chapters contain self-testing exercises but, as we often build on these problems in the text itself we have not removed the answers from the main text.

Additional comments to the Fifth Edition

There is a common cry uttered by academic and practising lawyers alike: 'Why can't the law stand still for a bit so I can catch up?' The reality is that all areas of law are in a constant state of flux, and legal reasoning is no different. Some modifications have only minor effect, some arise from innovations in the use of technology, and some have major impact, such as the ramifications of European legislation and case law.

In writing the first edition we forecast that European matters and forms of legal reasoning would become increasingly important to lawyers in the UK and begin to dominate legal method. That has proved to be case, and there are now few areas of law where the student, academic, or practitioner can afford to be ignorant of the points contained, particularly, in Chapter 10. Equally, we originally included some material relating to information technology—an area that had not been covered in books like this before; but the rate of change here has been staggering. It used to be the case that students were taken on a library tour in their first week of studies, perhaps given some simple exercises to do, and then that was it as regards the basics of legal research. No longer. One glance at the range of web sites available to lawyers (see Chapter 2) illustrates the need to master IT skills.

The most recent change, however, concerns the introduction of human rights principles into our law via the Human Rights Act 1998. It, perhaps, has not had the major impact on our law that many forecast. Nevertheless its introduction was a significant development and it does affect every area of law you will study.

We have also seen over the course of the last twelve years a clear shift in styles of interpretation used by judges when looking at statutes. There has been a steady move towards what is termed a 'purposive' approach to interpreting legislation, so that the legal method you will be trained in is in many ways quite different from that encountered by previous generations of students. Much of this owes its origins to the influences of European Community law. And here we should make a further point as regards the style of reference to European law which appears in this book. Throughout the text, after much agonising and consultation (including seeking the views of the relevant European organisations), we have decided to refer to the law emanating from Europe as *Community* law (or *EC* law). It has certainly become more common these days to refer to the *European Union* but the concept of a European Union is wider, and more politically biased, than the idea of the European Community. Thus although these term are now often used interchangeably, we have settled on *Community* (or *EC*) *law* because most of the law we are concerned with relates to that concept.

In writing this fifth edition we have sought to preserve the strengths of previous editions. It is still our firm belief, as we noted in the 1991 Preface, that the study of law is challenging but also immensely rewarding and enjoyable; we hope that you find it so.

James Holland
Julian Webb
February 2003

REFERENCES

DWORKIN, R. (1986), *Law's Empire* (London, Fontana Press).

SHERR, A., and WEBB, J. (1989), 'Law Students, the External Market and Socialization,' 16 *Journal of Law and Society*, 225.

Acknowledgements

This book would not have been possible, let alone have reached a fifth edition, without the support of many people. In particular, we would like to thank our colleagues at UWE, Bristol: Dr Adrian Chandler, Carol Crowdy, Julie Hamley and John Horrocks, and Tim Angell. Our thanks also go to a number of colleagues elsewhere: Dr Philip Leith of Queen's University, Belfast, Professors Phil Jones at Sheffield, David Miers at Cardiff, and Nick Wikely at Southampton Universities, all of whom have provided valuable comments which have influenced the contents of this book at one stage or another. We remain indebted to Professor Geoffrey Samuel of the University of Kent at Canterbury for access to his translations of material from the work of Villey, cited in Chapter 11. We must also acknowledge the unsolicited but much appreciated assistance of those university and college teachers who have shared their experiences of using *Learning Legal Rules* with us. You have helped us greatly in the preparation of this new edition. Finally, we must once again thank everyone at Oxford University Press both for their enthusiasm, and friendliness, but, particularly, our thanks must go to Jane O' Regan for her tolerance and professionalism.

Last but not least, our gratitude also goes out to our students, past and present, who over the years have been the victims of our particular attempts to introduce legal method skills into the law curriculum.

We owe a special word of gratitude to The Rt Hon Lord Templeman MBE, former Lord of Appeal in Ordinary, for agreeing to write the Foreword to this book; and for the continuing interest he has shown in our approach to the development of legal method.

The authors and publishers also wish to thank the following for permission to reprint copyright material: Butterworth & Co. (Publishers) Ltd for extracts from the *All England Law Reports*; The Controller of Her Majesty's Stationery Office for an extract from *Statutes in Force*; The Incorporated Council of Law Reporting for England and Wales for permission to reproduce *DPP* v *Bull* [1994], and Sweet & Maxwell Ltd for permission to extract *Pierrel* v *Ministero della Sanità* [1995] from *Common Market Law Reports*.

Table of Cases

1
Understanding the Law

1.1 Introduction

This first chapter sets out to introduce some fundamentals that will underpin your understanding of Legal Method. We do this by introducing you to the main sources of law that you will become familiar with as you work through this book: primarily *legislation* as well as other 'informal' categories of legal rules, and *case law* as it is developed by the courts. We will also look at the institutions responsible for making and shaping our laws—chiefly Parliament and the courts—and consider the impact of Europe on English (and United Kingdom) law. As regards the latter, we will discuss both our membership of the European Union and the more recent incorporation into 'British' law of rights derived from the European Convention on Human Rights. But, first, we will introduce a simple problem to help us focus on some of the issues this chapter will raise.

1.2 A Sample Legal Problem

A friend who is a shopkeeper has recently received a consignment of camping and other knives, including a small number of flick-knives. She is concerned that the police may take action if she were to display and sell these flick-knives to the public, and asks you for advice.

How can you find out if she would be breaking the law?

Obviously you need to know the law relating to flick-knives, displaying them in shop windows, etc. How do you go about this?

It is easy to assume that the 'law' can be found in one book; that somewhere there is a book which will give you the answer to every legal question you might pose. If this were true there would be little need for lawyers! Clearly it is not true. So a fundamental legal skill must be the ability to find the law. It is the purpose of both this and the following chapter to set you on the right road. Before we do that we need to consider a very basic question:

1.3 'What is Law?'

At first glance this seems a very simple, if not a rather strange, question to ask. After all, as the poet W.H. Auden said, 'The law is The Law' and we tend to know it when we see it. But it is also a question that philosophers and legal theorists have expended many pages in trying to answer. Why do you think that is? And what answers do you think they might have come up with?

Some of the philosophers' answers, reduced to their most basic form, are:

- Law is a system of rules laid down by a body or person with the power and authority to make law;
- Law is what legislators, judges, and lawyers 'do';
- Law is a tool of oppression used by the ruling class to advance its own interests;
- Law is a system of rules grounded on fundamental principles of morality.

Each of these characterisations has the capacity to tell us something useful about the nature of 'law' and how it operates—at least within 'Western' legal systems; whether each (or any of them) offers 'the truth' about law is a different question, and not one that we intend to dwell on here. We think 'what is law' is a useful question for *our* purposes for at least three reasons.

First, at its simplest, the ability to find the law presupposes that we know how to identify it: this leads us back to that fundamental question: 'what is law?' This chapter answers that question by looking at the 'institutional' sources of law, i.e. the bodies that have the power to make or interpret rules that have the authority of law. This is the easiest way of beginning to define 'law', and the most practical, though it is not the only way.

Secondly, even asking the question obliges us to think about how we conceptualise complex phenomena like 'law'. Being able to conceptualise a phenomenon and describe it in language is a crucial step on the path to understanding that thing and the ideas and beliefs which shape and are shaped by it. Our third reason for asking the question also flows from this: namely, that understanding in turn helps us to determine how we should make sensible or reasoned choices about what constitutes law in any given situation. This too can be a complex issue for philosophy, but it is also of real significance, for example, in assessing the perennial problem of whether and how we can determine if a law is 'good' or 'bad', and if it is bad, what we can (or should) do about it. We will touch on some basic issues of conceptualisation in **Chapters 3** and **4**, on 'Reading the Law' and 'Law, Fact and Language' respectively.

In this chapter, we will take the question 'What is law?' in two stages. First, we shall briefly distinguish law from other (what we call 'social') rules; then we shall explain what we mean by an 'institutional' source, and how that helps us to understand the law.

1.3.1 Legal Rules and Social Rules

Law, in the sense that we are using it, is definable as a system of rules. It guides and directs our activities in much of day-to-day life: the purchases we make in a shop, our conduct at work, and our relationship with the state are all built upon the foundation of legal rules. Of course, any society is governed by a mass of other rules which are not laws in the formal sense, but merely social conventions—perceptions of 'proper' behaviour. In reality, these are also means of controlling social conduct, but the different mechanisms employed to enforce these rules reflect different social values regarding the behaviour in question. Thus, while most of us would accept that anyone stealing the possessions of another, or possibly someone selling flick-knives, should be liable to a penalty under the criminal law, we might be rightly surprised to see someone in court for eating peas off their knife! Regulating the latter is not really so important to our society as to require the force of law.

Why some rules should be given the force of law and others not is another of those philosophical questions to which we do not have a full answer. Law certainly is not the same everywhere; it will reflect different values in different cultures and different epochs. Take laws governing adultery for example; in modern English law, a person who has a sexual relationship with another's spouse will incur no legal penalty (though he or she may end up being cited in a divorce case). In Islamic law, the *Qur'an* prohibits adultery by making it a crime, and subjects the parties to the *hudud* punishment of flogging or stoning (though the evidential requirements are so stringent that, unless the adultery is confessed, it is unusual for the full punishment to be handed out); in Ancient Greece, to give a historical example, a man who seduced another man's wife could face a claim for compensation, since he had violated the 'property' rights of his lover's husband. In a more deterrent mode, the seducer risked other physical penalties—the most widely used of which involved pushing radishes up his backside, or pulling out his pubic hair!

Thus, the different laws on adultery could be said to exist as a reflection of different religious or moral standpoints taken by the law; perhaps they also reflect diverse views of human sexuality, or the different status of men and women in a society. This cultural dimension of law is important in developing our understanding of why particular legal rules have developed, or why different 'legal traditions' (we will come back to this concept later in the chapter) have evolved in different countries. The cultural dimension has become increasingly important in legal education over the last thirty years or so. It is reflected both in the trend of studying law 'in context', i.e. in the light of the social, political, economic, or moral contexts that both shape and are shaped by the law, and in the development of specific subjects like Legal Anthropology and Comparative Law. One of the functions of this book is to provide a gentle introduction to the art of comparing legal traditions (see in particular **Chapters 4, 10,** and **11**), though we have not developed this dimension sufficiently for this book to constitute even a short introduction to Comparative Law as a subject in its own right.

1.3.2 The Institutional Sources of Law

Generally, laws are identifiable by the fact that they take a form which distinguishes them from social conventions. Their form tells us that they are derived from an 'institutional' source that is socially recognised as having the power to create law. Only laws so created can be said to be legally *binding* upon the individual, or even upon the state itself. Thus our first step in finding the law governing the sale of flick-knives would be to discover whether any of the legal institutions have had anything to say on the matter.

In English law there are three main institutional sources which we shall consider: Parliament, the courts, and the European Community. To these we can add a fourth, the

European Convention on Human Rights, though its impact to date has been more restricted than that of the other three. By taking them as our starting point, we are defining legal material by concentrating on the 'law-makers'. This is, perhaps, a slightly narrow basis. It does, however, emphasise the importance of what are often called the 'primary' sources, and distinguishes them from the 'secondary' or literary sources of law that provide only a commentary on or analysis of the rules (see **Chapter 2**).

1.4 Parliament

Parliament is significant for three reasons. First, it is the originator of what is probably the single most important modern source of law—that is, **statute law**. Secondly, through its legislative powers, Parliament is able to give law-making powers to other bodies, such as local councils and Government departments. This results in a form of law that is referred to as **delegated** or **secondary legislation**. Thirdly, Parliament's delegatory powers are being increasingly used to create sets of **informal rules** which operate within the framework of formal rules created by statute.

1.4.1 Statute Law

A statute is a document which contains laws made by Parliament. Each statute usually deals with a separate topic such as, e.g., the Theft Act 1968 or the Sale of Goods Act 1979. Statutes are now found in virtually all fields of law and regulate all sorts of activities. Some Acts affect our lives without us even knowing about them. For instance, how is the date of Easter calculated? For the answer to that one has to turn to a strange Act of 1750— The Calendar (New Style) Act. This Act determined many calendar calculations, including leap years and Easter. The strangest provision, however, came with the calendar itself. In 1750 Britain used the old Julian calendar. Many other countries had switched to the more accurate Gregorian calendar. There was a difference of eleven days between these calendars. When it was the end of September here, it was October elsewhere (as the Austrian and Russian armies discovered when they arranged to meet to fight Napoleon at the battle of Ulm and the Austrians turned up on their own eleven days earlier than the Russians). In 1750 Britain, the Julian calendar was wrong and a change had to be made. The question was: how? The Act provided the answer by stating that 2 September 1752 was followed by 14 September 1752. Eleven days were thus simply deemed not to exist! This led to riots in the streets; not least because some people were not getting birthdays in September 1752, and everyone was suddenly eleven days older.

Statutes are created directly by Parliament, following procedures laid down in both the House of Commons and the House of Lords. The details of that process belong more properly within a course on Constitutional Law, but it should be noted that a statute (also called an *Act of Parliament*) becomes law only after it has been introduced into Parliament as a 'Bill', been approved by Parliament, and has satisfied the formality of obtaining the Royal Assent. Once an Act has been passed it is unimpeachable, so far as English law is concerned. As Lord Campbell put it in *Edinburgh & Dalkeith Railway* v *Wauchope* (1842) 8 Cl & F 710: 'no Court of Justice can inquire into the mode in which it was introduced into Parliament, nor into what was done previous to its introduction, or what passed in Parliament during its progress.'

This rule is reflective of a wider principle which is referred to as the *Sovereignty of Parliament*. This is a rather legalistic way of describing Parliamentary dominance within the legal system. An Act of Parliament is the supreme form of English law; indeed until comparatively recently it could also be supreme for many other countries which were dependent territories of the British Crown, so that the Westminster Parliament has been significant in shaping much of the law of what is still described as the 'Common Law' world. The fact of supremacy is particularly important in Legal Method, since it is used to impose major limitations on the law-making powers of the judges, who will be reluctant to do anything that might be construed as usurping the law-making function of Parliament. The United Kingdom's membership of the European Community has almost certainly had an impact on the relationship between the courts and Parliament, particularly following the decision of the House of Lords in *R* v *Secretary of State ex parte Factortame (No. 2)* [1991] 1 AC 603; [1991] 1 All ER 70. We shall discuss this case further below (section 1.7.3), and in **Chapter 10**.

The growth of legislation has been a key feature of the English legal system over the last 100 or so years. It reflects the extent to which government has extended its control over our activities. This is particularly true of the legal developments that followed the emergence of the Welfare State in the 1940s. As a result, many important fields, such as employment, child care, and social security law, owe their modern existence almost exclusively to statute. This has, of course, meant that there has been significant growth in the volume of legislation actually in force. This is not just a matter of accumulation, because Parliament is also active in removing redundant or unwanted legislation from the statute books. Rather, there is clear evidence that the number of Acts being passed is increasing—by 20 per cent in the decade between 1964 and 1974 for example (Miers, 1986). If we take into account the length of legislation, that too suggests that there is an expanding statute book. Miers (1989) has also shown that the volume of legislation by this measure rose steadily from an average of 745 pages per session in the 1950s to 1,525 pages in the 1980s. All the available evidence suggests that this trend has continued unabated into the twenty-first century. Against this background there would therefore seem a fair chance that there is legislation somewhere governing the display and sale of flick knives.

1.4.2 Delegated Legislation

Acts of Parliament are not only a major source of law in their own right; they provide a legitimate means whereby Parliament can pass on, or delegate, its law-making powers to another body or person. Parliament's power of delegation has in fact been widely used for many years, but because its exercise is much less visible than the act of legislating, it is easy to lose sight of the importance of delegated legislation.

Most delegated legislation is published as **statutory instruments**; these are also sometimes referred to as *Regulations*. The volume of statutory instruments is considerable: 27,999 instruments were made between 1987 and 1997 (Page, 2001). Taking the important category of general instruments (that is, those that affect the general law, rather than some local or private interest) it is possible to say that, as a rough average, they have been passed at a rate of about 2,000 per year, thereby exceeding the number of Public Acts by a ratio approaching 20:1. Statutory instruments are not just quantitatively important. It is worth remembering that, in practice, the operation of whole areas of law, such as social security and immigration, is dependent upon a network of regulations, which will be of greater day-to-day significance than statute. For instance, the important rules governing employees' rights on the sale of a business are covered in the Transfer of Undertakings (Protection of Employment) Regulations 1981, a statutory instrument rather than an Act.

Delegation always requires the express authority of an Act of Parliament, which, in respect of any delegated legislation created under its authority, will be referred to as the *parent Act*. The parent Act will not only give authority to the process of delegation, but also will set the parameters of the delegated power. Sometimes these will be extremely wide and generalised, for example, where an Act provides that 'the Secretary of State may make such regulations as he sees fit', but equally they can be highly detailed and specific. For example, section 5(1) of the Social Security Administration Act 1992 required eighteen paragraphs and six sub-paragraphs to specify the powers available to regulate claims and payments of benefit. Practically, the ability to delegate carries great advantages, as delegated legislation can take effect more quickly, and deal more easily with technical detail, than statute law; however, Parliament does not maintain the same level of supervision over delegated legislation, so there is concern that those advantages are bought at some cost to the Constitution.

1.4.3 Informal Rules

Informal rules are mostly created by ministerial powers granted under the authority of statute. They go under a wide variety of names, such as Directions, Guidance, Circulars, and Codes of Practice. They are called informal because they can be contrasted with the formalities necessary to create an Act or statutory instrument, and because their structure and operation are also often less formalised. The bulk of this book is concerned with the formal rules, so we shall deal with informal rules in some detail here.

Do not let the term 'informal' lead you into thinking that these rules are unimportant. They play a significant part in the regulation of a wide variety of public bodies. Although it may seem rather odd that we should have such different types of rules, it can be argued that the difference in form is reflective of a genuine difference in function. The chief function of informal rules is to regulate official discretion. By discretion we mean, to quote Professor Galligan (1986:1):

> the extent to which officials . . . make decisions in the absence of previously fixed, relatively clear, and binding legal standards.

Discretion is of considerable importance in legal contexts. As we shall see, it is both difficult and often undesirable to make a legal rule so precise that there is only one way that an official could apply it. Few rules are so clear that they can be used like an on–off switch. The person using the rule cannot always say with certainty 'yes, it applies' or 'it does not apply here'. This means that officials must often resort to their own judgement in deciding whether a rule applies. Informal rules are instrumental in guiding officials in the use of their discretion, and can actually impose significant restraints upon it. At the same time, however, there is concern that the increasing use of such rules reduces the ability of Parliament and the courts to maintain a check on the activities of state bureaucracies.

To an even greater extent than delegated legislation, informal rules are a modern development in the English Legal System. The range of operation of such rules is almost as varied as the names they are called. Social workers, police officers, and social security officials, amongst others, all operate within a framework of such rules. Baldwin & Houghton (1986:239) have suggested that informal rules will fall into one or other of three categories:

Procedural rules: Many bodies lay down procedures for outsiders to follow— e.g. procedures for making a claim for social security benefit. Informal rules often play an important part in establishing these procedures, although, in practice, they are often the result of an amalgam of statute, statutory instrument, and informal rules.

Interpretative guides: These are 'official statements of departmental policy... expressions of criteria to be followed, standards to be enforced or considerations to be taken into account' (Baldwin & Houghton, 1986:241) which may be made available to citizens to inform them of their rights, etc. An example of such a guide is the guidance issued by the Inland Revenue to taxpayers.

Instructions to officials: Although akin to interpretative guides, these are often intended purely to give guidance to officials, not to citizens. This may mean that they operate as secret codes, though this is not always the case. For example, the *Adjudication Officers' Guide* used by social security officials is published and thus seems to fall between our two categories. It is intended primarily as official guidance, but can also provide useful information to the citizen on how the rules will be applied.

Informal rules do not apply to the public at large (so they would not be of immediate relevance to the problem we posed at the beginning of the chapter). Some are not published, while others are available publicly. Many will not be legally enforceable, but even here there is considerable variation. Consider, for example, the Codes of Practice created by the Home Office under powers in the Police and Criminal Evidence Act 1984. A particularly important one is Code of Practice 'C' governing the detention and questioning of persons held at a police station. It is not directly enforceable in the courts, by virtue of section 67 of the 1984 Act. This means that breaches of the Code are not themselves breaches of law; however, the Act does enable them to be used by a court to justify excluding any item of evidence that has been improperly obtained by the police (see, e.g., *R* v *Samuel* [1988] QB 615; [1988] 2 All ER 135).

In form, such rules will also vary considerably; often their structure is not so very different from the formal rules they support, but equally they may lack the detailed language of Acts and Regulations, and particularly the emphasis on internal definition often found in the latter. A particularly interesting example of the types of informal rule that exist is provided by the *Social Fund Manual*. This contains a two-tiered system of informal rules which are provided to officers of the Department of Social Security to assist in determining applications made by social security claimants for grants or loans for special needs. The distinction is made between 'Directions' and 'Guidance' in the scheme. The former, as the name suggests, have to be strictly applied by the officers, while the latter is intended only to be indicative, leaving the officer with some degree of choice in applying it to the claim at hand.

Differences in form, function, and language between rule-types are not merely a matter of esoteric interest, because those differences can affect decisions about the legitimacy of the rules. Thus, to take our example of the *Social Fund Manual*, the Directions, which are binding on officials, are couched in more detailed, imperative language, and possess a structure which is hardly distinguishable from conventional secondary legislation. The Guidance is less closely structured, less formal, and less peremptory in its language, reflecting its function of merely *guiding* officials in the exercise of their discretion. It is not surprising that the courts have used this difference in function and form to help determine the legality of such rules. When the Secretary of State published Guidance which used the mandatory language of the Directions, he was held to be acting in excess of his statutory powers—see *R v Social Fund Inspector and Secretary of State for Social Security ex parte Roberts, The Times*, 23 February 1990. To put it simply, guidance which directs officials to do something is no longer guidance.

Although legislation is extremely important, it cannot operate in isolation. Legislation requires implementation. On a day-to-day basis, that is the function of a wide variety of officials, whose job is either itself to carry out Parliament's commands or else to make sure that other organisations or private individuals are doing so. In this process, questions may be raised about the effect of a particular piece of legislation. Often these will involve technical questions of *interpretation*. On a day-to-day basis officials are constantly engaged in interpreting both primary and secondary legislation, but sometimes we require a more authoritative statement of what the law means. That process of interpretation is usually undertaken by the courts.

1.5 The Courts

The courts are not only important as interpreters of legislation, they are also the second major source of English law in their own right, through the development of the **Common Law**, a term which we first need to define.

1.5.1 The Meaning of 'Common Law'

This term is used in two ways:

> *To distinguish Common Law from statute:* 'Common Law' is used to describe all those rules of law that have evolved through court cases (as opposed to those which have emerged from Parliament) over the past 800 years. Despite the growth of statute,

English law is still generally understood in Common Law terms. By this we mean that the way in which we think about law, and categorise laws, is still heavily influenced by the old Common Law *forms of action* which determine what types of problem we now call 'contract', 'tort', etc.

To distinguish Common Law from other systems: Comparative lawyers have long used the term 'legal families' to group together legal systems which share certain common features. More recently, the term 'legal tradition' has become more popular as a way of thinking comparatively about different legal systems and cultures (see, e.g., Glenn, 2000). Tradition in this setting emphasises both the influence of (legal) history—the continuing presence of the past in shaping the law—and the complex, dynamic nature of legal culture. The philosopher Alasdair MacIntyre (1998) summaries this idea of a 'living tradition' as 'an historically extended, socially embodied argument, and an argument precisely about the goods that constitute that tradition'. In other words, 'tradition' becomes a way of understanding and explaining the norms and values that make up a particular conception of the legal world, and the ways in which that legal world embraces both continuity and change.

In the Western world, there are two dominant 'traditions' which we call Civil and Common Law (the letter being the oldest national law in Europe), though there are a number of legal systems, such as the Scottish, which reflect elements of both traditions. The term 'Common Law' is thus used as a means of defining all those legal systems in the world whose laws are derived from the English system. We use the term 'English' rather than 'British' with good cause. For reasons of history, not only Scotland, but also Northern Ireland, and even the Isle of Man and Channel Islands have evolved as separate legal systems from England and Wales (the Channel Islands, for instance, are part of Great Britain but not part of the UK or the EU). Although much of the legislation passed by the Westminster Parliament now governs the whole United Kingdom, there remain substantial differences in law and the legal processes that apply in the different jurisdictions that make up the British Isles. The process of devolution, which gives greater political and legal autonomy to Wales and Scotland, is likely to increase still further the variations in the law between different parts of the UK, albeit only in those areas of law that are within the competence of the new Welsh and Scottish assemblies.

The Common Law world remains extensive; it includes the Federal laws of the United States of America, and most existing or former members of the British Commonwealth, such as Australia, Canada, India, New Zealand, and Singapore, though in many such systems the English influence may coexist with elements of local customary law or even with other legal traditions, such as Islamic Law or Hindu Law (see, e.g., Glenn, 2000). This does not mean that these countries have all developed uniform responses to particular legal problems. To survive transplanting, the Common Law has had to respond to the different needs and conditions of each jurisdiction. This has often meant departing from the established (English) rules. Such variation is generally seen not so much as a dilution of the Common Law, but rather as a sign of its capacity to adapt (see, e.g., *per* Lord Diplock in *Cassell* v *Broome* [1972] AC 1027 at 1127; [1972] 1 All ER 801 at 871; *per* Lord Lloyd in the New Zealand case of *Invercargill City Council* v *Hamlin* [1996] 1 All ER 756 at 764–5). Courts, legislators, and lawyers in the Common Law world still share a more or less common approach to legal reasoning, and, as Lord Lloyd put it in *Invercargill*, a willingness to learn from each other. For example, it is not that uncommon, particularly in areas where the law is uncertain, for judges to refer to decisions from several Common Law jurisdictions, thereby enabling them to analyse a range of potential solutions to the problem.

1.5.2 The Contrast with 'Civil Law'

The term Civil Law describes those systems which have developed out of the Romano-Germanic legal tradition of continental Europe. It is the Civil Law tradition which dominates within the present European Community. Of the fifteen Member states, only two, the Republic of Ireland and the United Kingdom (subject to the *caveat* already noted), belong to the Common Law world (and of the other thirteen states which anticipate joining soon, none is a Common Law country either). As large sections of this book will be concerned with comparative issues between English and 'European' Law, it is worth taking a brief excursion at this point to highlight some of the features of these two legal traditions.

Underlying a number of practical variations there is, ultimately, a rather different way of thinking about law within each tradition. In Civilian systems (as they are called) one can conventionally identify a higher level of conceptualisation, reflected in a theoretically complex 'institutional basis' of Civil Law (see, e.g., Stein, 1984). This is sometimes said to create a more 'scientific' or rational legal system than the highly pragmatic tradition of the Common Law (cf. **Chapter 10** of this book). This has a number of practical implications.

First, it can be said that our dependence upon descriptive factual categories (the forms of action) may actually hold back new developments in English law, because we do not have the conceptual apparatus to incorporate change easily. This is sometimes seen as the key difference between the English and Roman traditions (e.g. Samuel, 1990).

Secondly, the modern Civil Law tradition is chiefly based upon principles of *codified* law. The modern process of codification in Europe is one that can be traced back to about the eighteenth century, though the structure of most Western European legal codes owes a major debt to the thinking of the ancient Roman lawyers, and particularly to the *Corpus Iuris Civilis* (meaning literally, 'the body of civil law') of the Emperor Justinian, who ruled from AD 527 to AD 565. The assumption underlying a codified legal system is that it is possible to create a set of texts containing an authoritative statement of the law, usually in the form of Civil and Criminal 'Codes', or sub-divisions thereof. Although English lawyers also talk about 'codifying' legislation, the term is used to mean rather different things in Common as opposed to Civil Law systems.

In the Common Law, a codifying Act is primarily a tidying-up operation. It is a piece of legislation which brings together all the existing law on a topic, both statute and case law, and converts it into a single entity—the codifying Act. An oft-cited example is the original Sale of Goods Act of 1893. The aim of tidying-up is one which codifying Acts share with the continental codes. However, by contrast with the continent, codification in England has been used as a limited means of imposing legislative coherence on a particularly problematic area of law, such as the sale of goods or the law relating to theft. What English codifications have not done is to produce a complete restatement of the whole of, say, Commercial or Criminal Law in a statutory form. Yet it is precisely the latter approach that has been adopted in the majority of Civilian systems. The codification of the English Criminal Law was first proposed by the Law Commission in its Report of 1985. However, its approach (see, e.g., Law Commission, 1992) has been to advance a far more gradual and particularistic codification process than originally envisaged (see generally de Búrca & Gardner, 1990; Gardner, 1992). This seems to suggest that we still have a long way to go before English lawyers are prepared to use codification as anything other than a discrete solution to a specific problem. For the English, codification has never been the key mechanism for organising and conceptualising the rules of law that go to make up a legal system.

Thirdly, it follows that, in theory, codification reduces the role of the Civil Law courts to simply interpreting and applying the law of the Code. Common Law lawyers have traditionally argued that Civilian judges have not had the dual roles of their Common Law counterparts; that is, being both interpreters of legislation *and* custodians of a distinct body of case law. In truth, that difference has probably been over-emphasised, so that we are in danger of missing the significance of case law in continental Europe. In many European states, the law (or part of it) is not fully codified—German administrative law is one such example—and most countries have their own systems of precedent, some of which are not so far removed from English practice. Paradoxically, perhaps, the way in which the Codes tend to be structured leaves European judges with far more discretion in interpretation than their English counterparts are supposed to have! We shall come back to this point in **Chapters 7** and **8**; but, for now, let us return to considering the details of that English system.

1.5.3 The Court Structure

In looking at the English courts as a source of law, it is important to draw two basic distinctions. One is the distinction between *trial* and *appellate* courts; the other is between *civil* and *criminal* courts.

The function of trial courts, such as the county court, is to hear cases 'at first instance': that is, to make a ruling on the issues of fact and law (this is a distinction that we shall discuss in detail in **Chapters 3** and **4**) that arise in the case. This distinguishes them from appellate courts, whose function it is to reconsider the application of legal principles to a case that has already been heard by a lower court. Some appeal courts also have jurisdiction to reconsider disputed issues of fact—i.e. disputes about the events leading to the legal action. Thus, any one case may well be heard by more than one court before the issues are finally resolved. Rights of appeal can be a complex subject in their own right, governed by a whole set of procedural rules; the detail of these falls outside the scope of this book, and we shall only outline the general principles that apply.

Trial and appellate functions are often combined within one court; the system is not simple enough for us to say that court X is solely a trial court, while court Y is purely appellate.

Civil and criminal law are significantly different in their aims, and employ different legal procedures. This latter point is particularly true of rules of evidence, for example. 'Evidence' describes the legal rules which control what facts may be proved, and the manner of their proving, before the courts. If you were to study the Law of Evidence, you would soon be struck by the greater evidential restrictions governing criminal as opposed to civil cases.

The term civil law (as opposed to 'Civil Law' as already considered) is used to describe all those areas of law which govern the relationship between legal persons—i.e. individuals and corporations—such as contract, employment, or tort (itself an umbrella term used to describe a whole variety of specific wrongs such as negligence, libel, and trespass).

Criminal law, by contrast, describes those wrongs which are sufficiently important for society, usually through the intervention of the state, to outlaw as crimes, and to impose special penalties on the wrongdoer (such as a fine or term of imprisonment). By and large there is a fairly clear distinction between those courts having civil and those having criminal law responsibilities (what lawyers call *jurisdiction*). **Figure 1.1** provides a basic guide to the structure of the English court system.

Let us now briefly consider the role of each of these courts. Fuller details of the courts' respective jurisdictions and operation can be found in textbooks on the English Legal System (e.g. Ingman, 2002; Slapper & Kelley, 2001). The diagram gives the position as at 1 January 2003 (source: The Lord Chancellor's Department website <http://www.lcd.gov.uk/judicial/judapp.htm>).

The House of Lords

The House of Lords is at the top of the hierarchy of English courts. It deals only with appeals, usually from the Court of Appeal, but, by a special procedure (called 'leapfrog'), it may also hear appeals direct from the High Court. Cases are normally heard by five judges, or, exceptionally, by as many as seven judges if the case is felt to raise issues of extreme importance—see, e.g., *Pepper v Hart* [1992] 3 WLR 1032; [1993] 1 All ER 42 and *R v Bow Street Metropolitan Magistrate ex parte Pinochet Ugarte* [1999] 2 All ER 97. These judges are known formally as Lords of Appeal in Ordinary, or less formally as the 'Law Lords'. The Lords have final jurisdiction over both civil and criminal appeals, but hear few cases by comparison with other courts—usually some ninety to 100 cases a year. This is primarily for two reasons. First, the House of Lords will only allow appeals in respect of cases which raise points of law of 'general public importance'—that means that there must be some significant area of doubt regarding the operation of a rule of law before the Lords will hear the case. Such cases are relatively few. Secondly, the cost of taking a case as far as the House of Lords is extremely high, and this may deter people from exercising the rights of appeal that they may have, unless their claims are financially assisted by the state.

The Court of Appeal

The Court of Appeal is divided into two Divisions, Civil and Criminal. The Civil Division will hear appeals from the High Court and county courts. Cases are heard by a minimum of two, but normally three, judges called Lords Justices of Appeal. As at 1 February 2003, of the five Heads of the High Court Divisions and thirty-six other Lords Justices of Appeal, only

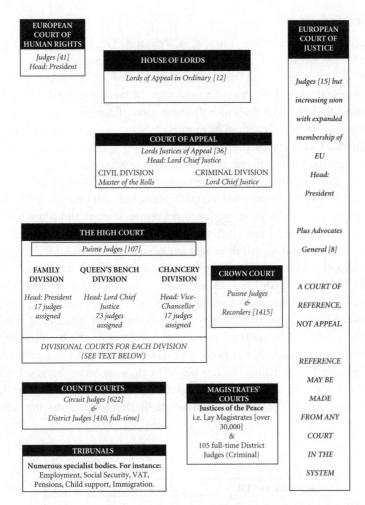

Figure 1.1 The Courts of England and Wales the ECJ and ECTHR

ten were women. For some years the first woman to be appointed (Dame Elizabeth Butler-Sloss) was also referred to as 'Lord Justice', but she (and the others) are referred to now as 'Lady Justice'. Female judges will tell you, however, that they are often referred to in all manner of ways. Thus, female District Judges should be called 'Ma'am', but 'Sir', 'Your Worshipfulness', 'Madam', and even 'Lovey', all betray various confusions or prejudices. The title Lord (or Lady) Justice is written as 'LJ' following the judge's name—hence 'Smith LJ'. The Civil Division is headed by a senior judge known as the Master of the Rolls. He (as yet there has never been a female Master of the Rolls) is referred to by whatever title is appropriate with the suffix 'MR'. The present incumbent is thus Lord Phillips of Worth Matravers MR.

The Criminal Division will hear criminal appeals against either conviction or sentence from the Crown Court. Criminal cases will normally be heard by at least two or three judges drawn from among the Lord Chief Justice, (currently Lord Woolf), the Lords Justices of Appeal, and the Judges of the High Court.

The High Court

This is the most complex of the courts to understand. The best way to grasp how it operates is to consider the trial functions of the various elements.

You can see in figure 1.1 that the Court is sub-divided into three divisions, each of which has a separate jurisdiction to hear cases at first instance (i.e. trials). These divisions are the **Queen's Bench**, which deals with the main areas of common law, such as contract and tort; **Family**, which deals with matrimonial cases and the wardship and adoption of children; and the **Chancery** Division, which deals chiefly with certain property, corporate, and tax matters. That seems simple enough, but now it begins to get more complicated. The English courts have long been important in the development and adjudication of both 'local' and international commercial disputes, not least because of Britain's (and particularly London's) historical importance as a centre of international trade and commerce. Because commercial law itself and the demands of court users have become increasingly complex and specialised, there has been a growing need for specialisation within the two divisions which have significant commercial law jurisdictions: Queen's Bench and Chancery. As a consequence, a number of specialist, commercial, trial courts have been created *within* each of those divisions, with judges being assigned specifically to those courts. The oldest of these is the Admiralty Court, which existed originally as a separate Common Law court in its own right, but was, in the late nineteenth century, amalgamated into a rather curious hybrid, the Probate, Divorce, and Admiralty ('PDA') Division. The functions of the old PDA division were dispersed across all three divisions when the present system was created. The other specialist courts are of relatively recent creation. Their location and jurisdictional responsibilities are represented in **Figure 1.2**:

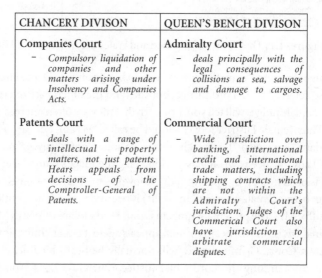

CHANCERY DIVISON	QUEEN'S BENCH DIVISON
Companies Court – *Compulsory liquidation of companies and other matters arising under Insolvency and Companies Acts.*	**Admiralty Court** – *deals principally with the legal consequences of collisions at sea, salvage and damage to cargoes.*
Patents Court – *deals with a range of intellectual property matters, not just patents. Hears appeals from decisions of the Comptroller-General of Patents.*	**Commercial Court** – *Wide jurisdiction over banking, international credit and international trade matters, including shipping contracts which are not within the Admiralty Court's jurisdiction. Judges of the Commerical Court also have jurisdiction to arbitrate commercial disputes.*

Figure 1.2 Specialist Courts of the High Court

There is also one specialist court that sits outside the divisional structure. This is the Technology and Construction Court, which was, until, 1998, known as the Official Referee's Court. It was a very restricted jurisdiction over building and engineering disputes, and, now, computer litigation.

In addition to these first instance jurisdictions, each division has appellate functions performed by a 'Divisional Court'. A Divisional Court will normally be presided over by two or three judges. The Divisional Courts of the Chancery and Family Divisions have jurisdiction over certain appeals from the county and magistrates' courts. The main function of the Divisional Court of the Queen's Bench Division has been to exercise what is called the 'supervisory jurisdiction' of the High Court; that is, the power to oversee the quality and legality of decision-making in inferior courts and tribunals. It also (occasionally) hears criminal appeals '*by way of Case Stated*' on points of law from the magistrates' courts and Crown Court. Following recommendations in the Bowman Review of the judicial review process, the Divisional Court of the Queen's Bench Division was renamed the 'Administrative Court' in October 2000. It now also has its own nominated 'lead judge' who is responsible for overseeing its work. Currently this is Mr Justice Scott Baker.

At first instance cases are heard by usually a single Puisne (pronounced 'puny') Judge, referred to as 'Mr Justice...' and written as, e.g., 'Brown J' (plural— 'JJ'). The title 'Justice Brown' is an American expression and not used in this country. As at 1 January 2003, there were six women judges (plus the President of the Family Division) out of a total of 107 sitting in the High Court. They are referred to as 'Mrs Justice', a status which seems to apply regardless of marital status—we do not have a 'Miss', let alone 'Ms Justice'. There appears to be no ruling on this as such, so, should the question arise, there is no reason why we could not follow the Irish precedent set by Miss Justice (Mella) Carroll.

The County Court

Whereas the High Court can trace its ancestry back to Norman times, the county courts are mainly nineteenth-century creations. Two types of judges sit in the county courts: Circuit Judges (the more senior) and District Judges. Work is divided amongst these judges on a set of procedural rules which are outside the ambit of this work. An appeal from the decision of a District Judge (the right to appeal is based on limited grounds) will go to a Circuit Judge. An appeal from the decision of a Circuit Judge goes to the Court of Appeal.

The High Court and the county court deal with the same sort of legal issues. The difference is that the High Court deals generally with the more legally complex and/or higher monetary value claims. For over a century, the jurisdiction of the two courts was determined by assigning a series of upper financial limits on the business of the county court. These limits varied between different forms of action (e.g. as between actions in contract and actions concerning land). Major changes to the procedure of the High Court and the county courts were introduced on 26 April 1999, following recommendations in *Access to Justice* (1996)—often referred to as the 'Woolf Report', after its author, the then Master of the Rolls, Lord Woolf. While much of the detailed application of these rules goes beyond the scope of this book, we will briefly consider some of the key changes in section 1.6, following.

The Crown Court

This court deals almost exclusively with criminal trials and appeals. Most of its case load involves the trial at first instance of the more serious criminal offences, such as homicides, serious physical and sexual assaults, and property offences involving loss or damage of a 'high value'. It is in this context that the Crown Court remains the only court in the English system in which a judge regularly sits with a jury. The function of the judge is to advise the jury on the law; the jury, however, remains the sole tribunal of fact, and it is for the jury alone to decide whether an accused is guilty or innocent as charged. The Crown Court has an appellate function whereby it also hears appeals from the magistrates' courts on issues of fact or law.

The Magistrates' Courts

Magistrates' courts are purely courts of first instance. The bulk of their caseload involves the trial of less serious criminal offences (in fact over 90 per cent of all criminal cases are tried by magistrates), though the courts also have a civil jurisdiction over liquor licensing, tax arrears, and some matrimonial matters. The magistrates' court is unique in that the great majority of cases are heard before Justices of the Peace—lay persons with little formalised legal training, though they are advised on the legal issues by a legally qualified Justices' Clerk. Legally qualified magistrates may sit alone to hear cases: they were formerly called Stipendiaries but now have the title of District Judge (Criminal).

Administrative Tribunals and other Courts

In addition to the formal courts, there is a plethora of administrative tribunals, many of which have been created only since the Second World War (though some, like the Commissioners of the Inland Revenue, are far older). They control a vast range of activities from the issuing of passenger licences to airlines, through employment disputes, to adjudicating on parking fines or the award of social security entitlement. Most of these tribunals have their own rules of procedure and are regulated by specific statutory controls. No tribunals have ever been created by the Common Law. The majority have relatively little contact with the traditional courts, though rights of appeal from some important tribunals exist, either to the High Court or to the Court of Appeal. Perhaps the best known tribunals are the Employment Tribunals (until 1998 known as 'Industrial Tribunals'). Appeals from these tribunals go to a specialist appeal forum known as the Employment Appeal Tribunal, and from there any appeal goes to the Court of Appeal.

In England and Wales there are a number of other local or special courts in existence, which are rather too specialised to merit discussion here. However, you should be aware of three other courts which, formally speaking, are not a regular part of the English court system, but are still of considerable importance to it. These courts are the Court of Justice of the European Communities, the European Court of Human Rights, and the Privy Council.

The **Court of Justice of the European Communities** (ECJ) is the final authority on points of interpretation of European Community law. It is not a court of appeal, but a court to which domestic courts or the European Commission can refer points of European law for clarification and ruling (see further section 1.7,). We shall also discuss its role and jurisdiction in greater detail in **Chapter 10**. The Court is commonly called the 'European Court of Justice' (ECJ), and you will usually see it referred to as this in textbooks and articles, though this is not its official title.

The **European Court of Human Rights** is the international court created by, and with power to adjudicate cases involving the application of, the European Convention on Human Rights (on which see section 1.6 and **Chapter 9**). It is a wholly separate institution from the ECJ, and the two should not be confused. Again we discuss the nature and role of this court more fully later, this time in **Chapter 9**.

The **Judicial Committee of the Privy Council** (normally abbreviated to just 'Privy Council') has a number of rather esoteric functions in the English Legal System, relating to matters such as Admiralty cases and appeals from the disciplinary decisions of the General Medical Council. Its jurisdiction has also recently been extended to include adjudicating on the 'legislative competence' of the Welsh Assembly and Scottish Parliament under procedures laid down by the Wales Act 1998 and Scotland Act 1998 respectively (see further **Chapter 9**). Moreover, as a relic of the British imperial past, it has held the function of a final court of appeal for cases from a number of Commonwealth jurisdictions. Much of that caseload has gradually been taken away from the Privy Council. Hong Kong has been the latest to remove rights of appeal to London, as a consequence of the colony's re-birth in 1997 as a 'Special Administrative Region' of the Peoples' Republic of China. Nevertheless, appeals to the Privy Council still exist in cases from Singapore (albeit only with the consent of parties to the litigation), New Zealand, and much of the Commonwealth Caribbean. Together with the British cases, these generate an annual caseload for the Privy Council which is not far short of that of the House of Lords.

The court's role continues to be controversial, particularly in Caribbean criminal cases, where it often constitutes the final court of appeal on death penalty cases. Calls for the abolition of its Commonwealth jurisdiction are perennial in most of the countries to which it still applies (e.g. for a summary of the debate in New Zealand, see McDowell & Webb, 2002:272–81). Arguments against the continuation of such rights of appeal include concerns that the Privy Council is too geographically and culturally remote, and perhaps too inclined to apply English legal thinking without taking sufficient account of local legal tradition. One the other hand, it is still argued by supporters of the Privy Council that its detachment remains a unique constitutional check on government in those jurisdictions.

Cases before the Privy Council are normally heard by the English and Scottish Law Lords. Judges from other Commonwealth states are entitled to preside, but that right is not always exercised. Given the status of the judges, Privy Council decisions may carry some considerable, albeit only persuasive, weight within the English Legal System, as well as being binding in the jurisdictions for which it remains the final court of appeal.

1.5.4 Precedent and the Common Law

The Common Law has not, as a system of rules, evolved from the totality of case law. It would be physically impossible to maintain records of and develop principles from every decision of every court that has ever heard a case. Rather, the origins of the Common Law can be traced back to the practice which developed in medieval England, whereby records of arguments used in the Royal courts were kept and circulated, at first unofficially, among the judges and practitioners. This practice gradually hardened into an officially sanctioned system of *precedent*, whereby important cases were recorded and subsequently used as authority for specific rules of law. As a reflection of that original practice, precedent is still created only by the superior courts—the High Court, Court of Appeal, and House of Lords, though some of the major tribunals have separately created their own internal systems of precedent, and where rights of appeal to the courts exist, they will also be bound to follow the precedents set. Precedent is, in theory, binding on all inferior courts (and tribunals). These include, chiefly, the Crown Court, magistrates' courts, and county courts; the details of our system of precedent will be discussed at much greater length in Chapters 5 and 6.

So, in advising our friend we would almost certainly have to take some account of case law, either because the legal rules concerned are actually a creation of the Common Law, or because the courts have considered the operation and effect of some relevant statutory provision. In advising her, we would not only have to know what cases (if any) existed, but also, by reference to the doctrine of precedent, assess what impact those cases might have on any future proceedings against her, which leads us onto our next point: what might those proceedings involve?

1.6 The Importance of Procedural Law

When someone goes to court, there are two kinds of law that need to be taken into account in managing their case. The first is what we call the **substantive law**, that is the specific rules which tell us what the law of contract or crime says about selling flick-knives (to continue with our example). The second is the **procedural law** which lays down the process by which a case is brought before the court, and how it is tried. The procedural law differentiates between civil disputes between individuals and criminal prosecutions brought by the state. Generally procedural and evidential rules tend to be rather more restrictive in the case of the latter, not least because an individual's liberty is often at stake. The details of procedural law are not widely taught in English law schools before the stage of professional training, but a basic knowledge of how cases come to court, and the systemic assumptions underpinning that process, is useful in understanding not just how the legal system works, but how and why cases get to court (and sometimes into the law reports) in the way they do. Let's begin, then, by contrasting the basic assumptions which underpin procedural law in the Common and Civil Law traditions.

One thing procedurally that virtually all Common Law civil and criminal courts (it is much less true of tribunals) have in common is the assumption of what is commonly called an *adversarial process*. This was described by Justice (1974:18) as:

> a fight, a pitting of strengths and wits against each other, a display of aggression mitigated only by the ritual of a complex set of rules and conventions.

This notion of 'trial by battle' is deeply embedded, both historically and psychologically, within English law. It has created a system in which, traditionally, it is the parties themselves who make the running in any case. It is they, not the judge, who select the facts and the legal issues upon which a case is to be fought. Traditionally, the role of the judge is thus, in theory, reduced to one of a passive umpire, overseeing proceedings and ensuring that the trial is pursued according to the rules of the legal game. Of course, this does not mean that the judge is a silent bystander; he is quite at liberty to interject, for example, either to test the quality of the legal arguments being put forward, to seek clarification of some point of fact or law, or to prevent an improper line of questioning. Even so, it is sometimes said that the system is of rather limited efficacy; that court cases are not about discovering the truth behind a case, but about ensuring procedural fairness. Defenders of the system argue that this way the law is doing the best it can. In *Air Canada* v *Secretary of State for Trade (No. 2)* [1983] 1 All ER 910, Lord Wilberforce put it in these terms (at 919):

> In a contest purely between one litigant and another, such as the present, the task of the court is to do … justice between the parties. … There is no higher or additional duty to ascertain some independent truth. It often happens, from the imperfection of evidence, or the withholding of it, sometimes by the party in whose favour it would tell if presented, that an adjudication has to be made which is not and is known not to be, the whole truth of the matter; yet if the decision has been in accordance with the available evidence, and with the law, justice will have been fairly done.

This traditional adversarial approach differs somewhat from the *inquisitorial* procedure in the majority of Civil Law systems, though those differences are often overstated. The inquisitorial process is typified by a far more pro-active judicial role than we would expect to find in a true adversarial system. The difference is most marked in civil cases. In criminal cases, there remains, as in France, for example, considerable emphasis on the spectacle of the trial, with its stress upon the examination of oral testimony presented to a full court in a public process, though in the case of serious crimes the role of the trial is diminished by extensive pre-trial judicial investigations. By contrast, the emphasis on public testimony is commonly much less in Civilian as opposed to Common Law civil proceedings (this is one reason why Civilian civil procedure is often described as 'bureaucratic' in style). Typically, it is the judge who makes much of the running. For example, he or she will be responsible for questioning witnesses and compiling a dossier of evidence; he or she will also be largely responsible for identifying the legal issues prior to the final trial. In many cases the judge will decide everything on paperwork alone and never hear from witnesses in person. As regards criminal matters, in France, for example, these functions will be performed by an 'investigating magistrate' known as the *judge de la mise en état* who has no precise equivalent in the Common Law.

The perception of the legal process is accordingly rather different. There is not an assumption, in Civilian systems, that the court's function is to vindicate the winner, to establish that one party has a legal right. Rather there is a more open and free-ranging search for 'truth'. This difference in perception affects the substantive procedures used. Because there is no perceived battle between two sides, there is less need to control inquisitorial proceedings by restrictive procedural and evidential rules (a point we shall explore in more detail in

Chapter 4). Whether it is more effective at finding the truth is debatable. As Feibleman (1985:34) points out, 'there is nothing in the world cheaper or more prevalent than the absolute truth. Everybody has one'. Nevertheless, it is common to draw quite a stark contrast between these two types of process, though in reality that is rather artificial. There have always been legal institutions in Common Law countries (including England) which adopt a form of inquisitorial process. Equally, there are Civilian legal systems (such as Italy) where adversarial procedure is much in evidence. There are in any event many specific procedures which have their parallel counterparts in both systems. Having said that, the emphasis upon an adversarial structure explains many of the specific concepts within, and reasoning processes governing, the English Legal System, as we shall see throughout this book.

That said, there are signs that (whether by coincidence or design) the gap is narrowing. This can particularly be seen by reference to the so-called 'Woolf Reforms' of the English Civil Justice system. We will now consider these briefly.

The progress of civil cases in England and Wales is subject now to a largely unified procedure governing both High Court and county court litigation. The rules are contained in two main sources: the *Civil Procedure Rules 1999* (CPR) and a range of supplementary *Practice Directions* issued from time to time by the courts to regulate their own procedure.

Proceedings are commenced by a claimant issuing a claim. This is a formal document submitted to the court and to the prospective defendant(s). Each potentially defended case is then allocated to a 'track' by the court. There are three tracks:

- a 'small claims track' for low-value cases which are normally dealt with by way of small claims arbitration in the country courts;
- a 'fast track' which is designed to deal expeditiously with the simpler, lower value cases (generally in the range of £5,000–£15,000), which will predominantly end up in the County Court; and
- the 'multi-track' which deals with the rest of the workload of the county and High courts—i.e. the higher value and more complex cases.

Many cases are managed according to 'pre-action protocols'. These prescribe a standardised range of steps and a timetable for the parties to bring a case to court. They are designed not only to ensure that there is less delay in civil proceedings, but also to achieve fuller disclosure of evidence at an earlier stage of proceedings than under the old rules. Regardless of whether or not a case is subject to one of the protocols, all cases are supervised by a judge, who is responsible for setting the timetable and managing the pre-trail stage of proceedings in conjunction with the parties. This increased emphasis on judicial case management makes our system look more like an inquisitorial one, though if one looks at the detail, there are significant differences still apparent. Moreover, examples of relatively high levels of judicial case management could be found, pre-Woolf, elsewhere in the common law world—in Australia, for example.

Taken together these measures were seen as critical by Lord Woolf to achieving his objective of increasing the efficiency of the Civil Justice system. First, they seek to ensure that cases are brought to court more expeditiously, because the parties are not only subject to a stricter timetable, but they also have less opportunity, and power, to use delay or other possibly doubtful tactics during the pre-trial stage to 'wear down' the opposition. Secondly, they encourage the parties to look more seriously at opportunities to resolve a case before it reaches court. They have achieved this in two ways:

- by loading more of the costs of bringing an action at an early stage (most litigators we have spoken to acknowledge that this has encouraged them to negotiate earlier, and to be less inclined to issue proceedings as a tactical device for getting the parties to take the dispute seriously), and

- by giving the judge managing the case more opportunities to encourage the parties to investigate settlement options: Again, this is an increasingly common trend across the developed world, as civil courts struggle to manage growing caseloads, and not a trend unique to the Common Law world. In France, similarly, civil procedure is being reformed to increase opportunities for conciliation and settlement within the court process (see Elliott & Vernon, 2000:130–1).

Following from this second point, the CPR has specifically given the judges powers to 'stay' (i.e. suspend) proceedings for up to twenty-eight days to enable the parties to use 'Alternative Dispute Resolution' (ADR)—see **Figure 1.3**, below—in an attempt to settle the matter. This power applies to all cases subject to the CPR, including even those public law matters coming within the jurisdiction of the Administrative Court—see *The Queen on the application of Cowl* v *Plymouth City Council* [2001] EWCA 1935.

ADR is an umbrella term which, in the context of the English Legal System, refers primarily to two dispute resolution techniques. These are:

- *mediation,* whereby a trained mediator, as a neutral third party, acts as a go-between, facilitating negotiations between the parties (see, e.g., Genn, 1999 for a simple introduction to mediation);
- *early neutral evaluation,* where a lawyer (usually a judge, or possibly a barrister) looks at the evidence in a case and presents their evaluation to the parties of how the case is likely to be decided by a judge.

ADR thus differs from court-based adjudication. The mediator or evaluator does not produce a decision as such, they are not 'judges' by a different name. They simply employ different techniques to enable or encourage the parties to reach their own private settlement outside the court. ADR is becoming much more widespread in the English Civil Justice system. A number of mediation schemes are now being operated in conjunction with the courts. Family mediation is widespread, and in fact has been increasingly used since its introduction in the 1970s. It has far less of a history in general civil proceedings, though a Commercial Court scheme has operated since 1993. Since the introduction of the CPR a Court of Appeal scheme has been established and a number of county court schemes piloted: for example, in the Central London County Court and the so-called 'Speed Mediation' alternative introduced for small claims at Exeter.

Figure 1.3 Alternative Dispute Resolution

GRIFFITH COLLEGE LIBRARY
South Circular Road, Dublin 8
Tel: 4150490/1/2 Fax: 4549265

The growth in ADR has some important implications for Legal Method as well as for the legal system more generally. The rise of ADR involves a substitution of private for public forms of dispute resolution. Mediated settlements are usually confidential to the parties and there is, by definition, no adjudication of a claim. Some commentators have raised concerns about the wider implications of this shift from public to private ordering. In the USA, for example, Professor Owen Fiss (1984) has thus argued that more private resolution of disputes reduces the power of law to articulate public values, to bring, in Fiss's words, 'a recalcitrant reality closer to our chosen ideals'. It might even be argued that too great a reliance on private and alternative forms of dispute settlement potentially reduces the opportunity for courts to establish points of principle through the public deciding of cases and the development of precedent. These are potentially significant criticisms of ADR, but at present they probably are not substantial problems in practice. In the UK at present, the impact of ADR is probably still not so great as to have a systemic effect of this magnitude. Indeed it seems likely that the costs of conventional litigation are still the greater disincentive to people exercising their rights and establishing legal principles over that 'recalcitrant reality'.

It is still too soon to be sure what impact the reforms to civil litigation introduced by Lord Woolf have had—or will have—on this adversarial approach. The reality of most civil litigation is that, pre-Woolf, there was already much more cooperation between the parties, and intervention by the judges, than textbooks would generally have you believe. Anecdotally, many practitioners suggest that the Woolf reforms may have done little more than formalise, and possibly speed up, that trend, notably by giving judges more extensive 'case-management' powers, and by increasing the pressure on litigants and their representatives to use ADR, rather than fight a case to the 'door of the court' and beyond. However, the Woolf reforms also strike at things such as the calling of expert witnesses, e.g., medical experts, engineering experts, etc., in some cases demanding that only one 'joint' expert is called. These sorts of changes may have a knock-on effect on how cases are argued—though they may never affect the real 'adversarial' battles which occur when litigants represent themselves.

Another consequence of the Woolf Reforms, of which you will need be to be aware, is that certain terms and phrases have been changed, apparently in order to make courts more 'user-friendly'. A law student, however, will have to be aware of both the new terminology and the old; the new because that is how the law is practised, the old terms because that is how the case reports prior to 1999 continue to describe matters. Many terms have stayed the same, e.g., Defendant. Here is a shortlist of some of the major changes:

Old terminology	New terminology
Plaintiff (*the person who brings the claim*)	Claimant
Affidavit (*sworn written evidence*)	Witness statement (in most cases)
Pleadings (*the legal basis on which the plaintiff is claiming against the defendant or the defendant is resisting the claim*)	Statement of case
Writ (*a formal document needed to start the case*)	Claim form

Interlocutory orders (*matters which arise before the actual trial, e.g., injunctions*)	Interim orders
County Court Rules and Rules of the Supreme Court (*the rules by which courts operate, e.g., time limits, papers to be served, etc.; included in 'The White Book' for the High Court and 'The Green Book' for the county court*)	The Civil Procedure Rules (*published by various publishers, including a new unified version of 'The White Book'*)
Mareva injunction (*an injunction which prevents the defendant dealing with certain funds*)	Freezing injunction
Anton Piller order (*an injunction whereby the plaintiff gains access to the defendant's premises to search for documents etc.*)	Search order

So much, then, for procedure and procedural reform. Before we close this chapter, there are two areas of European law which are having an increasing impact on the English Legal System, which we need also to consider.

1.7 English Law and the European Convention on Human Rights

The European Convention on Human Rights (ECHR) is an international treaty which was created in the aftermath of the Second World War. It has been signed by most European governments, including the UK, as a statement of their commitment to the protection of certain fundamental human rights, such as freedom from torture and slavery, freedom of religion, freedom of expression, and the right to a fair trial. The Convention is not one of the EU treaties and is no part of EC law as such. Its political governing body is a separate organisation called the 'Council of Europe'. All current EU members are members of the Council of Europe.

Whether or not individuals can enforce their rights under the ECHR within their own legal systems depends on the rules and structures of each legal system. Many, though not all, Western European legal systems are framed so that treaty obligations entered into by their governments are automatically incorporated into domestic (i.e. national) law. In that situation, a citizen could pursue a Convention right through the domestic courts. The legal position in Britain is different. Here, international legal rights can be directly enforced only where the treaty has been expressly incorporated into law. This normally requires an Act of Parliament. Although the courts and Parliament sometimes made reference to the ECHR in defining the scope of rights and duties under English law, there had been, prior to 1998, no express incorporation. Consequently, British citizens seeking redress under the ECHR had to rely exclusively on an international institution called the 'European Court of Human Rights' at Strasbourg. There have been a significant number of such cases on a variety of issues, including the freedom of the press; the rights of transsexuals to have public documents such as passports and birth certificates changed to record their 're-assigned' rather than 'genetic' sex; the detention and trial of 'political' prisoners in Northern Ireland; the use of corporal punishment in schools; and so on. Indeed, the British government has had a poor track record before the Court, having been found in violation of the Convention in a total of fifty cases (Greer, 1999:5); this has been one of the key reasons why the political pressure for incorporation of the Convention into English law steadily increased, though for many years neither Labour nor Conservative Governments had supported the move to incorporation as part of government policy.

That changed in 1996 when the Labour Party published an influential policy paper called *Bringing Rights Home*, proposing measures for the incorporation of the ECHR. This policy came to be reflected in Labour's 1997 election manifesto and its first legislative programme after that election. Consequently, after a sometimes rather bumpy ride through Parliament, the Human Rights Bill received the Royal Assent in November 1998. In addition the legislation devolving powers to the new Scottish and Welsh assemblies also contained provisions requiring those bodies to legislate consistently with the rights contained in the ECHR. The Human Rights Act 1998 (HRA) came into force in England on 2 October 2000. We shall explore the role of the Act in greater detail in **Chapter 9**.

The practical impact of the HRA is, as we shall see, quite difficult to quantify, though most commentators acknowledge that its potential is enormous. Not all of these comments have been positive. Lord McCluskey, in his Reith lecture, for example, warned that 'we are going to have to struggle to avoid being buried in new claims of right' (*Guardian*, 8 May 2000). In fact, the feared deluge of claims has not so far materialised. For example, only 19 per cent of cases received by the Administrative Court in the first fourteen months of the Act's operation raised HRA issues (see *The Administrative Court: Annual Statement by the Hon. Mr. Justice Scott Baker* at <http://www.courtservice.gov.uk/notices/divis/ACO-new-annual-statement.doc>). Nevertheless, for us, as lawyers, it creates a whole new set of concepts and rights which must be understood and developed through practice in courts and tribunals. But incorporation also has wider political and ideological significance too. Professor Keith Ewing (1999:79) has thus described the passage of the HRA as 'unquestionably the most significant formal redistribution of political power in this country since 1911, and perhaps since 1688 [the year of the original Bill of Rights]', while Sir William Wade (1998:532) had called it 'a quantum leap into a new legal culture of fundamental rights and freedoms'. As we will see, the Act has already had an impact on that part of legal culture we call 'legal method'. At the same time, there are things that the HRA will not do, partly because of the internal limits and restrictions built into the Act (see further Chapter 9), and partly because there is much that the ECHR itself does not do. Human rights remains a developing area of law, and many of our conceptions of fundamental rights have evolved and changed since the Convention was drafted nearly fifty years ago. There are new forms of human rights, some of which are not yet fully recognised or understood, and about which the ECHR is pretty much silent. These include:

- the rights of minority peoples, for example (see Gilbert, 1996);
- economic rights (so our seller of flick-knives could not use the HRA to argue that laws restricting trade in particular goods are an unwarranted restriction of her right to engage in a particular business) and cultural rights (Van Bueran, 2002); and

- so-called 'third generation' rights (Adjei, 1995: 34), which include the recognition of individual and community rights over the environment.

Whether incorporation of the ECHR will have any impact, positive or negative, on the development of such rights in English or UK law awaits the test of time.

Nevertheless, as we shall see in Chapter 9, just as the influence of EC law has gradually overtaken this book (as we predicted it would in the first edition), so too issues of human rights are taking on an increasingly pervasive role in shaping British law.

1.8 English Law and the European Community

The United Kingdom has been a member of the European Community (EC) since 1 January 1973. For three decades there has been a gradual, and perhaps irreversible mingling of European and English concepts within the legal system. The days are thus gone when anyone studying Law in this country could afford to concentrate only on English Law and the English Legal System. To this end we have dedicated **Chapter 10** of this book to the European influence and 'European Legal Method', though we have also sought to make some specific comparisons with Civil Law practices and institutions in each chapter. We have also, as here, tried to incorporate specific references to European Community institutions and legal method, where we have thought it helpful in appreciating the context in which our law now operates.

As a general point, our leaving the 'European Community dimension' until the penultimate chapter should not be seen as relegating the topic to an afterthought. The European influence is far too important for that. EC Law is generally taught as a subject in its own right in British law schools, and usually as a compulsory subject at that. However, it is also of much wider significance to the English Legal System, because of the constitutional relationship that now exists between the Community and Britain. It is not like studying, say, Contract Law where you might decide in your examination revision to ignore Chapter 8 on 'Illegality'. Experience has shown us, however, that a student (on whatever course and at whatever level) who is new to legal studies needs to become accustomed to and comfortable with English Legal System and Method before investigating other systems too deeply. In this chapter we shall simply introduce you to some basic EC concepts which will be developed more fully in the final chapter.

1.8.1 The Legal Foundations of the EC

The EC is an international organisation created by treaty in 1957 (the so-called 'Treaty of Rome' or 'EC Treaty'). This Treaty, as amended now by a number of other treaties (the latest of which is the Treaty of Amsterdam), remains the foundation of the Community. In legal terms, the Treaty is significant in two ways.

First, it created the institutions which enable the Community to function. These are the Commission; the Council of Ministers; the European Parliament; and the two Community courts. The Commission and Council wield both political and legal (i.e., law-making) power; the European Parliament, to date, has only a political, advisory function, and so is a very different body from the Westminster Parliament. The two courts are the Court of Justice of the European Communities (ECJ), and the Court of First Instance (CFI).

The Treaty gave to the Court of Justice powers to rule on matters of European Community Law brought before it by the Commission, or by a reference from a court within one of the Member States (this latter process is generally referred to as a reference for a preliminary ruling under Article 234—that being the provision in the EC Treaty creating the power). At this point we should note one impact of the Treaty of Amsterdam which came into force on 1 May 1999. As a result of this Treaty, most of the Article numbers in the original 1957 Treaty of Rome were re-numbered. Thus, Article 177 became Article 234. Consequently, from this point on we have cited all Articles of the EC Treaty under their new numbers.

Private individuals also have rights to bring actions before the Court, but these are strictly controlled by the terms of the Treaty. The Court of First Instance (CFI) has been in operation since September 1989. It was created under Article 11 of the Single European Act, which, despite its name, is a Community treaty and not a statute of any Member State. The CFI was created to take up some of the caseload of the ECJ. However, it presently has a restricted jurisdiction, concerned with competition law, staff cases, and certain cases arising from the European Coal and Steel Community Treaty of 1951. The CFI is of lower standing than the ECJ, and certain rights of appeal exist from its decisions to the Court of Justice.

Secondly, the Treaty is unusual in that it contains a number of provisions which give individuals (as opposed to nation states) substantive legal rights. A particularly important and well-known example is Article 239, which lays down a general principle that men and women are entitled to equal pay for work of equal value. This has been used in the UK to give rights to equal pay to women who have fallen outside the protection of our own sex discrimination laws (*Garland* v *British Rail Engineering Ltd* [1983] 2 AC 751; [1982] 2 All ER 402).

• At the time of writing there are fifteen Member States: Austria, Belgium, Denmark, Finland, France, Germany, Greece, Ireland, Italy, Luxembourg, Portugal, Spain, Sweden, The Netherlands, United Kingdom.

• There are a number of candidate countries, many of which will have been admitted by the time you are reading this: Bulgaria, Cyprus, Czech Republic, Estonia, Hungary, Latvia, Lithuania, Malta, Poland, Romania, Slovakia, Slovenia, Turkey.

1.8.2 EC Legislation

Apart from the substantive provisions of the Treaty, there are three types of laws emanating from the EC Commission or Council of Ministers:

Regulations: These are directly applicable in each Member State and take precedence over any conflicting provisions of domestic (i.e. national) law.

Directives: These are binding upon each Member State 'as to result', but not as regards methods of 'implementation'. What this means in plain English is that each state is obliged to pass such laws as are necessary to give effect to a particular Directive, and then usually within a specified period of time. The Commission may commence proceedings against a state for failure to implement within the required period, but generally a Directive may not be enforced by or against private organisations or citizens *before* it is implemented as, say, an Act of Parliament or statutory instrument.

Decisions: These are binding only upon the Member State(s) or individual(s) to whom they are addressed; they thus tend to have a much narrower field of application than either Regulations or Directives. They take effect from the date at which they are notified to the addressee. You should be careful not to get caught up in some terminological confusion. Decisions as referred to here are a species of legislation; they should not be mistaken for the decisions of the Court of Justice, which have a distinct legal status.

1.8.3 The European Dimension of English Law

The EC is not unusual in owing its existence to an international agreement. Many multinational organisations of states are created in this way. What makes the EC unique is that the Treaty itself creates rights and obligations which are enforceable not only within the institutions of the EC (as just considered), but before the national courts of each Member State.

In English law the enforceability of the EC Treaty and of legislation emanating from the EC Institutions (such as Directives) is guaranteed by the European Communities Act 1972— an Act of the Westminster Parliament. Although the effects of that Act are still widely debated by EC and British constitutional lawyers, it seems increasingly to be accepted that, by passing the Act, Parliament has, to a limited extent, ceded some of its sovereign power to the EC. How much power is probably impossible to quantify, but we seem presently to be upon the threshold of an important new stage in the legal relationship. In July 1990, following a reference to the CJEC, the House of Lords prevented the Secretary of State for Trade from implementing provisions of the Merchant Shipping Act 1988; see *R v Secretary of State for Transport ex parte Factortame (No. 2)*–[1991] 1 AC 603; [1991] 1 All ER 70.

The House of Lords, in delivering the reasons for its decision, concentrated upon the issues of granting 'interim relief' until the question finally came to court. By so doing their Lordships avoided the necessity of discussing the implications of their decision to disapply the Act. This case is undoubtedly of constitutional significance. Prior to the decision in *Factortame (No. 2)* no English court, in modern times, had accepted that it had the power to disapply an Act of Parliament. Indeed, in the original *Factortame* case the House of Lords had expressly denied that such power existed—see [1990] 2 AC 85; [1989] 2 All ER 692. Although the issue in the *Factortame* cases was a rather technical, preliminary point regarding the powers of the court to grant 'interim relief' (that is, to give a provisional remedy to a claimant to protect his interests until the case is heard on the substantive issue), the effect of *Factortame (No. 2)* is far more general. It now seems incontestable that, in cases where there is a conflict between principles of directly enforceable Community law and national law, Community law must prevail, regardless of the source of that domestic law. To EC lawyers, this is hardly a shock, since it reflects one of the founding principles of the Community legal order—the principle of supremacy of EC law. As Lord Bridge explained in *Factortame (No. 2)* ([1991] 1 All ER 70, at 108):

> [the principle of supremacy] was certainly well established in the jurisprudence of the Court of Justice long before the United Kingdom joined the Community. Thus whatever limitation of its sovereignty Parliament accepted when it enacted the European Communities Act 1972 was entirely voluntary. Under the terms of the 1972 Act it has always been clear that it was the duty of a United Kingdom court, when delivering final judgment, to override any rule of national law found to be in conflict with any directly enforceable rule of Community law. ... Thus there is nothing in any way novel in according supremacy to rules of Community law in those areas to which they apply and to insist that, in the protection of rights under Community law, national courts must not be inhibited by rules of national law from granting interim relief in appropriate cases is no more than a logical recognition of that supremacy.

Another recent case illustrates the constitutional significance of the 1972 Act: *Thoburn* v *Sunderland City Council* [2002] EWHC 195; [2003] QB 151; [2002] 4 All ER 156. The case concerned the conflict between section 1 of the Weights and Measures Act 1985 and, amongst other Statutory Instruments, the Units of Measurement Regulations 1994 (which had implemented Council Directive 80/181 Art. 1, as amended by Council Directive 89/617 and which were stated to be made in the exercise of powers conferred by s. 2(2) and (4) of the European Communities Act 1972). The 1985 Act had permitted the continued use of imperial and metric measures in selling goods loose in bulk (e.g., bananas on a market stall). However, the 1994 Regulations meant that the continued use of imperial measures for trade in such goods was permitted only until 31 December 1999. Thereafter the use of the pound as a primary indicator of weight was forbidden. The arguments before the court related to the doctrine of implied repeal and, in particular, whether the 1985 Act had impliedly repealed the European Communities Act 1972 section 2(2) to the extent that the latter empowered the provision of subordinate legislation which was inconsistent with it.

Laws LJ held that the 1985 Act had not impliedly repealed section 2(2). Section 2(2) is what is sometimes called a 'Henry VIII' clause (a reference to ideas of absolute monarchy): it allows secondary legislation to override primary legislation for the purposes of implementing EC law. The appropriate analysis of the relationship between EC and domestic law, said Laws LJ, required regard to be given to the following propositions:

(1) each specific right and obligation provided under EC law was by virtue of the 1972 Act incorporated into domestic law and took precedence. Anything within domestic law which was inconsistent with EC law was either abrogated or had to be modified so as to avoid inconsistency;

(2) the 1972 Act was a constitutional statute which could not be impliedly repealed.

Exactly what is meant by a 'constitutional statute' is something which you will cover in Public Law or Constitutional Law courses but Laws LJ indicated that these were Acts which governed the relationship between the state and the individual and enlarged or diminished fundamental constitutional rights. These types of statute could never be impliedly repealed and the 1972 Act was one of these. Further discussion of this topic is outside the scope of this book, but it is fair to say that this statement is controversial.

The *Factortame* and *Thoburn* cases illustrate how English and European case law is developing in response to the new legal order established by the EC. But it is important to remember that that legal order is also capable of undergoing change. The scope of Community law today is significantly greater than thirty years ago, when the UK joined the Community. It is more than likely that, in another twenty years, we shall see a legal order that is significantly different from that which exists today.

One implication of this is that, for the lawyer, it is becoming increasingly difficult to identify clear points of demarcation between national and Community law, and to find areas of national law which are wholly unaffected by EC law. Even areas like Criminal Law and Family Law are beginning to be shaped more by a European influence. One illustration of this is the extent to which EC law is beginning to address issues of corporate and transnational crime. So, for example, the EU has issued two Money Laundering Directives (one in 1991, implemented in the UK through the Criminal Justice Act 1993 and associated regulations, the other in 2001) aimed at coordinating across the EU measures to deal with attempts by criminals to use financial institutions and professionals such as lawyers and accountants to 'launder' the financial proceeds of their activities. Another graphic, and highly emotive, illustration of the more unexpected impact of EC law relates to the Irish laws on abortion.

The Irish Constitution contains, in Article 40, a specific provision protecting the life of the unborn child. The effect of this is to make abortions illegal within the Republic, except in cases where policy dictates that the risks to the life of the mother justify the termination. On the face of it, it is hard to see what connection could exist between such constitutional rights and EC law. However, in 1992, the Irish High and Supreme Courts were asked to rule on the Constitutional legality of Irish citizens travelling to England, where abortion operations are lawfully available on less restrictive grounds than in Ireland—see *Attorney-General* v *X* [1992] 2 CMLR 277. The case concerned a 14-year-old girl who had become pregnant after being raped. Relying on the Irish Constitution, the Irish Attorney-General sought an order preventing her and her family from travelling to England in order to have the pregnancy terminated. In the High Court, the applicant relied in part on the decision of the Court of Justice of the European Communities in Case C–159/90 *Society for the Protection of the Unborn Child* v *Grogan* [1991] ECR I–4685; [1991] 3 CMLR 849 and argued that, if it did prevent travel in this way, the Constitution was contrary to EC law, as contained in Article 50 of the Treaty of Rome and Directive 73/148 (on access to services across the Community). The High Court rejected this argument, but *not* on the basis that EC law did not apply to the issue. Rather, the Court relied on Article 8 of the Directive, which allows Member States to restrict travel in cases where public policy so dictates.

Attorney-General v *X* was ultimately determined in the applicant's favour on other grounds by the Supreme Court, which did not rule on the point of EC law. That left the High Court's decision as precedent on this point. But the story does not quite end there. In a further Irish High Court case, *SPUC* v *Grogan (No. 2)* [1993] 1 CMLR 197, the applicant sought to overturn *Attorney-General* v *X* in the light of a further Community law development. When the Maastricht Treaty on European Union (see **Chapter 11**) was signed, it contained a specific Protocol guaranteeing freedom to travel to obtain abortion services within the EC. The applicant in *Grogan (No. 2)* thus argued that, as the Irish Government was a signatory to the Protocol, the policy arguments relied on in *Attorney-General* v *X* could no longer apply. This argument was also rejected by the High Court. The applicant could not rely on the Maastricht Protocol itself, as it had yet to be implemented by national law.

To complete the picture, it is worth noting that *Grogan (No. 2)* was ultimately overtaken by developments on the political front. Throughout 1992 the Irish Government had been busy (both at Community and at domestic levels) trying to find a solution to the constitutional dilemma it now faced. These activities culminated in national referenda in November 1992, which put to the people of Ireland three questions concerning their rights (i) to legal abortion within the Republic; (ii) to travel outside Ireland in order to obtain abortion services; and (iii) to obtain information within the Republic about abortion services available abroad. The outcome of this process was that the liberalisation of the abortion laws was rejected by a majority of about 2:1, but the right to travel and right to information were both supported by a clear majority of voters. As a result the Government introduced Amendment No. 14 to the Irish Constitution which qualified Article 40.3.3 so as to make it clear that this did not restrict the freedom of Irish citizens to travel abroad, thereby averting any direct clash between the Irish Constitution and the Maastricht Treaty.

Thus we have a clear example of an area of law, concerning what most people would regard first and foremost as a high *moral*, rather than *economic*, issue in which EC law is not only becoming increasingly significant, but will ultimately override contrary domestic rules of law. Whether the EC should become so involved in determining the fundamental rights and freedoms of citizens remains a moot point, and one which much of the literature on Community law has left underdeveloped.

So, to return to our flick-knife example, if our concern was whether there are any controls on the importation of flick-knives, or whether this was an unfair restraint on cross-border trade, then we might well have to consider Community law. Nevertheless, despite the continuing expansion of European law into new areas, the question as raised would be unlikely to require research into the European dimension.

1.9 CONCLUSIONS

In summary, therefore, in solving any legal problem, including the one set at the beginning of this chapter, we need to be aware of the many dimensions of English law. Any advice we give must take into account the kind of issue with which we are dealing. Is it a question of criminal or civil law? Have we considered all relevant Acts (if any), and checked on the existence of any secondary legislation? What about case law? Are there any human rights implications? Have the courts said anything about the matter, either in interpreting a relevant statute or in applying rules of Common Law? Does the problem have an EC dimension? It is only by appreciating this context that we can, ultimately, find the relevant law to solve our problem. In practice, of course, you quickly overcome the need to run through the kind of checklist we have just presented. Your knowledge and understanding of substantive areas of law will help to make the job of researching legal issues much simpler. Even so, no one can retain sufficient detailed knowledge to make legal research redundant. The next chapter is intended to help you develop the basic research skills necessary to find the law on any basic legal problem.

REFERENCES

ADJEI, C. (1995), 'Human Rights Theory and the Bill of Rights Debate', 58 *Modern Law Review* 17.

BALDWIN, R., and HOUGHTON, J. (1986), 'Circular Arguments: The Status and Legitimacy of Administrative Rules', *Public Law* 239.

DE BÚRCA, G., and GARDNER, S. (1990), 'The Codification of the Criminal Law', 10 *Oxford Journal of Legal Studies*, 559.

ELLIOTT, C., and VERNON, C. (2000), *The French Legal System* (Harlow: Longman).

EWING, K.D. (1999), 'The Human Rights Act and Parliamentary Democracy', 62 *Modern Law Review* 79.

FEIBLEMAN, J. (1985), *Justice, Law and Culture* (Dordrecht: Martinus Nijhoff).

FISS, O. (1984), 'Against Settlement', 93 *Yale Law Journal*, 1073.

GALLIGAN, D. (1986), *Discretionary Powers: A Legal Study of Official Discretion* (Oxford: Clarendon Press).

GARDNER, S. (1992), 'Reiterating the Criminal Code', 55 *Modern Law Review* 839.

GENN, H. (1999), *Mediation in Action* (London: Calouste Gulbenkian Foundation).

GILBERT, G. (1996), 'The Protection of Minorities under the European Convention on Human Rights' in Dine, J., and Watt, B. (eds.) *Discrimination Law: Concepts, Limits and Justifications* (London and New York: Longman).

GLENN, H.P. (2000), *Legal Traditions of the World* (Oxford: Oxford University Press).

GREER, S. (1999), 'A Guide to the Human Rights Act 1998', 24 *European Law Review* 2.

INGMAN, T. (2002), *The English Legal Process* (9th edn., Oxford: Oxford University Press).

JUSTICE (1974), *Going to Law: A Critique of English Civil Procedure* (London: Stevens).

LAW COMMISSION (1985), *Codification of the Criminal Law*, Law Comm. No. 143 (London: HMSO).

—— (1992), *Legislating the Criminal Code—Offences Against the Person and General Principles*, Law Comm. No. 122 (London: HMSO).

MCDOWELL, M., and WEBB, D. (2002), *The New Zealand Legal System: Structures, Processes and Legal Theory* (3rd edn., Wellington: Butterworths).

MACINTYRE, A. (1988), *Whose Justice? Which Rationality?* (Notre Dame, Ind.: University of Notre Dame Press).

MIERS, D. (1986), 'Legislation, Linguistic Adequacy and Public Policy', *Statute Law Review* 90.

—— (1989), 'Legislation and the Legislative Process: A Case for Reform?', *Statute Law Review* 26.

PAGE, E. (2001), *Governing by Numbers: Delegated Legislation and Everyday Policy-Making* (Oxford: Hart Publishing).

SAMUEL, G. (1990), 'La notion d'intérêt, en droit anglais' in Gerard, P., Ost F., and van de Kerchove, M., *Droit et Intérêt* (Brussels: Facultés Universitaires Saint-Louis) iii.

SLAPPER, G., and KELLY, D. (2001), *The English Legal System* (5th edn., London: Cavendish Publishing).

STEIN, P. (1984), *Legal Institutions: The Development of Dispute Settlement* (London: Butterworths).

VAN BUERAN, G. (2002), 'Including the Excluded: The Case for an Economic, Social and Cultural Human Rights Act', *Public Law* 456.

WADE, W. (1998), 'Human Rights and the Judiciary', *European Human Rights Law Review* 520.

2

Finding the Law

Let us begin by considering again the problem of the shopkeeper, which we introduced in **Chapter 1**. We now know that the answer to her question lies somewhere in either exist-ing legislation, or in case law, or perhaps in a combination of the two. We also know that there is a vast amount of that primary material to be searched.

How do we go about finding the law on a particular issue? That is a question of developing the appropriate skills to do the job—what we would call 'library and research skills'. Law is above all else a library-based subject. You must be prepared to spend a substantial amount of time doing library-based research. This chapter is intended to provide an introduction to such skills. It is by no means complete, as lack of space prevents us from considering a number of sources—notably a number of British Gov-ernment publications, and sources of International Law. You may find the more detailed account of research sources provided by Dane & Thomas (1995) or by Clinch (2001) of assistance with specific problems. Most law libraries keep reference copies of these works.

2.1 Getting Started

The starting point of any research depends upon a number of variables. It depends, of course, upon the level of your existing knowledge of law. Once you have mastered the basic principles of a subject, research becomes a little easier, in so far as the parameters of your research will become much more clearly defined—there are possibilities that you will be able to exclude from the outset, for example.

To be an effective researcher, you need to develop some sense of how lawyers think about legal issues (e.g. the terminology they use, and so on). It is a question of becoming familiar with the way in which we structure and classify information. This does mean that, to start with, legal research can be sometimes slow and frustrating as you try to find your way around the material. Persevere—it becomes easier with experience.

The context may also define the level of research you need to undertake. Are you read-ing to fill in the background of a subject, to enhance your own understanding, or to pro-vide a detailed study of some issue or point of law? Each of these exercises may require rather different research strategies (we develop this further in **Chapter 3**), and may influ-ence your choice of sources. Lawyers have essentially two types of library sources: what we call **literary** and **primary** sources. These may be further subdivided. Accordingly, we have split the discussion into three constituent parts, covering:

(a) literary sources

(b) case law

(c) legislation.

We have then separately considered the special issues governing the use of:

(d) EC law

(e) electronic information retrieval systems.

2.2 Literary Sources

In practice, the simplest way to begin researching a problem is to find a book about it. The term 'literary sources' is used to describe books about law, as opposed to books of law, which contain 'official' copies of legislation or case reports. Literary sources are sometimes also referred to as *secondary* sources, to distinguish them from books of law, which are *primary* sources. Be careful that you do not confuse the term secondary meaning literary with other uses of the term, particularly in relation to secondary legislation. We shall discuss the use of literary sources under two headings: legal encyclopedias, and textbooks and journals.

2.2.1 Legal Encyclopedias

Encyclopedias are usually designed to provide a reasonably complete statement of the law in a concise form. They come in a variety of shapes and sizes. Many of them are subject-specific—so, for example, there are encyclopedias on Consumer Protection, Social Welfare Law, Employment Law, and so on. Most of these are large looseleaf volumes designed mainly for legal practitioners.

One of the most valuable starting points, particularly if you are researching a topic about which you have little or no existing knowledge, is the legal encyclopedia called *Halsbury's Laws of England*. The current edition (the fourth) was completed in 1986, though some of its fifty-six volumes have been revised and reissued since then. The whole work is regularly updated by a loose-leaf *Current Service* volume. *Halsbury's Laws* covers all areas of English Law, by summarising the present state of the law with references to the relevant case law and statutes. The quality of its coverage is generally good, but it is not exhaustive! Searching *Halsbury* involves using four distinct elements.

The index

To use *Halsbury's Laws*, you must begin by looking through the index, which takes up two separate volumes by itself. Like any index, it operates by identifying and referencing what we might call *key words*, so the first step has to be to think of the kind of terms that the index might use to identify the problem we are interested in. Once you hit on the right key word (which often involves a process of elimination) the index will give you a set of references to another volume within the series. Thus, if we were interested in problems related to arsenic poisoning, we could look up 'arsenic' in the index; we would find:

> ARSENIC
> > control, **18**, 1111
> > importation in food, **18**, 1181

Each of these references gives us an indication of the context in which arsenic is being discussed, followed by (in **bold**) the number of the volume in which it appears, and then the paragraph—not page—number. Often, the paragraph number will be followed by a little 'n', which indicates that the reference is to a footnote to that paragraph. Note that the index is published every two years only. This does mean that it can be seriously out of date at the time you are using it—hence the importance of the Noter-Up and volume indexes.

Sometimes you will not find a reference to the subject you are looking for. Be careful that you do not assume that there is, therefore, no legal material on that point; it may be that you are not using the correct research strategy. For example, the reference to arsenic says nothing about its use in homicide cases. Obviously, it would be silly to assume that it is perfectly lawful to kill someone by arsenic poisoning—so the answer must be that you are not looking for the right thing. In a homicide case, the fact that the murder was committed by poisoning is not of itself likely to be legally significant, so you would need to consider what it is about that particular method of committing the crime that is important. For example, it might be important because the person accused has previously been convicted of offences involving arsenic poisoning; so what you really want to know is whether, as a matter of procedure, you can use that information in court. In short, you must have a clear idea of what you are looking for and why.

The main volumes

From the index of *Halsbury*, you can go direct to the main volume which is relevant, and make a note of what appears there. Rarely you may find that, particularly if a volume has been reissued, paragraph numbers will have changed, or perhaps for some other reason the main index seems to be wrong. In that case, it is worth checking the index which appears in the back of the main volume, as that may give you a different paragraph number. From the main volume, you must go first to the *Cumulative Supplement*, and then to the *Current Service* to update your search.

The Cumulative Supplement

This is searched by looking for the relevant reference to the main volume. Any updates will appear under the same paragraph number. The *Supplements* are published annually and contain all updates to the main volume, up to their own date of publication. It is therefore necessary to use only the latest *Supplement*. Thus, if you followed up the arsenic reference to Volume 18, paragraph 1111, you would find that, at the time of writing, the latest *Supplement* refers to a variety of amendments affecting the Arsenic in Food Regulations, passed in 1990 and 1992.

The Current Service

This provides an update on everything that has happened since the publication of the last *Supplement,* in the form of 'Monthly Reviews' and a 'Noter-Up' section. The *Current Service* is searched by using the *Key* which appears at the front of that volume. This is another kind of index. Again, we must look up the original volume and paragraph reference—say the reference to control of arsenic (**18**, 1111). If it appears, there will be separate references opposite to the relevant Monthly Review and/or the Noter-Up which are filed in the *Current Service* volume.

So, *Halsbury* may well be a good starting point for researching our friend's problem. But you must remember that the first step is to think about how lawyers would describe it. We know that she is concerned about her liability for offering those knives for sale, so what are the likely key words? We suggest that there might be a number of possibilities. 'Sale of knives' might be too specific, but perhaps there may be something under 'Knife', or even 'Weapon', or possibly under the general concept of 'Sale of Goods'? Those are all possible key words that might be worth exploring. Can you think of any others?

2.2.2 Books and Journals

In terms simply of quantity, textbooks are the main literary source of law. We conventionally make a distinction between academic and practitioner texts. That distinction is a bit arbitrary, as many books may be as useful to the practitioner as to the academic lawyer, but, to generalise, academic texts tend to be less concerned with matters of procedure, and to offer a more critical perspective on the law than practitioner texts. Many academic texts now take a specifically *contextual approach* to law; that is, an approach which attempts to place law in a social, political, or economic perspective, rather than just concentrate on what we call the *black-letter* law—i.e. the rules themselves. Accordingly, the answers you find may well reflect the function of the text and the perspective of the author on the subject.

Law journals also take a wide variety of forms. Some, such as the *Law Society's Gazette,* are primarily practitioner journals, which will contain articles of interest to legal practitioners on matters of substantive law or practice management; they will also normally maintain an element of updating, with short casenotes and information about recent or planned legislation. Many of the more 'heavyweight' journals, such as the *Law Quarterly Review,* for example appeal to both practitioner and academic audiences. Of these, the majority have some kind of specialist focus—hence we have titles like the *Journal of Business Law, Industrial Law Journal,* and *Journal of Social Welfare and Family Law.* Others, such as the *Modern Law Review, Cambridge Law Journal,* and *Journal of Law and Society,* have a broad coverage of subject matter, but a primarily academic outlook. Most of the main journals have adopted a similar format, with each containing a number of leading articles, plus shorter articles on cases or new legislation, and book reviews.

2.2.3 Finding Literary Sources

As a starting point in your studies you will almost certainly be given guidance on what texts are required for the course, though for most purposes you will be expected to read more widely than just the required or recommended text. So, sooner rather than later, you will be required to look for other sources (both textbooks and journal articles) from which to work. There are a number of ways of going about this.

In relation to textbooks, start with a library catalogue. All libraries have a catalogue of their collections, either as a card index or in a computerised form. It will be normal for such catalogues to be indexed by subject, as well as by author. A search of the subject catalogue for 'Criminal Law', for example, should quickly guide you to the main books on the subject. However, this is a fairly crude technique that is just a means of getting started. Catalogues contain only general search terms, so you could not use one to find, for example, any law books containing references to flick-knives!

A more thorough way of checking on what has been written on a subject is to use one of the commercially produced indexes of law books published. The most widely used is entitled *Law Books in Print* and gives details of all British and American law books currently in print. Books found this way, if not held by your library, can usually be obtained through an inter-library loans scheme. However, this is usually worthwhile only if you are doing a sustained piece of research, say for a project or dissertation, as such loans can take several weeks to arrive.

Searching for journal articles is not so straightforward. Most libraries will have a catalogue of periodicals and journals; but this will only tell you which journals the library carries, without giving any indication of their specific contents. There are, however, a number of published indexes to help you. These are:

The Legal Journals Index: This commenced publishing only in 1986, but it contains full details of all the legal journals published in the United Kingdom, and so provides an extremely valuable research resource. It is indexed according to both subject matter (with a brief summary) and name of author. Cases and Acts of Parliament which have been the subject of a commentary are also indexed under their title. It is also available in computerised form as part of the CLI internet service (see below).

Current Law: This is published monthly, and most libraries carry bound volumes (called the *Current Law Year Book*) back to its commencement in 1947. Recent articles can be found under each subject heading, and the *Year Book* contains a separate index thereto. The range of journals covered is not exhaustive, so this is less useful than the *Legal Journals Index*. It does, however, provide some assistance in tracing articles before 1986.

Index to Legal Periodicals and *Index to Foreign Legal Periodicals*: These are both American publications. The former is an index to all American journals, plus a selection from Britain, the Republic of Ireland, and the Commonwealth; the latter indexes articles on international and comparative law, and on the municipal law of all countries which do not appear in the *Index to Legal Periodicals*. (See Dane & Thomas, 1995:60–1.)

Other social science indexes: There are a number of specialist indexes which can be used to discover law-related material written from the perspective of other academic disciplines. In particular, the *British Humanities Index* and *Social Sciences Index* are useful in this respect.

Often textbooks and articles will also make reference to other journal publications, and these can often be valuable in researching a particular topic. In this context particularly, though it applies more generally as well, you should note that certain standard abbreviations are used in the citation of journal articles. Thus, for example, an article in the *Modern Law Review*, volume 53, beginning at page 116 would be cited as (1990) 53 MLR 116. Another in *Public Law* would be cited as [1990] PL 183. Each citation depends on the form adopted by the particular journal, so it takes a while to get used to the different citations. Do be precise in their use. This is not just a matter of pedantry, it is a way of ensuring that we are all 'speaking the same language' and that references can be easily traced. A guide to legal abbreviations has been written by Donald Raistrick (1981); and a list of the main abbreviations in use is also contained in Appendix 1 to Dane & Thomas, and on the web site that accompanies this book.

2.2.4 How Authoritative are Literary Sources?

Literary sources do not really contain 'the law'; they contain the author's interpretation of it. This is reflected in the way, historically, the courts have used them. By and large, the courts have been rather reluctant to place reliance on secondary sources in coming to decisions—though exceptionally, *Halsbury's Laws* have long been cited before the courts. Indeed, at one time, it was the practice that no living author could be cited in court—a rather curious rule which seemed to suggest that death gives an author authority which he or she never had while alive! This restriction has largely fallen into disuse, and some well-established texts are now quite widely cited.

It is relatively unusual to see journal articles cited as being influential on the court's decision, but even here there is evidence that the courts' attitude to citation has significantly relaxed in recent years. A few examples of the latter practice can be seen from the House of Lords decisions in *Morris* v *Beardmore* [1981] AC 446; [1980] 2 All ER 753, where Lord Edmund-Davies quoted with approval a casenote by Geoffrey Samuel in (1980) 96 LQR 12, in *R* v *Shivpuri* [1987] AC 1; [1986] 2 All ER 334, where the House acknowledged the influence of the late Professor Glanville Williams's criticism (in [1986] CLJ 33) of their earlier decision on the law of attempts in *Anderton* v *Ryan* [1985] AC 567; [1985] 2 All ER 355, and, in the recent case of *R* v *A* [2001] UKHL 25; [2001] 2 AC 45, where their Lordships referred to a number of academic analyses of the procedural rules governing the bringing of evidence of a complainant's previous sexual experiences in the trial of various sex offences.

2.3 Finding Cases

The operation of our system of precedent is dependent upon us being able to find out what the courts have said about any given question. This means that we must have a record of the courts' decisions. These records are referred to as 'law reports'.

Whenever possible you are recommended to look at actual reports of cases rather than just to accept the interpretation given in textbooks. This section is intended to give you some guidance to the English system of law reporting, and then to help you find and update specific cases.

2.3.1 Law Reporting

The tradition of law reporting is very ancient in the English Legal System, though many of these early reports are now regarded as highly unreliable. In essence the law reports can be divided into two historical phases, pre- and post-1865.

Before 1865, there were two main sources of case reports:

Year books: Established about 1285, these continued in existence until 1535. They were probably derived from the notes of cases taken by student advocates. Consequently they are not consistently reliable: would you want to rely on your notes as law reports? They are often difficult to read and make relatively little sense to anyone except a legal historian.

Private reports: Sometimes called 'Nominate Reports' because each series is named after the counsel who compiled them. Hundreds of reports appeared in this era. The same case could be reported by a range of reporters, and in such cases it is not unusual for the contents, even the decision, to vary as between reports! The advantage of these reports, however, lay in the evolution of more precise methods of recording judgments, e.g., Burrow's Reports introduced the idea of a 'Headnote' (a summary of the facts, decision and reasoning—a device which is used in every report today) in about 1765. Some were good, e.g. Coke's Reports [1600–58]; some were not so, e.g. Espinasse's Reports [1793–1807], of whom it was said: he was deaf; he heard only half of what went on in court, and reported the other half. These reports are now collected together in *The English Reports*. These require a search technique all of their own, and you are advised to read Dane & Thomas before you attempt to search for a case in the English Reports. Cases from the nominate reports are still cited, though increasingly rarely. Some of the most important have also been reprinted in a series called the All England Law Reports Reprint (cited as All ER Rep), which contains a selection of cases from between 1558 and 1935.

Even after 1865, there remains no single 'official' (i.e. state sponsored) source of law reports in the English Legal System. This is yet another respect in which our system differs from much of continental Europe. For example, in France there are separate criminal and civil series of the *Bulletin des arrêts de la Cour de Cassation* (the final court of appeal in most civil matters) dating back to 1798, while in Germany there are about twelve current sets of official law reports; these tend to be published separately by reference to the particular court in which the cases were heard. Thus, e.g., the Supreme Court (*Bundesgerichtshof*) and Constitutional Court (*Bundesverfassungsgericht*) reports constitute separate series.

In England, in 1865, a body called the Incorporated Council of Law Reporting (ICLR) introduced what is now recognised as the main source of law reports. The Council is still responsible for these today, though there are a number of other organisations which publish various law reports, as well as a body of case law that is never published. We shall consider each of these in turn.

The Law Reports and alternatives

The so-called 'Law Reports' consist of Queen's Bench Reports (abbreviated to QB), Chancery (Ch), Family (Fam), and Appeal Cases (AC). This broadly reflects the division of work between the superior courts, as Queen's Bench, Chancery, and Family Reports will contain reports of both High Court and Court of Appeal decisions. Appeal Cases contain chiefly House of Lords and Privy Council cases. The Council also publishes the Weekly Law Reports (WLR), which are relied upon by many practitioners.

There are other reputable reports not published by the Council. The All England Law Reports (All ER), published by Butterworths, is a prime example. These are probably the most widely used alternative. Indeed, many smaller law libraries in the UK and abroad rely purely on the All England Law Reports, which are also available electronically through All England Direct—cited as All ER (D). Both the Weekly Law Reports and the All England Reports are published in weekly parts as well as annual bound volumes. Electronic versions of all the law reports are available from a range of sources, discussed in section 2.

The Times Newspaper

The (London) Times is the only English newspaper that has maintained a regular and consistent practice of reporting legal cases. These can be cited and provide a useful means of keeping abreast of current developments. Arguably the value of these has been diminished by the increased availability of both summaries of cases and full text reports on the internet, particularly since the introduction of 'Daily Law Notes' by the ICLR (see below, 2.).

The Law Reports are generally preferred to other reports in the case of any conflict. This is because judgments in the Law Reports are revised either by the judges themselves or with their cooperation. This should ensure that they are a more reliable source of what was said. However, the opportunity for correction enables a judge sometimes to introduce changes to the text which may reflect what he meant to say, rather than what he said. This is, perhaps a rather more controversial practice, though in some cases it has enabled judges to amend or clarify their reasoning in the light of criticisms directed at the unreported transcript—see, e.g., Lord Denning's judgment in *Ghani v Jones* [1970] 1 QB 693, and Jackson (1970:3).

Conflicts between the various law reports are comparatively rare, but not wholly unknown. For an example you might like to look at the reports of *Davies v Swan Motor Co. (Swansea) Ltd* [1949] 2 KB 291 at 319; [1949] 1 All ER 620 at 629, where there is a small but confusing discrepancy in the reporting of the judgment of Evershed LJ. See if you can spot it!

Specialist Reports

More particularly, there are many and varied specialist reports such as the Criminal Appeal Reports, Reports of Patents Cases, and Industrial Cases Reports. These are of considerable assistance to subject specialists. A list of the majority of such reports can be found in Dane & Thomas.

Unreported cases

The reporting of cases is still largely a matter of choice by the editor of the particular series of reports. There are still cases, even in the higher courts, which go unreported. This does not mean that they are wholly irrelevant. Transcripts of unreported Court of Appeal cases are available to judges and practising lawyers, and unreported cases can quite properly be cited to a court.

Occasionally the editors of the law reports have got it badly wrong by excluding a case which subsequently proves to be important. This happened in 1973, for example, with the case of *Mesher* v *Mesher*, which introduced a new kind of 'property adjustment order' for use in divorce cases. Initially the case had been picked up only by *The Times* (a point that seems to have been forgotten as the case is widely cited as unreported). Even so, the Mesher Order (as it was called) became very popular with the divorce courts, with the result that the case was belatedly reported in the All England Law Reports in 1980 (see *Mesher* v *Mesher and Hall (Note)* [1980] 1 All ER 126).

2.3.2 How to Find a Case

In attempting to find cases there are a number of different strategies which may be adopted depending on the information you have.

First, a case can most easily be found by its name and the reference to its location in the law reports. Taken together, these provide a means of identification as unique as a finger-print. The name of any case in English law is normally based upon the parties involved— hence some of the case names we have already seen, such as *Mesher* v *Mesher* or *R* v *Shivpuri*. The case reference is more properly called its **citation**. The most common form of citation of any case will be made up of the following elements:

	YEAR	VOLUME (if any)	REPORT	PAGE
Thus				
	[1989]	2	QB	123

tells us that the case is to be found in volume 2 of the Queen's Bench Law Reports for 1989, beginning at page 123. There is one significant variation on that, which affects the style of citing dates and volume numbers. Some series of law reports in the last century, and a few modern sets, have consecutively numbered volumes, year by year—e.g., the case of *Bowker* v *Rose* which is reported only in (1978) 122 Sol Jo 147. Theoretically, the date there is not significant—we could find that case merely by knowing that it is in volume 122 of the *Solicitor's Journal*. For that reason, where the set of reports is consecutively numbered, the date is cited in round brackets. If the date is in square brackets, it is vital to the finding of that case, because any subsequent volume number will only refer to volumes *within that particular year.*

The style of citing cases is, as with journal citations, rigidly adhered to. You may find the system rather complex and confusing at first, but it will soon become familiar. We have already indicated the main reports, with their abbreviations, above. If you need help, fuller lists of specialist, and of American and Commonwealth, reports with their abbreviations can be found in Raistrick and in Dane & Thomas. The new method of citing cases available on the various Internet sites is dealt with later in this chapter, in the section *Using Computerised Information Retrieval Systems*.

Cases can be found, within reason, even if you only know the name. These days this is most easily done using the electronic, internet-based resources discussed in section 2.6.1. However, if you are using paper resources, this can be done by finding the citation in the *Current Law Case Citators*. These cover the period since 1947 through a mixture of bound volumes and paper supplements for the most recent years. Note that, since the 1991 issue, the citator has been rearranged into two parts. Part I contains English cases, while Part II contains those cases formerly digested in the Scottish section of the citator. All reported cases are listed in the citator in alphabetical order, based upon the first-named party to the case. The citator will then give a list of all citations of that case, and a reference to a summary of the case in the relevant annual volume of *Current Law*. There are limits to this strategy. It is sometimes possible to find a case this way even if you only know the first-named party—so long as it is not a particularly common name, like Smith! It is not practicable to find cases where you only know the second-named party, as these are not separately identified. It may also prove difficult to find cases if you are unaware of the spelling—if possible do try to keep an accurate note of case names handy when undertaking research—some, such as *Spettabile Consorzio Veneziano* v *Northern Ireland Shipbuilding Co.* (1919) are likely to tax any but the most exceptional memory. The criteria for naming cases are more fully discussed in **Chapter 3**.

2.3.3 Updating Cases

Once you have found your case, it will be necessary to check whether it is still relevant, unless it is exceptionally recent. As we shall see in later chapters, cases are not immutable. They may be rejected by higher courts, distinguished in other cases, or otherwise discussed in some way that may be relevant to your research.

To find out what has happened to a particular case, you can either use electronic resources or turn again to the *Current Law Case Citators*. For the history of older cases the *Citators* may be the only option. In addition to the citations of the case named, the citator also charts its subsequent history. If a case pre-dates 1977, it is still worth checking the later citators, as they will tell you when the case has been most recently considered. If it appears, it will still be necessary to go back to the earlier citator, as the whole history will not be given in the latest entry. The form of reference in the citators is broadly the same so, to give a *fictitious* example, the citators may have the following entry:

- in the 1947–76 edition:

  Balderdash v *Ballyhooley* [1966] QB 201; [1966] 2 WLR 32; 130 JP 789; [1966] 1 All ER 468, CA . . . *Digested* 66/571: *Approved* 76/552.

- and, in the 1977–88 edition:
  Balderdash v *Ballyhooley* [1966] *Distinguished* 87/579.

This tells us that the case of *Balderdash* v *Ballyhooley* appears in the *Current Law Year Book* of 1966 at paragraph 571; that it was approved of by a later case, which is digested in the 1976 *Year Book* at paragraph 552, and that it was distinguished in 1987 by the case digested at paragraph 579 (note that in the later citator you do not get the original case reference; this should help to remind you to look it up in the earlier citator, if you have not already done so). By looking up those references it would be possible to get the names and citations of all those cases and, if necessary, to trace their history using the citators.

For very recent cases, it is normally sufficient to use the monthly parts of *Current Law*, by searching through either the abbreviated case citator, to be found near the centre of each monthly issue (if you know the case name) or the relevant subject headings. These subject headings also form the basis of a more detailed index which can be found at the back of each bound volume of the *Current Law Year Book*.

2.4 Finding and Updating Legislation

Legislation, you will recall, can be divided chiefly into Acts of Parliament and Statutory Instruments. The publication of each of these is a separate activity, so separate search techniques are required.

2.4.1 Acts of Parliament: The Sources

Before we begin, one important thing you need to know about an Act is the way in which it is cited. Like cases, Acts of Parliament have a unique signature. This is not based solely upon their name (or **short title** to use the technical term), however. Many different Acts share a common name—for example, there are presently five statutes in force bearing the title 'Criminal Justice Act'. This means that the year in which the Act became law will be crucial in identifying it. Additionally, every Act passed has a 'chapter number' which may also be used in its identification. In practice, it is quite possible to find legislation by reference to the year and chapter number alone. The citation of an Act as '1988 c. 33', for example, could refer only to the Criminal Justice Act 1988.

Until comparatively modern times, Acts were not formally given short titles (though such titles were quite widely used on an informal basis) so that all legislation was identified by chapter number and **regnal year** (that is, a number assigned to the year in which it was passed, counting it from the first year of that monarch's reign). Hence, the famous Poor Law Amendment Act passed in 1834 was properly cited as '4 & 5 Will. IV c. 76'. This indicates that it was the 76th statute passed in the Parliamentary session which overlapped the fourth and fifth years of William IV's reign.

The tradition of citing regnal years gradually declined after the Second World War, and the system was formally dropped in 1963. Since there are numerous older Acts of Parliament still in force, the old system of citation cannot be wholly disregarded. However, do remember that when writing about any statutes it is conventional now to refer to them, wherever possible, by their short title and date only.

Acts of Parliament are published in a variety of series. The initial responsibility for publication lies with the Stationery Office which, as the government printer, is required to publish individual copies of all statutes as they are passed. These are ultimately brought together in the annual bound editions of the *Public General Acts and Measures*. In addition to the government printer's versions, there are a number of other series which are worth knowing about. The most widely available of these are the *Law Reports: Statutes, Halsbury's Statutes*, and *Current Law Statutes Annotated*.

Law Reports: Statutes

This rather incongruously named collection is also published by the Incorporated Council of Law Reporting—hence the title. The contents are not annotated or revised, and so they do not provide anything different from the Stationery Office copies.

Halsbury's Statutes of England

This provides a partner series to *Halsbury's Laws*, containing an annotated version of all legislation presently in force, organised by subject. It is therefore the main resource for discovering whether legislation exists on any topic.

Search techniques are similar to those employed in respect of *Halsbury's Laws*. If you begin with the *General Index*, this gives you a wide range of key words, each of which will refer you to a volume and paragraph within the main collection. If you are looking for a specific statute by title, you can take a short-cut by referring instead to the Alphabetical List of Statutes at the beginning of the *Table of Statutes and General Index*. Any revisions which post-date the publication of the relevant main volume will be traceable to the *Cumulative Supplement* and, for recent changes, to the *Noter-up* binder. The text of very recent legislation will appear, alphabetically by subject, in one of the five binders of the *Current Statutes Service*; it can be found by reference to the alphabetical list of statutes at the front of the *Service*.

Current Law Statutes Annotated

All Acts are published in a loose-leaf format soon after coming into force. Of these, those which the editors judge to be sufficiently important are annotated by someone who is a specialist in that area of law. The annotations are not part of the Act, and do not, of course, have any legal effect, though they can be very useful in explaining the background, scope, and operation of the Act. During the course of each year, bound volumes of the *Current Law Statutes Annotated* are published; they are printed in order, according to the chapter numbers of the Acts.

2.4.2 Statute Law Search Techniques

Focusing on paper resources for now, *Current Law* is of some basic assistance in finding out what has happened, as it will contain a brief description, under the relevant subject heading, of any legislation passed during the year. It is not sufficiently detailed to be of substantive help, but it can make you aware of legislation which you would not otherwise have known about. Sweet & Maxwell also publish the *Current Law Statute Citators*. There are three bound volumes, containing information on all legislation passed in 1947–71, 1972–88, and 1989–95 respectively and a soft-back copy for 1996 onwards. These provide a valuable means of updating statutes. Each citator is organised chronologically by year and chapter number (it also gives the title). Any changes to an Act are then listed *section by section*. This is important; it means that to use the citator most effectively you need to know not only the short title and chapter number, but also the specific parts, or *sections*, of the Act that you wish to trace.

Suppose, for example, you wish to discover what has happened to section 1 of the Criminal Evidence Act 1898 (c. 36). You would check the various citator volumes (you need to check each of them as they are not cumulative), and then, to be completely up to date, you would check entries in any individual *Year Books* published since the last citator and the loose parts for the current year. The information is displayed in a particular format, for example, against 1998 c.36 the 1972–88 Citator has the following entry:

s. 1, amended: 1979, c. 16, s. 1; repealed in part: 1982, c. 48, sch. 16; 1984, c. 60, s. 80, sch. 7.

This shows that part of the section is amended and other parts are no longer in force (*repealed*), by virtue of the *sections* (s.) of and *schedules* (sch.) to the Acts cited. To work out the detailed effect of those amendments, you would, of course, have to compare the various texts. The titles of those later Acts either can be found elsewhere in the Citator, or you could go direct to the relevant volumes of the *Public General Acts*, or *Current Law Statutes Annotated*.

As we suggested in **Chapter 1**, legislation does not stand alone, but is explained and applied through case law. One question, therefore, might be whether we can discover what case law exists on a particular statutory provision, if we only know the details of the Act. In this respect, *Halsbury's Laws* may be a valuable starting point, as this will usually refer to both statute and case law underlying any legal proposition. The *Current Law Legislation Citator* also lists important cases under the relevant sections of each Act. Thus, to take the example of the 1898 Act, the 1989–95 citator shows not just textual amendments, but gives references to a number of court decisions where section 1 has been applied. These citations can be followed up in the manner suggested above. In the later Citators cases appear by name, though in the 1947–71 volume cases are identified only by their reference in the *Current Law Year Books*. The reference comprises two elements, the year and paragraph number, in the form '60/766'. This is sufficient to enable you to trace it to the relevant passage in a Year Book, where you will find the full citation.

Since the House of Lords decision in *Pepper v Hart* [1993] 1 All ER 42, the courts have also been entitled to refer to the Official Reports of proceedings in Parliament (*Hansard*) as an aid to construction in cases where the language of the Act is unclear (we discuss the parameters of this principle further in **Chapter 8**). This means that lawyers today need to be familiar with the research techniques necessary to make sense of the legislative history of an Act. The potential scale of this change is indicated by the fact that *Pepper v Hart* affects not only Acts passed since 1993, but *all* Acts in force.

Every Parliamentary Bill has to go through both the Commons and the Lords before receiving the Royal Assent and becoming law. In this process, the Bill will normally be introduced by its promoter at the so-called Second Reading stage, where you may find some general statements about purpose or legislative intent; it will also be debated before both Houses, sometimes briefly, sometimes in some detail. It will also be analysed clause by clause in Standing Committee—this is often the most useful part of the process for our purposes, as in *Pepper* v *Hart* itself. You need to check all of these stages. The following research strategy should work in most cases (see Tunkel, 1993:18 for further information and alternative approaches).

For established legislation, the best starting point is the *Current Law Statutes* version of the Act. This will give you all the *Hansard* references to debates in both Commons and Lords. It will also generally (though not always, especially with older Acts) refer to the discussion in Standing Committee. An alternative source for that information is the Stationery Office's *Catalogue of Government Publications*, issued in monthly parts.

Current Bills, or very recently enacted legislation, can be followed through Parliament *via* the *Current Law* monthly parts, which contain a 'Progress of Bills' section. The House of Commons *Weekly Information Bulletin* (paper or internal version) and Lawtel (if you have access) are good alternatives. All of these are quicker than wading through *Weekly Hansard*!

Once you have identified the relevant debates, etc., these can be followed up through *Hansard*. This is bound in separate volumes for the Commons and the Lords, by Parliamentary session rather than calendar year. There is also limited availability in electronic form. Each volume is indexed and there are separate sessional indexes too. Current developments can be tracked through the paper parts of *Weekly Hansard*. The main *Hansard* Commons series does not include reports of Standing Committees. These are published as a separate series.

2.4.3 Statutory Instruments

Statutory instruments are also published by the Stationery Office, separately, in the annual bound volumes of *Statutory Instruments* (entitled, until 1948, *Statutory Rules and Orders*), and in electronic form.

The main alternative (paper) source for statutory instruments is *Halsbury's Statutory Instruments*, a multiple-volume set organised by subject, with a Current Service containing instruments passed since the publication of the bound volumes. *Halsbury's* contains information on all instruments in force, though not necessarily in a full-text form. Summaries may also be found under the appropriate subject headings in *Current Law* and the *Current Law Year Books*.

Note that statutory instruments also have their own mode of citation, which is made up of their title, the year in which they were passed, and the instrument number.

So, for example, the Income Support (General) Amendment Regulations of 1988 are cited as SI 1988/663.

2.4.4 Legislation of the Scottish Parliament and Welsh Assembly

Under the devolution Acts, the Scottish Parliament and Welsh Assembly each have the power to create legislation in their own right. The Welsh Assembly may make only secondary legislation, in the form of statutory instruments (see s. 66(2) of the Government of Wales Act 1998). The Scottish Parliament, however, can create primary legislation also. This primary legislation is known as 'Acts of the Scottish Parliament' (s. 28(1) of the Scotland Act 1998). Both sets of legislation are published independently of the laws passed by the Westminster Parliament, and are available electronically as well as in paper form.

2.5 Finding EC Law

Because the EC has separate law-making institutions from the United Kingdom, it is hardly surprising that much Community law is found in locations distinct from those we have so far discussed.

However, elements of Community law can often be found in the kind of sources we have already considered. Both *Halsbury's Laws* and *Halsbury's Statutes* have volumes specifically on European Community law, while a looseleaf *Encyclopedia of European Community Law* has been published since 1973. A rather less daunting encyclopædia is *Croner's Europe*. This was designed to provide a legal and business reference work for managers in the run-up to the Single Market in 1992, and beyond. In so doing, it provides an accessible guide to the European institutions and to much substantive Community law, and can thus be a useful point of first reference.

In addition to occasional articles in the journals already considered, there are now quite a number of journals which specialise in EC law matters. These include the *European Law Review, Common Market Law Review*, and *Legal Issues of European Integration*. Articles on the Community may also be found in the main journals of International Law, such as the *International and Comparative Law Quarterly*. These all appear in the *Legal Journals Index*.

The various English law reports increasingly contain cases concerned with EC law—where the English courts are considering the application of Community law either *ab initio*, or in response to a preliminary ruling of the European Court of Justice of the European Communities (ECJ). Furthermore, it is becoming more common to find decisions of the ECJ (particularly, though not exclusively, those involving the UK) reported in the usual English law reports—e.g., Case 171/88 *Rinner-Kühn* v *FWW Spezial Gebäudereinigung GmbH and Co. KG* [1989] IRLR 493, which we shall consider in detail in **Chapter 10**.

Despite this, there are a number of specific sources of EC law with which you ought to be familiar.

European Court Reports

The European Court Reports (cited as ECR) are the official reports published by the ECJ. The Reports are available in all the Community languages, including English, but the demands of producing multiple translations of every case does mean that there are substantial delays between the Court handing down its decision and that case being reported. In the early 1990s, the time lag was such that even the first reports—in French—were taking over a year to appear in the ECR. Since 1994, steps have been taken to reduce delays by excluding the Report of the Hearing from the published version, and also by excluding most staff cases heard by the CFI from publication in the ECR.

Following the creation of the CFI in 1989, the ECR has been divided into two parts: ECR I, which reports decisions of the ECJ, and ECR II, which contains decisions of the CFI.

Common Market Law Reports

The CMLR are an 'unofficial' series published weekly in English by the European Law Centre. They cover cases before the Court of Justice and the Court of First Instance, and before national courts within the EC. Although unofficial, the relative speed of publication makes them largely preferable to the ECR, though they do not report every case before the ECJ or CFI.

Both series are indexed by subject and case name or number. The case number is an important feature of ECJ decisions. The proper mode of citation is to give the case *number* first, followed by its name, and then the citation of any report. Thus for example, one of the leading cases on the impact of EC membership on national sovereignty, is properly cited as Case 6/64 *Costa* v *Ente Nazionale per l'Energia Elettrica (ENEL)* [1964] ECR 585. The case number, it can be seen, contains two elements: the actual number at which the case was listed (here, no. 6) and the year in which the application or reference was made (64—indicating 1964). Since the creation of the Court of First Instance, a new element has been introduced into the citation of cases. Now all cases have the prefix 'C–' or 'T–'. This indicates that the case was listed, respectively, either before the ECJ or the CFI.

Note also that the year contained in the case number will not be the same year that judgment was given, or that the case was reported. For example, the reference for a preliminary ruling in *R* v *Secretary of State ex parte Factortame Ltd* was made in 1989. The case therefore received the number C–213/89. Judgment by the ECJ, however, was not handed down until June 1990. In fact, several years may elapse between the reference and the case being heard. You should also be aware that some English textbooks do not adopt the full European mode of citation, and either disregard the case number or place it after the names of the parties.

The Official Journal

The *Official Journal* (OJ) is the primary organ of legal information within the Community. Mastering the OJ is also one of the major challenges of researching Community law. It is made up of several sections, of which the most important are referred to as the *L* and *C Series*.

The *L Series* contains a record of all Community legislation. This covers the text of all the treaties, their protocols, and amendments, and also other legislative measures. In respect of the latter, it is published and indexed in two parallel sequences, one containing Regulations, which, under Article 191 of the EEC Treaty, must be published in the *Journal*, the other contains all other (non-obligatory) legislation. Though there is no legal requirement that this be published, it is accepted practice that all Directives appear, as do some Decisions. Each piece of legislation will have its own identifiers. Like cases, each Regulation, etc., has an 'act number', so, for example, the important Equal Treatment

Directive of 1976 (on sex discrimination) is cited as 'Directive 76/207' (i.e. number 207 of 1976). The same format applies to Decisions. That numerical sequence is reversed in respect of Regulations, hence we speak of 'Regulation 1408/71', not 71/1408. Full references should also indicate the institutional source of the legislation (Commission or Council) and the Treaty of its origin (EEC, ECSC, or EURATOM—see further **Chapter 10**). *Journal* references to legislation are usually cited by year, series, issue number and page. For example, the 1985 Product Liability Directive is found at [1985] OJ L210/29— meaning *L Series*, issue number 210, of 7 August 1985 (note that the date of the citation is to the OJ reference, not the date that the act was passed, that appears in the long title to the act).

The *C Series* covers a wide range of information generally falling under the heading of 'Communications'. In particular, it includes the text of legislation proposed by the Commission (but not yet law, such as Draft Directives), and both the listings of cases to appear before the ECJ and brief summaries of decisions handed down by the Court. The OJ is quite a useful source of basic information on Court decisions, as the summaries may appear in advance of any full reports. Cases reported in the *Journal* are usually cited in the same form, thus, [1990] OJ C146/9 refers to Case C–70/88 *European Parliament* v *Council of the European Community*.

The chief difficulties in using the *Journal* are twofold. First, it is published almost on a daily basis, which makes for a vast amount of information accruing over a relatively short space of time. It is not re-issued in a bound form, so that physically locating specific copies of the OJ can be a time-consuming business. Secondly, searching for information in the OJ is made more difficult by the limitations of the index. The index is issued monthly, and consolidated into annual parts. It is divided into two separate sections, an Alphabetical Index and the Methodological Table.

The Alphabetical Index is a subject-based index for use where you do not have a full reference (or any reference) to a legislative act or case. The limitation of the Index is that it does sometimes adopt a rather odd choice of key words, so that some terms you would expect to find simply do not appear. In an attempt to overcome the difficulties of getting to grips with the appropriate 'Eurospeak', there is a further volume, which contains the rather Orwellian-sounding 'Eurovoc Thesaurus' (properly called the *Official Journal: Annex to the Index: Eurovoc Alphabetical Thesaurus*). This lists most conceivable search terms, and then gives the actual key word that you should look up in the Alphabetical Index.

References in the Alphabetical Index take the following form:

Document No.   OJ Reference   Legal Form

The document number refers to the case or act number. You do not need to know the legal form to find a document in the *Journal*, but this will tell what the reference is to, e.g., that it is a Commission Directive, or a decision of the Court of Justice. The OJ reference in this Index is listed in the form 'C1/212/10'; indicating, in order, the series, issue number, and page.

The Methodological Table is far simpler to use, provided you have full references. Acts and cases are indexed separately. All legislative acts are listed in numerical order, and all cases by the year in which the application was made, and then the case number. The Table separately records cases in one of three categories; those listed before the Court; those in which judgment has been given, and those which have been withdrawn before a hearing.

Other legislative sources

In addition to publication in the OJ, the Community has published a consolidated volume of the Treaties, entitled *Treaties Establishing the European Communities* (1987). There is no official equivalent in respect of other Community legislation, though there are a number of student texts which contain selections of source documents, for example, Rudden and Wyatt's *Basic Community Laws*, and Nigel Foster's *EC Legislation*.

2.6 Using Computerised Information Retrieval Systems

The basic problem facing any legal researcher is that the law library only expands, it never contracts. Payne (1983) put it more graphically:

> The Ten Commandments consist of 120 words, the Magna Carta 63 Clauses and the American Declaration of Independence 500 words. The Common Market regulations concerning duck eggs run to no fewer than 120,000 words!

Since the 1970s, the availability of computerised legal information retrieval (IR) systems has been presented as a possible solution to the problems created by this glut of information. The advantages of such systems are fairly obvious. They have the potential to store, with relative ease, large quantities of information in electronic form, as a *database*. This information can also be searched thoroughly and accessed far more quickly than by traditional means.

The amount of computer-based legal information has grown exponentially since the early 1980s. The earliest systems to develop were those which required *on-line* searching, i.e., using a dedicated terminal or modem to connect, via the public telephone network, to a commercial database in another location. Since the early 1990s, this form of information retrieval has increasingly been supplemented (or supplanted?) by newer technologies—notably compact disc (CD) and the Internet (see below). The majority of information retrieval sytems, whether CD or on-line, also allow downloading of information to paper copy or a diskfile. Today the internet is without doubt a primary means of accessing current legal information. Much of this information can be accessed using a good search engine like 'Google' and it does not require the level of training that commercial service providers like Lexis prefer. Consequently, in this chapter we intend to focus primarily on internet resources.

2.6.1 Commercial Systems

The main on-line legal information systems available in the UK are LexisNexis, Lawtel, and Westlaw; the same or similar services exist in many other Common Law jurisdictions.

The **LexisNexis** database is probably the most extensive, containing over three billion documents. It includes full-text case reports of most cases reported in England and Wales since 1945; all public general Acts and statutory instruments in force; Scottish, Irish, Australian, and New Zealand law reports; decisions of the ECJ; some French cases and legislation (in French), and extensive American materials. Since January 1991, LexisNexis has also incorporated the Celex database of EC secondary legislation in its INTLAW library. For more manageable searching this material is broken down into two tiers of segments. At the first level, these are called 'libraries'. Each library is then sub-divided into a set of files. It is possible to search only one file of one library at a time. Thus to search the English case database it is necessary to enter first the 'ENGGEN' library and then the CASES file. The system enables you to browse the range of libraries and provides on-screen help, so accessing files is not difficult.

Unlike LexisNexis, which provides mostly full-text research and retrieval, **Lawtel** relies far more on summaries, with the result that some aspects of the system are far more geared to updating and preliminary rather than in-depth research. The main data available include: summaries of statutes passed since 1980; summaries of cases, both unreported and from the main generalist and some specialist law reports (from 1980 on); summaries of Parliamentary Bills, Green and White Papers; details of commencement dates, repeals, and amendments to statutes passed since 1984; a European law database; and an index of articles published in the main practitioner journals. One particular feature of Lawtel is that it contains a 'Daily Update' section, giving a brief description of all new documents added to the database in the last twenty-four hours. Lawtel, like most specialist database services, is a subscription service, and so requires a username and password to obtain access. Although originally developed, like LexisNexis, to use its own specialist software and terminals, Lawtel is now accessible across the Internet, using any normal PC and Internet browser (see further below). The website address is *www.lawtel.co.uk*

Westlaw, like Lexis, is originally a US-based service and also provides access to an extensive full-text retrieval system. It is divided into a set of databases which are divided in part by topic (as regards much of the US Federal law) and by jurisdiction. There is also an extensive range of text and periodical secondary sources (though again, like LexisNexis, the journals are primarily North American). In most respects Westlaw and LexisNexis perform similar functions, the screen appearance is different for each, each uses its own search techniques and protocols (though these are in fact similar in many regards), and each system has its own particular strengths and weaknesses.

In addition to these various sources of legal information, there are also a number of bibliographic databases which can be useful to academic lawyers as a research tool for finding secondary sources. One of the most widely used in academia is the BIDS database, which provides a detailed, international source of references in the Sciences, Humanities, and Social Sciences. The database, which incorporates references to some 7,000 journals and published conference proceedings, is updated regularly and can be searched on a year-by-year basis. BIDS contains some legal material, though primarily articles which have an interdisciplinary dimension.

2.6.2 Law on the Internet

The massive improvements in both communications and database technology over the last decade have unleashed the potential for sharing large quantities of information across computer networks at high speed and relatively low cost. The Internet is the most obvious and talked-about example of this phenomenon. The Internet is simply a loose conglomeration of computer networks which is built around a common communication system, or 'messaging protocol' in the jargon. It was developed in the American defence industry in the late 1960s and has expanded to incorporate, first, the international academic community and, from there, a growing number of commercial and individual users in some 160 countries. Estimates suggest that the number of Internet users worldwide increased from about 20 million in the mid-1980s to over 40 million in 1995.

There are a number of Internet features which are of use to lawyers. First, the Internet is a powerful medium for disseminating information rapidly and to a potentially infinite number of users, through the use of electronic mail (*e-mail*), *lists*, and *bulletin boards*. E-mail is simply a mechanism for sending messages to another user or group of users; it is probably the primary means of written communication within commercial and academic organisations, and is increasingly being used for formal business communications between organisations too. Although different 'hosts' (i.e. the local networks which feed into the Internet) may use different software, and therefore adopt slightly different ways of accessing the Internet, communication is made possible by a common system of addressing messages—much as we have a standard way of addressing letters that go through the ordinary postal system. Thus users are identified by their username (the form this takes tends to be defined by the protocols of the host) and the name of the host to which they are connected—our own institutions, for example, are 'uwe.ac.uk' and 'wmin.ac.uk', so someone at UWE could be contacted by sending mail to them as, for example, 'j.smith@uwe.ac.uk'. The limit of this system is obvious—you need to know an address and username to send a message. This is overcome to varying degrees by list and bulletin-board services. List services are essentially electronic mailing lists or discussion groups. They are run from hosts on the Internet using a range of software, the most common being 'listserv' and 'listproc' programs. Users need to subscribe to a specific list by sending the appropriate subscription message, in return for which they will normally obtain a range of services, including a listing of other subscribers, the ability to obtain a digest of list messages and to access an archive of list data, as well as the obvious capacity to send and receive messages via the list. Most law lists are hosted by academic institutions in the USA or UK and tend to be defined around special interest groups, e.g., bioethics, criminal justice, data protection law, law and economics, public law, etc. Bulletin-board services sound rather similar, though technically they are not. They enable subscribers to communicate in a kind of 'open space' in the network, where any other subscriber can read and comment on messages left. Bulletin boards exist on all kinds of topics. They can be a useful way of tapping into know-how that is otherwise unpublished, or they may be a complete waste of time and (cyber)space! There are a number of bulletin boards on legal matters, mostly based in the USA.

The most important feature of the internet (indeed for most people it is pretty much synonymous with the internet) is the *World Wide Web* (WWW). To get access to the internet you require a number of things, most of which will be already sitting on the computer you are using; you need special 'browser' software, such as 'Netscape' or 'Microsoft Internet Explorer', to access the Web an internet service provider (ISP) actually to connect you to the Web and e-mail services. Once connected, you can conduct searches using a generalist 'search engine' such as *Alta Vista, Google, Lycos,* or *Yahoo*. The techniques you use for searching are discussed in the next section. There are also a growing number of sites that provide 'portals'. These are a kind of gateway to the internet, which means that, rather than searching the whole net at random each time, you can use the basic subject index created by a portal site to get you closer to what you want (for example, a lot of portal sites now have 'legal services' as a discrete category). You should be aware that the quality of different portals varies, and none of them is likely to give you access to anything other than a relatively small amount of the available information—usually the most popular sites make it onto portal listings, but these may be no more than 15–20 per cent of the sites available. Even so, this can still be a very large amount of information!

Documents installed on WWW use 'hypertext' (or more sophisticated variants on this theme), that is a kind of document structure which enables users to browse the database using highlighted keywords, concepts, or graphics called 'markers' to move within and between documents. These function rather as we might use the index to browse through the relevant parts of a book. This makes WWW much more interactive than some elements of the Net. A growing number of legal organisations have used WWW to generate 'home pages' giving information about their activities; for example, both the (English) Law Society (*www.lawsoc.org.uk/*) and Bar Council (*www.barcouncil.org.uk*) have their own websites. Most UK law schools have also created WWW pages, mostly as a mechanism for advertising courses and other activities, though a number of them also maintain list of law-related web links.

There is a growing number of electronic journals available, for example *E Law*, established by Murdoch University in Australia at *www.murdoch.edu.au/elaw* and *Global Legal Studies* (at Indiana University) which is available on the Web at *www.law.indiana.edu/glsj/glsj.html*. The *Web Journal of Current Legal Issues* (cited as Web JCLI) was the first UK law journal launched on the www, in 1996. Based at Newcastle University's web site, it can be accessed at *www.webjcli.ac.uk/*. It was followed, in 1997, by the *Journal of Information, Law and Technology*, which is to be found at *www.elj.warwick.ac.uk/jilt/*

Apart from journals, a large number of primary legal data can now be accessed across the Internet, including legislation, case law, and international legal materials. Much of this is freely accessible (i.e., not as a subscription service), as the following table of useful web sites shows. It is also absolutely essential when navigating the WWW to be careful when typing the address you want. There are generally no spaces between letters or symbols, and even one typing error is usually enough to prevent access. Also be warned that site addresses can and do change, and although site administrators ('webmasters' in Net-speak) will generally create new links to steer you in the right direction, we cannot guarantee that **Table 2.1** will remain accurate until the next edition! Check *our* website at Oxford University Press for changes!

Table 2.1 Useful 'free' websites for legal research

Legislation:	www.hmso.gov.uk/acts.htm	Full text of Public General Acts of the Westminster Parliament, since 1996, (c.1), Local Acts from start of 1997. Draft and final (full text) statutory instruments from 1997 on.
	www.bailii.org	The British and Irish Legal Information Institute's full text database of UK statues (1988–), Northern Irish statutes (1945–), Irish Statutes (Republic) (1922–) and Acts of the Scottish Parliament. Also a range of English, Scottish, Irish, and Welsh statutory instruments.
	www.parliament.the-stationery-office.co.uk/	Full text of Bills presented before Parliament in the current session, with an indication of the stage reached.
Case Law:	www.bailii.org	Full text of decisions of the HL, PC, CA (all from 1996–) and the High Court (from various start dates, though none before 1996).
	www.parliament.the-stationery-office.co.uk/	Full text versions of all House of Lords judgments since 14.11.96.
	www.courtservice.gov.uk/judgments	Selected full text judgments from the CA and High Court only (cases selected by the judges for reporting here).
	www.lawreports.co.uk	Incorporated Council of Law Reporting site, containing its 'Daily Law Notes' feature. This service, updated daily Monday–Friday provides summaries of important new decisions of the ECJ, HL, CA and High Court prior to their appearing in the published Law Reports series.
	www.europa.eu.int/cj/en/index.htm	European Court of Justice: contains text relating to the ECJ, cases decided by the ECJ and CFI since 17.6.97 and a weekly list of recent proceedings (opinions and judgments).

	www.echr.coe.int	European Court of Human Rights: searchable full text database of cases. Also has full text of the Rules of the Court and the ECHR and its Protocols.
UK Parliament:	*www.parliament.uk/hophome.htm*	Gateway to House of Lords and House of Commons websites, with information on their functions and activities, and access to the Information Offices of both Houses. Can also be used to access Parliamentary publications.
	www.parliament.the-stationery-office.co.uk/pa/ld/ldhansrd.htm	Full text of the House of Lords Hansard (debates) from 10.6.96.
	www.parliament.the-stationery-office.co.uk/pa/cm/cmhansrd.htm	Full text of House of Commons Daily Hansard (debates); complete from the start of session 1997/98.
Other useful sources	*www.worldlii.org*	New site (officially launched November 2002) containing some 270 databases of legal information from 48 jurisdictions in the UK and Ireland, the USA, Canada, Hong Kong, South Africa, Australasia and the South Pacific. Also provides links to over 15,000 law-related websites around the world.
	www.findlaw.com	Law portal site indexing information on US law and practice, including government and public interest sites, law firms, and the university Law Review Project, which provides electronic access to a significant number of US academic law journals.
	www.open.gov.uk	Gateway to a vast range of sites created by UK central government departments (including the Lord Chancellor s Department and the Home Office), government agencies and local authorities. Of variable utility.
	www.homeoffice.gov.uk/hract/	The Home Office's guide to human rights under the auspices of the Human Rights Unit.

Apart from the free sites there are a number of subscription Internet services useful to lawyers. Lawtel, as we have seen, is one of those. The subscriber elements of Sweet & Maxwell's Current Legal Information (CLI) site provide an excellent resource (at *http://smlawpub.co.uk*). CLI contains electronic versions of the Legal Journals Index, Current Law Case and Legislation Citators, from 1977 and 1989 onwards respectively, the Financial Journals Index, the digest of Current Law Cases (1986 to date), and the Badger 'grey paper' index which digests and abstracts law-related material from journalistic and some other secondary sources.

As this brief survey indicates, the amount of legal information on the Internet is growing exponentially—most of the free sites identified here have emerged only in the last five to six years, and we see no indication that this trend is about to stop. This does not necessarily mean that we are on the brink, as some computer pundits seem to suggest, of a kind of 'informational Nirvana', but it may not be many years before the knowledgeability of law is determined far more by access to computer resources than to conventional libraries—though it may take rather longer before we see a wide range of legal data on the Internet being routinely cited in the courts!

2.6.3 Search Techniques

Most of the internet and CD-based systems have little in the way of organising or indexing, other than into broadly thematic but large-scale libraries of data. Rather, most systems use a technique of matching key words or phrases entered by the user to the text contained in the database. In technical terms this usually involves a system of what is called 'boolean searching' (see Leith, 1991). This involves fairly simple word-matching techniques, so that, for example, if you search for cases containing the word 'knife', that is precisely what you will get—all cases in which the word knife appears, regardless of its legal significance. This is probably the greatest practical limitation of such systems, as it means they are not very effective if you are trying to research concepts, particularly concepts which are difficult to define.

An example of such is 'good faith', which is an important concept relating to Contract Law (see further **Chapter 10**). However, it is extremely difficult to define, is not always identified by name, and arises in a range of legal contexts, as well as being a term that may be used colloquially. As a result it is almost impossible to construct an effective boolean search related to that concept.

Against this, these systems do have the advantage of being *interactive*. It is not necessary to get one's search terms exactly right first time; it is quite possible to modify a search request in response to the information that one has received from the system already. In developing search terms, it is important to note that various systems use particular words to enable you to structure your request with some degree of precision. These special words are normally referred to as *connectors* or *logical operators*. This means that those particular terms will not actually be searched for, but will tell the system how your search terms relate to each other. The main connectors can be described diagrammatically as shown below.

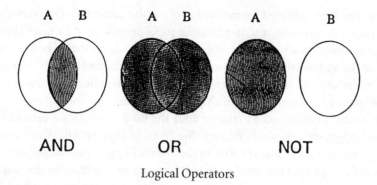

Logical Operators

As you can see, there are essentially three ways in which search terms can be connected; we have identified them by the most commonly used connectors AND, OR, and NOT (the precise terms used and variety of connectors will vary from system to system):

- AND will search documents for terms A and B, and will retrieve those only where *both* terms are discovered (here represented by the shaded area in the two circles. LexisNexis and Westlaw also have a rather more sophisticated proximity connector which enables you to specify the maximum number of words you want separating your search terms, e.g. 'cat w/3 dog' in LexisNexis will retrieve only those documents where 'cat' occurs within three or fewer words either side of 'dog' (whereas AND will retrieve any documents where both your research terms occur, regardless of proximity).

- OR will retrieve all documents containing *either or both* search terms A and B.

- NOT enables you to search for term A, but *excludes* documents which also contain word B.

The technicality of boolean searching undoubtedly limits the research utility of electronic systems, and may well be one reason why it is estimated that boolean searching alone may retrieve as little as 25 per cent of the relevant information from a system (Poynder, 1994). A number of search engines such as 'Google' and information retrieval systems, including LexisNexis and Westlaw, have developed a facility for *natural language searching*, which enables you to enter search terms in 'natural language' or 'free text' as it is sometimes called—in other words 'plain English', if you prefer. The process of keyword selection and pattern matching is then completed by the software. Natural language searching is not necessarily superior to boolean. Most natural language systems simply convert into boolean by selecting those words that appear to be searchable. The selection mechanism tends to be relatively crude, so a natural language search can actually throw up more irrelevant material than a well-constructed boolean search.

2.6.4 Citing Electronic Sources

As we indicated above, there has been a massive expansion in the number of case authorities now available through web sites. Equally, cases are now reported very quickly after judgment has been delivered (sometimes even on the same day). One very common problem has arisen: how do you cite particular pages or sections of the case? This second point is important for any advocate when attempting to direct the judge to a particular passage in the authority, as there has been no common method adopted in presenting reports in electronic format; moreover, the printout of pages (usually without number- ing) will often vary according to which printers, typefaces, or computers are used. In response to this problem, on 11 January 2001 the Lord Chief Justice issued a *Practice Direction (Judgments: Form and Citation), The Times,* 16 January 2001. This directed that all judgments, as from 11 January 2001 in the Court of Appeal (and subsequently in the High Court), adopt what is termed a 'neutral' form of citation. Whether the judgment is eventually reported in the printed law reports or not, each case will be given a specific reference number and paragraph numbers which will appear in both the electronic and printed forms of the report. The paragraph numbers do not start and stop with each judge's judgment, but run throughout the case report sequentially, thereby facilitating searching in electronic form, and the comparison of electronic and paper versions. The practice of neutral citation has also been taken up by the House of Lords and Privy Council.

The electronic citations thus adopted take the following form:

- **UKHL** for the House of Lords;
- **UKPC** for the Privy Council;
- **EWCA** for the Court of Appeal followed by 'Civ' or 'Crim' respectively for the Civil and Criminal Divisions;
- **EWHC** for the High Court (followed by the abbreviation for the Division of the High Court, or 'Admin' for the Administrative Court).

Each case is given a unique number by the court administrators. For example, the cita- tion for the judgment in the Court of Appeal (Civil Division) case of *Smith* v *Jones* (which we will say is the tenth case in 2003 to be decided by that court) appears as: *Smith* v *Jones* [2003] EWCA Civ 10. The official number (here, 10) will now always have to be cited on at least one occasion whenever a reference is made to *Smith* v *Jones* in later cases. If refer- ence is to be made to, say, paragraph 59, the citation becomes: *Smith* v *Jones* [2003] EWCA Civ 10 at [59]. Multiple paragraph references will take the form of: *Smith* v *Jones* [2003] EWCA Civ 10 at [1], [7], and [30]–[42].

Once the judgment has been reported in the printed reports the neutral citation will appear in front of the familiar citation from the law reports described earlier in this chap- ter: thus, *Smith* v *Jones* [2003] EWCA Civ 10 at [42]; [2003] QB 113 at [42]; [2003] 1 All ER 88 at [42]. Note that the paragraph number is referred to throughout, though it appears that some judges still prefer citing the page rather than paragraph number when referring to the reported version of a case. The neutral citation must always be used on at least one occasion when the authority is cited in a later judgment. Other than that, the Law Reports produced by the Incorporated Council of Law Reporting are still judi- cially preferred in the High Court and Court of Appeal, and should be cited where available—*Practice Direction (Judgments: Form and Citation) (Supreme Court)* [2001] 1 WLR 194. This was confirmed most recently in *Bank of Scotland* v *Henry Butcher and Co (a Firm)*, *The Times*, 13 February 2003, where the Court of Appeal, faced with an extremely ill-prepared case, not only re-emphasised the requirement to refer to The Law Reports rather than citing other published versions but also indicated in very strong language how the Court would take a dim view of lawyers who did not comply with all relevant practice directions on the proper preparation of material and the use of authorities.

2.6.5 Unreported Cases and IR Systems

The electronic availability of cases, has significantly reduced the significance of the distinction between reported and unreported cases. Dearth of authority is thus potentially replaced by excess.

As long ago as 1983 Lord Diplock, in *Roberts Petroleum Ltd* v *Bernard Kenney Ltd* [1983] AC 192; [1983] 1 All ER 564, sought to restrict severely the use of unreported authorities made available by electronic transcripts, even though they are verbatim reports of the official record. His Lordship's complaint was that the relative ease of accessing such cases by computer had led lawyers increasingly to cite cases that established no new or important principle. This extra material was seen to cause a greater waste of time.

Clearly, there is some merit to the core of his Lordship's argument, to the effect that lawyers should only cite cases that actually lay down or explain a principle of law. However, there are plenty of reported cases that, at best, provide only a gloss on established principles, so the problem does not apply solely to unreported cases. Furthermore, if we were to take Lord Diplock's argument to its logical extreme, then, even more than now, we would be creating a situation where the law reporter, not the court, becomes arbiter of what is law, and to that extent only, his lordship's suggestion is of limited assistance.

2.7 Concluding Remarks

In this chapter we have introduced you to the main resources and techniques required to undertake both conventional paper and electronic legal research. These are extremely important skills, both academically and practically speaking. Research skills are emphasised both in the Quality Assurance Agency's 'Benchmark' statement of skills required of the law degree, and in the requirements of the Law Society and Bar at the professional stage of training. But you will not get proficient in these skills just by reading this book. We have provided you with a start, and a reference resource to dip into if you get stuck; that is all. As with all skills, mastery lies in action, not reading! Get familiar with your library and get comfortable with the technology—the days are now long gone when any lawyer—academic or practising—can afford to be a technophobe!

Finally, before moving on to **Chapter 3**, you will find a couple of exercises based upon some of the material in this chapter, and intended to help you test your research skills.

EXERCISE 1   Flick-knives for sale

If you were wondering whether you would ever find the answer to the problem we have used to develop the themes of this book, now is *your* chance to find out. See if you can find answers to the following questions. If you can, you will have the basic material to advise our fictitious friend.

QUESTIONS

(a) Using the index and main volumes to *Halsbury's Laws*, find the volume number and paragraph containing information on criminal liability for the display and sale of flick-knives.

(b) Using any appropriate research strategy, what is the current **statutory** provision governing that liability?

(c) Can you find any **cases** on the interpretation of that provision?

(d) Using your research, what is your advice?

ANSWERS

(a) There are in fact two alternative references to flick-knives. One reference, indexed under '*Offensive weapons, manufacture, sale, hire etc.—restrictions*' refers you to vol. 11, para. 174. Alternatively, the index also lists '*Flick-knife, offences as to*'. This refers you to a separate source in vol. 47, para. 379. However, as vol. 47 was reissued in 1994, this reference is now totally inaccurate.

(b) Volume 11 of *Halsbury* refers you to the Restriction of Offensive Weapons Act 1959 s. 1(1), as amended. In vol. 11, the latest amendment noted refers to the Criminal Justice Act 1988. At the time of writing, no further updates appear in the 1996 *Cumulative Supplement* or the *Noter-Up*. Searches could also be made using the title of the 1959 Act in either the *Current Law Statute Citator*, or *Halsbury's Statutes*, though the latter would be a rather more long-winded process.

(c) Volume 11 mentions no cases; that is misleading, they do exist! The *Current Law Statute Citators* are more helpful. The 1989–94 citator lists no cases. The 1972–88 citator mentions two cases in 1983: *Gibson* v *Wales* and *R* v *Simpson*. The 1947–71 citator lists only *Fisher* v *Bell*—the case which led to the first amendment of the 1959 Act. These could be followed up (if required) in outline using the *Current Law Year Books*, or in full through the various law reports.

(d) Your advice should take into account that, though initially it was not an offence to offer a flick-knife for sale (*Fisher* v *Bell*), the Act has been amended. As a result it is now an offence not only to sell, but also to have on display or in one's possession, a flick-knife for sale.

EXERCISE 2   (Un)equal treatment?

Imagine you are working in a law firm. Your principal is in a hurry, and has asked you to do some research for her. She is concerned with a problem on equal pay, and recalls that there was a case listed before the ECJ sometime in 1989, in which the European Commission was seeking to question the compatibility of the UK Sex Discrimination Act 1975 with EC law. She cannot remember the case number, nor when the Court actually delivered its judgment. Can you:

(a) find it in the *Official Journal*?

(b) give her the case name and number?

(c) find out what has happened to it since?

ANSWERS

(a) As you do not know the case number and may be uncertain of the name, it would be best to use the OJ's Alphabetical Index. You should have started with the Annual Edition for 1989. There are a number of search terms you might have tried, such as equal pay, or sex discrimination, but neither of those would have helped. In fact the case fitting that description is listed twice, under 'equal rights for men and women' and under 'equal treatment'. These refer to OJ Cl/192/13: i.e. *C Series*, No. 192, p. 13.

(b) If you follow up that reference in Issue 192 of 1989, you will find it refers to case 202/89 *European Commission* v *United Kingdom*.

(c) The reference you have looked up tells you only that the case has been presented; it is silent as to any judgment. To find a reference to the judgment, you need to use the Annual Edition for 1990. As you have the case number now, it would be easier to search the Methodological Table (though you could use the Alphabetical Table, it is rather more long-winded). This will tell you whether the case has been decided or withdrawn. In fact, the case was withdrawn on 28 December 1990—see [1990] OJ C326/18.

REFERENCES

CLINCH, P. (2001), *Using A Law Library* (2nd edn., London: Blackstone Press).

DANE, J., and THOMAS, P. (1995), *How to Use a Law Library* (3rd edn., London: Sweet & Maxwell).

JACKSON, R. (1970), 'Police Search—Law Reports—Law Reform by Precedent', *Cambridge Law Journal* 1.

LEITH, P. (1991), *The Computerised Lawyer* (London: Springer-Verlag).

LLOYD, I. (1986), *Legal Databases in Europe* (Amsterdam: Elsevier).

PAYNE, R. (1983), 'Lawtel: a Prestel based legal retrieval service' in *The Progress in Legal Information Systems in Europe* (Strasbourg: Council of Europe).

POYNDER, R. (1994), 'Beyond Boolean', *Information World Review*, July/August, 14.

RAISTRICK, D. (1981), *Index to Legal Citations and Abbreviations* (Abingdon: Professional Books).

TUNKEL, V. (1993), 'Legal Research after *Pepper* v *Hart*', 90 *Law Society's Gazette*, 12 May 1993, 17.

3

Reading the Law

One of the key factors which distinguishes law from the social rules we considered in **Chapter 1** is its nature as written text. Law derives at least some of its authority and power from the status that this confers (for a critical development of this argument see Goodrich, 1986:21–4).

Much of this book is concerned with principles of interpretation—both of statutes and of cases. At its heart, any process of interpretation is one of reading. Reading is an activity that can be carried on at different levels. If you have ever studied literature you will be familiar with the idea of reading as a search for layers of meaning. On this basis, for example, one does not find in Dickens's *Hard Times* just the story of the characters involved, but also a powerful critique of mid-Victorian social values, and a particular attack on the doctrine of Utilitarianism which dominated that age.

Legal texts can similarly be seen as displaying layers of meaning. These layers broadly correspond to the three questions that we might ask about a legal text, what we call the *What, How & Why* of law, that is:

(a) *What* kind of law is it?

(b) *How* does it affect existing law?

(c) *Why* was it made?

At the first level (*what*), the form of the document itself tells us something about it. If, for example, it takes the form of an Act of Parliament, we know that it takes precedence over case law.

At another level (*how*) we must work out what it is actually about; this is a matter of constructing meaning from the text, though, again, the way in which legal documents are put together can sometimes help us in this task.

At a third level, legal texts contain a deeper meaning, which may help us to answer the question *why* the law has developed in such a way. Legislation has a history which may reflect particular economic, political, or social values. Court decisions may also reflect a variety of underlying influences, for example: the values which the legal system has traditionally served; the prejudices of a particular judge; or the perceived internal logic of the case-law system. Asking *why* may involve an element of historical analysis (e.g. to see how a law has developed over the years—though note that, traditionally, reading the law has been treated as a largely ahistorical process), or a consideration of governmental or judicial policy-making. This will help us to understand the reasoning behind the court's decision in a case, or why an Act with those particular provisions was passed at that particular time.

In this chapter, we shall consider primarily the questions *what* and *why*. In looking at the structure of legal rules, we may occasionally trespass on the territory of *how*, though that will generally be left to later chapters. In so doing, we have broken this chapter down into four sections: reading statutes; reading cases; reading literary sources; and, lastly, we shall take the step from reading to writing about law.

3.1 Reading Statutes

Once a bill has received the Royal Assent it becomes an Act of Parliament. An Act is a public document and must be published by The Stationery Office; it will also, as we have seen, be published in a variety of other sources, including *Statutes in Force*. A copy of such an Act is reproduced below.

3.1.1 The Elements of an Act of Parliament

Any modern Act of Parliament will take the following form (each number here corresponds to that on the illustration):

(1) Short Title

(2) Citation

(3) Long Title

(4) Date of Royal Assent

(5) Sections

(6) Marginal Note

In addition to these, copies of the statutes may also contain:

(a) Enacting formula

(b) Textual amendments and annotations

(c) Date of Commencement

(d) Schedules and Tables

We shall now consider each of these in the order in which they appear in the Act. The numbers or letters in bold text after each heading refer to the illustration.

Long and short titles (3) & (1)

Older Acts contain a *Preamble* which introduces the legislation, often in some detail, and usually explaining why it had been passed. This device is not used in modern statutes.

Modern Acts will have both a **long** and **short title**.

- The long title describes the general scope of the Act.
- The short title is for convenience of citation.

(1)   **PUBLIC LAVATORIES (TURNSTILES) ACT 1963 (c. 32)**   (2)

Ss. 1,2

(3)   An Act to make it the duty of local authorities to abolish turnstiles in public lavatories and sanitary conveniences.   [31st July 1963]   (4)

1.—(1) Every turnstile in any part of a public lavatory or public sanitary convenience controlled or managed by a local authority, or in any entrance or exit of such a public lavatory or convenience, shall be removed not later than six months after the passing of this Act; and after the passing of this Act no turnstile shall be (5)   installed in, or in any entrance or exit of, any such public lavatory or convenience.

Abolition of turnstiles.   (6)

(2) It shall be the duty of local authorities to ensure that the provisions of this Act are complied with notwithstanding anything in any other Act, whether public or local.

(3) If any local authority in England and Wales fail to discharge a duty imposed on them by the foregoing provisions of this section, that duty shall be enforceable, on the application of [¹the Secretary of State], by mandamus.

(4) There shall be paid out of moneys provided by Parliament any increase attributable to this Act in the sums of payable by way of Rate-deficiency Grant or Exchequer Equalisation Grant under the enactments relating to local government in England and Wales or in Scotland.

(5) In this section the expression "local authority" means, in England and Wales, a local authority within the meaning of [²the Local Government Act 1972], a local authority within the meaning of the London Government Act 1939 or the Common Council of the City of London and, in Scotland, the council of a county, the town council of a burgh or a district council.

1972 c. 70.
1939 c. 40.   (b)

2.—(1) This Act may be cited as the Public Lavatories (Turnstiles) Act 1963.

Short title and extent.

(2) This Act shall not extend to Northern Ireland.

¹ Words substituted by virtue of (W.) S.I. 1965/319, arts. 2(1), 10(1)(a), Sch. 1 Pt. 1 and (E.) 1970/1681, arts. 2(1), 6(3)
2 Words substituted by virtue of Local Government Act 1972 (c. 70), s. 272(2)   (b)

Figure 3.1 A Public General Act from *Statutes in Force*

As neither provides more than the most general indication of what the Act is about they are of very little help in deducing the scope or meaning of legislation. By contrast, the Preambles to the older Acts are used as an aid to interpreting those particular Acts (see **Chapter 8**). This difference may seem rather odd; why should a preamble be of use when the long title is not? The answer lies in the fact that they serve diverse functions.

Consider, for example, an Act you may meet in the Law of Contract: the Unfair Contract Terms Act 1977 (referred to here as UCTA). The short title does not tell you, in fact, that the Act is concerned with exclusion clauses in contracts. The long title is not much more help. It states:

> An Act to impose further limits on the extent to which under the Law of England and Wales and Northern Ireland civil liability for breach of contract, or for negligence or other breach of duty, can be avoided by means of contract terms or otherwise, and under the Law of Scotland civil liability can be avoided by means of contract terms.

In this way, they are perhaps analogous to the label on a jam jar. If you look at a jar, you will usually find the title in large letters on the front—STRAWBERRY JAM—but that does not really tell you what is in the jar. It does no more than broadly identify the product to us. You need to look much more closely to find that the jar does not just contain strawberries and sugar, but also, say, pectin, citric acid, and sodium citrate, and often a collection of 'E numbers' as well. So it is with an Act. To find out what it is really about you need to look at the contents (i.e. the operative sections) in detail. By comparison, preambles served to give the courts some notice of Parliamentary intent, though even then, this was often in rather vague terms.

This does not mean that the long title is wholly useless; it will give you a general indication of the scope of the Act and, together with the contents list which sometimes precedes it (headed *Arrangement of Sections*), it can be helpful in establishing a sense of the Act's contents and structure when *skim reading* (see below).

Citation (2)

Statutes obviously have their short title and the year of their creation cited, but, as we explained in the previous chapter, they also have what is known as a **Chapter number**. If a Statute was the 50th to be passed in 1977 then it will have that number. This is a means of reference only.

Royal Assent (4)

No Statute is law until assented to by the Monarch. The date of assent is given in the Statute—in UCTA it is 26 October 1977. Frequently this is the date on which the Act becomes law. However, the Act may state that all or part of it will come into effect at a later date (in UCTA's case this was 1 February 1978) or at a date to be appointed by the appropriate minister. Different parts of the Act can thus come into effect at different times. Obviously this may have important practical consequences for the advice lawyers give. Inevitably it can make life very complicated, where you need to know which rules have been superseded already, which have not, and which are going to be, and when!

Enacting formula (a)

Although not always reproduced in *Statutes in Force* (they are missing from our example), these are introductory words which appear in every Act stating that both Houses of Parliament and the Monarch have passed the Act. The form of words used is identical in every case, and is of long historical standing. They are of little practical legal significance, though the publication of the Act with these words is taken as conclusive evidence that the Act has been passed and is good law.

Sections (5)

All Acts are divided into sections—these are usually cited in an abbreviated form as s. 1 or s. 2, or (in the plural) ss. 2 and 3. Sometimes it may be possible to perceive a logical development of concepts as the sections progress, but this is not always the case, so you may, in resolving a single problem find yourself starting at section 1, which is qualified by something in section 3, which contains terms defined in section 45 and repeals part of an earlier enactment listed in Schedule (sch.) 4! We provide further discussion and specific examples of how statutes are organized in **Chapter 7**.

Each section will often be divided into **subsections**—cited as section 1(1) or section 1(4). After subsections we can have **paragraphs**—cited as section 1(1)(a) or section 1(2)(g); and even **sub-paragraphs**, as in section 1(1)(a)(i). Section 3 of UCTA has such a division. If you have ever tried to draft the rules of a committee or a game you will appreciate that this device can be used to split up ideas or clarify particular points. Thus, each separate section of an Act may deal with a separate issue (though these sections may often remain closely related), and each sub-section (etc.) within a section may express a different aspect of that issue. For example, if you have a definition section, it may be that the phrase to be defined has more than one statutory meaning, in which case you could use a different sub-section for each meaning.

Often, you will also find that groups of sections dealing with the same point have *headings* and that very large groupings are divided into *parts*. These titles are of little significance; they are essentially a form of indexing. At best they will indicate some general thematic coherence among the sections under that heading, but they have virtually no value as an aid to interpretation.

Marginal notes (6)

Most Acts display marginal notes as a kind of quick reference mechanism to help you find the section you want. They are generally, like headings, thought to have little legal significance; though there is judicial disagreement over whether, as a last resort, both marginal notes and headings may be used as indicative of the general purpose of the section(s) to which they refer (cf.—which means compare—*Chandler* v *DPP* [1964] AC 736; [1962] 3 All ER 142 and *DPP* v *Schildkamp* [1971] AC 1; [1969] 3 All ER 1640). In any event, it is an issue which seldom arises.

Amendments and annotations (b)

In *Statutes in Force*, it is normal for any amendments to an Act made subsequent to its passing to be incorporated into the text. As in the illustrated Act, the amendments are shown within square brackets. These amendments are cited as being part of the Act, and have the full force of law. Any footnotes or commentary annotated to an Act (as, e.g., in *Current Law Statutes Annotated*) do not form part of the Act and, of course, have no direct legal effect.

Date of commencement (c)

Acts will normally have a specific commencement section near to the end of the statute. It may either state that the Act, or parts of the Act, will come into force on a specific date or dates, or that it comes into force on a date to be fixed by the relevant government minister. On the latter occasions the normal form of words runs more or less as follows:

> ... this Act shall come into force on such day as the Secretary of State may by order appoint; and different days may be so appointed for different provisions or different purposes of the same provision ...

This gives the minister *carte blanche* in deciding what comes into force and when.

Schedules (d)

Schedules (the term may be abbreviated to 'sched.' or 'sch.') can be found at the end of most Acts of Parliament. Schedules are parts of an Act that provide more detail regarding sections or groups of sections. Sometimes they give examples of how to calculate things contained in the Act, such as pensions, tax assessments, and so on; sometimes they simply expand upon phrases; sometimes they define phrases; or sometimes they contain detailed amendments of earlier legislation. As such, they may be quite detailed, perhaps even exceeding the length of the rest of the Act. Each provision within a schedule is called a **paragraph**, and there may also be **sub-paragraphs**. So, a provision is properly cited in the form 'sch. 1 para. 3(a)'.

A schedule, normally the last, tells you which earlier Acts the present statute repeals. This is important because, generally speaking, once an Act is passed it remains in force until repealed by another Act. This is why vestiges of the Witchcraft Acts were still in force as late as 1951 and why other such anachronisms remain 'on the Statute book'. By an odd quirk it also meant that, in English law, the USA did not gain its independence until 1963!

Note, here, that though lawyers sometimes talk of Acts being 'obsolete', there is no formal basis upon which an Act could be disapplied by the courts simply because it has become old or out-of-date. At most it can be argued that a statute should not apply to a novel situation, because that situation was not within the original legislative intent; this reflects what is sometimes called *the principle of contemporary exposition*: see *Aerated Bread Co.* v *Gregg* (1873) LR 8 QB 355. In this case Blackburn J refused to apply provisions of the Bread Act 1836 regarding 'fancy bread' to the plaintiff's product, because at the time the Act was passed, the term had a very specific meaning, which could not be applied to the disputed product some thirty-six years later.

Some obsolete legislation is periodically repealed by the passing of Statute Law Revision Acts, which are purely administrative measures intended to tidy up the statute book.

3.2 Reading Cases

In this section we will look first at the form of English reports and then of European Union cases.

3.2.1 English Law Reports

Like statutes, modern English law reports tend to follow a standard format, similar to the illustration (see the following page) from *Finnegan* v *Clowney Youth Training Programme Ltd* [1990] 2 All ER 546. Running down the pages, you will find:

(1) The name of the case.

(2) The court in which it was heard.

(3) The names of the judge(s) presiding.

(4) The hearing date(s).

(5) The headnote.

(6) Notes of cross-references to *Halsbury*.

(7) A list of cases referred to.

(8) Details of the appeal.

(9) The names of counsel appearing in the case.

(10) The judgment(s) (not shown).

(11) Letters in the margin.

Some of these are quite self-explanatory, so we will be selective in the points we discuss.

The name of the case (1)

It was said in **Chapter 2** that English case names follow the names of the parties involved. In this respect, Common Law case citations tend to differ from the forms adopted in many Civilian systems, which often adopt a more anonymous, administrative title, based usually on the court, and a case number or date, though this is not always so. The French, for example, use both styles. Cases before the *Cour de Cassation* are cited by giving an abbreviated version of the division concerned (*civile, criminelle, sociale, commerciale*), the date of the decision and its location in the relevant reports, *les recueils généraux*, known as the *Recueil Dalloz, Recueil Sirey,* and the *Juris-Classeur Périodique*.

Conversely, decisions of the *Conseil d'Etat* are cited by a case name. By comparison, the English system sounds simple, but, as is so often the case, that impression is misleading; there is a wide array of forms that the case name can take. These forms can themselves tell us quite a lot about the nature of the case.

In *civil* cases the normal mode of citation is the name of the person bringing the case or appeal (**claimant**, formerly **plaintiff** or **appellant**) first followed by the name of the **defendant** (or **respondent** in an appeal): thus, '*Smith* v *Jones*'. The 'v' means *versus*, that is 'against' (reflecting the adversarial nature of the process); it is usually spoken as 'and',

546   All England Law Reports   [1990] 2 All ER

(1)

Finnegan v Clowney Youth Training
Programme Ltd

a

HOUSE OF LORDS (2)
LORD BRIDGE OF HARWICH, LORD GRIFFITHS, LORD ACKNER, LORD OLIVER OF AYLMERTON AND
LORD LOWRY
(3)
2 APRIL, 17 MAY 1990
(4)

b

Northern Ireland – Employment – Discrimination against a woman – Provision in relation to retirement – Female employees required to retire at 60 whereas men retiring at 65 – Northern Ireland and English legislation identical – English legislation passed before adoption of EEC equal treatment directive whereas Northern Ireland legislation passed subsequent to directive – Whether Northern Ireland provision passed to implement directive – Whether Northern Ireland c *provision to be construed differently from English provision – Whether unlawful discrimination for women to be required to retire earlier than men – Whether necessary to refer question to European Court – Sex Discrimination (Northern Ireland) Order 1976, art 8(2)(4) – Council Directive (EEC) 76/207, art 5(1).*

European Economic Community – National legislation – Construction – Construction of legislation d *relating to death or retirement – Determination of case not dependent on question of Community law – Whether court should make reference to European Court.*

(5)
In February 1986 the employee, who was employed by the employer as a supervisor, was told that she would be required to retire on 1 April 1986 following her sixtieth birthday on 22 March. Her request to be allowed to continue working beyond her sixtieth birthday was refused and her employment was duly terminated on 1 April. The employee *e* made a complaint to an industrial tribunal alleging that she had been unlawfully discriminated against by the employer on the grounds of sex, contrary to art 8(2)ᵃ of the Sex Discrimination (Northern Ireland) Order 1976, in that she had been forced to retire at the age of 60 whereas male employees retired at 65. The employer relied on art 8(4)ᵇ of the 1976 order, which *f* provided that art 8(2) did not apply to provisions relating to death or retirement. The tribunal upheld the complaint and awarded the employee compensation, on the ground that art 8(2) and (4) had to be construed consistently with art 5(1)ᶜ of Council Directive (EEC) 76/207 (the equal treatment directive), which prohibited discrimination in working conditions, including conditions governing dismissal, on grounds of sex. The employer appealed to the *g* Court of Appeal in Northern Ireland, which allowed the appeal on the ground, inter alia, that art 8(2) of the 1976 order was to be given the same meaning as identical legislation in England which had been construed as permitting discrimination in retirement ages. The employee appealed to the House of Lords, contending, inter alia, that the English legislation was distinguishable since it had been passed before the equal treatment directive was adopted whereas the 1976 order had not been made until after the adoption of the directive, so that the order had to be construed in the light of the directive. The employee also requested *h* the court to seek a preliminary ruling from the Court of Justice of the European Communities (11) under art 177 of the EEC Treaty on the question which arose on the appeal.

Held — (1) Since art 8(4) of the 1976 order was in identical terms and in an identical context to the English legislation it must have been intended to have identical effect and should not be presumed to have been made for the purpose of implementing the equal

---

a   Article 8(2), so far as material, provides: 'It is unlawful for a person, in the case of a woman employed by him at an establishment in Northern Ireland, to discriminate against her . . . (*b*) by dismissing her, or subjecting her to any other detriment.'
b   Article 8(4) provides: 'Paragraphs . . . (2) do not apply to provision in relation to death or retirement.'
c   Article 5(1) is set out at p 548 *h*, post

---

a treatment directive, notwithstanding that the order was made subsequently to that directive. It followed that although the employee's compulsory retirement at the age of 60 was a contravention of art 8(2) of the 1976 order, since it discriminated against her on the grounds of sex, it was a provision in relation to death or retirement which fell within the exception permitted by art 8(4) and therefore did not constitute unlawful discrimination. The employee's dismissal therefore did not contravene art 8(2). The appeal would accordingly be dismissed

b (see pp 551 *a b d* to *f h* to p 552 *b*, post); *Duke v GEC Reliance Ltd* [1988] 1 All ER 626 applied; *Marshall v Southampton and South West Hampshire Area Health Authority (Teaching)* Case 152/84 [1986] 2 All ER 584 considered.

(2) Since it was for the United Kingdom courts to interpret the 1976 order and since the equal treatment directive did not have direct effect between citizens the determination of the appeal did not depend on any question of Community law. Accordingly, a reference

c to the European Court under art 177 was not necessary (see p 551 *h* to p 552 *b*, post).

Notes

For discrimination against employees, see 16 Halsbury's Laws (4th edn) paras 771·2, 771·5, and for cases on the subject, see 20 Digest (Reissue) 588-593, *4495-4515*.

For Community provisions on equal treatment of employees, see 52 Halsbury's Laws (4th

d edn) paras 21·13, 21·17.   (6)

For references to the Court of Justice of the European Communities for a preliminary ruling, see 51 ibid paras 3·79-3·81.

For the EEC Treaty, art 177, see 50 Halsbury's Statutes (4th edn) 325.

Article 8 of the Sex Discrimination (Northern Ireland) Order 1976 corresponds to s 6 of the Sex Discrimination Act 1975. For s 6 of the 1975 Act, see 6 ibid 702.

e

Cases referred to in opinions

Burton v British Railways Board Case 19/81 [1982] 3 All ER 537, [1982] QB 1080, [1982] 3 WLR 387, [1982] ECR 555, CJEC.

Duke v GEC Reliance Ltd [1988]1 All ER 626, [1988] AC 618, [1988] 2 WLR 359, HL.

f Litster v Forth Dry Dock and Engineering Co Ltd [1989] 1 All ER 1134, [1990] AC 546, [1989] 2 WLR 634, HL.   (7)

Marshall v Southampton and South West Hampshire Area Health Authority (Teaching) Case 152/84 [1986] 2 All ER 584, [1986] QB 401, [1986] 2 WLR 780, [1986] ECR 723, CJEC.

Note [1966] 3 All ER 77, [1966] 1 WLR 1234, HL.

g Pickstone v Freemans plc [1988] 2 All ER 803, [1989] AC 66, [1989] 2 WLR 634, HL.

von Colson and Kamann v Land Nordrhein-Westfalen Case 14/83 [1984] ECR 1891.

Appeal

Frances Finnegan (the employee) appealed with leave of the Court of Appeal in Northern Ireland against the decision of that court (Hutton LCJ and Mac Dermott LJ) on 28 November

h 1988 allowing the appeal of the respondent, Clowney Youth Training Programme Ltd (the employer), by way of case stated by an industrial tribunal (J E Maguire chairman) sitting at Belfast on 23 November 1987 in respect of its decision that the employer had unlawfully discriminated against the employee on grounds of sex, contrary to the provisions of art 8 of the Sex Discrimination (Northern Ireland) Order 1976, SI 1976/1042, in compulsorily (8)

j retiring the employee at 60 when comparable male employees were allowed to work until the age of 65. The facts are set out in the opinion of Lord Bridge.

Patrick Coghlin QC and *Seamus Treacy* (both of the Northern Ireland Bar) for the employee. (9)

Patrick Markey QC and *Brian Kennedy* (both of the Northern Ireland Bar) for the employer.

Their Lordships took time for consideration.

Figure 3.2 An English Law Report

hence 'Smith and Jones'—spoken citations can thus sound confusing if there are more than two parties, as you will have a multiplicity of 'ands', one of which is a 'v'!; if Jones were to lose his case and appeal, the form of citation should switch to '*Jones* v *Smith*'. For an apparently unfathomable reason this does not always happen. Four other forms of civil citations crop up with some regularity.

First, in shipping cases (a number of which come up in contract and commercial law), it is a convention to abbreviate the case name to that of the ship involved, so, for example, the case of *Compania Financiera Soleada SA, Netherlands Antilles Ships Management Corp. and Dammers and van der Heide's Shipping and Trading Co.* v *Hamoor Tanker Corp. Inc.* (1981) is mercifully known as *The Borag*. That abbreviation will be sufficient to find the case in most books or citators.

Secondly, cases may appear in the form '*Re Smith*' (where '*Re*' roughly means 'concerning'). This form arises in some property cases, particularly those relating to trusts or the estates of deceased persons. It is also used in cases where the court is considering its wardship jurisdiction (where the court effectively takes ultimate control over the affairs of a child). In the latter cases the name of the child will not normally be disclosed, and the case citation will appear as '*Re M*', for example. They are usually indexed under the name referred to, not under '*Re*'. (There are also some other situations where the court will not disclose the names of the parties, so that cases are identified by an initial letter, in the form of '*A* v *B*'.)

Thirdly, you may come across cases cited as '*In B*' or '*In E*'. These cases arise in the law relating to wills and estates. '*In B*' stands for '*In Bonis*' (in the goods of). '*In E*' stands for '*In the Estate of*'. The distinction arose because, prior to the 1897 Land Transfer Act, personal representatives could only deal with deceaseds' goods, not their land. The citations reflect this. The equivalent cases nowadays use the form '*Re*', so it is increasingly unlikely that you will come across this form of citation.

Lastly, another form appears where the Administrative Court has exercised its public law jurisdiction judicially to review the administration or an inferior court. These cases are cited in the form '*R* v *Bloggs ex parte Smith*'. This is the only context when the Crown ('*R*') is commonly cited in civil proceedings. It reflects the fact that technically the action has been taken by the Crown, on the application of some other party, under what are, historically, the *prerogative* powers of the Crown. The term *ex parte* properly denotes someone who is outside the proceedings. In this situation it seems rather peculiar, though strictly correct, as it identifies the person who made the application for judicial review. As part of the move to simplify and adopt 'plain English' in the courts, there is some trend now to replace *ex parte* with its English equivalent. Consequently you may see cases cited in the form '*R (on the application of Jones)* v *Director of Public Prosecutions*'.

Criminal cases are normally cited as '*R* v *Smith*'. The '*R*' stands for *Rex* or *Regina* (Latin for king and queen) denoting the state's role as **prosecutor**; the accused is normally cited as the **defendant**. The oral form of the citation is 'the Crown against Smith', although it is usually abbreviated to just *Smith*.

Once again, there is a variety of alternative forms. Some criminal prosecutions can be commenced only with the approval of one of the government's law officers—the

Attorney-General (A-G) or the Director of Public Prosecutions (DPP). In such cases that official's title will appear instead of the Crown as prosecutor. Some cases, notably those which commenced in the magistrates' courts before the Crown Prosecution Service was set up in 1985, bore the name of the (police) prosecutor (see, e.g., *Albert* v *Lavin* [1982] AC 546; [1981] 3 All ER 878). This principle still applies in those very rare cases where a member of the public brings a private prosecution.

The court and presiding judge(s) (2) and (3)

These are perhaps of greater significance than you might at first think. Given that our system of precedent depends upon a ranking of courts, we need to know whereabouts in the 'batting order' this particular case is placed. Furthermore, in cases before the House of Lords, Court of Appeal, and a Divisional Court of the High Court, it will be normal to have more than one judge presiding. Sometimes the number, and even the status, of the judges presiding will influence the weight of that decision.

The headnote (5)

This does three things. First, it provides a brief statement of the **material facts** of the case. By facts we are talking about the description of events leading up to the case (see further **Chapters 4** and **6**); the term *material* denotes those facts which the judge considered important in deciding the case (we discuss the concept of materiality in detail in Chapter 6). Secondly, it will normally indicate the legal issues (usually called the **questions of law**) to be considered by the court. Thirdly, the headnote contains a summary of the court's decision on the issues of fact and law (as appropriate), including details of any *dissenting* judgment (where one or more judges disagree with the majority view).

It will also frequently give some indication of the effect of this decision on existing case law. This is indicated by the use of the following terms in conjunction with the citation of the relevant case:

Affirmed: this indicates that the court has agreed with the decision of a lower court in respect of the *same* case.

Applied: this means that a court has regarded itself as bound by an earlier decision, and has therefore employed the same reasoning in the instant case. The alternative would have been to *distinguish* the earlier case (below).

Approved: this is used where a higher court states that another case before a lower court was correctly decided.

Considered: this seems to be something of a residual category. If the court has discussed a reported case (particularly one decided by a court of equal status) but not reached any dramatic conclusion about its application, then it will probably appear as 'considered'.

Distinguished: an earlier case will be distinguished where a court has no power (or no wish) to overrule it, but does not want to apply it either. The court will therefore find some ground for saying it is different, and should not be followed. Distinguishing is an important category as it provides one of the main mechanisms by which the Common

Law refines the scope of legal principles. Distinguishing may be restrictive or non-restrictive. Where it is *restrictive*, the act of distinguishing will materially affect the scope of the earlier authority; where it is non-restrictive, the court is simply saying that there is a material difference, but not one that will affect the ambit of the rule for the future. For example, in *Rickards* v *Lothian* [1913] AC 263, Rickards was the landlord and manager of property occupied by Lothian and other tenants. Lothian ran a bookselling business on the second floor. One night, water overflowing from a tap left running on the fourth floor ran down into Lothian's premises, causing considerable damage to his stock. It was established that the accident was not caused by Rickard's negligence. Lothian consequently sought to bring an action under the tort of *Rylands* v *Fletcher* (1868) LR 3 HL 330 which, regardless of fault, makes the occupier of land liable for damage caused to another by the 'escape' from his property of anything likely to do harm, provided that the use of the land was 'non-natural'. Hence in *Rylands* v *Fletcher* itself, the claim was founded on the 'escape' of water from a reservoir constructed on the defendant's land—this construction being declared a non-natural use of the land. By contrast, in *Rickards* v *Lothian*, although there was an escape of water, the Privy Council held that the provision of a bathroom with running water was *not* a non-natural use of the defendant's property. Consequently this case could be distinguished from *Rylands* v *Fletcher* on its material facts, precisely because there was no non-natural user in the later case. This was, therefore, a **non-restrictive** distinction.

Now, suppose the facts had been slightly different. Assume that instead of an escape of water, the damage in *Rickards* had been caused maliciously by a trespasser who set fire to the property. This would clearly be a non-natural use, but the court might, arguably, still not allow Lothian to recover, because the case could again be distinguished from *Rylands* v *Fletcher*. In *Rylands*, the non-natural use was authorised by the owner, in our new version of *Rickards*, it was not. If the court was so to hold, this would be an example of **restrictive** distinguishing. We would now say that liability under the principle in *Rylands* v *Fletcher* was restricted to those cases where the use was authorised by the owner or occupier of the land.

Overruled: this is used to show where a court has rejected and invalidated an earlier decision of a court of lower (or sometimes equal) status to itself. The power to overrule is thus limited by a court's position in the hierarchy. Sometimes, as an alternative to overruling, you will see the comment '**Not followed**'. This is used where the decision in question is persuasive authority, for example, from another jurisdiction. 'Not followed' does not affect the status of the precedent within its own jurisdiction, but it will certainly cast doubt on the value of that decision within the jurisdiction that has declined to follow it.

Reversed: this is the opposite of affirmed. It means that the higher court has decided that the lower court in the *same* case came to the wrong decision.

Although the headnote is intended as a summary of the whole case, it is not authority for anything within the case. It is simply a *résumé* provided by the publishers of the report. Though they are usually fairly reliable, mistakes are sometimes made. For example, in *O'Grady* v *Saper* [1940] 3 All ER 527, which concerned an appeal from an action originally brought against an employer in respect of unpaid wages during the employee's absence for sickness, the headnote reads:

> *Held*, the facts proved showed by implication that there was no agreement that the respondent should be paid wages while absent through illness and he was not entitled to recover.

This significantly distorts the contractual point which was made in that case. What the court actually said was that the respondent (the employee) could not recover because there was an implied contractual term that he was *not* to be paid wages during any sick leave. So be careful in relying upon the headnote of a case—it certainly should not be used as a substitute for reading the judgments.

List of cases (7)

Most law reports will contain two separate lists. The first is a list of cases cited by the judge(s) in the judgment. That list is useful if you are trying to discover how the courts have subsequently used a particular decision. In other words, it provides a list of possible precedents used in that case. The second list (if there is one) will refer to additional cases cited in argument by counsel. Since the judge has not cited them, they are obviously of much less significance, but they can sometimes be worth considering if you are under-taking detailed research into the rationale of a decision, as they may show up points that the judge has apparently ignored or rejected, but without formal consideration of the case in the written judgment.

Details of the appeal (8)

Here the report gives a short history of the case, stating the parties, the previous hearing(s) of the case, and usually the legal findings which form the basis of the appeal.

There are a number of basic points regarding appeal terminology that we can deal with here. In most cases, the case will refer simply to an 'appeal', which may be an appeal on a point of law, or fact, or both depending upon the jurisdiction of the court. However, there are three particular procedures that you may confront quite frequently, which require a little more explanation.

(a) Appeal by way of case stated: this most commonly arises in appeals from the magistrates' court to the High Court, either where the applicant believes the magistrates have made an error of law (e.g., misinterpreted a statute) or acted outside their jurisdiction. The magistrates state a case by submitting to the High Court a statement of facts found by the justices, together with the question(s) of law or jurisdiction on which guidance is sought. The High Court may then come to its own decision on the issue, or refer the case back to the magistrates for reconsideration in the light of the High Court's opinion. Further rights of appeal exist on a case stated. These lie directly to the House of Lords in criminal cases. A good example of the whole appeal process is provided by the case of *Albert* v *Lavin*, already mentioned. The law report includes the form of words used by the magistrates to state a case concerning police powers of arrest for a breach of the peace. In civil cases the appeal is normally to the Court of Appeal. In *Finnegan* v *Clowney Youth Training Programme Ltd* the appeal shows that a case was stated by an industrial tribunal to the Court of Appeal in Northern Ireland. This particular procedure is unique to the Northern Irish system, though there are a number of contexts in which an English civil case can be stated for the High Court, these tend to be rare.

(b) Interim application: in civil proceedings an interim application (formerly called an interlocutory application) is an application to the court for some kind of temporary order that will take effect until the case comes to a full trial at a later date. Such applications most commonly arise as requests for an *injunction* (an order requiring the other party to do, or stop doing, something). They are thus meant to preserve the *status quo* until the trial. Interim applications will normally be heard by a single judge in the High Court, with a right of appeal to the Court of Appeal.

(c) 'Leapfrog appeal': under Part II of the Administration of Justice Act 1969, a civil case may exceptionally move from the High Court direct to the House of Lords. This is colloquially referred to as a 'leapfrog appeal'. It may only be used where:

(a) the case involves a point of law of general public importance relating to the interpretation of primary or secondary legislation, and

(b) the High Court is bound on that point of law by a precedent of the Court of Appeal or House of Lords, and

(c) the House of Lords grants leave to appeal.

The procedure seems to be used in few cases (see Drewry, 1973).

The names of counsel (9)

Historically, the only lawyers entitled to appear before the High Court and above were barristers. Changes to the rules are contained in the Courts and Legal Services Act 1990, section 27, which came into force in January 1991. This extends rights of audience to solicitors who have undergone additional advocacy training.

In the majority of cases before the higher courts, each side will be represented by two barristers, a leader and a junior counsel. Until late 1977, this was a formal requirement where the leader was a 'QC' (Queen's Counsel). Now a QC may appear alone, though she or he can decline to do so. The change in rules seems to have made comparatively little difference in practice.

The judgments (10)

The judgments are the most important part of any case, and as we shall see in **Chapters 5 and 6**, they are crucial to the operation of the English doctrine of precedent. It is normally the practice that, where there is more than one judge sitting, each is entitled to deliver his own opinion on the case. The first judgment given tends to be that of the senior judge presiding. However do not assume that because it is first it is therefore the 'main' or 'leading' judgment. Indeed, where there are multiple judgments, it can be dangerous to assume that any one has precedence over the others—though sometimes you can get an intuitive sense that one judgment is the most significant, perhaps because the other judges refer to it extensively, or because it seems to be the most comprehensive or to provide the best analysis. The judges following may then either give a full judgment of their own, either supporting or dissenting from the decision of one or more of the other speakers, or give a brief *concurring* judgment, which may be no more than 'I agree'. The chief exception to this practice is the Privy Council, where a unanimous or majority opinion is presented by one judge alone, and only dissenting voices from that have a separate right to be heard.

So far as the formalities of judgments are concerned, there appear to be none of any real significance, though there are many points of style, particularly in respect of forms of address. Titles are always given—a matter of style which is normally followed in academic writing, though the judges are also strong on ritual courtesy. A fellow judge is seldom anything less than 'learned' even where the discussion of his judgment strongly suggests that the speaker considers him to have the reasoning powers of a codfish. In deference to their exalted position, Law Lords can usually expect to be both 'noble and learned'.

The style of judgments tends to be quite individual. Some judges adopt a clear narrative pattern; Lord Denning was a prime, in his later decisions one might say an extreme, example of this style, whereby the facts and the law are woven into a continuous 'story'. Others have a far more formal style, which can produce some very dense prose indeed. A more recent innovation by some judges is to break up the text with headings and subheadings, which can much improve the clarity of the argument contained therein.

One final feature of English cases, which differentiates our process from that of most other countries, is the high proportion of *extempore*, or 'off the cuff', judgments. It is common practice in the High Court, though less common in the Court of Appeal, for judgment to be given either immediately after the conclusion of argument, or following a brief adjournment. Judges in these courts have the power to **reserve** judgment, that is, to go away, think about the issues, and present a full written judgment at a later date. The House of Lords will always reserve its decisions. In the former courts it is for the judges to decide. A number of factors, including the judge's self-confidence, or views of the complexity of the case, and particularly the pressures of his or her caseload, will influence that decision. Despite some judicial and academic doubts about the quality of unreserved as compared with reserved judgments, it would seem that the practice of giving unreserved judgments is set to continue for the foreseeable future.

Where a judgment in the law reports has been reserved, that is usually indicated, at a point just preceding the judgment(s), by the abbreviation '*Cur. adv. vult*.' This is short for *Curia advisari vult*, meaning 'the court wishes to be advised'. Judgments in the Lords are preceded by the more mundane: 'Their Lordships took time for consideration.' Presumably it would be inappropriate for the House of Lords even to pretend to take advice on the law!

Letters in the margin (11)

These are a useful addendum to the page number, which may be cited in the form 'p. 123a'. (Note also that, conventionally, the 'p.' denoting the page can be dropped when citing pages of the law reports.) Taken together they can be used to locate more accurately a piece of text which is being referred to in court, in the headnote to a law report, or in an essay, and so on. As we noted in **Chapter 2**, it is now also the normal practice that paragraphs are numbered continuously throughout the published version of the judgments, a practice that reduces the significance of the pagination and marginal lettering when citing cases.

3.2.2. European Reports

As we also noted in **Chapter 2**, decisions of the ECJ and CFI are reported in two main series of reports available in the UK—the *European Court Reports* and the *Common Market Law Reports*. There are slight but mostly insignificant differences in the way in which these two sets of reports are laid out. For our purposes, therefore, it is sufficient to focus on just one version—the *Common Market Law Reports* (CMLR). To do this we have chosen Case C–83/92 *Pierrel SpA* v *Ministero della Sanità* [1995] 1 CMLR 53, a decision on a point of conflict between Italian law and Community law governing the marketing of pharmaceuticals; the issues in the case are not significant for our purposes, the structure of the report is. Rather than take you through each element of the report, we have highlighted only the significant differences from an English law report:

(1) The boxes

(2) The court and chamber

(3) The personnel

(4) Date of judgment

(5) The headnote

(6) Advocates appearing

(7) Advocate-General's Opinion (not shown)

(8) The judgment

The boxes (1)

This is a particular feature of the CMLR. The *Reports* include cases from courts of national as well as international jurisdiction, and the publishers therefore needed to develop a system which would make it clear to readers in any country what the status of a decision was. This is the system they devised. The box on the left indicates the class of court as follows:

> ECJ—the Court of Justice of the EC
> CFI—the Court of First Instance of the EC
> EFTA—the Court of the European Free Trade Association

For courts of national jurisdiction, the CMLR identify decisions according to the level of the court in the national hierarchy. Level I thus indicates a court of first instance, or trial court; Level II covers all intermediate courts (like the English Court of Appeal); and Level III indicates a final court of appeal (e.g. the House of Lords). The use of this system enables us roughly to gauge and compare the relative significance of decisions of national courts on points of Community law.

The box on the right of the page indicates the court's jurisdiction, e.g., 'EEC' for courts with jurisdiction across the Communities, or 'UK-England' for English courts, etc.

(1)   (1)

| ECJ* | | EEC | 1993
                                                                        ——
PIERREL SpA AND OTHERS *v.* MINISTERO DELLA SANITÀ   *Pierrel SpA*
           (Case C–83/92)   *v.*
                                                            Ministero
                                                           della Sanità
BEFORE THE COURT OF JUSTICE OF THE EUROPEAN COMMUNITIES   (2)   ——
                  (5th CHAMBER)   European
                                                            Court of
                                                            Justice

(*Presiding*, Moitinho de Almeida P.C.; Joliet and Rodríguez (3)
Iglesias JJ.)
Herr Carl Otto Lenz, *Advocate General.*

                                            7 December 1993 (4)

Reference from Italy by the Consiglio di Stato under **Article 177**
EEC.

Provisions considered:
   Dir. 65/65
   Dir. 75/319
   Dir. 83/570
   Dir. 92/27

> **Regulation of trade. Pharmaceuticals.** Article 21 of the (5)
> Pharmaceuticals Specialties Directive 65/65 means that the
> suspension or revocation of a marketing authorisation for a
> proprietary medicinal product may be decided only on the
> grounds laid down in that directive or other relevant provi-
> sions of Community law. [23]
>   CLIN-MIDY SA *v.* BELGIAN STATE (301/82): [1984] E.C.R.
>   251, [1985] 1 C.M.L.R. 443, *confirmed.*
> **Regulation of trade. Pharmaceuticals.** National rules,
> according to which marketing authorisations for proprietary
> medicinal products which are not used within a specified
> period are to lapse, breach the Pharmaceuticals Specialties
> Directive 65/65, as amended. [30]

  * This box indicates the court or, for national systems, the class of court which
delivered this judgment. The box on the right indicates the country or jurisdiction
to which the court belongs.

The Court *interpreted* the Pharmaceuticals Specialties Directive 65/65, as amended and
supplemented by Directives 75/319, 83/570 and 92/27, *in the context of* Italian legislation
which provided that authorisations to market proprietary medicines lapsed if they were
not used within 18 months *to the effect that* the grounds laid down by the directives for the
revocation or suspension of such authorisations (which did not include failure to use
them within a specified period) were exhaustive, *that* the lapse of an authorisation was
analogous to a revocation since they both resulted in termination, and so *that* the Italian

legislation breached the directive, it being irrelevant that it had been amended after the national court's **Article 177** reference.

> Professor Luigi Ferrari Bravo, Head of the Department of (6) Contentious Diplomatic Affairs at the Ministry of Foreign Affairs, assisted by *Oscar Fiumara* and *Francesco Guicciardi*, Avvocati dello Stato, for the Italian Government.
>
> *Luis Ines Fernandes*, Director of the Legal Department of the Directorate-General for the European Communities at the Ministry for Foreign Affairs, *Maria Luisa Duarte*, Legal Adviser at the Directorate-General for the European Communities, and *Cláudio Monteiro*, Legal Adviser at the Directorate-General for Medicinal Products, for the Portuguese Government as *amicus curiae*.
>
> *Antonio Aresu*, of the Legal Service of the E.C. Commission, and *Virginia Melgar*, a national official seconded to the Legal Service, for the Commission as *amicus curiae*.

The following case was referred to in the judgment:

1. CLIN-MIDY SA v. BELGIAN STATE (301/82), 26 January 1984: [1984] E.C.R. 251, [1985] 1 C.M.L.R. 443.

The following further cases were referred to by the Advocate General:

2. GUNA SRL v. E.C. COUNCIL (C–437/92), not yet decided.
3. ANGELOPHARM gmbH v. FREIE UND HANSESTADT HAM-BURG (C–212/91), 25 January 1994: [1994] 1 E.C.R. 171, [1994] 3 C.M.L.R. 573.
4. MARLEASING SA v. LA COMERCIAL INTERNACIONAL DE ALIMENTACIÓN SA (C–106/89), 13 November 1990: [1990] 1 E.C.R. 4135, [1992] 3 C.M.L.R. 305.

The following additional cases were referred to in argument:

5. ALGERA v. COMMON ASSEMBLY (7/56 & 3–7/57), 12 July 1957: [1957–58] E.C.R. 39.
6. RE THE MARKETING OF MEDICINES: E.C. COMMISSION v. ITALY (C–145/82), 15 March 1983: [1983] E.C.R. 711, [1984] 1 C.M.L.R. 148.

TABLE OF PROCEEDINGS	PAGE
Opinion of Lenz A.G., 15 July 1993	58
Judgment of the European Court of Justice, 7 December 1993	64
Language of the proceedings: Italian	

Figure 3.3 A Decision of the ECJ

The court and chamber (2)

The formal title of the court is given together with, where appropriate, the chamber in which it is heard. This is not a reference to the English practice of hearing some (mostly interim) applications in private in the judge's office (called 'chambers'); rather it refers to the procedural process of assigning the case to a particular group of judges. Each of the EC Courts is divided into chambers. The ECJ and CFI may therefore choose to sit either as a chamber or as a 'plenary' (full) court. A plenary court may hear cases either as a *Petit Plenum* of eleven judges, or as a *Grand Plenum* of fifteen. The ECJ consists of six chambers. The two largest each have seven judges, though only five will actually preside over a particular case. These are then sub-divided into four further chambers, having three or four judges each. Each smaller chamber sits as a panel of three. The chamber system has evolved as a means of dealing with the ever-increasing workload of the Court. Between 1980 and 1993, 1,464 judgments were delivered by chambers as against the 1,126 decisions of the plenary Court (based on figures in Brown & Kennedy, 1994:413). The ECJ itself determines whether to hear proceedings in plenary session or as a chamber, and, if the latter, whether as a chamber of three or five. This decision is taken by the Court at the close of the written proceedings, and after the Advocate General has been heard. It is based simply on an assessment of the importance or difficulty of the issues raised. Member States and any Community institutions involved in the proceedings can require the trial to be conducted before the full Court. The CFI, with a total of twelve judges, operates in a very similar fashion, and is also divided into chambers of three or five judges, though, unlike the ECJ, it has only rarely exercised its power to sit as a plenary court.

The personnel (3)

There are a number of key personnel within the ECJ. In addition to the judges, there are the Advocates General and the Registrar of the Court. We will consider each of these roles in turn.

There are fifteen judges at present: one from each Member State. Under the terms of the Treaties, the judges are appointed for a renewable term of six years:

> from persons whose independence is beyond doubt and who possess the qualifications required for appointment to the highest judicial offices in their respective countries or who are jurisconsults of recognised competence. (Brown & Kennedy, 2000:46)

The effect of this condition is to enable judges to be appointed either on the basis of professional expertise and seniority (the first option), or on the basis of academic scholarship (the second option). The alternative nature of these qualifications is particularly significant in the British or Irish context where, unlike most continental jurisdictions, academics *per se* are not elegible for domestic judicial appointment. To date, however, the UK has not nominated a judge who would not satisfy the first option, though two of the judges have also held chairs at British universities. David Edward, for example, was both a Scottish QC and Salveson Professor of European Institutions at Edinburgh University before his appointment, first to the CFI, and then, in 1992, to the ECJ.

Each chamber of the ECJ has a president elected annually by its members (in practice, this means that each judge serves as President in rotation). The ECJ as a whole also has one judge who is elected President of the Court for a (renewable) three-year term. The President of the Court presides at plenary hearings and has ultimate responsibility for the judicial administration of the Court. Other than the Presidents, all judges rank equally, though seating positions in court are determined by 'seniority in office'—in effect, length of service as a judge.

Each case has assigned to it a *Judge-Rapporteur*. This is a judge nominated by the President of one of the smaller chambers to undertake the preparatory inquiry phase once an application has been lodged with the Court. The *Judge-Rapporteur*'s role is akin to that of the investigating magistrate in civilian court procedure, i.e., to undertake an inquiry and produce a report on the case for the Court to consider (see, e.g., Edward, 1995:549ff for a fuller explanation of the processes involved). This report is used by the Court to determine procedure for the hearing of the matter—e.g. what witnesses (if any) may be called, whether the case is heard by the chamber to which it was assigned, or by a chamber of five judges or plenary court. The *Judge-Rapporteur* is also normally present at oral hearings, and is entitled to put questions to the advocates.

The *Advocates General* are perhaps the most distinctive element of the proceedings, having no equivalent in Common Law procedure. Their role clearly reflects the Civilian origins of the Court and its early links (both procedural and personal) with the French *Conseil d'Etat* (see further Vranken, 1996:40–8).

The idea of an Advocate General is a familiar one in continental legal systems. The Advocate General is an 'adviser' to the court, performing a task which might be likened to 'sifting' through the law on behalf of the Court in each case. Article 222 (formerly Art. 166) of the EC Treaty describes his function thus:

> It shall be the duty of the Advocate General, acting with complete impartiality and independence, to make, in open court, reasoned submissions on cases brought before the Court of Justice, in order to assist the court in the performance of the task assigned to it in Article 220 [formerly Art. 164, which makes the ECJ responsible for ensuring that 'in the interpretation and application of this Treaty the law is observed'].

In practice this means that the Advocate General receives all the details of the case from the parties, investigates the law relating to the issues raised, and delivers his opinion on the case to the Court as to what decision it should reach. He sits with the judges on the Bench (opposite the Registrar) but plays no part in their deliberations. He delivers his opinion after the case has been heard by the Court, and often at a later hearing.

Thus, the Advocate General is very much a part of the Court, and is subject broadly to the same conditions of appointment, tenure, salary, etc., as the judges (indeed, over the years, a number of Advocates General have become judges, and *vice versa*). In a sense, then, in true Civilian style both Advocates General and judges are part of the same Community *magistrature*. In much the same way, in France we see a functional distinction between judges of the *siège* (i.e. those who sit in judgment 'on the bench') and judges of the *parquet* (the 'floorboards') who take responsibility for the prosecution of cases, but this does not alter the fact that both are part of the career judiciary. (The analogy is not exact, of course, as the ECJ has no direct equivalent of the *parquet*.)

Note that since 1982 there is no hyphen in the spelling of Advocate General, except when referring to the possessive case, thus: The Advocate General said...but The Advocate-General's opinion was... The plural of an Advocate General is Advocates General. This distinction is not a popular question on games shows.

The procedure governing cases before the CFI is slightly different. When the CFI sits in plenary session, an Advocate General is always appointed. Such appointment is not necessary where a case is heard before a chamber of the CFI, though an Advocate General may be appointed in such cases on the authority of the Court in plenary session (Arts. 18–19, *Rules of Procedure, Court of First Instance*).

Lastly, there is the *Registrar*, who is in charge of the court Registry (i.e. its administration) and deals with the procedure and administration of the court. His role is perceived as something more important than the title would imply under our system—he even sits with the judges in court, but takes no part in the decision. There are also two Assistant Registrars who take day-to-day responsibility for the administrative and judicial sides of the Registry's work respectively.

Date of judgment (4)

Note that, unlike the English reports, no separate hearing dates are given, assuming that there has been an oral hearing. In practice, in some 15 to 20 per cent of cases before the ECJ, the oral hearing is dispensed with under procedures introduced in 1991 (Edward, 1995:555). Note that the ECJ always reserves its judgment.

The headnote (5)

The form of a headnote differs substantially from that used in English law reports. Opening with a reference to the procedure whereby the case reached the Court (here, Art. 177—now Art. 234—Reference) and citations of the relevant Community legislation, it then identifies the subject matter of the case, together with references to key paragraphs in the judgment (in square brackets) and refers to any authority cited in the judgment— but *not* authorities referred to by the Advocate General.

The Advocates (6)

Parties before the ECJ must normally be represented by a lawyer. In addition, in reference proceedings, legal representatives from other Member States having an interest in the ruling may submit observations to the Court in both the written and oral proceedings. The Commission also always submits observations in reference proceedings. In the *Pierrel* case, observations were received from the Commission and from the Portugese Government only.

Advocate-General's Opinion (not shown)

The Advocate-General's opinion is an important part of the case, and one that has no direct counterpart in the English legal system. In his opinion the Advocate General will normally go through the facts, the law, and various authorities (including case law and academic commentary), and usually in far more detail than does the judgment of the Court. Practically speaking, therefore, it makes a lot of sense to read the opinion before the judgment, as that will (especially if the opinion is followed by the court) give you significant insights into the development and rationale of the law.

The Advocate-General's opinion is not part of the Court's judgment and is in no sense 'binding' either on the court to which it is presented or on any other later court. In English terms it is therefore best seen as having persuasive authority, and it is quite common practice for Advocates General to cite each others' opinions. The division between the Advocate-General's opinion and the judgment has become rather more blurred by the modern practice of the judges in some cases simply to adopt the opinion in its entirety by 'direct reference', and has been criticised accordingly (see Brown & Kennedy, 2000). For an example of the practice, see Case C–284/91 *Suiker Export v Belgium* [1992] ECR I–5473. Whatever the procedure, estimates suggest that the Advocate-General's opinion is followed in something like 70 to 85 per cent of cases (Vranken, 1996:61).

The judgment (not shown)

There are two particular points to note about the style of judgments of the European Courts.

First, all decisions are *collegial*. A decision is reported as a decision of the court, without the individual (or idiosyncratic!) voices we associate with English judgments. Collegiality also means that, following the Civilian tradition, there is no provision for dissenting judgments. Decisions will follow the majority reasoning if unanimity cannot be achieved, but, unlike the Common Law approach, no record of the minority view is retained to trouble posterity.

Secondly, the form and style of the decision are also rather different from those found in English law reports. To start with, the judgment is presented in the form of numbered paragraphs, a practice which has only recently been adopted by English Courts. These provide a reference point when citing the decision. Note also that the actual ruling of the Court always appears at the end of the judgment. It is usually quite short, and is identified by the opening phrase 'On those grounds...' from the French *pour ces motifs*, which is used in the original version of the reports. There are some other relatively minor stylistic differences between reports which can reflect the age of the case (the principles governing the format for judgments were relaxed in 1978) or small variations in 'house-style' between the ECR and CMLR. They are not significant for our purposes. So much, once again, for the formalities, and now to a more substantial issue.

The contents of the judgment also appear distinctive to lawyers of the Common Law tradition. But this is not just a matter of style—it reflects the different legal cultures involved, and particularly assumptions about the judicial function. Unlike the rather more rhetorical approach of many English judges, the language used by the European Courts tends to be more measured, if not downright flat. This is sometimes said to reflect the compromise nature of many decisions and is a consequence of the collegiality principle. If a camel is a horse designed by committee, European judgments can sometimes be the judicial equivalent of the camel. Judgments are also relatively short. This is not least because they commonly lack the detailed factual and legal analysis which is the feature of many English judgments and of the Advocate-General's opinion. Very few cases are cited in support of the decision (though references to case law have become more common in recent years) and judgments rarely make any direct reference to the opinions of Advocates General—not even the opinion given in that case. This is not to say that EC decisions suffer from a lack of rigour or rationalisation: they are presented in a very logical, developmental form in which point follows point in a seemingly inexorable sequence. This form of presentation can sometimes make European decisions easier to read and understand than their English counterparts, but it does mean that points of uncertainty or argument get rather lost in what is packaged as a rational, deductive process (we explore some of the reasons behind this approach in **Chapter 11**). It can also mean that the Court is often reluctant to explore the implications or boundaries of the law beyond the issues directly raised by the case at hand. This contrasts with English practice, where judges will frequently speculate on the scope or implications of a particular ruling. Lawyers asking the question '*what if...*' of the ECJ will seldom find guidance in the judgment. Arguably this has meant that the Court has actually generated a lack of legal certainty through an unwillingness to provide fuller reasoning of its decisions in cases like *Francovich* (see, e.g., Bebr, 1992) and *Faccini Dori* (see our discussion of these cases in **Chapter 10**).

3.3 Reading Books and Articles

How do you read a book or article?

This may seem like a silly question, but it is not. Educational research has shown that many of us are very inefficient in the way we approach academic reading. Given the time pressures you will face as a student it is vital that you develop an efficient technique. One that is worth trying is commonly called **SQ3R** (see, e.g., Williams, 1989:4–5). It describes a sequence of five steps you should follow when looking at books and articles: Survey, Question, Read, Recall, and Review.

3.3.1 Survey

Start by getting a 'feel' for the publication and its potential usefulness. You can do this by looking at the following:

The title

Yes, we are starting with the obvious, but mind that it is not so obvious that you overlook it! The title may tell you a lot about the author's aims. Consider, for example, what you might be able to tell about the contents from the following (real) book titles:

> *The Law of Contract*
>
> *A Casebook on Contract*
>
> *Nutshells—Contract Law*
>
> *The Rise and Fall of Freedom of Contract*
>
> *Contract Law—Questions and Answers*
>
> *Understanding Contract Law*
>
> *Sourcebook on Obligations and Legal Remedies*

Similarly, phrases in titles or subtitles like 'a student's guide', 'a critical approach', or 'handbook' can also help indicate the level of difficulty or type of approach being taken.

The 'blurb', editorial or abstract

Books almost invariably have a brief summary of their aims or arguments on the back cover or inside the jacket (if hardback). This is often written—or at least revised—by the author and should provide a reasonable indication of what the book is about, though do not forget that it is also written with the aim of selling the book! Similarly, some, though by no means all, journals either contain an editorial summarising the contents of the particular issue or require authors to provide a brief summary or 'abstract' of their article which gives a guide to the contents. This may provide a useful framework around which you can organise your own notes from your reading.

The date of publication

In a book this is given on either the face or obverse of the title page. In a constantly changing field like law, recency of publication is important. Most law books will become progressively more out of date as time goes on. Always check the date of publication and be prepared to update accordingly. If the book is more than three or four years old, it is often worth checking a publisher's catalogue to see if there is a later edition or finding a more up-to-date alternative. With journal articles, the problem is more acute. These are not generally updated by revised versions and it can be difficult to check for accuracy other than by returning to primary sources. The older the article, the more careful you may have to be. Having said that, there is no general rule that can tell us when a piece of legal writing is past its 'sell by' date.

Contents page

A quick check of the contents page can also give a useful overview, not just of the bare contents of a book, but of how the material is structured and used. It is a curious reflection on academic cultures that many North American law journals will publish much longer articles than their British or European counterparts. In the USA particularly, articles of 25,000 words or more are not uncommon. It is perhaps unsurprising therefore that in the American journals major articles will normally have their own table of contents.

Preface

A lot of readers will skip the preface or introduction and just focus on the main text of a book. This is often a bad idea. Most prefaces, etc., are written by authors expressly as a way of explaining the thinking behind their books.

3.3.2 Question

Worthwhile reading requires more than staring at the page and trying to soak up the contents like a sponge. You *must* ask yourself questions both before and during your reading. Consider first your objectives in reading the text: what is it you want from this book or article?

• Are you looking for an overview of a topic?

• Are you trying to answer a specific question or legal problem?

• Are you looking for a critical perspective on the law or the context in which it has evolved?

Use these to focus and crosscheck your reading.

3.3.3 Read

Think about how you have been using this book. Have you read everything we have written? Has your reading been all at the same speed, or to the same depth? In fact, it is highly unlikely that you have read every word, and even if you have you will have varied the depth and pace of your reading. You are almost certainly using a range of reading techniques already, according to the purpose for which you have been reading at the time. It is worth thinking about how you might harness those techniques to make yourself a more efficient and productive reader. In practice we suggest there are three stages to effective reading:

(a) *Skim* the text for an overview. This can often be best achieved by taking the text a paragraph at a time. When skim reading it is often sufficient to read just the opening sentence or two of each paragraph. Let us explain why. Most well-constructed paragraphs can be split into three elements (this idea is useful in developing your writing skills too): an opening sentence or two, incorporating the 'topic sentence'; an explanatory or discursive middle element; and a closing sentence, which commonly serves to develop the topic sentence as well as to complete the paragraph. The topic sentence is crucial; it provides the main idea of the paragraph and all other sentences develop it and are dependent on it to some degree. Consider the following paragraph as an example (we have given each sentence a number, in brackets, for reasons which will become apparent in a moment):

> Lord Woolf has proposed fundamental and radical changes to the way litigation should be conducted. [1] His diagnosis is that civil justice is in crisis because (among other things) it takes too long, costs too much money and, even when people win, they are unhappy with the process. [2] Although this analysis is far from new, I agree with it. [3] I also agree with Lord Woolf that radical change is needed, not cosmetic surgery. [4] However, reforming the civil justice system for the better 'ain't easy'. [5] This is why, despite some sixty reports in England on aspects of civil procedure since 1851, there has been no lasting solution to the twin problems of cost and delay. [6] The same is true of North America. [7] Our predecessors were neither foolish dullards nor acting in bad faith; reform is simply very difficult. [8] The challenge is not simply to propose change: it is to propose reforms which significantly improve the current position. [9] (Watson, 1996:63)

Here the topic sentence is the first sentence: it tells us that the subject of the paragraph is Lord Woolf's proposals for the reform of civil justice. The later sentences relate back to the topic sentence (TS), albeit at different levels, to expand on or explain the theme it introduces. By identifying the TS, we can quickly spot the focus of that paragraph and thus decide whether to ignore it or return to it for a further reading and analysis. In longer paragraphs it can sometimes be helpful to skim the last sentence or two as well, to help us see where the argument is going.

(b) It follows, then, that the second stage is to *identify* those elements of the text which need to be read in detail. Do not make notes at this stage, other than to identify the bits to which you will return. You need to concentrate on understanding the text at the level of an overview first. Only once you have done this are you really ready for the next stage.

(c) *Read in detail.* This is never the first stage in effective reading. Indeed, you will often find that there is material you will never have to read in detail because by surveying the text and skim reading you can establish that *it is of absolutely no use to you whatsoever.* If you start by reading in detail, you risk wasting time on something that is of little or no practical help, whatever its intrinsic worth may be!

Reading in detail will usually involve two distinct processes:

(i) reading for understanding; and

(ii) reading critically.

Again we will take each of these ideas in turn.

You can really know something only if you understand it. Reading for understanding is therefore a central part of the learning process. Often you will find understanding does not come easily. The ideas represented in a piece of writing may be complex; sometimes they may not be clearly expressed. It may be necessary for you to work hard at unpicking the meaning. Here again, it is often helpful to work through the text a paragraph at a time. If you can make sense of the structure and order of the writer's ideas at this level, you will have a better chance of grasping their meaning. There are better ways of doing this than staring at the page and waiting for inspiration.

Think back to what we said about paragraph organisation in the section on skim reading. You will recall that we said that all sentences in a paragraph relate back to the topic sentence (TS), but at different levels. So there will be sentences which are directly subordinate to the topic sentence (Level 2 sentences), but also other sentences which illustrate or modify the Level 2 sentences and so are subordinate to them (Level 3 sentences) and, in more complex paragraphs, so on. Maughan & Maughan (2002:35–7) have shown how we might use a tree diagram more effectively to identify this relationship and thereby to extract the meaning from a paragraph (see **Figure 3.4**). We suggest that this technique can help us to untangle long and complex paragraphs. We can, however, start with a straightforward example, using the extract from Garry Watson's paper quoted above. If we apply their approach here, we get a structure that looks like this (the numbers in brackets correspond to the sentence numbers in the text):

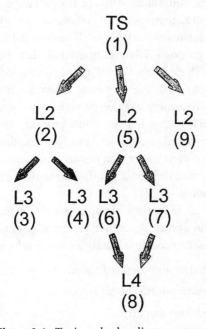

Figure 3.4. Topic and subordinate sentences

Thus Sentence 1, the TS, introduces the main theme:

Lord Woolf has proposed radical reforms.

This is developed by Sentence 2 (L2):

Woolf says reform is necessary because of delays etc.

which is then modified by Sentences 3 and 4 (L3):

I agree with Lord Woolf.

Sentence 5 (L2) returns to the topic sentence to qualify it:

But reforming civil justice is not easy.

The statement in Sentence 5 is then justified by Sentences 6 and 7 (L3):

Just look at the impact of previous attempts in the UK and N. America

and Sentence 8 (L4) then emphasises the point by saying, in effect:

and it was not for want of trying.

Lastly, Sentence 9 returns to the TS with a final modification that is crucial to the later development of the argument:

Proposing radical reform is one thing: making a difference is another.

It is quite possible that you would analyse this, or any paragraph, slightly differently from us. That is because it is ultimately your interpretation of what the writer is saying, and which sentence is subordinate to which may well be debatable. That relationship is not really important for our purposes. What is important is that you can see a logical structure to the paragraph which establishes, develops, and ultimately modifies or transforms a basic theme. Once you can see that development, it becomes much easier to understand what the writer is trying to achieve. We do not suggest that you need to work through everything as systematically as this, but you would probably find this technique helpful with any material you are struggling to understand. Note also that in our analysis we have used paraphrases of Watson's text, rather than verbatim quotations. This too is deliberate— the process of translating another person's words into your own is also an important step on the path to understanding.

If your purpose is critical, in that, for example, you are attempting to analyse or challenge the ideas presented by a particular author, your reading must be directed to that purpose. In that case you must consider how the author has developed his argument. Has he:

(a) made any unsupported or unrecognised assumptions?

(b) reached conclusions unsupported by his argument?

(c) ignored counter-arguments that exist?

Often, a comparison of different texts can help you sort out the range of arguments and counter-arguments which exist. Do not fall into the trap of being dependent upon a single book or article when constructing any kind of critical analysis. Literary sources may also be of assistance if you are attempting some critical analysis of a case or statutory provision.

Lastly, always remember, when reading, what your purpose is. If you are unsure, stop, think, and read again.

3.3.4 Recall

In the recall phase you are really trying to test yourself on what the text was about. It is at this point that you should begin to make notes.

Note-taking is an integral part of effective, detailed reading. Simply photocopying text and going through it with a highlighter is a poor substitute for the kind of mental processing of information that takes place when making notes on your source material. Do *not* take verbatim notes as you read. Read first, then make your notes. Obviously longer pieces of text need to be broken down into manageable chunks for this technique to work—no one can make meaningful notes on a whole book at one, two, or even three sittings! But why not make notes as you read? We advise against this for three reasons. First, it is difficult to assess just how critical any part of the text is before you have completed the whole; you are therefore more likely to misrepresent your source this way. Secondly, delaying note-taking encourages you to think about what you have read. Thirdly, it reduces the likelihood of one kind of *plagiarism,* that is of quoting someone else's work without attribution. This is an academic cardinal sin, and a ground for failure under the academic regulations of every law degree we have come across. However, it can be very easy to confuse quoted or paraphrased material from your own notes if you are not careful about maintaining that distinction. If you must take down verbatim extracts, make sure it is clear to you what is quoted material and what is not. Williams (1989:30) also suggests the following guidelines for good note-taking practice:

(a) *Record your source:* Make sure that you keep a note of the full reference for your source material. You will need this for any works you cite in your bibliography, and you may need to locate it again. Note the author(s), the title, publisher or journal name, year, and page reference(s). If it is a library book it can save time later if you note the library (shelving) classification too. If you are doing an extended piece of project work, where you are likely to have a large number of references, it may be helpful to note each reference on individual index cards which can be stored as a permanent record. Alternatively, there are a number of cheap 'shareware' computer programs which can enable you to produce an electronic index of references that can be downloaded to a document file for wordprocessing.

(b) *Show the main ideas clearly:* What are the key points/arguments to come out of the text? Identify them! Show also how the main ideas are linked and what supporting points are used for each.

(c) *Be brief:* Do not take copious notes unless you have to. It may be better to take brief notes at first, and come back to the source later if more detail proves necessary.

(d) *Be selective:* Avoid lengthy illustrations, asides, etc. If an example helps you to understand a point, outline it briefly. Make a note of the page reference of any examples you are uncertain about using.

(e) *Leave notes well spaced on the page*: This enables you to fill in with more detail later on (if necessary).

3.3.5 Review

Williams also suggests (at 5) that the review process has two elements. One is retrospective, the other prospective. First, you can quickly review the first four stages of **SQ3R** to check your progress:

- *Survey* the whole text to remind yourself of the structure.
- *Question*—what was your purpose? What were the specific questions to which you wanted answers?
- *Read* the text by skimming only. Are there any points you have missed?
- *Recall*—check your notes. Are there any gaps? Have you found answers to your questions?

From here you need, lastly, to think about what you will do with your notes. It may be that they will serve a one-off purpose, contributing to an essay, say. Even so, it is worth putting them aside for a day or two, to see if they still make sense or whether they need further revision or correction. However, it is more likely that they will form part of your knowledge bank for the future (for end-of-year examinations perhaps), in which case you will need to consider what future strategies of review and refinement you intend to adopt as part of your preparation for that event.

EXERCISE 3   **SQ3R Squared**

Ask yourself the question, 'How can the SQ3R method improve my study skills?'. Now, using SQ3R, work through the relevant sections of this chapter, and see what answer you come up with.

  Of course, we are not going to give you an answer to this one—that is for you to decide! Having said that, the technique is tried and trusted, and most people should get something of value from it. You should consider trying SQ3R out on an assignment. Do not be put off just because it may take you longer than your conventional research and reading methods. The time invested should pay off in the long run, both in terms of greater conceptual understanding as you progress through your course and in terms of better (and, it is hoped, easier) preparation for examinations.

3.4 From Reading to Writing

The processes of reading and note-taking will often be the precursor to a specific writing task—an essay or examination script. In this section we will consider briefly the techniques involved in basic, academic legal writing.

3.4.1 Writing Essays

Writing essays is essentially about two things.

  First, it is about conveying *information*. Any essay you are asked to write will require you to tell the reader what you know about the subject under discussion. In conveying that information there are three cardinal rules:

Be accurate

Try to be as precise as possible in the information you put down. Vagueness is a sure sign of a lack of understanding or insufficient thought. If it is not possible to give an accurate statement of the principles involved (perhaps because the law is in a muddle), then say that there is no single answer and *clearly distinguish any alternatives that seem to exist.*

Accuracy is also about clarity of meaning. Style is important because a good style enhances the clarity of your exposition; in the end your arguments can be only as good as your ability to express them. Do not ignore the fact that language has its own rhythm, and this can often guide you to sentences or phrases which do not work. Some people find that reading work aloud helps in this, because if a phrase sounds wrong, it probably is wrong. This is not recommended practice in a library!

It is equally important to avoid jargon or words you do not understand. Do not be like the famous Mrs Malaprop, with her 'nice derangement of epitaphs'. If in doubt use a dictionary, or a thesaurus if you want to bring in alternative vocabulary. A good guide to a simple writing style remains Sir Ernest Gowers's *The Complete Plain Words*, which was originally written for the Civil Service. One can only assume it has fallen into some disuse among its original audience, but if you are worried that you write like a (bad) civil servant, it is recommended reading.

Be relevant

Do not introduce something you know to be irrelevant into an answer. There is a great temptation to throw every possible bit of information you have at the question, and hope that some of it is right (what many teachers call a 'shotgun' approach). This does not look impressive, as it again suggests a lack of forethought. Keeping to what is relevant is not magic; it is simply a question of familiarity with and understanding of your material. If you have taken the time to analyse the question, and thought out what is expected of you there should be no need to adopt such an approach.

Be concise

In our experience, teachers do not award marks on the basis of the number of pages filled. It is obviously impossible for us to state what the 'average' acceptable length of an essay is, as criteria vary from course to course and year to year. You should always be guided by your tutors as to what is required. If you are given an indication of the appropriate length, then any significant shortfall normally indicates that something is missing.

Brevity is not, ultimately, just about the number of words you use; it is about how you use them. Again, it is a matter of clarity. Clarity is best achieved by short sentences and the proper use of paragraphs. Remember that a sentence should always make sense, and that each separate issue you discuss deserves its own paragraph. Sentences full of long words do not impress unless they convey a meaning not otherwise possible. Lawyers, perhaps more than any other profession, have a reputation for pomposity. It is a reputation that is not wholly undeserved. Formal legal writing is still perceived to be very different from everyday English. Indeed, there are those who suspect that its connections with the

English language are little more than coincidental! This is because, at its worst, it not only uses technical terms outside the general language, but also uses forms of language and phrasing that are archaic, and often redundant—documents full of jargon interspersed with the occasional 'whatsoever', 'wheresoever', 'heretofore', and 'hereafter'. In a brilliant parody, James D. Gordon III (1991:1689) offers a classic example of such 'legalese'; a lawyer's translation of the phrase, 'I give you this orange':

> Know all men by these presents that I hereby give, grant, bargain, sell, release, convey, transfer, and quitclaim all my right, title, interest, benefit and use whatever in, of, and concerning this chattel, otherwise known as an orange, or citrus orantium, together with all the appurtenances thereto of skin, pulp, pip, rind, seeds and juice, to have and to hold the said orange together with its skin, pulp, pip, rind, seeds and juice for his own use and behoof, to himself and his heirs in fee simple forever, free from all liens, encumbrances, easements, limitations, restraints or conditions whatsoever, and all prior deeds, transfers or other documents whatsoever, now or anywhere made to the contrary notwithstanding, with full power to bite, cut, suck or otherwise eat the said orange or to give away the same, with or without its skin, pulp, pip, rind, seeds or juice.

Fortunately, this kind of 'supernatural incantation' (to borrow Gordon's phrase) is becoming far less common in legal practice, where there is a growing tendency to simplify documents and to move towards a system of 'plain English' drafting (see Adler, 1990). Although mastery of technical legal language is a requisite for both the study and practice of law, jargon used for its own sake has no place in the law school. Do not let your choice of words turn your work into a parody of legal language.

Secondly, essay-writing is about constructing an *argument* based on the information you have acquired. Essay questions inevitably ask you to structure your material in one way or another. The clue usually lies in the first or last words of the question: 'Consider critically'; 'Discuss'; 'Evaluate', and so on. The greatest failing of all is to miss the significance of those words and simply 'write all you know' about a topic without bringing any critical faculty into play.

The key thing to remember about argument in academic writing is that there are certain conventional rules about what constitutes a 'good argument'. If you have had little or no previous experience of this type of writing, it is something you will certainly need to think about, and practise. The Open University (1985) has published a guide to study skills, which includes a section on the techniques of argument. It can be found in many academic libraries, and gives a more detailed discussion than we can provide here. We can briefly summarise the techniques, however:

(a) A good argument requires authority: it is insufficient to rely on your own value judgements or 'commonsense'. Any arguments you advance must be supported by authority from primary or literary sources. Your own value judgements do not constitute evidence of how things work. Value judgements also personalise the debate so that your arguments lack a sense of objectivity. You may bring an element of value judgement into play in a conclusion, for example, where you have to choose between two established alternative arguments, but even then you should indicate why one argument is to be preferred. Your preference should be supportable on rational grounds, not just on the basis that 'I think it is the better answer'. Commonsense is of no more worth than one person's value judgement. An argument is not necessarily true because the proponent believes most other people would support it.

(b) A good argument is built up carefully: in developing an argument it is important to have a plan of where you are going. Arguments need to be developed gradually. A good essay comprises three elements: INTRODUCTION—DISCUSSION—CONCLUSION.

Your introduction should explain what you are setting out to do. Your discussion should display the relevant information, derived from the appropriate sources, and show clearly on what side of the argument each piece falls. The conclusion should sum up the main points you have made and make clear your conclusion regarding the question asked. Keep these separate functions clearly in mind. Do not fall into the trap of presenting a lengthy ramble through the detail of the law, followed by a final paragraph containing a number of disparate critical remarks. That does not constitute an argument!

(c) You may find it helpful when planning an answer to reduce your plan to a diagrammatic form. Space precludes us from exploring the options in any depth, but you should be aware that there are a number of techniques you can use, including 'flow charts' and 'decision trees', which help you to construct a logical framework for ideas or processes, and 'mind maps' (see Buzan, 1989) which provide, it is said, a less formally structured way into a problem, and therefore a less restrictive and more powerful way of identifying the issues and making connections between ideas. For examples of how each of these can be used to support legal problem-solving, see Maughan & Webb (1995:chap. 3).

A final word of warning: good planning and good writing technique can never wholly disguise a lack of content. It can, however, enable you to use your knowledge to its best effect. Failure to abide by the basic rules can be met with the kind of indignity once meted out to an attorney by the United States Supreme Court. The Court returned a brief with the instruction that a whole new set of papers be filed in a form that was 'logically arranged...concise and free from burdensome, irrelevant and immaterial matter...' (*Gilchrist* v *Interborough Rapid Transit Co.* (1929) 279 US 159). We hope that none of your work receives a similar epitaph!

3.4.2 Answering Legal Problems

In studying law you will encounter what law teachers call 'problem questions' for the first time. The basic techniques of introduction and discussion which we have already considered apply to problems as much as essays, but you must be aware of the fact that you are dealing with a different kind of question.

The essence of any problem question is that it requires you to analyse some fictitious fact-situation and consider questions of legal liability that it creates. The precise scope of your answer will depend on what you are asked to do. The facts will normally be followed by some such request as 'Discuss'; 'Advise Ann'; or 'Advise Ken of his liability to Lee'. Do not ignore this; questions of standpoint and objective are as important to the student as the practitioner; so, in dealing with problems always remember who you are advising and what you are trying to do. For example, it may be that the problem concerning Ken and Lee also involves a third party, Mary. But if you have not been asked about Mary's rights or liabilities, it would be a serious error to discuss them.

Problem questions are usually constructed on a number of levels. Chiefly, this enables teachers to differentiate more clearly between the various qualities of answer. Most will therefore have one or two major issues, plus a number of less obvious legal points, or 'twists' to the facts which, for example, could distinguish the events from an earlier case which you might cite as a precedent. Particularly in examinations, it can be difficult to sort out the factual material and assess its legal implications in the time available. There is no instant solution to this. The answer lies in having a good working knowledge of the relevant law (this helps you to identify those facts which will have legal significance), and in adopting a systematic approach to the question.

By 'systematic' we mean that you must learn to use the question to help construct an answer. Let us explain. Most problems involve a sequence of events, so that x happens, followed by y, then z. Often x, y, and z have separate legal consequences, so by following the facts as laid down you can explore the consequences of each event, as it 'happens'. This should help ensure that you do not miss elements of the question completely. Sometimes, of course, one fact becomes relevant only when linked with something else which appears later in the question. So long as you make the right links, and do not lose sight of them, the same technique can apply. Again, you may find using 'mind maps' helps you to keep track of facts and the legal issues they raise. Above all else, developing a good problem-solving technique takes practice; do not miss out because of a lack of it! To help you we have included a specimen problem and outline answer as Exercise 17 in **Chapter 8**.

Finally, whatever you are writing, remember two cardinal principles.

First, there is one vital ingredient in any writing—WILL POWER! Unfortunately, essays do not write themselves, and a tutor's patience is rarely infinite. The hardest part of any piece of writing is actually to sit down at your desk and begin. It is much easier to go and make the tenth cup of coffee that evening, or to sit down and read that fascinating article on law reporting in thirteenth-century Outer Mongolia. Such delaying tactics can reflect a whole variety of difficulties—from a lack of confidence to total boredom with the subject matter; though normal human inertia is probably the most common cause. We cannot pretend to have a magic cure, but offer the following advice:

(a) Find a period in which you can work reasonably undisturbed. Time to think and plan is normally vital to producing good written work, particularly as careful planning can remove much of the apprehension that surrounds the writing process. Also try to ensure that you have a relatively long period in which to compose the actual essay. It is not advisable to try and cram writing into odd half-hours scattered through the day.

(b) The hardest parts to write are often the introduction and/or the conclusion, so leave these until last. Draft the various points of your argument first, then come back to the finishing touches. Probably the worst thing you can do is to try and finalise your opening sentence before anything else has been written.

(c) Pace yourself. Many of us justify leaving things to the last minute on the basis that we 'work better under pressure'. That is nearly always a myth. Perhaps some of us *only* work under pressure; but it is rarely the best that we can do. Instead it is usually hurried and full of half-developed ideas that sound fine at 2.00 am, but are much less convincing in the cold light of day.

Secondly, you should never miss an opportunity to check your work before submitting it. Many minor errors can be found this way. It also gives you an opportunity to review your own writing critically, and make sure that it does make sense. A student who begins an essay on the cost of litigation with the sentence 'Litigation is expensive, particularly if the defendant contests the case' will probably be given the benefit of the doubt; but repeat that sort of error too often in one piece of work, and the marker will inevitably question your understanding of the subject.

3.5 CONCLUSION

There is perhaps a danger at this stage of having replaced the myth that the law can be found in one book with another, more sophisticated version, which says that law is simply about constructing a solution from a variety of written sources. Provided your research is adequate, and you understand how to go about reading what you have found, you will come up with the answer. To an extent there is some truth in that, but the reality is rather more uncertain.

In practice, the process of reading the law does not operate in a vacuum; it is not an arid activity, but one that is applied in real legal disputes. Going to law is not simply a case of lawyers dusting down the appropriate statutes and cases, and reading them (though that will inevitably be part of it); it is, at its heart, a process of reconstructing disputed events ('the facts') and proposing a legal solution to them. The implications of this reality on *our* reading of the law is, in part, the subject of the next chapter.

EXERCISE 4   Attempting the impossible

Before attempting this exercise you are advised to read and make notes on:

(a) The case of *R* v *Shivpuri* [1986] 2 All ER 334—an important case in both Criminal Law and Legal Method. You are advised to use the All England report, as the answers make specific reference to that version.

(b) The introductory parts and s. 1 of the Criminal Attempts Act 1981.

Make sure that you understand the basic context of the dispute—i.e. what the case was about; why it was before the particular court hearing the case; what that court decided; and why. Once you have done so, you should be ready to test your comprehension against the following questions.

1. Starting with the Criminal Attempts Act, let us check your basic information:

    (a) What is its full citation?
    (b) When did it receive the Royal Assent?
    (c) What is the subject of Part I of the Act?

2. Is the short title (Answer YES or NO to each of the points opposite)?

(a) an accurate statement of what the Act is about?

(b) capable of assisting our interpretation of the Act?

3. Answer TRUE or FALSE to each of the points opposite.

Section 1 of the Act:

(a) makes it a statutory offence to attempt to commit an indictable offence;

(b) seeks to exclude from criminal attempts any significant steps towards a crime where the offence is in fact impossible to complete;

(c) includes within the definition of an attempt any acts of an accused which he believes would involve the commission of a crime, but which, if completed, would not, in reality, be criminal.

4. Turning to *R* v *Shivpuri*:

(a) Which court's decision appears in the report cited?

(b) In which court(s) had the case appeared previously?

5. Which of the statements opposite contain(s) a material (i.e., important) fact (there may be more than one)?

(a) The accused believed he was carrying heroin or cannabis?

(b) The substance in the suitcase was not a prohibited drug?

(c) The full offence of 'dealing' could not be committed?

6. Which of the statements opposite reflects the legal issue(s) at the root of the appeal? Again, there *may* be more than one right answer:

(a) Whether a merely 'preparatory' action constitutes an attempt in English law.

(b) Whether it is possible to be convicted of attempting to commit an offence where the facts make its actual commission impossible.

(c) Whether the requirement that the accused acted 'knowingly' mean that the prosecution must prove that the accused *knew* it was a particular controlled drug.

7. Do the judges all agree on the outcome of the case (YES or NO)?

8. Was that outcome:

(a) that the appeal was upheld on the question of attempting the impossible?

(b) that the appeal was dismissed because the judge had wrongly advised (*misdirected*) the jury?

(c) that the appeal was dismissed on the question of attempting the impossible?

(d) that the appeal was dismissed on *both* issues (i.e., attempting the impossible and on the misdirection of the jury)?

9. What was *Shivpuri's* impact on the standing of the earlier decision in *Anderton* v *Ryan?* Did it:

(a) Overrule *Anderton* v *Ryan?*

(b) Apply it?

(c) Distinguish it?

ANSWERS

1. (a) It is cited as the Criminal Attempts Act 1981, c. (i.e., *chapter*) 47.

   (b) It received the Royal Assent on 27 July 1981 (the date given just below the long title).

   (c) Simply 'Attempts etc'! This is to distinguish it from the repeal of the so-called 'sus' laws created under the Vagrancy Act 1824, which form the subject of Part II (see the 'Arrangement of Sections' and long title).

2. (a) is correct; it is a brief but accurate description.

   (b) does not correctly state the principle: if you got this wrong, think back to the 'Strawberry Jam' analogy used earlier in this chapter.

3. (a) **TRUE**: this is the combined effect of subsections (1) and (4)—the latter restricts liability only to *indictable* (i.e., serious) criminal offences.

   (b) **FALSE**: this statement actually reverses the effect of subsection (2) which deals with cases of 'factual impossibility'—e.g., the situation where A attempts to poison B with a substance which is, in fact, harmless.

   (c) **TRUE**: this is the most difficult to work out. Subsection (3) is concerned with the intention of the accused. So long as the accused intends to commit the offence, it does not matter that, because of some mistake on his part about the law, what he does is not a crime. A widely cited example is the situation where A has sexual intercourse with B, believing her to be under the legal age of consent. Technically, A has committed the offence of attempting unlawful sexual intercourse, even though B is not in fact 'under age'.

4. (a) The House of Lords.

   (b) The Crown Court and Court of Appeal—see 335i.

5. This comes close to being a trick question! All three of (a), (b), and (c) would have been material questions of fact. That this is the case with (a) and (b) should be reasonably evident. The accused's belief and the nature of the substance are both material to the question of attempting the impossible; they are both matters which are proved by evidence. Item (c) is rather more difficult. The *definition* of an offence is a matter of law; but that is not the point here. Here the issue is one of *proving* that the accused could not commit the offence. That, we suggest, is a matter of fact.

6. (b) and (c) are both correct. Statement (b) is probably the more obvious answer, but the issue identified by (c) also arises, e.g., at 339b *per* Lord Bridge. (a) is incorrect; though this point has arisen in a number of cases, it was not critical here—see e.g., Lord Bridge at 342g.

7. Yes is the right answer, though they do not necessarily arrive at the same outcome for the same reasons. If you got this one wrong it is probably because you have confused the *result* of the appeal with the *reasoning* used by the judges to come to their decision (see further the answer to Question 9). They should always be kept separate in your mind.

8. (d) is the correct answer. The misdirection point is less obviously a ground of the appeal, but it is raised by the defence and discussed by the House of Lords. They held that though there had been a technical misdirection, it had caused no miscarriage of justice, and so could be disregarded under their lordships' statutory powers—see Lord Bridge at approximately 341d–h.

9. The correct answer is (a). The decision of the House was unanimous in this respect; though Lords Hailsham and MacKay state that they would have been content to distinguish *Anderton* v *Ryan* (see 337b and 345h), they do not actually dissent from the judgment given by Lord Bridge.

REFERENCES

ADLER, M. (1990), *Clarity for Lawyers* (London: The Law Society).

BEBR, G. (1992), 'Case Law', 29 *Common Market Law Review*, 577.

*BROWN, L. N. and KENNEDY, T. (2000), *The Court of Justice of the European Communities* (5th edn., London: Sweet & Maxwell).

BUZAN, T. (1989), *Use Your Head* (Revd. edn., London: BBC Books).

DREWRY, G. (1973), 'Leapfrogging—And a Lord Justice's Eye View of the Final Appeal', 89 *Law Quarterly Review* 260.

EDWARD, D. (1995), 'How the Court of Justice Works', 20 *European Law Review* 539.

GOODRICH, P. (1986), *Reading the Law* (Oxford: Blackwell).

GORDON, J. (1991), 'How not to Succeed in Law School', 100 *Yale Law Journal* 1679.

MAUGHAN, C. and MAUGHAN, M. (2002), 'Legal Writing' in J. Webb *et al.*, *Lawyers' Skills* (Oxford, Oxford University Press).

—— and WEBB, J. (1995), *Lawyering Skills and the Legal Process* (London: Butterworths).

OPEN UNIVERSITY (1985), *Preparing for the Social Sciences Foundation Course* (Milton Keynes: Open University Press).

RENTON COMMITTEE (1975), *The Preparation of Legislation*, Cmnd. 6053 (London: HMSO).

VRANKEN, M. (1996), 'Role of the Advocate General in the Law-making Process of the European Community', 25 *Anglo-American Law Review* 39.

WATSON, G. (1996), 'From an Adversarial to a Managed System of Litigation: a Comparative Critique of Lord Woolf's Interim Report' in R. Smith (ed.), *Achieving Civil Justice* (London: Legal Action Group, p. 63).

*WILLIAMS, K. (1989), *Study Skills* (Basingstoke: Macmillan).

4

Law, Fact, and Language

In any legal argument that gets to court someone wins and someone loses. So why are people prepared to go to court when statistically they may only have a 50 per cent chance of success? There may be many more or less rational reasons, but usually a litigant will go to court only if advised that he or she has an arguable case. So what is it about legal disputes which means that *both* parties can be sufficiently certain of the 'truth' of their claim and the legal merits of their case to go to court, even though only one of them can win? Surely their lawyers read the same law?

The answer to this conundrum lies in the difference between the law in books and the law in practice. In practice, legal disputes are often affected by a range of variables that are not wholly predictable. In this chapter we shall explore some of these variables through two key factors. These tell us much about how legal disputes are actually *constructed* in court. The factors we consider are the relationship between:

(a) law and fact, and

(b) law and language.

We shall close the chapter by attempting to pull those two strands together in a discussion of how these elements combine to give the judges a high degree of flexibility in deciding cases.

In exploring these issues, it is important to bear in mind that the range of problems discussed probably does not affect all cases, and certainly does not affect them to the same degree. The greatest difficulties arise in those cases which are conventionally described as 'hard cases', that is, cases for which there is no clearly recognised or accepted legal solution.

4.1 Law and Fact

Law does not operate in a vacuum. Obviously, legal disputes only arise out of factual situations—e.g., a boundary dispute between neighbours or an assault by one person on another. This means that such disputes will always involve a mixture of law and fact— e.g., to prove in negligence that X has acted in breach of his or her duty of care, requires us to establish as a matter of *law* that there is a duty of care governing X, and that on the *facts* X has broken that duty.

We can define 'questions of fact' as all questions which attempt to prove what happened. They are established by various types of evidence, e.g., oral witness statements, forensic evidence, etc. 'Questions of law' arise in connection with legal principles that may be argued in a case (e.g., what is the definition of 'theft'), together with any procedural matters (e.g. the jurisdiction of a particular court). We can explore the practical importance of this a little more deeply.

4.1.1 Using the Law/Fact Distinction

Our experience with both undergraduate and postgraduate students shows that it can be very difficult to grasp the implications of the law/fact distinction.

The difference between questions of law and of fact is used in three ways:

To define the function of judge and jury

In many courts it is lay people who act as assessors of fact (notably as a jury in some criminal trials, and in tribunals), whilst judges deal with the legal problems. One needs to be sure which issue is decided by which person(s).

However, in many criminal and virtually all civil cases, the function of the jury as **tribunal of fact** (as it is called) has been taken over by judges. They will be responsible for ruling on both law and fact in the case before them. They are legally obliged to keep those functions separate within their own minds. This may seem an odd requirement, and in reality it sometimes requires the kind of mental gymnastics that even experienced judges can find difficult to maintain! However, it does emphasise that the determination of the issues of fact is separate from the ultimate issues of law before the court.

To establish rights of appeal

This applies particularly to the higher courts, where appeals on issues of fact are commonly outside the jurisdiction of the appellate court.

To establish the boundaries of precedent:

As we shall see in Chapter 6, only a decision on a point of law is capable of creating a binding precedent for use in later cases.

4.1.2 The Limits of the Law/Fact Distinction

Although it is easy enough to provide an abstract definition of fact and law, they can be difficult concepts to apply on a case-by-case basis. Given its significance, the difficulty we have in distinguishing between law and fact may seem rather surprising. We argue that, at its root, it is difficult because English lawyers have traditionally treated the question 'what is fact rather than law?' as context-specific. In other words, different approaches have been applied in different situations. This may enhance the flexibility of the courts' response to that question, but it can make it difficult for anyone actually learning the law. As a guide, but nothing more, we suggest that the following broad principles need to be considered:

Normally, the question is resolved by the substantive law

The statutory or common law rules governing a particular issue may well make explicit that a certain matter is a question of fact, rather than law, or *vice versa*. Again, the issue is complicated by a lack of consistency. Thus, for example, for many purposes the issue of 'reasonableness' is treated as a matter of fact—as in the uses of the 'reasonable man test' in both civil and criminal law (see, e.g., *Qualcast (Wolverhampton) Ltd* v *Haynes* [1959] AC 743; [1959] 2 All ER 38). Conversely, on a criminal charge of malicious prosecution, the question whether the accused had 'reasonable cause' to bring the prosecution is a question of law for the judge.

Similarly, further complexity can be caused by the courts' recognition that many issues may raise mixed questions of fact and law. For example, in cases of defamation it is necessary for a claimant to establish that the words used by the defendant had a defamatory meaning, and that they were defamatory to the claimant. The issue of defamatory meaning is a question of law, while the requirement of actual defamation of the claimant is one of fact. Again, there are no general guidelines to recognising where an issue raises such mixed questions—it is purely a matter where we have to be guided by the substantive law.

Special principles govern questions of interpretation of words

The meaning of words can be a question of fact or law. It is now well established that the *ordinary* meaning of words is a matter of fact. In *Brutus* v *Cozens* [1973] AC 854; [1972] 2 All ER 1297, the House of Lords had to decide whether an accused who had disrupted a tennis match at Wimbledon as a protest against the presence of a South African player at the tournament had been properly convicted of using 'insulting behaviour' likely to occasion a breach of the peace, contrary to section 5 of the Public Order Act 1936 (now repealed). Their Lordships noted that the Act did not define the word 'insulting', nor was there anything to suggest that the word was to be given any special or technical meaning. Therefore, they held that 'insulting' was to be given its ordinary meaning (which they did not attempt to explain), and that the question whether behaviour was insulting was a question of fact to be determined by the magistrates.

One final point, which may be causing you some confusion, needs to be considered. In establishing this principle of interpretation, the courts have arguably extended the concept of 'fact' beyond its most obvious usage, which reflects the normal idea of facts as events which may be proved by evidence from 'eye-' or 'ear-witnesses'. This principle will often have the effect of excluding debates about statutory meaning from the process of appeal, or, in public law matters, the process of judicial review. This must be contrasted with those situations where the courts will, as a matter of *law*, find some *implied meaning* within the words of a statute or other document. Thus, in a famous American case, *Riggs* v *Palmer* (1889) 115 NY 506, the question was whether the beneficiary under a will was entitled to take his bequest, despite the fact that he had murdered the testator. The local wills legislation was silent on the issue, but the Ohio Supreme Court disqualified the beneficiary by applying the long-established principle that a wrongdoer should not benefit by his own wrong. This, the court said, should be implied into the legislation. (A similar principle has been established in English law: see *Re Sigsworth* (1935), discussed in Chapter 8.)

So, given these principles, the next logical question is, how do we actually establish the facts in a case?

4.1.3 Proving the Facts

The first job of the court must be to establish the existence of the facts alleged within a given case. That does not mean that all the possible issues of fact will actually be considered. A feature of the adversarial process is that the legal contest is managed by the two sides involved. (We have already seen in Chapter 1 how the Woolf reforms have limited some aspects of adversariality, but those changes do not impact on the argument presented here.) It is therefore common practice for the parties to sort out in advance the scope of their dispute. This applies as much to questions of fact as it does to questions of law, so that it is not uncommon for certain facts to be agreed or admitted before a case comes to trial. For this reason we conventionally talk of '**material facts**' as a way of denoting those facts which remain at issue and which will subsequently form the basis of the judge's decision. Assessing the materiality of facts is chiefly dependent upon the legal issues involved in each case. A knowledge of substantive law is always required, because the substantive law will tell us what facts the parties are required to establish to win their case. What appears to be material to a client is often immaterial to the lawyer, and *vice versa*. This does not always help the lawyer–client relationship!

Let's now try to illustrate the issue of materiality by way of a simple exercise:

EXERCISE 5   'On your bike', or the case of the missing bicycle

Andrea has a bright red bicycle which she rides to school every day and leaves unsecured in the bike shed. One afternoon, after classes have ended at 4 pm, she discovers that her bicycle is missing. She reports this fact to the headmistress. By 4.30 pm the bike has mysteriously been found outside Andrea's home. Ben tells Andrea that he saw her friend Caroline riding a red bike at about 4.15 pm.

Which of these facts would you consider important in assessing whether Caroline had attempted to steal the bicycle?

(a) that the bike has been taken from Andrea, apparently without her knowledge, and

(b) Caroline was seen riding a red bike at a time consistent with the theft.

Others might, of course, be relevant in assessing the veracity of Andrea or Ben as witnesses, though that is a slightly different issue.

Are these sufficient to support the conclusion that Caroline is a thief?

Certainly not, though that is a possibility, there is still relatively little to connect Caroline to the theft. If Caroline was unable to explain Ben's evidence, then our hypothesis that Caroline is the thief would be strengthened. If she merely denied the allegation we would be little further forward. There is at present insufficient evidence to say 'beyond reasonable doubt' that Caroline took the bike.

There are a number of other explanations, some more plausible than others, that need to be explored, e.g.:

(a) Andrea had forgotten that she had not gone to school by bike that day.

(b) Caroline has a red bike of her own, and was seen riding that.

(c) Ben had mistakenly identified Caroline.

(d) Ben had taken the bike, and blamed Caroline to hide his own guilt, and so on . . .

The facts we have are therefore far from conclusive (see further the section on the burden of proof, below).

This example enables us to expand upon some of the points made so far. It highlights that the facts in any given case are unlikely to be of equal importance, and that their significance will often depend on their interrelationship with other facts in the case. Assessing what facts are material will depend in part on our ability to create an overall picture of events. For example, the statement that Andrea rides her bike to school every day does not appear to be particularly relevant to the legal issues—unless our inquiries lead us to discover that force of habit had caused her to forget that today her mother had driven her to school. Do not forget that experience and knowledge of the law will also play a part in establishing what facts are relevant and material. Thus, in the bicycle case above, once we know that the legal definition of theft requires that the thief has an intention to deprive the owner of that property permanently, Caroline's intentions regarding the future of the bike (assuming she took it) acquire a whole new significance—did she mean to keep it, or was she just borrowing it? This also illustrates an important point about the relationship between law and facts, which is that their dependence works *both ways*. We need a good knowledge of the facts to create a viable legal argument, but at the same time, we need knowledge of the law to sort out the legally relevant facts from the mass of information that will surround a case. We shall return to the relationship between law and fact later in Chapter 10.

The process whereby the material facts are established is referred to as one of **proof**. There exists within any legal system a variety of procedural rules governing what facts may be proved. Such rules vary from system to system in their restrictiveness. English rules of proof are widely regarded as amongst the more restrictive, though the rules regarding proof in civil cases tend to be less strict than in criminal procedure. Put briefly, the basic evidentiary requirements for proof of a fact are that it is *relevant and admissible*, and that the evidence is sufficiently strong to satisfy the *burden of proof*. We shall consider these points separately.

Relevance and admissibility

A fact will be **relevant** if it enables the court to reach a conclusion on any of the issues before it. In practice facts are often like the pieces of a jigsaw, where you cannot make out the picture until it is nearly complete; so it may be difficult for the court to see where the proof of a single fact is leading. This means that counsel may legitimately be asked to justify why a particular fact should be admitted.

Admissibility is a technical rule. It provides the courts with a means of excluding evidence that is relevant, but for some reason is inherently so unreliable that the court should refuse to be swayed by it. The best example of this is probably the rule in criminal evidence excluding a concocted confession under section 76 of the Police and Criminal Evidence Act 1984.

Admissibility in English law is complicated by the fact that it operates by means of a mass of exclusionary rules and exceptions thereto—incidentally, it is in this respect that the rule is frequently contrasted with the less restrictive systems operating in most of continental Europe. There, though the question of relevance remains fundamental, admissibility operates more on an assumption of 'freedom of proof'. 'Freedom of proof' requires a wide judicial discretion to admit or exclude evidence as the case demands, rather than the adherence to strict rules of evidence.

Questions of relevance and admissibility will depend, in part, upon the standpoint and objectives of the person using the information. To put it simply: what facts are important may well depend upon whether you are acting for a claimant or defendant; in either case you will seek to emphasise those facts which support your case, and play down, discredit, or even seek to exclude those which support your opponent. In that respect facts do not represent an objective truth, but sometimes an accurate, or sometimes a crude, estimate of the most convincing version of events.

The burden and standard of proof

The emphasis in law on notions of proof and probability is also a way of acknowledging that facts are not as concrete as they may seem. All cases, whether Criminal or Civil, are decided according to the **burden of proof**. This too is a complex subject, and too intricate for full discussion here, though some basic points can be made. The burden of proof places the responsibility for establishing a particular fact on its proponent, so that if A claims that B injured her by his negligent driving, it is up to A to make out a case. The requirement of proof means that facts must be established to the satisfaction of the court, but this does not mean absolute certainty. It will be relatively unusual for facts in a case to be *conclusive*.

The term **conclusive** is one which needs to be used with great caution. Technically, evidence is conclusive only where, by virtue of a rule of law, it cannot be contradicted—a widely cited example is the rule of law treating a child under the age of 10 as incapable of committing a crime. This technical meaning is thus different from the popular sense of the term, where it is used to describe evidence that effectively clinches the case. In reality, what is popularly called 'conclusive' is no more than evidence which carries a very high degree of probability. Lord Guthrie (amongst others) has made the obvious point that, '[o]utside the region of mathematics, proof is never anything more than probability' (*Nobel's Explosives Co.* v *British Dominions General Insurance Co.* 1918 1 SLT 205 at 206). Consequently, to ensure certainty and consistency in law, we specify not just the burden but also a **standard** of proof, which is a way of asking the tribunal of fact to consider whether the evidence presented on a particular allegation of fact is strong enough for the proponent to satisfy the tribunal on that point. In civil cases we generally require proof 'on a balance of probabilities', i.e. proof that the version alleged is simply more probable than not. In criminal cases a 'higher standard' is required, of 'proof beyond reasonable doubt'; it is sometimes said that this means that the trier of fact must be 'certain, so that they are sure'. What these abstract concepts come to mean in individual cases remains somewhat uncertain. The use of terms such as 'proof beyond reasonable doubt' may often work to disguise the extent to which conclusions about the facts of a case are subjective. Put simply, it is not easy to draw the boundaries between doubts which are reasonable and those which are not.

For example, criminal cases in particular may turn on questions of identification. Witness A may say that the person she saw looked like the accused X, whereas witness B may have given a different description. Identification is a question of fact, but do not let the terminology fool you; in establishing whether X is the guilty person, the court will be working in part from a whole range of conscious and unconscious perceptions regarding the person of the accused and the veracity of the witnesses, only some of which are reducible to rules of law, in an attempt to establish 'the facts'. Let us now consider how problems of establishing the facts may have disturbed the verdict in a real case.

4.1.4 The Case of William Wallace

At the time our story begins, in 1931, William Wallace was a 52-year-old insurance collector living in Anfield, Liverpool, with his wife Julia. They had been married for about seventeen years. They were known as a quiet, rather formal couple, with relatively few social acquaintances. Wallace was an unremarkable man, except in respect of his beliefs. He was a follower of Stoicism, a virtually dead philosophy based upon the *Meditations* of the Roman general, Marcus Aurelius; as Wallace wrote in his diary: 'For forty years I have drilled myself in iron control and prided myself on never displaying an emotion outwardly in public.'

Wallace was a regular chess player at a club in the city. On the evening of Monday, 19 January 1931, the captain of the club took a telephone message for Wallace from 'R. M. Qualtrough', leaving an address and a request for Wallace to visit at 7.30 the following evening. When Wallace arrived at the club half an hour later, he said that he had not heard of Qualtrough, but took a note of the address, assuming the call was in connection with his insurance business.

The following evening, Wallace left home sometime between 6.30 and 6.50 pm, caught a tram at 7.06 to his supposed destination, where he spent over half an hour looking for Qualtrough's address. It did not exist. He caught the tram home, where he was seen by his neighbours at 8.45, trying to enter the house. He explained that, unusually, both back and front door were locked, and he could get no reply from Julia. On trying the back door again, it opened. Inside was Julia's body; she had been beaten to death with an iron bar. The front bedroom of the house had been ransacked and £4 removed from the cash-box in which Wallace kept the monies he collected (though this was subsequently discovered inexplicably stuffed into a vase in the upstairs of the house).

An immediate search of lodging houses, the railway, cafes, and clubs in the area revealed no one who might be the murderer. Furthermore, the fact that there was no evidence of a forced entry to the house, or of a struggle between killer and victim, suggested either that Julia was taken wholly by surprise or that she knew her murderer. The police felt that they were left with two possible suspects.

The first was Gordon Parry, a former colleague of Wallace's, who had a record of petty theft and a reputation as a womaniser. Rightly or wrongly, this was sufficient to make him an initial suspect. He knew Julia; the layout of the Wallace's house; and that normally, on a Tuesday night, the cashbox would have contained over £100—the sum of Wallace's weekly collection. He might also have held a grudge against Wallace, who had caught Parry helping himself to insurance money that he was supposed to be collecting. However, Parry had an alibi. His girlfriend had told the police that they had been together the whole evening. He was dropped from the police enquiries.

The second suspect was Wallace himself. The police had by now heard rumours that the relationship between the Wallaces was far from happy, though this Wallace strenuously denied. There remained no clear motive for the killing. However, Wallace also seemed abnormally calm; he was observed, while being questioned by the police on the night of the killing, casually leaning over Julia's body to flick cigarette ash into an ash tray. This behaviour almost certainly aroused some suspicions. Did the police have a cold, calculating killer in their midst?

But didn't Wallace, like Parry, have an alibi? In a sense he did. Several witnesses, including a police officer, had spoken with Wallace in his search for Mr Qualtrough. However, there was no reliable assessment of the time of Julia's death. One pathologist put it at about 6 pm; another at 8 pm. It was not inconceivable that he had killed his wife before leaving for his appointment with the fictitious Qualtrough. Indeed, Qualtrough could have been a creation of Wallace's own plans. The telephone call to the chess club which created the whole alibi had been traced to a telephone box only some 400 yards from the Wallaces' house. Even so, how could the police deal with the fact that no blood was found on Wallace after such a ferocious killing? They surmised that he had worn only a macintosh, found partially burnt under the dead woman's body, to commit the killing. As traces of blood were found in the bathroom, this seemed to suggest that whoever had killed Julia had stopped in the house long enough to try to wash the blood off.

On 2 February Wallace was charged with his wife's murder. He was committed for trial before the Liverpool assize in April 1931. At the trial, the Crown pressed its case in a manner that was later described as 'oppressive'. Counsel claimed that Wallace had planned the entire thing, to the extent of faking his own alibi; witnesses were called attacking Wallace's demeanour; to all this he listened, impassively. The defence countered by emphasising the circumstantial nature of the evidence; the limited time Wallace would have had to commit the crime, clean himself up, and leave for his appointment, and the fact that the macintosh could as easily have been burnt by the gas fire in the room as by some deliberate act of the killer—this view, it was argued, was supported by the fact that Julia's skirt had been partially burned by coming into contact with the fire, presumably as she fell. On the fourth day of the trial, the jury retired to consider its verdict.

Obviously it is impossible to recreate accurately the atmosphere and arguments of a capital trial in a few short lines, but from the outline here, what would you expect that verdict to be? Innocent or guilty?

For Wallace, the answer came quickly. After retiring for an hour, the jury returned a verdict of guilty. He was sentenced to death. The day after his trial he was told that he was due to be hanged on 12 May. His lawyers immediately entered an appeal against his conviction. His appeal was heard on 18 and 19 May (sentence having been postponed) by the Court of Criminal Appeal. After what must have been a mercifully short judgment for Wallace (who was present at his appeal), the Court handed down its decision—see *R v Wallace* (1932) 23 Cr App Rep 32. The conviction was quashed on the basis that it was unsupported by the evidence. He was free to go.

So, how was it that the trial court had convicted Wallace? The Court of Criminal Appeal (*per* Lord Hewart CJ at 35) made it clear that no fault lay with the judge; the problem was evidential. This was a case of considerable difficulty and doubt, where much of the evidence was consistent with both innocence and guilt. In the end, the jury had (in the eyes of the appeal court) simply got it wrong.

The conviction was thrown out on the basis that the prosecution had not satisfied the burden of proof. They had failed to exclude the possibility that someone else had committed the murder. The reasons behind Wallace's conviction by the jury are difficult to ascribe, and of course, we shall never know the real answer, but it is submitted that there are a number of likely possibilities. Taken together these may help account for what was, with hindsight, a perverse verdict.

First, the jury itself lost sight of the differences between fact and speculation. A court is not concerned, as Lord Hewart said in *Wallace*, 'with suspicion, however grave, or with theories, however ingenious'. The prosecution case was full of ingenious theorising—for example the assertion that Wallace had worn the coat found under Julia's body to commit the murder and then sought to burn it—but few of these hypotheses could finally be substantiated.

Secondly, contemporary accounts indicate that there was a powerfully *presented*, aggressive, case by the prosecution. This, ironically, was probably aided by Wallace's own stoicism. His air of detachment in the courtroom probably did little to gain him sympathy, and may have helped foster the image of a cold and calculating killer. The defence also alleged that the police had been unduly obstructive to the preparation of their case (though this view was not supported by the Court of Criminal Appeal, more recent research suggests that it may have had greater foundation than was then realised, or acknowledged—see Wilkes (1984)). Taken together these might have served to distort the perceived strength of the prosecution case. The significance of questions of presentation and style will be further considered under the heading 'law and language' (below).

Thirdly, there is also evidence that the defence miscalculated badly in the presentation of its case by failing to apply to the judge to have the prosecution case rejected for a lack of evidence. This point illustrates rather graphically how much can depend on the forensic skills of the lawyer rather than upon either the actual facts or law in a case. A great deal, perhaps too much, in the adversarial process can depend upon tactics and techniques of argument.

4.2 Law and Language

The legal process is intrinsically bound up with language. The popular image of law is one that emphasises the oral element of legal tradition, that is, the process of argumentation before a court. Even the reality, which for most practising lawyers is rather more prosaic than television would have us believe, is still a world in which legal documents fill up much of the day. Words thus dominate the legal landscape; this is hardly surprising, because without language there could be no law. As Bernhard Grossfeld argues: 'Law certainly uses language, but language is the stronger' (1990:99). In the context of legal methods and techniques, there are two issues that need to be addressed; one essentially theoretical, the other more practical. These are the relationship between language and power, and the problem of the flexibility of language.

4.2.1 Law, Language, and Power

It is widely recognised that there is a substantial gap between legal and 'everyday' language. In some respects, that gap is narrowing as lawyers are being encouraged to use more naturalistic language (e.g., the changes in terminology introduced by the Woolf reforms, discussed in Chapter 1), but the continued relevance of old statutes and precedents means that what are really archaic forms of language are still in legal use, though it has to be said that lawyers are not wholly innocent in the perpetuation of this gap. The law has always tended to be a conservative institution, and the traditional usage of legal jargon has often been presented as part of the attraction or mystique of law. Some terms still in use, such as *autrefois convict* or *mandamus*, reflect law's origins in the language of the medieval aristocracy or the church; others illustrate specialist usage of quite ordinary words—e.g. the meaning given to the term 'consideration' in Contract Law. This specialist language has to be learned. There is no escape.

However, the existence of a distinct 'legal language' has wider social effects than just making the law student's life rather difficult. Here we shall discuss two important examples of those wider effects:

Law as camouflage

The extent to which law relies upon its own language is a very basic indication of the closed nature of legal argument. The term 'mystification' is used as a description of the way in which the language of the law defines who can participate in legal argument. The need to develop the 'special' skills of a lawyer has the effect of excluding non-lawyers from entering into legal discourse, with, it is argued, consequent limits upon the ability of citizens to gain access to justice. The special use of certain forms of language also serves to disguise rather than enhance our understanding of the legal system. This reflects what Grossfeld describes as 'law as camouflage' (1990:47). He gives a simple example of this from the United States' Constitution which, until amended after the American Civil War, contained rights to slave ownership. Despite this, the term slavery was constantly avoided in the legal terminology; instead slavery was always called the 'particular institution'.

In practice, the process of disguise may often be far more sophisticated. In the early Common Law, for example, we talk of the way in which actions could be based on 'legal fictions'—fictional pleadings which did not reflect the true dispute but were used to overcome technicalities and give a suitor access to the courts. A more modern analogy would be the way in which proof of marriage breakdown (particularly 'unreasonable behaviour') will be (to some extent) artificially constructed in divorce proceedings. Here it is employed to put an end to a marriage which, in reality, both parties wish to escape from, but without the restriction of separating and waiting for two years to obtain a divorce by consent. The use of the term 'unreasonable behaviour' thus camouflages the true workings of one aspect of the law of divorce.

This facet of language creates difficulties not only for the lay person, but also for lawyers outside the system. Getting past the camouflage is one of the major problems lawyers face in reaching an accurate understanding of a foreign legal system. Hence legal language is an important symbol of the power of law itself both to define, deliberately or otherwise, who may exercise legal rights, and to disguise the uses of law by those within the system from those outside. We would suggest that there are also other, more immediate ways in which use of language involves a significant exercise of power. This also enables us to posit formally the links between law, fact, and language in the title of this chapter.

Facts, power, and the legal process

We have already shown that facts are not plucked out of the air, ready-made. They need to be described—a process which, of course, requires language. Hanson (1959) makes the fundamental point that language and fact are dependent upon each other. This leads us to the conclusion that the way in which facts are described, not surprisingly, governs our perception of the nature of those facts. Linguistic differences thus can be said to affect the 'reality' created. Consider the example of the Eskimo language which contains many different words to describe types of snowfall. We could imagine a situation where a witness is asked to describe the weather conditions at a particular time. The picture of the facts painted by an English-speaking witness saying 'it was snowing hard' would then be very different from the presumably more graphic image created by an Eskimo witness speaking his or her own language.

In the legal environment, the ability of a witness to communicate what she or he has seen will be of great importance, because it is that act of communication which creates the facts of the case. Of course, not all witnesses share the same degree of linguistic competence, least of all in a pressured, artificial, setting such as a court. Stories are often presented in a broken, fragmentary way; narrative patterns can become distorted by lawyers' attempts to discredit testimony. Witnesses can become confused and uncertain.

Variations in presentation can have a dramatic effect on the court's perception of witnesses' credibility, and thence of the court's structuring of the facts. In a study in the early 1980s, O'Barr and his colleagues (1982) analysed the way in which different language styles emerged in court. They identified in particular a difference between 'powerful' and 'powerless' speech. Powerless speech, they found, was typified by the use of more qualified statements; deferential speech styles, hesitation, and other factors which did not affect the nature of the facts contained in testimony, but changed its presentation. In one experiment in particular, the researchers recorded the same information on tape, changing only the language style and the gender of the speaker. The witnesses giving information in a powerful style were rated by subjects as significantly more convincing, trustworthy, and competent than those whose linguistic style was 'powerless'. Subjects also tended to rate women speakers generally as being less powerful than men—even on the basis of identical material. Clearly, therefore, the medium can be as significant as the message itself.

4.2.2 The Flexibility of Language

The English language has over the last two or three hundred years become virtually the first global language. It is spoken in some form by, some estimates suggest, nearly one billion people around the world. Influenced by many different cultures, it has become one of the richest and most complex languages in the world. The current *Oxford English Dictionary* lists some 500,000 words in recognised use (though many may be highly obscure). This represents probably the most extensive vocabulary of any modern language. Buried somewhere within its midst are the many terms that constitute what might be called 'legal English'; but lawyers do not operate exclusively in a linguistically closed environment. Legal discourse must involve large numbers of 'ordinary' English words as well. Given the apparently huge range to choose from, one would have thought that a high degree of precision should be attainable. Unfortunately, this is not always the case.

It is said that legal rules suffer from a problem of indeterminacy, meaning that it is often difficult to predict the scope of those rules. Neither the judges nor Parliament will necessarily provide you with exhaustive explanations of what they mean to say, and much of the indeterminacy of laws is traceable to the flexibility of legal language. Some of that indeterminacy can be avoided by precision—the *correct* use of language (so far as is possible) is vital to the work of a lawyer. At times it is easy to be overly cynical on this matter: to say that lawyers are simply playing with language. But, trite though it sounds, words are all that a lawyer has at his or her disposal. Though whether changes to legal forms of language could reduce the scope for ambiguity, or whether our problems are inherent in the generally flexible and imprecise nature of language, remains a hotly debated question.

Problems in establishing meaning affect two stages of the legal process. Meaning must be considered at the point of drafting any legal document, and also subsequently at the stage of interpreting that document. The essence of the problem is that the law has tended to assume that meaning can be safely ascertained only from the document itself. In many situations we have little alternative. If a court is interpreting the contents of a will, for example, it may have little choice in the matter. The document may have been drafted twenty or thirty years ago; the person whose wishes it contains (called the testator) will be dead, and the memories of others involved at the time (if they can be found) may be unreliable. In practice, in such situations, the courts may resort to oral evidence or other documentary evidence that could shed light on the testator's intentions, but that tends to be a last resort. As we shall explain in Chapter 8, special rules govern statutes as opposed to other documents, but the starting point is essentially the same.

There is, however, an element of artificiality in this approach. The belief that we can establish the meaning of a document purely from the words used seems to assume that we can overcome two discrete problems: first, the difficulty of ascribing meaning to individual words; and, secondly, the problems created by the need to interpret more complex syntactic structures.

The meaning of words

To understand the problems of meaning we need, once again, to think about the relationship between legal and everyday language. We have already said that legal discourse involves the use of both specialist and general language. Knapp (1991:10) suggests that the relationship can be described diagrammatically as follows:

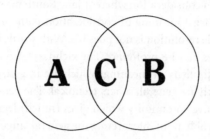

These two circles represent three linguistic subsets. Group A represents words used only in the general language; group B contains words used in legal language only, and group C represents words which are common to both legal and general English. On this basis, group (B + C) represents the sum of the legal language. These sets and subsets are open; their boundaries will change over time. New words will be developed to reflect technological and other changes in society. Words may actually move across the dividing line between the general and the legal language (as an example of the latter, Knapp cites the phrase 'corrective measures'—a general expression which had acquired a specific legal meaning in some of the former socialist states). We shall see in Chapter 8, in the context of statutory interpretation, that major difficulties can arise in ascribing a meaning to the words used in an Act of Parliament or in delegated legislation. We shall also see how the courts have developed principles of interpretation in an attempt to deal with this. Without anticipating too much of that discussion, it can be said that primarily the courts start from the assumption that words should be given their ordinary, everyday, meaning unless the context suggests a special or technical meaning is intended. It is an approach that has wider applications than just statutory interpretation. Courts are regularly engaged in thinking about the meaning of words in interpreting contracts and other written documents, and in applying rules of common law to specific cases. In such situations, lawyers face three major problems in respect of the meaning of words. These are:

(a) Dealing with *semantic ambiguity*: to say that words should be given their ordinary commonsense meaning is not always as simple as it sounds. Many words have more than one meaning, and it can be difficult to resolve which of a number of shades of meaning is intended in a particular legal document.

This problem may be especially acute in respect of words in subsets A and C, above. A feature of terms used only in legal language (subset B) is their tendency to be used in a manner that is unequivocal. By and large, legal language can convey very precise meanings—at least to other skilled users of legal language.

By contrast, where words exist in both legal and general usage (i.e. words in Knapp's subset C), there may be quite distinct ordinary meanings; that is, an ordinary everyday meaning and an ordinary legal meaning—like the term 'consideration' for example. In some instances such a range of meanings may be a cause of confusion. It may be difficult to determine which of the meanings is intended. Though the problem of meaning often can be resolved by looking at the linguistic context (for example, if a written contract contains the phrase '... in consideration whereof Jane Smith pays Alan Brown £200', it is pretty obvious that the legal meaning of consideration is the one intended), there are times when such a simple resolution is not possible. With words in subset A (the general language) the difficulties can be profound. The richness of our language means that many words have a multiplicity of meanings which are in general usage, or a range of meanings, some of which are general, others technical. The general language also lacks the common interpretative community which gives (much) legal English its precision. So, how do we resolve problems of interpreting the general language?

It may be argued that these problems can be resolved if we can accept that most ambiguous words have a core meaning that would be widely accepted as the most ordinary meaning of the word. However, to do that we have to accept the idea that a particular word does have a distinguishable core or standard meaning, and this itself may be highly debatable in some specific cases. Consider the following as an example of the problem:

> Let us suppose that in leafing through the statutes, we come upon the following enactment: 'It shall be a misdemeanour, punishable by a fine of five dollars, to sleep in any railway station.'... Suppose I am a judge, and that two men are brought before me for violating this statute. The first is a passenger who was waiting at 3 am for a delayed train. When he was arrested he was sitting upright in an orderly fashion, but was heard by the arresting officer to be gently snoring. The second is a man who had brought a blanket and pillow to the station and had obviously settled himself down for the night. He was arrested, however, before he had a chance to go to sleep. (Fuller, 1958:664)

The word 'sleep' in this example is clearly ambiguous. It can denote both the actual state of being asleep, and the action of spending the night in some place in order to sleep. Which is the core meaning? The words themselves are of comparatively little assistance to us in such cases, and it will normally be necessary to look to the context in which the language is used in order to construct some kind of settled meaning for the word being used. Often, it will be sufficient to consider other parts of the same document, which may make it clear, either expressly or by implication, what meaning is intended.

In Professor Fuller's example, it would not be too difficult to argue that such legislation would really be aimed at sleeping in the second sense we have identified. The Act would thus catch tramps and others entering the railway station with the intention of using it as a shelter for the night, without making genuine passengers who 'nod off' waiting for a train guilty of an offence. But, just as we have created an argument in support of the second meaning, could not another lawyer create an argument supporting the first? It is quite possible for lawyers to construct contradictory but equally viable arguments as to why one or other meaning or inference should be applied. In cases of true ambiguity, it is almost impossible to say that there is a particular right answer. Fortunately such instances are comparatively rare.

(b) Attempting to explain meaning: where problems with interpretation of a word arise, it is easy to assume that such problems can be resolved by simply explaining that word in different terms. In fact, that process is not always easy, and may create a new and unexpected set of difficulties.

One way of trying to define a word is to use a **synonym** for it. Synonyms are not ambiguous in themselves, but they often arise out of attempts to avoid ambiguity. A synonym is one word which has the same meaning as another. Sometimes it is tempting to use a synonym in the hope that it will carry a clearer sense of what is intended than the original word. Thus, in *Brutus* v *Cozens* [1973] AC 854; [1972] 2 AUER 1297, counsel sought to define 'insult' by reference to its dictionary definition and by the substitution (*per* Lord Kilbrandon at 1304) of terms such as 'insolence' or 'affront'.

In using synonyms two difficulties can arise. First, given the flexibility of language, it can be dangerous to assume synonymous meanings exist, particularly if one is dealing with technical legal concepts. Take the term 'fraud' for example; this is widely used in both civil and criminal law. The ordinary meaning connotes, according to the *Shorter Oxford English Dictionary*: 'Criminal deception; the using of false representations to obtain an unjust advantage . . .'. Thus, in ordinary usage fraud could be considered synonymous with deception. In law the terms are not synonymous, however. Buckley J distinguished fraud and deception in the case of *Re London and Globe Finance Corporation Ltd* [1903] 1 Ch 728 at 733:

> to deceive is by falsehood to induce a state of mind; to defraud is by deceit to induce a course of action.

So, a person may be deceived without being defrauded in the eyes of the law. Secondly, even if the word is a good synonym for the one which it replaces, it will rarely advance our understanding—as Lord Kilbrandon pointed out in respect of our earlier examples from *Brutus* v *Cozens*, such words are all equally 'as much, or as little, in need of interpretation'. In short, synonyms are not really of great value as aids to understanding.

If synonyms are unhelpful, should we seek to explain concepts by the use of some alternative formulation? This may be a superficially attractive way for us to deal with uncertainty of meaning, particularly where ordinary words carry within them complex notions of probability or desirability. But it is an approach that carries a real risk of increasing misunderstanding, as research has shown. Consider now the meanings of the set of words in our next exercise.

There is not, of course, a set of right answers to this task. Do not be surprised if you find considerable disagreement. When this same exercise was attempted by a group of forty executives on general management courses at a business school, it was found that there was a high level of overlapping between ranks, and hence considerable inconsistency between respondents. Thus, for example, the term 'expected' was on average placed the second most uncertain term in the list; its position for individual respondents nevertheless ranged from first to sixth. 'Unlikely' came bottom of the average rankings, but its range of ranks varied from third to tenth! In fact, the variation was such that only three out of the forty respondents produced identical lists (Moore & Thomas, 1988:127–8).

EXERCISE 6   **The uncertainty of uncertainty**

The following ten expressions are all used as verbal measures expressing some degree of uncertainty. They are not ordered in any deliberate ranking:

Probable

Quite Certain

Unlikely

Hoped

Possible

Not unreasonable that

Expected

Doubtful

Not certain

Likely

Now place these in rank order from 1–10, starting with the term that is MOST UNcertain and descending to the LEAST UNcertain. If you can, do this as a group exercise, so that each of you compiles his or her own list WITHOUT DISCUSSION; then compare your list with those of other members of the group. What do you find?

In case you are wondering, the above exercise does have important implications for legal decision-making. If, in a legal environment, we attempt to define a word or phrase by using some alternative formulation, there is no guarantee that our audience will give our words the same meaning as we intended. This has, in fact, been borne out by research into jury trials (LSE Jury Project, 1973), where 'jurors' have been asked to respond to what lawyers perceive to be equivalent ways of expressing the burden of proof. Needless to say, the subjects of the research did not always agree that the alternatives were equivalent at all!

(c) Interlingual ambiguity: as law becomes an increasingly international and therefore interlingual phenomenon, it is to be expected that a new crop of linguistic problems will arise. These difficulties tend to take a number of forms, but share a common basis in our (in)capacity to translate legal concepts from one jurisdiction to another. We shall focus on two specific issues here: interlingual synonymy and homonymy.

We have already considered problems of synonymy within a legal language. Between different languages, problems of synonymy arise where terms that appear to be synonymous in fact are not. In the most extreme cases, terms may have direct linguistic equivalents in another language, but in fact mean very different things. Knapp (1991:14) uses the example of the term *lichnaya sobstvennost* in Soviet law. This could be translated literally into English as 'personal property', but the English and Soviet legal notions of personal property are, as Knapp puts it, 'mutually incomparable'. Our translation would therefore be highly misleading. A rather less extreme, but not less difficult, problem arises where there is only a partial overlap of meaning. For example, English law uses the term 'easement' to describe certain rights that one person may acquire over another's land—such as a right of way. French law recognises the similar concept of *servitude*—but although there is some common ground between the concepts these terms denote, they are not identical. Easement would not provide a precise translation of the term *servitude* and *vice versa*.

A similar problem arises with legal homonyms (a homonym is a term which is either phonetically or in written form more or less identical to a word in another language). Again, these may convey very different ideas through the same term. Knapp (1991:15) uses the example of the term 'magistrate' and its homonyms. In English, 'magistrate' refers to a very particular kind of judge, sitting in the magistrates' court. In French, *magistrat* refers more generally to the professional judiciary, and as Weston (1991:109–10) shows, the term is extremely difficult to translate accurately into English, though at least the English and French terms do have judging in common! By contrast, the Czech term *magistrát* has nothing to do with the judiciary. It refers to a city administration—a kind of city council. Of course, just to increase the confusion, what is a misleading homonym for some comparisons is not necessarily so for others—the French *magistrats* and Italian *magistrati* are similar institutions.

Although this all sounds very academic, such interlingual problems are of practical significance. In multilingual legal communities such as the European Union, problems of translation and of linguistic and conceptual equivalence arise at the stages of drafting and interpreting legislation (see respectively Chapters 7 and 10 of this book where the EC legal context is developed more fully). These difficulties can occur both at national and supra-national levels. Interlingualism may also need to be addressed in domestic courts when dealing with matters established by international treaty, or when applying conflicts of law rules—e.g. in dealing with international trade matters or with the recognition of foreign divorces.

Interpreting syntax

In law, a second level of difficulty emerges out of syntax, by which is meant the grammatical use of words. Lawyers do not just have to work out the meaning of individual words; words are, of course the constituent parts of more complex linguistic structures, such as phrases and sentences, and in reality these can create separate problems from those which arise in the interpretation of a single word. The primary difficulty is that which has been called **syntactic ambiguity**. This phrase is used to describe the alternative constructions that are created by the use of qualifying phrases and dependent clauses within a sentence or paragraph. Bryan Niblett (1980:10–11) explores this problem by drawing a comparison between the syntax of a legal proposition and that of a computer program. Both constructs can suffer from what computer programmers call the 'dangling else' ambiguity. Niblett presents us with the following expression to illustrate this:

> if (condition 1) then if (condition 2) then
> (statement 1) else (statement 2)

If we consider this expression it does not take long to work out how the ambiguity arises. If conditions 1 and 2 are satisfied, there is no problem, since statement 1 obviously applies; but what if neither condition is satisfied, or only condition 1? When does statement 2 come into play? The ambiguity is there because we do not know from this expression to which *then* the *else* is an alternative. The ambiguity thus does not depend upon the words used but upon the way the expression is structured. Syntactic ambiguity is a particular problem of statute or delegated legislation. In practice, such instances of ambiguity have to be resolved by the courts choosing one of a number of competing interpretations, or sometimes by Parliament amending the ambiguous construction.

This can be seen from another of Niblett's examples, taken this time from a real statute, namely, the Guard Dogs Act 1975. Section 1(1) of the Act provides:

> A person shall not use or permit the use of a guard dog at any premises unless a person ('the handler') who is capable of controlling the dog is present on the premises and the dog is under the control of the handler at all times while it is being so used *except while it is secured so that it is not at liberty to go freely about the premises* (emphasis added).

The phrase in italics in that section is a classic example of the 'dangling else'. Does it qualify the whole of the foregoing section, or does it just qualify the requirement that 'the dog is under the control of the handler at all times . . .'? Just by looking at the words themselves, either answer is acceptable. The Divisional Court in *Hobson* v *Gledhill* [1978] 1 WLR 215; [1978] 1 All ER 945 was faced with exactly that conundrum. The accused used three Alsatian dogs to guard his premises. There was no handler present on the premises, but the dogs were secured and could not move freely about the property. If our first interpretation was correct, then no offence had been committed; the dogs were secured, so no handler was required. But if the second construction was correct, the accused would be guilty of an offence under the Act. Even if the dogs were secured, it was necessary to have a handler on the premises. The court decided the case by taking the first interpretation, a process which it justified by reference to a principles of statutory interpretation, which we shall consider in the next section.

More complex forms of ambiguity may arise, particularly within lengthy legal documents, where there is a contradiction between provisions. This is not, strictly speaking, a problem of syntax, just inconsistent drafting. However, it will raise difficult questions about which of the two conflicting provisions should prevail.

4.3 Fact, Language, and the Judicial Construction of Cases

In the next four chapters of this book we shall be looking at the rules or principles that have been developed, chiefly by the courts, to assist in the interpretation and use of existing statutory and common law authorities. The purpose of this chapter has been to get you to consider the background against which such principles operate. This is not simply a question of setting the scene. Many of those principles exist precisely because of the linguistic difficulties we have discussed in this chapter, and are there to provide guidance to the courts in overcoming such difficulties.

At the same time, however, it would be wrong to assume that such principles create a highly structured body of rules which can dictate with a high degree of certainty how issues, and hence legal cases, will be resolved. Cases are ultimately constructed in the courtroom. In *Hobson*, for example, the court was able to justify its decision by reference to a principle of statutory interpretation, which requires ambiguity in a statute imposing criminal liability to be construed in favour of the accused. However, as we shall see in later chapters, the majority of these principles are not hard-and-fast rules of law which the judge can apply only one way. Such principles provide a framework. They are part of what circumscribes and defines the boundaries of 'acceptable' legal argument. Nevertheless, they are mostly broad and leave much to the wisdom of the particular judge in each case. This means that judges have a considerable degree of discretion in choosing the principles they apply, and hence the meanings they give to statutes and other legal documents.

Similarly, though true semantic ambiguity can be a major problem, flexibility in assigning meaning to words provides another source for the exercise of discretion. This has both positive and negative effects on the development of English law. On the one hand, problems of precision in definition may be such that judges and draftsmen become reluctant to define a word at all, or else avoid the issue by taking the 'ordinary meaning' approach of cases such as *Brutus* v *Cozens*. On the other hand, the lack of a precise definition may be equally indicative of a positive decision not to impose what might be an unduly restrictive definition on a particular concept. Whether this is desirable is ultimately a political rather than legal question, but it does have a legal cost in that a lack of formalised definitions can sometimes allow the law to develop without the internal coherence and consistency that we might expect. So what, ultimately, dictates how a judge's discretion is applied?

Of course, there is not a straightforward answer to that question! To understand what is going on here, and at the same time to help explain the dilemma with which we opened this chapter, we need to touch on the nature of legal argumentation, a subject we will return to in greater detail in **Chapter 11**.

4.3.1 Interpretation and Justification in Legal Argument

Legal argumentation is a particular kind of activity that exists only in language and in the specific process of communication in legal settings. Putting it at its simplest, we can say that legal argument requires actions of both interpretation and justification.

Legal argument is posited first on interpretation. By this we don't just mean statutory interpretation—though that will be part of it. Interpretation provides meaning to a whole range of legal texts—statutes, law reports, the formal statements of case which are the basis for bringing a court action, and so on (one can include oral testimony here as well, as it is commonly reduced to writing as part of the preparation for a trial). The range of possible interpretations of such documents is itself defined by the norms and practices of legal interpretation—another way of putting this would be to think of legal interpretation as the product of the specific 'interpretative community' of the law. Interpretation is the first step in legal argument because interpretation defines what is being argued about, both as regards the rules in a case and the facts to which they apply. It is the means of establishing a basic consensus of understanding out of which we can define the issues about which there is dissensus, and thus a need for argument.

Next, legal argument requires some kind of grounding in reasons which provide a *justification* for the position being taken. Again, in relatively simple terms, legal justification can adopt broadly one of two forms (see Summers, 1978). First, it can be *consequential*, that is, it focuses on the goal, outcome, or consequences of legal action. Consequential reasoning thus seeks to justify a decision through a balancing of the different interests affected in a case. This can be seen, for example, in judicial references to public policy. Thus a court may refuse a claim for compensation because to allow it would risk swamping the courts with similar claims, or because to do so would impose an unacceptable burden on actual and potential defendants. Secondly, it can involve what Summers calls '*rightness reasons*'. In other words, the justification can be found by reference to objective and sometimes, perhaps, universal rights or principles (e.g., 'torture is wrong') which are said to apply in this case.

The role of the lawyers and the judge, therefore, is

(1) to construct an interpretation out of a set of contingent facts; some this interpretation will be agreed or assumed; other elements will be the subject of argument, with a decision on the 'true' facts to be made by the tribunal of fact;

(2) to provide justification for an outcome which is permitted on normative grounds and

(3) which provides a compelling story that integrates the facts with the law in a manner that is both normatively and 'narratively coherent' (Jackson, 1988), i.e. in which there is a good 'fit' between the facts and the legal outcome.

If we focus now on the role of the judge within this system we can begin to see how discretion arises, and how we are justified in talking about the judicial construction of cases.

4.3.2 Discretion, 'Judicial Style', and the Construction of Cases

The idea that there are acceptable forms of legal argument both constrains and creates the scope for judicial discretion, since it gives the judge some, sometimes considerable, freedom of interpretation and freedom of justification. The critical question may thus be how far is the judge prepared to push his or her freedom within or even beyond the boundaries of what is acceptable? This, we suggest, in large part comes down to a question of what we may call the 'judicial style' of the judge. This question of judicial style will be significant in determining how a judge handles a case, including the way in which he or she uses precedent—see Llewellyn (1960)—or principles of statutory interpretation (a point to which we shall return in Chapter 8). We can illustrate the operation of judicial style, first, by reference to two decisions on the law of negligence.

In negligence, it is necessary for the plaintiff to show that the injuries suffered are 'reasonably foreseeable' if the claim is to succeed.

In *Bradford* v *Robinson Rentals Ltd* [1967] 1 WLR 337; [1967] 1 All ER 267, the High Court had to deal with an unusual claim. In this case, the plaintiff was claiming in respect of frostbite suffered as a result of driving his employer's unheated van during an exceptionally harsh winter. On these facts, the plaintiff succeeded in his claim; the employer was negligent in allowing the plaintiff out in such a vehicle and the plaintiff's injuries were a reasonably foreseeable consequence of that action, despite the fact that the precise kind of injury suffered was uncommon in England.

In *Tremain* v *Pike* [1969] 1 WLR 1556; [1969] 3 All ER 1303, the plaintiff, a farmworker, contracted a rare disease called Weil's disease which is caused by the sufferer being infected by an organism found in rats' urine. His claim was that his employer had been negligent by allowing the rat population on the farm to grow to such an extent as to place his health at risk. The court did not deny that such behaviour was negligent, but it refused the plaintiff's claim on the basis that the *type* of injury was not foreseeable. What was foreseeable was a more obvious kind of 'rat injury' such as a bite. In effect, the court held that you cannot foresee a rare disease.

Is the latter decision inconsistent with the former? If the approach in *Bradford* had been followed in *Tremain* there would certainly be grounds for suggesting that contracting Weil's Disease is no less foreseeable than contracting frostbite. But the court in *Tremain* was not bound by *Bradford*; the judge consequently had greater freedom of justification in applying the reasonable foresight test than he might otherwise have done. The difference thus lies not in the actual tests used, but in the attitude to the test displayed by the two courts. In the second case, the judge took a very restrictive (and consequentialist) view, requiring that the precise *type* of injury should be reasonably foreseeable. In *Bradford*, the judicial view was more relaxed. It was foreseeable that some kind of injury would follow from being thus exposed to the extreme cold, and that was taken to be sufficient. It was not necessary that the precise nature of the injury should be foreseen.

Judicial style may also affect the way in which facts are used. We have already confronted the idea that facts in law are not a wholly objective truth. They are in part constructed within the courtroom and may be affected by a whole variety of highly subjective factors; for example, the presentation by counsel, the language and appearance of witnesses, or the ability of the jury (or judge?) to comprehend the issues. We have also noted that the judge is, in many cases, the arbiter of fact. We suggest that questions of judicial style might thus also influence the reception and interpretation of those facts.

In two studies, by Jackson (1988) and Twining (1990), the judgment of Lord Denning in *Miller* v *Jackson* [1977] QB 966; [1977] 3 All ER 338 has been considered. Although the two authors adopt different standpoints, they have both used *Miller* critically, as an example of how judges may manipulate a case through the statement of facts. We have used an extract from that judgment as the basis for the final exercise in this chapter.

EXERCISE 7   It's just not cricket!

Consider the following passage taken from Lord Denning's judgment in *Miller* v *Jackson* (pp. 340–1):

> In summer time village cricket is the delight of everyone. Nearly every village has its own cricket field where the young men play and the old men watch. In the village of Lintz in County Durham they have

their own ground, where they have played these last 70 years...The village team play there on Saturdays and Sundays. They belong to a league, competing with the neighbouring villages. On other evenings after work they practise while the light lasts. Yet now after these 70 years a judge of the High Court has ordered that they must not play there any more. He has issued an injunction to stop them. He has done it at the instance of a newcomer who is no lover of cricket. This newcomer built, or has had built for him, a house on the edge of the cricket ground which four years ago was a field where cattle grazed. The animals did not mind the cricket. But now this adjoining field has been turned into a housing estate. The newcomer bought one of the houses on the edge of the cricket ground. No doubt the open space was a selling point. Now he complains that, when a batsman hits a six, the ball has been known to land in his garden or on or near his house. His wife has got so upset about it that they always go out at weekends. They do not go into the garden when cricket is being played. They say that this is intolerable...And the judge, much against his will, has felt that he must order the cricket to be stopped; with the consequences, I suppose, that the Lintz Cricket Club will disappear. The cricket ground will be turned to some other use. I expect for more houses or a factory. The young men will turn to other things instead of cricket. The whole village will be much the poorer. And all this because of a newcomer who has just bought a house there next to the cricket ground.

From this statement can you:

(a) predict Lord Denning's decision on the law: did he find in favour of the cricket club, or of the Millers?

(b) distinguish fact from supposition within that case.

ANSWERS

The answer to (a) will probably come as little surprise. Lord Denning found in favour of the cricket club. He held that there was no actionable nuisance by the club, and discharged the injunction. His lordship was not, in the end, wholly successful in carrying the rest of the Court of Appeal with him. The other two judges found that there was an actionable nuisance; however, only one of them felt that it was such that an injunction (a discretionary remedy) should be granted, so that Lord Denning was in a majority in favour of dismissing the injunction granted by the High Court.

Is it not rather odd that we can guess the final decision from what is supposed to be a statement of facts? Yes—if one assumes that the facts are supposed to be a fairly objective part of the process. Lord Denning's comments illustrate, as Twining notes, the way in which facts can be formulated so as to advance a particular argument, albeit that, here, Lord Denning's formulation is far more explicitly biased than one would normally expect from a judge. Jackson argues that his technique is strongly rhetorical. Through its choice of language and a range of rhetorical techniques, it builds an image of a rural community bound together by its love of cricket; it is an idyll that is threatened by an outsider who can destroy that traditional way of life. The effect is to create a narrative framework 'laden with disapproval' (at 96).

In respect of (b), the construction of a narrative built upon both fact and supposition is another aspect of Lord Denning's attempt to carry us along to his conclusion. He thus creates a picture of socially undesirable consequences that might flow from the continued injunction: the replacement of the cricket ground with houses or a factory; the fear that young men will turn 'to other things' which, though remaining unspoken, are clearly undesirable. These are, of course suppositions, without evidence; they should not impinge on the case, and yet they do.

In saying that judicial style is an important determinant of cases, we are not suggesting that judges have, in effect, a free rein to decide cases as they think fit. As we have said at various points in this chapter, judges (and lawyers) operate within a culture which creates limits on what is acceptable practice. The existence of objective rules and principles, applied within a setting which expects decisions to display at least some normative and narrative coherence, means that in most cases there will be one story and one outcome that is more 'correct' than another. Indeed, one reason why Lord Denning's judgment in *Miller* v *Jackson* has been so extensively criticised is precisely because he stepped beyond the boundaries of acceptable judicial argumentation, and challenged the perception, perhaps even the ethical expectation, we have that a judge will maintain his or her air of neutrality.

While the framework of rules and principles within which judges operate does impose some constraints on them, clearly it may not always be sufficient. Does this matter? Should the judges be made more constrained, more accountable for their decisions? Before you dismiss this question as irrelevant to legal method, consider the role of the guiding principles of precedent and interpretation that make up much of this book. To what extent are these self-imposed, and therefore capable of revision from within the judiciary itself? As Llewellyn (1960:53) pointed out: a sense of legal tradition may guide lawyers, but it is the lawyers who may reshape and mould it for the future. Who should decide whether the lawyers are right to do so?

REFERENCES

FULLER, L. (1958), 'Positivism and Fidelity to Law—A Reply to Professor Hart', 71 *Harvard Law Review*, 630.

GROSSFELD, B. (1990), *The Strength and Weakness of Comparative Law* (trans. T. Weir) (Oxford: Clarendon Press).

*HANSON, N. (1959), *Patterns of Discovery: an Inquiry into the Conceptual Foundations of Science* (Cambridge: Cambridge University Press).

JACKSON, B. (1988), *Law, Fact and Narrative Coherence* (Roby: Deborah Charles Publishing).

*KNAPP, V. (1991), 'Some Problems of Legal Language', 4 *Ratio Juris* 1.

LLEWELLYN, K. (1960), *The Common Law Tradition* (Boston, Mass.: Little Brown).

*LLOYD-BOSTOCK, S. (1988), *Law in Practice* (London: British Psychological Society/Routledge).

LSE JURY PROJECT (1973), 'Juries and the Rules of Evidence', *Criminal Law Review* 208.

NIBLETT, B. (1980), 'Computer Science and Law: An Introductory Discussion' in B. Niblett (ed.), *Computer Science and Law: an Advanced Course* (Cambridge: Cambridge University Press).

O'BARR, W., et al. (1982), *Linguistic Evidence: Language, Power and Strategy in the Courtroom* (New York: Academic Press).

SUMMERS, R. (1978), 'Two Types of Substantive Reasons: The Core of a Theory of Common Law Justification', 63 *Cornell Law Review* 707.

TWINING, W. (1990), *Rethinking Evidence: Exploratory Essays* (Oxford: Basil Blackwell).

WESTON, M. (1991), *An English Reader's Guide to the French Legal System* (New York/Oxford: Berg).

WILKES, R. (1984), *Wallace: The Final Verdict* (London: Grafton).

5

The Doctrine of Judicial Precedent

5.1 Introduction

In this chapter we begin to deal with case law in depth. In the study and practice of law we seek to analyse legal principles; and the 'principles' in English law are derived from pure case law or from case law dealing with statutes. Indeed, it is often said to be a strength of English law that it is built upon the concrete examples of case law rather than hypothetical models. This contrast with the European approach, which does depend upon 'models', will be drawn and expanded upon later. As regards the Common Law fixation with a case-by-case development of the law, it is worth noting the observations of Lord MacMillan that, unlike the Civil Law lawyer, the Englishman

> has found that life is unconformable to any fixed theory and that principles always fail because they never seem to fit the case in hand, and so prefers to leave theory and principle alone. (1937:81)

We shall explore the significance of this statement over the next two chapters.

The doctrine of judicial precedent is concerned with the importance of case law in our system. It is really the lawyer's term for legal experience. We all tend to repeat things we have done before: law is essentially no different. If one case has decided a point of law then it is logical that that solution will be looked at in the future. The American judge, Oliver Wendell Holmes Jnr, once said that 'The life of the Law has not been logic; it has been experience'. Miles Kington put it another way in *Punch*: judicial precedent means 'A trick which has been tried before, successfully.'

But if judicial precedent is simply experience in legal jargon, why does it deserve our attention? Why can we say that, during your training in law and afterwards, you will have to possess a clear understanding of the intricacies of judicial precedent? The answer lies in the fact that the term 'experience' only begins to describe the situation.

First, even when a layman uses the term 'precedent' there is an implication that what was done before should be done again—that a starting point in trying to solve a problem is to see what examples exist where this (or similar) problems have been tackled before. The example—the precedent—is at least a good guide and probably will be followed. This achieves consistency, if nothing else. And the corollary is that people making decisions are often afraid to do something in case 'it creates a precedent'. As MacCormick states:

> To understand case-law... is to understand how it is that *particular* decisions by particular judges concerning particular parties to particular cases can be used in the construction of *general* rules applying to the actions and transactions of persons at large. (1987:155)

In other words, combining the remarks of Lord MacMillan and MacCormick, the principles of English law are derived from observing the development of a line of particular cases on a particular topic. This is a key factor in English law. Because English lawyers are so avidly fixed on case law, principles do not develop unless claimants bring cases. Academics and practitioners may speculate on the development of legal principles, but it takes real-life cases to settle them. And the judges in each case, to a greater or lesser extent, draw upon the principles established in those earlier cases in reaching their decision. For instance: imagine that a case in 1920 decided that any person selling parrots was under an implied contractual duty to ensure that the parrot could talk. A layperson reading about this case might think it interesting, especially if he has just bought a dumb parrot. A lawyer, however, immediately starts to think of the ramifications of the case: what is the significance of the case? How does it stand with other cases? What level of court made the decision? Thus, to the lawyer, the case presents further questions:

(a) Would this principle still apply if the pet shop owner clearly told the customer that the parrot could not talk?

(b) Does the same principle apply to related birds such as budgerigars?

(c) Should the principle apply to other birds?

(d) Wider still, is there a general principle to be found in the case which might mean that a similar duty (say as to standards of health) might apply to other animals?

Thus, as MacCormick indicates, the particular case concerning parrots may consequently be seen as giving birth to a more general principle on the duties owed by pet shop owners to their customers, e.g., that they owed a duty always to deal in good faith. It is not beyond speculation that the same principle might one day then be applied to sellers of other types of goods such as televisions or cars. Eventually a textbook writer will sum up the case law in one general statement on the duties owed by vendors of goods. Looking back at the history of the cases, we might find that one case concerning a mute parrot is now applied to all cases on defective merchandise.

5.2 The Idea of Binding Precedent

We now need to add one further ingredient. It is this: an important and distinctive element of English law is that the reasoning and decisions found in preceding cases are not simply considered with respect or as a good guide, but can be **binding** on later courts. This is known as the principle of *stare rationibus decidendis*; usually referred to as *stare decisis*. It translates simply as 'Let the decision stand'. *Stare rationibus decidendis* is the more accurate statement because, as we shall see, it is the reasoning (*rationibus*) that is the vital binding element in judicial precedent. However, nobody actually refers to it this way.

What *stare decisis* means in practice is that when a court makes a decision in a case then any courts which are of equal or lower status to that court **must** follow that previous decision if the case before them is similar to that earlier case. So, once one court has decided a matter other inferior courts are bound to follow that decision.

You must be careful here: the 'decision' of a case can mean a number of different things. At its simplest, the 'decision' is that X won and Y lost. Thus X and Y are (subject to any appeal) bound by that decision; this is referred to as *res judicata* (a matter which has been adjudicated upon). But when we use the word 'decision' in the context of legal analysis we are referring to something much wider. We are referring to the *whole* reasoning process that went into deciding that X won—we are referring to *why* X won; and we shall explore how we set about this below.

So, first, you must be aware right at the start that legal reasoning is not simply a process of matching one case against another; it is not merely a question of drawing analogies. There will always be differences in the facts of the two cases, if nothing else. As precedent is founded on comparing cases a primary question is: how significant are the differences? Just because the facts of two cases are apparently similar does not mean they should be decided in the same way. You would not, for instance, say that if a tabby cat called Henry miaows like a banshee, then every other tabby cat called Henry will do so too.

We can translate this into something more realistic and legally orientated:

EXERCISE 8   **Zebras on the North Circular**

Let us say that in *case (1)* a man driving a Ford Mondeo runs over an old lady who was law-fully using a zebra crossing. The man is held to be liable in negligence.

Let us say that in *case (2)* a woman driving a BMW runs over an old man who was crossing the road. Should she be found liable, too, or do you need to ask some further questions? If there are other questions, what might they be?

We do not present a formalised answer to this, because we wish to explore the ramifications of the issues it raises; but you may check your ideas against the comments which follow. We have seen in earlier exercises that a proper assessment and analysis of factual detail is essential to the application of rules. You might wish to know, for instance, what were the weather conditions in each case; were either of the drivers speeding; was the old man crossing the road at a safe point?

All these matters will come out in the evidence given by the parties. The judge will decide, on the strength of the evidence, which version of the 'truth' he or she believes. The judge will then apply the law (i.e. the judicial precedents) to the facts of this case to decide whether the defendant is liable to pay damages to the claimant. The more similar the facts of this new case are to existing precedents, the easier it is for the judge to decide that the law which is found in those precedents applies to the new case; the more the new facts differ from existing precedents (or raise completely novel points), the more difficult it will be to find a match. As you will see much later in this book (in Chapter 11) there are various reasoning techniques a judge may employ (reasoning by induction, deduction, analogy, or even through policy considerations) but the basic idea is he or she has to decide whether the new case should be decided in the same way as the older cases. This leads us to ask: what similarities or differences in the facts might be significant here?

Are the cases, for instance:

(a) sufficiently similar that the decision of *case (1)* should be applied in *case (2)?* or

(b) sufficiently different that the decision of *case (1)* should not be applied (never mind be considered binding) in *case (2)?* or

(c) are the factual differences of minimal significance? or

(d) are the facts different, but the principle underlying the decisions in the cases similar? Here you need to be sure what was the principle that was established in the first case: does the reasoning—*'why?'*—in the first case apply to the second?

In the next chapter we shall explore in more depth how we assess the *'why?'* in a case. For the moment, imagine that when you read the report of *case (1)* you found that the House of Lords had pronounced that whenever a driver injures a pedestrian, irrespective of how careless the pedestrian was, the driver is to be held to be at fault. This would mean that, whatever the differences in fact between *case (1)* and *case (2)*, it looks as if the driver will be liable because the **general** principle established in *case (1)* would apply. On the other hand, perhaps the principle in *case (1)* was that drivers will be held to blame if pedestrians are using a zebra crossing. If that is the principle established in *case (1)*, it is arguable that it should not apply to the facts of *case (2)*.

5.3 Establishing the Principle in a Case

As can be seen from the above, the doctrine of judicial precedent is not simply a mechanical process of matching similarities and differences. It is not merely a science of comparisons for it embodies the art of interpretation; the art of propounding the **principle** to be derived from each case. It also involves the lifeblood of a lawyer: argument. We will deal with this aspect of precedent in depth in the next chapter. However, by way of introduction we can look at one—case from the nineteenth century (the one which appears in the box below: *Household-Fire Insurance* v *Grant*) and see how it was treated as a precedent when cases, which at first sight seemed quite similar to it, came before later courts.

Household Fire Insurance Co. v *Grant*
(1879) 4 Ex D 216

Grant made an application in writing to the company for shares. A deposit was paid, the remainder to be paid within twelve months. The company allotted shares to Grant and posted the allotment to him. The letter never arrived. The company later went into liquidation and the liquidator sought the balance of Grant's application which was still outstanding. Grant maintained he had no contract with the company because his offer had not been accepted. No contract would mean no liability to pay. The company maintained that the offer had been accepted when their letter of acceptance had been posted even though it never arrived.

In case you have not studied Contract Law yet (or are not going to) we should explain that a contract is formed when there is an offer which is accepted, without the addition of new terms, by the other party. A person making an offer is termed the *offeror*; the person receiving the offer is the *offeree*. The general rule is that acceptance has to be communicated by the offeree. There is no contract simply because, in his or her own mind, the offeree is willing to accept. However, a major problem arises when the parties are not face to face. If they communicate by post, for instance, when does the acceptance take place? Should it be when the letter of acceptance is posted by the offeree, or only when it arrives with the offeror?

By the end of the nineteenth century there existed a number of authorities on what is now termed the 'postal rules' of acceptance in contract. These stretched back to *Adams* v *Lindsell* (1818) 1 B & A 681, but the key case under scrutiny was to be the House of Lords case of *Dunlop* v *Higgins* (1848) 1 HLC 381; 9 ER 805. In this case Dunlop wrote to Higgins offering to sell some iron, reply to be by return of post. The offer was accepted by Higgins in a letter but bad weather delayed the post. In the meantime there had been an increase in the price of iron. It would have been in Dunlop's interest if no contract had been concluded with Higgins because then Dunlop would still own the iron and be able to sell it to other customers at the new (higher) price. The House of Lords decided otherwise: a contract existed when the letter of acceptance was posted.

In *Household Fire Insurance* v *Grant* all three judges in the Court of Appeal analysed whether *Dunlop* v *Higgins* applied to the case before them. Thesiger LJ said that the decision in *Dunlop* v *Higgins* rested 'upon a principle which embraces and governs the present case'. To say that the acceptance takes place when the letter is posted and arrives late (as with *Dunlop* v *Higgins*) but not if it never arrives (as with *Household Fire*) would be illogical. The principle was, therefore, that once the letter of acceptance was posted the parties were bound. Of course, the offeree would have to convince a court on the facts that his had happened; but that point of evidence was irrelevant to the legal principle.

When Bagallay LJ looked at *Dunlop* v *Higgins* he concluded (at 227–8):

> I think that the principle established by that case is limited in its application to cases in which by reason of general usage, or of the relations between the parties . . . or of the terms in which the offer is made, the acceptance of such offer by a letter through the post is expressly or impliedly authorised.

Thus the principle in *Dunlop* v *Higgins* was seen by Bagallay LJ as being more limited than Thesiger LJ's approach; but on the facts Bagallay LJ decided that the present case still fell within the rule.

Bramwell LJ dissented. He thought there was *no contract* because the letter never arrived. He argued that *Dunlop* v *Higgins* had been completely misinterpreted; at best it was authority for the rule that acceptance takes place on posting only where the letter arrives (albeit late and within a reasonable time).

So the same authority was used by two Lords Justices to find for the company; but they had quite different interpretations of what *Dunlop* v *Higgins* really decided. The same case was also used by Bramwell LJ to argue a completely different conclusion—showing at least that simply knowing about the existence of a case is not enough; you must be able to argue its relevance or irrelevance to the case in hand. This means that you must read cases in depth. In this chapter we shall concentrate on the position where the facts are sufficiently similar that the cases are 'alike'. How will the doctrine of *stare decisis* affect our analysis? In answering this question it becomes important that we should look at the mechanical side of precedent. The courts stand in a defined hierarchy: which courts are **bound** to follow the decisions of which other courts? This is not usually perceived as the most stimulating part of legal studies, but understanding the workings of *stare decisis* depends upon having a sound grasp of the court structure. In turn, an efficient system of precedent depends upon dependable law reporting. You should familiarise yourself with the court structure and know how to use a law library. You will find these matters explained earlier in this book, detailed in any text on the English legal system, and nearly every Law course now includes instruction on how to use a law library. These are hardly the thing examination questions are made of, but a lawyer who cannot describe the structure in which the law operates, or find the law, will lose credibility fast.

5.4 The Mechanics of *Stare Decisis*

The system of precedent itself involves a fair degree of detail, but the basic principle to keep in mind is that the precedents created by superior courts bind lower courts and, generally, courts of equal status. We considered the basic court structure in **Chapter 1** (at **1.5.3** and **Figure 1.1**). You are advised to refer to that diagram to see the relationship of the courts discussed below.

One other idea you need to bear in mind is that not all precedents are binding. For if some precedents are binding there must be others which are not. These we call **persuasive** precedents. **Persuasive** precedents arise out of a number of contexts:

(a) Decisions of *lower* courts cannot bind. They may be persuasive.

(b) Decisions of the High Court at first instance (i.e. the trial stage) are persuasive authority for later cases in the High Court.

(c) Decisions of the Judicial Committee of the Privy Council (see below).

(d) Decisions of the Scottish and Northern Irish courts.

(e) Decisions of other courts within the Common Law world: see, e.g. the use of the Australian case of *Sutherland Shire Council* v *Heyman* (1985) 60 ALR 1 in *Murphy* v *Brentwood DC* (1990), detailed below.

5.4.1 The House of Lords

The decisions of the House of Lords bind all lower courts. There has been a long debate as to whether decisions of the House of Lords should bind a future House of Lords. For some 100 years the Law Lords considered themselves bound. This was changed by the *Practice Statement (Judicial Precedent)* [1966] 1 WLR 1234 where it was said that though the doctrine of being bound had many commendable points: 'too rigid adherence to precedent may lead to injustice in a particular case and also unduly restrict the proper development of the law.'

Thus the Lords can depart from their own previous decisions; but they will do so only in rare circumstances. Remember that the House of Lords is the highest court in the land (save, in a quite different way, on European Community law matters). Its pronouncements (only about 100 a year) must be seen as creating an air of certainty in business dealings, in criminal law, in land law, and so on. Changing its mind may do 'justice' to a particular case, but at a cost. For instance, if you are conducting complicated contractual negotiations based on a decision of the House of Lords, it is somewhat annoying to find that, having concluded the deal, the law relating to that contract has suddenly been changed by a new House of Lords' decision. One of the authors can bear testimony to this.

However, despite this, the Law Lords will change their minds. Such occasions are rare, but here are a few cases which show this in action (see also the excellent analysis of this topic in Harris, 2002).

British Railways Board v Herrington [1972] AC 877; [1972] 1 All ER 749

The Lords faced a number of nineteenth-century and early twentieth-century decisions wherein they had held that there was only a limited duty of care in negligence owed to children who trespassed onto property. This duty was that the occupier should not act recklessly with regard to children whom he knew to be there; and public policy dictated that there was no duty at all to keep out such children or to make the premises safe for them. Since then changes in perceptions of public policy and the development of the law of negligence had altered the approach to the whole topic of responsibility for negligent actions. Thus their Lordships felt able to ignore the earlier decisions and impose on British Railways a duty of care in keeping railway line fences repaired.

Miliangos v George Frank (Textiles) Ltd [1976] AC 443; [1975] 3 All ER 801

The House of Lords had previously decided that all awards of damages in an English court had to be made in sterling. In this case, however, because of changes in international trade and the status of sterling they felt the time had come not to adhere to their previous decisions.

R v Shivpuri [1987] AC 1; [1986] 2 All ER 334

The case concerned the law as to criminal attempts. A decision of the House of Lords one year earlier (Anderton v Ryan [1985] AC 567; [1985] 2 All ER 355) had received great criticism. In R v Shivpuri the House of Lords changed its mind on whether it was possible to attempt to do the impossible. This is a rare example of the House of Lords overturning its own decisions **simply because it felt the earlier decision was wrong**. Usually the Lords look for wider policy considerations.

In Food Corp. of India v Antclizo Shipping Co. [1988] 1 WLR 603, [1988] 2 All ER 513, Lord Goff (on behalf of the court) stated that their Lordships would not depart from a previous House of Lords' decision unless:

(1) it felt free to depart from both the reasoning and decision of the earlier case; and

(2) such a review would affect the resolution of the actual case before them and not be of mere academic interest.

At first sight this is an extremely limiting pronouncement. Point (2) means that the House of Lords will not be prepared to overrule one of their previous decisions, even if they think it wrong, unless by doing so this would affect the case before them. It is not their job to write textbooks on Law, but to decide real cases before them. Their Lordships will, in these circumstances, refuse to overrule their decision because that point is only of academic interest. This is what happened in *Antclizo*, and is in keeping with the spirit of the 1966 Statement. However, it is worth noting that in *Shivpuri* and a later case named *R* v *Howe* [1987] AC 417; [1987] 1 All ER 771 the overruling took place even though some of their Lordships thought the cases under review could be distinguished on their facts.

Point (1) involves the court in a detailed scrutiny of the earlier case in question. What the Law Lords appear to be saying is that not only must the decision be judged to be incorrect; so too must the reasoning. The problem here is that Lord Goff's reasoning seems to be that if the Lords find the decision to be wrong but the reasoning correct they will not interfere with the case. This then means that they will be agreeing with a case where the final conclusion does not match the analysis. It is rather like a maths exam where an answer, $2 + 2 = 5$, is marked correct because the reasoning (though clearly not the result) is sound. This seems puzzling. For further discussion, see Harris (1990:135).

But the *Antclizo* case does allow us to say one further thing, to which we shall return. That is, when a case first appears, stating a principle of law, one can never really be sure of the impact the case will have. At the instant it appears, when there are no other cases which have attempted to apply it, one can only speculate as to its impact. One famous example is a case called *Junior Books* v *Veitchi* [1983] AC 520; [1982] 3 All ER 201. When this case was decided many lawyers believed it had cleared the way for major changes in legal thought. A decade later the case had all but fallen into oblivion.

There is thus no one principle by which the House of Lords sets about overturning its precedents. In *Murphy* v *Brentwood District Council* [1990] 3 WLR 414; [1990] 2 All ER 908, for instance, their Lordships were again prepared to overturn one of their previous decisions (*Anns* v *Merton London Borough Council* [1978] AC 728; [1977] 2 All ER 492). There are various reasons given by their Lordships for why they were prepared to make this decision. Lord Mackay, the Lord Chancellor, felt that the earlier case was taken as a preliminary issue of law so that the facts had not been considered in detail. The case may have worked in theory but did not relate to real facts. Lord Keith looked at *Sutherland Shire Council* v *Heyman* (1985), an Australian case which had rejected *Anns*, as well as US cases which had analysed the cases on which *Anns* itself was based and proved these to be faulty. Thus, departure from *Anns* could be justified on the ground that the case was 'unsatisfactory'. Lord Oliver also noted academic criticism of the decision in *Anns*. *Antclizo* was not mentioned in the case.

Indeed, *Antclizo* itself appears to have become one of the 'lost' cases along with *Junior Books* v *Veitchi*. The case, for instance, makes no appearance in *Pepper (Inspector of Taxes)* v *Hart* [1992] 3 WLR 1032; [1993] 1 All ER 42, in which the House of Lords overturned a long-established principle on the sources that could be referred to in interpreting a statute. For the moment at least *Antclizo* appears to have gone to ground.

In 1998–9 a novel twist was added to this area in the case of *R* v *Bow Street Metropolitan Stipendiary Magistrate, ex parte Pinochet Ugarte (Amnesty International and others intervening)* [1998] 4 All ER 897. This case concerned the legality of extraditing former Chilean President Pinochet to Spain to face various charges of torture and murder. The matter went before the House of Lords, which decided by majority that Pinochet could be extradited. However, one of the Law Lords (Lord Hoffmann) had connections with Amnesty International, one of the parties allowed to make representations in the proceedings. These connections had not been declared by Lord Hoffmann (who found against Pinochet). Thus the decision was questionable, but there was no established mechanism for overcoming this. In the circumstances, the House of Lords decided to review their decision by way of a re-hearing of the appeal: [1999] 2 All ER 97. It is doubtful, however, that such a procedure will be used again in the near future; though it is noticeable that in practice many judges at all levels now make very clear announcements at the start of cases of potential conflicts of interest (e.g. that they were once instructed by one of the parties when they were barristers in practice).

5.4.2 The Court of Appeal

The importance of this court, both because of its place in the hierarchy and because of its heavy workload, means that you need to be aware of how it deals with precedent. Most of the important cases you will deal with in your studies were reached by this court or its predecessors such as the Court of Exchequer Chamber.

There are two important questions concerning the Court of Appeal and the notion of *stare decisis*.

(a) To what Extent is the Court of Appeal Bound to Follow Decisions of the House of Lords?

Strictly speaking the answer is always. But there have been campaigns in the Court of Appeal to overcome the principle. The principal crusader was Lord Denning MR (who, sadly, died in 1999 aged 100). His retirement signalled a halt to the conflict.

The *per incuriam* campaign

In his major attack Lord Denning advocated that if a House of Lords decision had been made *per incuriam* it need not be followed. *Per incuriam* means that a court failed to take into account all the relevant and vital statutes or case authorities and that this had a major effect on the decision. The analogy might be made with the writing of a scientific paper. Let us say a famous scientist produces a theory, and that a few years later it is discovered that his research was faulty: he had not read two of the leading papers. Would you say there are grounds for arguing that the theory should be open to scrutiny or even doubt?

The *per incuriam* rule is a well-established technical rule; but you must be careful here. *Per incuriam* does not simply mean the earlier court got things wrong. It only means there was a significant oversight. As we shall see later in this chapter, not only must there have been a failure to take account of relevant authorities; that fault must also have been such a major defect that it seriously affected the reasoning in the case and would have affected the outcome. So, with the example of the scientist, if it is now discovered that if he had researched thoroughly and read the two leading papers this would still have had no effect on his theory, the fault is a technical one of methodology and does not affect the conclusions drawn.

Lord Denning MR tried this form of reasoning in *Broome* v *Cassell* [1971] 2 QB 354; [1971] 2 All ER 187. Lord Denning persuaded the other members of the Court of Appeal to reach a decision which was contrary to that of an earlier House of Lords decision, *Rookes* v *Barnard* [1964] AC 1129; [1964] 1 All ER 367. Lord Denning pointed out that *Rookes* v *Barnard* was a decision made *per incuriam* because it had failed to consider even earlier House of Lords authorities.

However, when *Broome* v *Cassell* went to the House of Lords, the Law Lords rebuked Lord Denning for adopting such a rule because they believed he had plainly looked for an excuse not to adhere to *stare decisis*. As Lord Hailsham, the then Lord Chancellor, said:

> I am driven to the conclusion that when the Court of Appeal described the decision in *Rookes* v *Barnard* as decided 'per incuriam' or 'unworkable' they really only meant that they did not agree with it...[I]n the hierarchical system of courts which exists in this country, it is necessary for each lower tier, including the Court of Appeal, to accept loyally the decisions of the higher tiers. [1972] AC 1027, 1054.

The 'lapsed rule' campaign

Let us say that the House of Lords reached a decision some years ago based upon a particular rule or set of facts, e.g., that damages in English courts can be given only in sterling because of the stability of the currency and established forms of procedure. Now let us say that the reason for the rule has disappeared: the forms have changed and sterling has lost its stability. Should the precedent created by the House of Lords be followed even though the whole basis of this precedent has disappeared?

This was the question considered by the Court of Appeal, led by Lord Denning, in *Schorsch Meier GmbH* v *Hennin* [1975] QB 416; [1975] 1 All ER 152. Like so many things in law, a Latin maxim describes the rule thus: *cessante ratione legis, cessat ipsa lex* (with the reason for the rule ceasing, the law itself no longer exists). On this occasion the Court of Appeal was split. Lord Denning and Foster J agreed that a 1961 decision of the House of Lords had run its course. That earlier case, *Re United Railways of Havana and Regla Warehouses* [1961] AC 1007; [1960] 2 All ER 332, is referred to as the *Havana* case. In fact, the rule that damages should be awarded only in sterling seems to have existed for over 300 years. Lawton LJ, however, did not recognise that the Court of Appeal had such power and found himself bound to follow the House of Lords.

This case did not go on appeal to the House of Lords. However, as we shall see below, the House of Lords soon had opportunity to comment on this issue in a case named *Miliangos* v *George Frank (Textiles) Ltd* [1977] Qb 489; [1976] 3 All ER 599; and once again disapproved Lord Denning's attempts to vary the notion of *stare decisis*. As you will have noted above, however, their Lordships did overrule their own previous decisions on the same grounds proposed by Lord Denning, i.e. the 'lapsed rule' idea.

Thus one is forced to say that the campaigns failed. It is for the House of Lords to change its mind; not for the Court of Appeal to decide the issue for it. On the positive side, this helps to create certainty. Equally, such strict adherence to *stare decisis* may increase costs (because of the need for further appeals), as well as appearing to invite the veneration of rules whatever the logic or perceived justice. This is an age-old problem in law: balancing the need for certainty with the desire for the law to be flexible.

(b) To what Extent is the Court of Appeal Bound by its Own Previous Decisions?

The basic rule is that it is bound. Some exceptions were given in the leading case of *Young* v *Bristol Aeroplane Co. Ltd* [1944] KB 718, 723 by Lord Greene MR. Thus:

The Court of Appeal can choose between its own conflicting decisions

Such conflict should not arise in an ideal world, but it does, and Lord Greene MR did not explore *which* of the conflicting decisions should be followed. Academic and judicial debate over the years tended to indicate that a later Court of Appeal faced with this problem would probably be free to decide which authority it should follow, with the result that the one not chosen is overruled (for a full debate see Cross (1991:144)). If a general rule has emerged it has been that the latest case would probably be followed in preference to the earlier decision.

The situation can occur for a number of reasons; the most usual ones are:

- because the Court of Appeal does not hear one case at a time (there may be two or three hearings going on at the same time in different courtrooms in the Strand, before different members of the court). These cases may involve similar legal principles and the various courts may reach different conclusions which later appear contradictory;

- it is also possible that some earlier cases may not have been reported;

- equally, one court may look at the previous decisions and consider them distinguishable for one reason or another whilst another may think they are not distinguishable and should be followed (which highlights the point we have made before on this being a matter of interpretation rather than pure science).

It was this last reason that gave rise to the problem in *Starmark Enterprises Ltd* v *CPL Distribution Ltd* [2001] EWCA Civ 1252; [2002] 4 All ER 264. The case concerned a rent review clause in a lease of property. Two earlier Court of Appeal decisions (which we shall simply call decisions 1 and 2) had followed on from, considered, and applied an earlier decision of the House of Lords. The two Court of Appeal cases appeared to be in conflict. In *Starmark* the landlord argued that decision 2 (the latest) was unsupportable and decision 1 should be preferred; alternatively, that decision 2 was distinguishable on the facts from the present case; it should therefore be ignored and, again, decision 1 should be followed. The tenant argued that there was no conflict between decisions 1 and 2 and decision 2 was entirely consistent with the original House of Lords approach; equally, the facts in the present case and decision 2 were indistinguishable and so decision 2 plainly had to be followed.

Kay LJ decided that decisions 1 and 2 did conflict and that he preferred the views expressed in decision 1 (which was also the minority judgment in decision 2) and was bound to follow the reasoning in decision 1. Arden LJ held that decisions 1 and 2 involved the same principle and could not be reconciled; it was not possible to distinguish them.

Her Ladyship agreed with Kay LJ and held that decision 2 was faulty and should not be followed. The final judge, Peter Gibson LJ, stated at [97]:

> Where the ratio of an earlier decision of this court is directly applicable to the circumstances of a case before this court but that decision has been wrongly distinguished in a later decision of this court, in principle it must be open to this court to apply the ratio of the earlier decision and to decline to follow the later decision. In my judgment the majority of this court in [decision 2] wrongly distinguished [decision 1]. The ratio decidendi in [decision 1]...should in my judgment have been applied in [decision 2] and is decisive of this case.

Thus, in *Starmark*, the latest authority was not followed. Kay LJ's remark (at [3]) perhaps sums up the frustration of encountering conflicting decisions, when he said: 'It is unfortunate that over 15 years after ... [decisions 1 and 2] ... were decided, the legal effect of a common provision in a rent review clause is still unknown. This is the common law at its least impressive.'

It is also worth noting that Lord Denning led another attack on what he clearly perceived to be the fetter of *stare decisis* in the case of *Davis v Johnson* [1979] AC 264; [1978] 1 All ER 1132 (HL); [1978] 2 WLR 182; [1978] 1 All ER 841 (CA). This was not an instance of cleverly adopting rules to excuse departure from precedents. Here, Lord Denning sought to apply the 1966 Practice Statement to the Court of Appeal as well as the House of Lords. The argument was that, if the Court of Appeal could simply depart from previous decisions when justice demanded (as the House of Lords can now do), this would save wasting time and costs of further appeals to the House of Lords. Once again, however, the attempt failed (not least because Lord Denning had conveniently forgotten that procedures already existed whereby a case could be allowed to 'bypass' the Court of Appeal for this very reason: see **5.6** below).

If its own previous decision has been overruled expressly or impliedly by the House of Lords it need not be followed

Thus if the order of cases ran:

- Court of Appeal's *decision*
- House of Lords' decision (disapproving the Court of Appeal's reasoning)
- Your case in the Court of Appeal

then the Court of Appeal in your case **must** follow the House of Lords and not the first Court of Appeal decision

But this does not answer the question which path should be chosen where the order of cases is:

- House of Lords' decision
- Court of Appeal's *decision 1* (which, for some reason, is contrary to the earlier House of Lords' decision)
- Your case in the Court of Appeal

Now the Court of Appeal is caught between two rules: one saying it is bound to follow its own previous decisions, the other that it is bound to follow the House of Lords.

This situation arose in *Miliangos* v *George Frank (Textiles) Ltd*. Only a year after the Court of Appeal (in the *Schorsch Meier* case) had ignored earlier House of Lords authority and decided to award judgment in a currency other than sterling, the same issue came before the Court of Appeal again. Should it follow its decision in *Schorsch Meier* or follow the decision of the House of Lords which had been bypassed in *Schorsch Meier*? You may wish to speculate as to which answer, which strand of *stare decisis*, you think should be the most appropriate.

The Court of Appeal in *Miliangos* chose to follow its own previous decision and not the House of Lords. When the case went before the House of Lords their Lordships agreed that judgment could be given in a currency other than sterling, thereby overruling their own previous decision; but took the opportunity to criticise Lord Denning's approach in the *Schorsch Meier* case for ignoring the doctrine of *stare decisis*. However, to add to the confusion, whereas Lord Simon in the House of Lords agreed that the Court of Appeal in *Miliangos* should have follow its own precedent created in *Schorsch Meier*, Lord Cross felt that the Court of Appeal in *Miliangos* should have ignored its own precedent in *Schorsch Meier* because that decision was in conflict with the earlier House of Lords decision! So the short answer is: nobody really knows.

As a side point, it is interesting to note that Lord Greene's statement in *Young* v *BAC* (that the Court of Appeal is bound by its own decisions) actually conflicts with some earlier Court of Appeal decisions which stated that the Court of Appeal was *not* bound by its own previous decisions. The sort of panic that this can send a student into should be avoided; Lord Greene's words reflected the history of the Court of Appeal since its creation and are generally taken as gospel today.

The court is not bound by its own decisions found to have been made *per incuriam*

We have discussed the *per incuriam* rule to some extent already. For some reason this rule appeals to students and it tends to be used on many occasions (usually incorrectly). It is worth repeating, therefore, that it does not mean that the court made a mistake. The fact that the case being examined had weaknesses in argument, or in the judgment, does not make the decision *per incuriam*. Thus in *Morelle* v *Wakeling* [1955] 2 QB 379; [1955] 1 All ER 708, Lord Evershed MR limited the use of the *per incuriam* rule to cases where:

• there was ignorance of authority which would have been binding on the court; *and*

• that ignorance led to faulty reasoning.

To this the Court of Appeal has added that the rule can be applied only where, had the court reviewed these authorities, the court *would* (not just might) have reached a different decision. Thus in *Williams* v *Fawcett* [1986] QB 604; [1985] 1 All ER 787 and *Duke* v *Reliance Systems* [1987] ICR 491; [1987] 2 All ER 858 the Court of Appeal has shown itself ready to use the *per incuriam* rule regarding its own decisions, but with reservations.

In the case of *Rakhit* v *Carty* [1990] 2 WLR 1107; [1990] 2 All ER 202, the Court of Appeal was faced with the situation where a Court of Appeal decision (*decision 1*) was plainly *per incuriam* as it had missed some vital statutory provisions. *Decision 1* had been followed without question in another Court of Appeal case (*decision 2*). Could the present Court of Appeal still declare *decision 1* to be *per incuriam* and therefore *decision 2* of no binding effect? Lord Donaldson MR said (at 208):

> If, therefore, that court [*in decision 2*], having all the relevant authorities before it, had concluded that [*decision 1*] was rightly decided, I would have felt bound to follow it, leaving it to the House of Lords to rectify the error.

As this was not the case, the Court of Appeal in *Rakhit* v *Carty* declared *decision 1* to have been reached *per incuriam*, thereby invalidating both *decision 1* and *decision 2* as precedents.

The latest pronouncement by the Court of Appeal on this matter confirms all that has been said above: *Peter Limb* v *Union Jack Removals Ltd and Honess* [1998] 1 WLR 1354; [1998] 2 All ER 513 (see **5.7** below).

5.5 Are there any other Exceptions to the Application of *Stare Decisis* to the Court of Appeal that have Emerged since 1944?

The short answer to this is: yes, but not many.

(a) The Criminal Division of the Court is traditionally more relaxed on *stare decisis*, especially where an individual's liberty is at stake. This seems a little strange, given that the House of Lords usually espouses the view that it should rarely change its mind on criminal law matters in order to promote certainty! See, for instance, its reluctance to change its mind in *R* v *Shivpuri*. But then, in the hands of the House of Lords rests the final appeal; which is the very issue that caused all the controversy discussed above.

For further explanation on this topic, see *R* v *Spencer* [1985] 1 All ER 673 and note Pattenden (1984:592). The Court of Appeal addressed this issue again in *R* v *Parole Board* [1992] 2 WLR 707; [1992] 2 All ER 576. The case concerned the right to see documents submitted to a parole board. The Court applied the principle that, where liberty is at stake and injustice might occur, *stare decisis* was not applicable. However, the Court of Appeal found the earlier precedents distinguishable in any case so that the comments on *stare decisis* were not strictly necessary.

(b) If, in exceptional cases, the House of Lords cannot review a decision of the Court of Appeal then the Court of Appeal can choose not to follow its own precedent: *Rickards* v *Rickards* [1989] 3 WLR 748; [1989] 3 All ER 193.

(c) Where a previous decision has been disapproved by the Judicial Committee of the Privy Council then (though Privy Council decisions are not part of the court structure) the Court of Appeal may depart from its own decisions. This has occurred on a few occasions, most notably in *Doughty* v *Turner Manufacturing Co. Ltd* [1964] 1 QB 518; [1964] 1 All ER 98, where the Court of Appeal chose to follow a Privy Council decision (*The Wagon Mound*) rather than its own previous ruling on the same matter in *Re Polemis*.

(d) Where the previous decision was on an interim matter (previously called inter-locutory matters) and heard by only two judges this will not bind a full Court of Appeal (i.e. three or more judges sitting): *Boys* v *Chaplin* [1968] 2 QB 1; [1968] 1 All ER 283. An interim decision concerns pre-trial matters. For instance, if there is a dispute as to procedure this will be an interim matter. Some issues depend on interim matters and the main case never actually comes to court. One example is where an employer points to a clause in an employment contract which seeks to stop an ex-employee working for another in the same business once that employee leaves the company. This is known as 'restraint of trade'. If the employer had to wait for a full hearing it would be pointless because the restraint usually lasts for about a year and the case could take longer than this to come to court. The employer will therefore seek an injunction, which (if granted) will prevent the employee from working for the other company until the full case can be heard. The reality is, however, that if the employer obtains the injunction the full case rarely gets heard.

Connected with the idea of interim appeals is an issue which is only just being explored. Two-judge Courts of Appeal have become more common in recent years, mainly for administrative reasons. On the whole they tend to hear mainly appeals from interim decisions as before, plus appeals from county courts. However, cases have arisen which were not interim matters but proved to be important decisions (e.g. *National Westminster Bank* v *Morgan* [1983] 3 All ER 85, *Harris* v *Wyre Forest District Council* [1988] QB 835; [1988] 1 All ER 691, and *Interfoto Picture Library* v *Stiletto Visual Programmes Ltd* [1988] 2 WLR 615; [1988] 1 All ER 348). The *Interfoto* case, as we shall see, had the added complication of judges agreeing on the decision but disagreeing on the reasoning. A two-judge Court of Appeal is accorded the same powers of creating biding precedent as a full court of three of five: *Langley* v *North West Water Authority* [1991] 1 WLR 697; [1991] 3 All ER 610.

We have not yet had a case where a two-member Court of Appeal has failed to agree on the decision. If this happens one presumes the court will apply the old maxim used by the House of Lords: *semper praesumitur pro negante.* This means that the presumption is always in favour of the negative, which means that the appeal fails. A fascinating example of this arose in *Charter* v *Charter* (1874) LR 7 HL 364, where four of their Lordships were divided evenly as to the outcome and the remaining member died without leaving an opinion.

5.6 Does Every Case have to be Heard by the Court of Appeal before it can Proceed to the House of Lords?

Fortunately the answer is no. If the Court of Appeal is bound by the House of Lords and itself then a system which demanded it hear every case anyway would be ludicrous. Thus a civil case may be allowed to go on appeal from the High Court to the House of Lords, bypassing the Court of Appeal. This is known as the 'leap-frogging' procedure. However, if the case began life in the county court then an appeal from that court lies to the Court of Appeal, not the High Court; thus the 'leap-frogging' procedure would be irrelevant.

It is only fair to say that however much writers and judges try to explain the system on a rational basis, there will always be some uncertainty and some cases that simply break the rules. For one thing we have yet to consider in depth how one case can be distinguished from another so that the precedent in question (and therefore the application of *stare decisis*) is sidestepped. For another, judges occasionally surprise everyone with an admission that they were wrong in an earlier case (see Lord Denning in *Dixon* v *BBC* [1979] QB 546; [1979] 2 All ER 112, discussing his earlier judgment on the same issue in *BBC* v *Ioannou* [1975] ICR 267; [1975] 2 All ER 999). This is reassuring when considered in the context of human frailty, but likely to set a practising lawyer's teeth on edge; and is little consolation to the party in the overruled case who originally lost (and probably paid costs). Even more surprising, perhaps, was Lord Denning's admission in one case that his own reasoning in an earlier case (which he now wished to avoid) was not legally correct, but that he had reached that earlier decision to do justice—'It was not really [a case which fell within the definition of dismissal] ... but we had to stretch it a bit', he commented. The comment occurred in *Western Excavating* v *Sharp* [1978] ICR 221, 227; [1978] 1 All ER 713, 718 in relation to *Marriott* v *Oxford and District Co-operative Society Ltd (No. 2)* [1970] 1 QB 186; [1969] 3 All ER 1126.

It is also worth commenting at this stage that (as we noted above in discussing the House of Lords overruling itself), when a decision of a higher court alters the law by overruling a line of established precedents, that decision does not merely affect the law from that moment on. The court setting the new precedent is stating the law as it *always has been*. Thus, commercial contracts concluded on the old law are in danger of being open to a different interpretation from that intended when they were formed; so too, property deals, licences, employment contracts, and so on. Therefore, one part of the work of lawyers is to review these earlier matters in the light of the new decision. This *retrospective* effect of precedents has been made abundantly clear in the House of Lords case of *Kleinwort Ltd* v *Lincoln Council* [1998] 4 All ER 513. In this case, the House of Lords overruled long-established Court of Appeal authorities and abolished the rule that money paid under a mistake of law could not be recovered. Their Lordships were agreed that the idea of retrospective effect means that once the law has been changed it applies not only to the case in hand but to all subsequent cases coming before the courts even though the events in question occurred before the previous authority was overruled. What they were not in agreement over was how this applied to the actual case on whether a mistake of law arose *at the time of the contract* when the law was later changed; on this they were divided 3 : 2 in favour of saying there was a mistake of law.

A question often posed by students is whether the aggrieved party in the case which has been overruled can now revive the case with the cry, 'There you are, I was right all along'. The answer is no. Parties to a case have to lodge an appeal within time limits. If these have expired it is unfortunately too late to do anything about it.

5.7 Precedent in the Higher Courts: Summary

In discussing the *per incuriam* rule above we noted the case of *Peter Limb*. That case also made some general comments on precedent and the Court of Appeal. Brooke LJ stated that there were five main principles to be derived from the authorities:

(a) Where the court has considered a statute or a rule of law having the force of a statute, its decision stands on the same footing as any other decision on a point of law.

(b) A decision of a two-judge Court of Appeal on a substantive appeal (as opposed to an application for leave) has the same authority as a decision of a three-judge or a five-judge Court of Appeal.

(c) The doctrine of *per incuriam* applies only where another division of the Court has reached a decision in ignorance or forgetfulness of a decision binding upon it or of an inconsistent statutory provision, and in either case it must be shown that if the court had had this material in mind it must have reached a contrary decision. In *Cave v Robinson Jarvis & Rolf* [2001] EWCA Civ 245; [2002] 1 WLR 581 the Court of Appeal expressed the view that the decision in question had to be 'manifestly wrong' before it would be declared *per incuriam*.

(d) The doctrine does not extend to a case where, if different arguments had been placed before the Court or if different material had been placed before it, it *might* have reached a different conclusion.

(e) Any departure from a previous decision of the Court is in principle undesirable and should be considered only if the previous decision is manifestly wrong. Even then it will be necessary to take account of whether the decision purports to be one of general application and whether there is any other way of remedying the error, for example by encouraging an appeal to the House of Lords.

Lastly, it is worth noting a trend over recent years for the Court of Appeal to bunch together issues arising in a number of cases, set aside a specialist panel to look at all the cases, hear a selection, and issue general guidelines on the area. This has mainly happened in connection with procedural matters (*Peter Limb* was such a case). It happened again in *Bannister* v *SGB plc* [1998] 1 WLR 1123; [1997] 4 All ER 129 (which was also the first Court of Appeal decision to be published on the Internet immediately after the decision was given, so that all 200-plus affected parties could know the outcome as soon as possible). And, interestingly, in *Greig Middleton & Co. Ltd* v *Denderowicz* [1998] 1 WLR 1164; [1997] 4 All ER 181 (which was on the same issue as *Bannister*) the Court of Appeal took the opportunity to add as annexes to the *Greig* judgment some reserved judgments in other related cases and to produce a revised judgment of *Bannister*, directing that it would be the revised version which should appear in the Law Reports.

5.8 Other Courts

5.8.1 Trial Courts

All courts which are lower in status than the Court of Appeal (such as the High Court, Crown Court, magistrates' court, county court, and the various tribunals) are bound by *stare decisis* in the normal way. It should be noted, however, that the important tribunals also have their own appellate tribunals (e.g. the Employment Appeal Tribunal for employment tribunals) which often incorporate their own variations on the rules of right to appeal and the binding nature of precedent within that system. Courts like the Crown

Court are trial courts, dealing for the most part with fact and evidence rather than questions of high legal analysis. They do not, therefore, create precedent. There is, however, some attempt to follow the reasoning employed in courts of the same level, e.g., as between divisions of the High Court. In *Colchester Estates (Cardiff)* v *Carlton Industries plc* [1984] 3 WLR 693; [1984] 2 All ER 601 it was stated that the latest decision should be preferred provided it was reached after full consideration of the earlier decisions. An example of this in operation arose from a decision of Butler-Sloss J (as she then was) in *Re Cherrington* [1984] 1 WLR 772; [1984] 2 All ER 285 which was not followed in a case on exactly the same point (*Re Sinclair* [1984] 3 All ER 362) because there had not been a full discussion of all the issues in *Re Cherrington*.

5.8.2 Divisional Courts

For mainly historical reasons the High Court has a supervisory and limited appellate jurisdiction over the trial courts (sometimes called 'courts of first instance'). Each division of the High Court—Queen's Bench, Family, and Chancery—has what is termed a 'Divisional Court'. Thus:

(a) The Divisional Court of the Chancery Division can hear appeals from a county court in bankruptcy cases.

(b) The Family Division may hear appeals on guardianship matters from either the magistrates' courts or county courts.

(c) The most common appellate function relates to the Queen's Bench Division. Say a party to a criminal case in a magistrates' court wishes to appeal on a question of law from the magistrates' decision. This can be done by asking the magistrates to **state their case**, i.e. to set out their legal reasoning, and the issue goes before the Divisional Court of the Queen's Bench Division. This is therefore known as an 'appeal by way of case stated'. A full re-hearing (e.g., an appeal against the conviction relating to fact rather than law) of the case would go to the Crown Court. An appeal by way of case stated can also lie in limited circumstances, from the Crown Court to the High Court.

These Divisional Courts are bound by *stare decisis* in the usual way as regards decisions of higher courts. When it comes to Divisional Courts binding themselves, the rule is similar to that used in the Court of Appeal: on civil matters they are bound but not necessarily so on criminal issues: *R* v *Govenor of Brockhill Prison* [1997] 1 All ER 439, 451.

5.8.3 Judicial Committee of the Privy Council

At one time this was the final court of appeal for the courts of the British Empire. Its decisions were therefore treated with great respect, even though technically they have never created precedents under English law for English cases. However, for the most part the court has been (and is) made up of the Law Lords. Consequently, if the Judicial Committee of the Privy Council reached a decision on a point of law (relating, say, to Australia) which was similar to English law, its reasoning would be very persuasive (see, for instance, *Doughty* v *Turner Manufacturing Co. Ltd*, mentioned above, where the Court of Appeal followed a Privy Council decision rather than its own authority). The jurisdiction of this court is now very limited indeed, but you should watch out for decisions made earlier this century.

5.8.4 The Court of Justice of the European Communities

Though **Chapter 10** deals extensively with the European influence and 'European Legal Method', specific reference to European Community institutions and legal method is needed here to explain the context in which our law now operates. As we said in **Chapter 1**, leaving the 'European dimension' until the last chapter should not be seen as relegating the topic to some form of afterthought.

Throughout this book you will see that both the 'European' way of dealing with cases (the procedure) and the technique of analysing cases (the legal method) are quite different from our approach. This is because the system used by the Court of Justice was created by countries (e.g. France and Germany) which rely on the Civil (or Roman) Law system. For various reasons our Common Law system developed separately from the Civil Law system used on the Continent. As Britain did not join the Community until 1973 there is minimal (but perhaps growing) Common Law influence to be seen in the Court of Justice.

The final court to note then (one of increasing importance) is the European Court of Justice (ECJ). Today we tend to think only of the European Community (the EC—also known as the European Union or EU), but prior to the EC there existed the European Coal and Steel Community (ECSC), founded under the Treaty of Paris 1951. The Court of Justice began life as the Court for the ECSC and therefore pre-dates the European Community. The Court of Justice became part of the European Economic Community (as it was then known) when that Community was founded under the Treaty of Rome 1957. It remained the Court of Justice for the ECSC and became the court for the other Community created at the same time as the Economic Community, viz. the European Atomic Energy Community (Euratom).

There are four major institutions which are common to all the European Communities: the Court of Justice, the Parliament, the Commission, and the Council. We will deal with the institutions in depth in **Chapter 10**. Note that the Court of Justice is commonly referred to as the 'European Court of Justice' or the 'European Court'.

We have listed below a few general points on the Court of Justice which you should bear in mind when reading about the legal method used in English law. For a more detailed description of the Communities and the Court of Justice we recommend reference be made to Steiner and Woods (2000) and Brown and Kennedy (1994).

Most of the law you will deal with in your studies will be 'pure' English law; but this will become less true over the years: see Lord Denning MR's famous statement in *HP Bulmer Ltd* v *Bollinger SA* [1974] Ch 401, 418; [1974] 2 All ER 1226, that 'when we come to matters with a European element, the Treaty is like an incoming tide. . . . It cannot be held back'. Remember here, however, that we are dealing with the Court of Justice, not the way individual countries' legal systems work.

What is the jurisdiction of the ECJ?

The Court of Justice exists to ensure that in the interpretation and application of the Treaty of Rome the law is observed. It is therefore the supreme authority on the interpretation of the law relating to the European Community. It deals only with the interpretation and validity of Community-generated law. Therefore, unless the law in question was generated by the European Community (and there are various ways this can occur), the Court of Justice has no jurisdiction. Many criminal law matters, for instance, are questions of domestic law and have nothing to do with the European Community.

However, as seen in Chapter 1, the impact of Community law is growing. As well as dealing with general agricultural matters, administrative law, company law, etc., its effect can now be seen in everyday life such as employment rights and social law. Thus an increasing number of matters fall within the jurisdiction of the Court of Justice.

How does a case come before the ECJ?

Actions may be brought against individuals, Member States, or the institutions of the Community. We will concentrate in this book on the most common way in which a case will come before the Court of Justice—a reference to the court for a *preliminary ruling* under Article 234 of the EC Treaty.

Under Article 234, any country's domestic courts or tribunals can ask the Court of Justice for a ruling on Community law; but it is that domestic court or tribunal which implements the decision.

It is for the court to decide whether it wishes to refer a matter to the Court of Justice and there are various rules relating to this which we shall explore later. The national court is only asking for an authoritative interpretation of that particular part of Community law. It does this by posing questions in the abstract; it does not ask for the solution to the particular case before it.

Article 234(3) states that a court or tribunal *shall* refer the matter where, as against that court's decision, there is no judicial remedy under national law. So, any court has a discretionary power to refer a case to the Court of Justice and if a court is the final appeal court it *must* refer the matter. Thus the House of Lords should in theory be bound to refer all cases to the Court of Justice which involve a problem of Community law. The House of Lords does not, however, refer all relevant cases to the Court of Justice. This is because it is required to do so only if it considers that such a referral is 'necessary'. What 'necessary' means we will have to leave until **Chapter 10**. Suffice it to say here that for a national court to decide that it is not 'necessary' to refer the matter basically requires that the provision has already been interpreted by the Court of Justice in previous references made by courts in Member States or the correct application is obvious to the national court.

A key point to note here, however, is that the use of Article 234 **is not an appeals procedure**. The Court of Justice does not decide the case, it merely gives its interpretation of Community law. Most importantly, however, the Court of Justice is the *only* court that can authoritatively interpret Community law. The domestic court has then to apply the ruling as it sees fit to the case in hand.

Does the ECJ use a system of judicial precedent?

A major distinction between how European lawyers (and courts) reason and the reasoning of Common Law lawyers is the use of *stare decisis*. European lawyers are, traditionally, merely persuaded by precedent. The same is true of the Court of Justice.

Obviously, as Stein has said, 'Every legal system has case law in the sense that the scope of the rules is illustrated by their application to a set of facts' (1984:85), but this is not the same thing as holding to a doctrine of precedent. Further, any legal system seeks to avoid inconsistencies; but, as we have seen, this is certainly not the same as holding to a strict doctrine of *stare decisis*. For whereas the Common Law relies on declaring law only when the occasion requires it (i.e. through litigants bringing cases), the Civil Law system relies heavily on Codes: written, logical, reasoned, and systematic statements of principles of law. As Lord MacMillan observed:

> From these principles the whole law [can] be deduced, and with the aid of these principles the law [can] be methodised and arranged. It is the conception of order, logic and reason in the regulation by law of human affairs. (1937:79)

Cases, in simple terms, become examples of applications of the Code; hardly the stuff of which *stare decisis is* made.

The Codes vary in form and technicality of language. The language employed in the French Code is aimed more at the layman than is the case with the German Code, for instance. Now, the Civil Law lawyer bases his argument on the explicit or implicit statements in the written law (the Codes and academic writing), not overtly on the opinions given in earlier cases. Developing this point, reliance on the Codes and the principles stated therein drives the Civil lawyer away from an obsessive interest in the facts of earlier cases. It is the issue that matters. The Common Law lawyer, on the other hand (as we shall explore in the next chapter), holds tightly to the concept of 'material facts' and the importance of individual cases.

Indeed, the predominance of issue over fact has to be the pattern of thought employed by the Court of Justice because the function of the court is to *interpret* Community law. As the court is required only to answer abstract questions from the national court and does not make decisions in a particular case, so the facts of a case (which are so important to the English law lawyer in distinguishing one case from another) take on less significance. This does not mean the facts are ignored, because it is almost impossible to answer a legal question without some reference to the context in which it has arisen. But it does mean that our system of *stare decisis* cannot apply to the Court of Justice. Further, the court is the final court on these questions and the only thing that can alter such a decision (other than the court changing its mind at a later date) is an alteration made to the Treaty itself. As annual minor alterations to the Treaty are an impossibility—major or complete revisions for political reasons are the only likely source of alterations—the court has to favour flexibility over certainty.

However, it is worth noting here the point we made above that the Court of Justice, in trying to define when it is 'necessary' for a domestic court to refer a matter to the Court of Justice, has stated that it would not be necessary if (amongst other things) the provision in question had already been interpreted by the Court of Justice. This at least shows the value of precedent in any system; but it does not mean that the Court of Justice is moving towards our system of *stare decisis.*

5.9 Impact of Human Rights Legislation

We noted in **Chapter 1** that the Human Rights Act 1998 came into force in October 2000. As well as affecting how statutes are to be interpreted, it is also possible that this Act will have a significant effect on the standing of some precedents. We shall explain this in greater depth in **Chapter 9**, but for the moment we can say that all Common Law rules and precedents that are incompatible with Convention rights are potentially open to challenge, especially if those precedents relate to the interpretation of statutory provisions. Further, the Act expressly requires the British courts to *take into account,* among other things, the judgments, decisions, and advisory opinions of the European Court of Human Rights, thereby adding another court to our system of precedent.

5.10 CONCLUSION

Both the Common Law and the Civil Law traditions utilise the concept of precedent. No case has a meaning by itself; each case stands in a relationship to other cases. Like tracing one's ancestors, therefore, it is at least theoretically possible to go backwards in time, step by step, to see how a complicated principle emerged from perhaps a single case. It is not uncommon to find gross inconsistencies or jumps in logic, but for the most part the changes will be evolutionary rather than revolutionary. Inevitably one will face the same problem as with the 'Big Bang' theory of how the Universe began: what came before the original case?

Sometimes the answer is that the seminal case derived its principle from a mixture of other cases on related (often barely related) principles: see, for instance *Rylands v Fletcher* (1868) LR 3 HL 330. On other occasions the principle may be derived from ancient Roman, Greek, or Biblical laws. Or the source may lie in a perception of fundamental rights and wrongs, such as laws prohibiting murder. Often the answer lies in works written by eminent scholars centuries ago—their views on the law being accepted by judges in later cases and then set as legal doctrine by the mechanisms of judicial precedent. The fact that these initial cases or scholarly writings were illogical, have exceeded their 'best before' date, or have been misinterpreted does not mean that they can be easily upset.

Much of this reification of (sometimes) archaic principles is due to the fact that there is a world of difference between merely recognising the source and value of precedent and the concept of *stare decisis.* The great value of the doctrine of *stare decisis* is that it provides certainty. On the other hand, there are dangers: first, that in order to avoid the conclusions of *stare decisis* courts are sometimes forced to find hair-splitting distinctions between cases; secondly, the doctrine limits flexibility and can make unassailable some principles which should have been abandoned long ago.

A rare example of a long-established legal concept being overturned can be found in *R* v *R* [1991] 3 WLR 767; [1991] 4 All ER 481. In *R* v *R*, public policy, together with historical and social considerations, came under review. This case concerned 'marital rape' and posed the question whether a husband could be criminally liable for raping his wife if he had sexual intercourse with her without her consent. The idea that a man would not be guilty in these circumstances could be traced back to Sir Matthew Hale in his *History of the Pleas of the Crown* written in 1736. Texts and cases since that time had taken this proposition as an accurate expression of the law (which it probably was in 1736). In *R* v *R*, however, the House of Lords took the opportunity to restate the law concerning marital rape and declared that the husband could be guilty of rape in these circumstances. As Lord Keith said: 'The common law is... capable of evolving in the light of changing social, economic and cultural developments.'

You may, however, ask yourself one final simple question: why should we stand out from the rest of the legal world with our fixation that once a superior court has decided a matter an inferior court *must* follow it?

REFERENCES

*Brown, L.N., and Kennedy, T. (1994), *The Court of Justice of the European Communities* (4th edn., London: Sweet Maxwell).

*Cross, R. (1991), *Precedent in English Law* (4th edn., Oxford: Clarendon Press).

Harris, B.V. (2002), 'Final Appellate Courts Overruling their Own "Wrong" Precedents: the Ongoing Search for a Principle', 118 *Law Quarterly Review* 408.

Harris, J.W. (1990), 'Towards Principles of Overruling—When Should a Final Court of Appeal Second Guess?', *Oxford Journal of Legal Studies* 135.

MacCormick, N. (1987), 'Why Cases have *Rationes* and What These Are', in L. Goldstein (ed.), *Precedent in Law* (Oxford: Clarendon Press).

MacMillan, Lord (1937), *Law and Other Things* (Cambridge: Cambridge University Press).

Pattenden, R. (1984), 'The Power of the Criminal Division of the Court of Appeal to Depart from its Own Precedents', *Criminal Law Review* 592.

Stein, P. (1984), *Legal Institutions: The Development of Dispute Settlement* (London: Butterworths).

Steiner, J. (1995), *Enforcing EC Law* (London: Blackstone Press).

*——, and Woods, L. (2000), *Textbook on EEC Law* (7th edn., London: Blackstone Press).

6

How Precedent Operates: *Ratio Decidendi* and *Obiter Dictum*

6.1 Introduction

The concept of *stare decisis* provides us only with the ground rules of precedent. It tells us that one court must follow the decision of a superior court when dealing with similar cases. It describes the environment in which our system of precedent operates. What it cannot tell us is **when** two cases are sufficiently similar that the doctrine should be applied.

If the facts of cases were identical we would have no problem. But the facts change from case to case; sometimes in an obviously major way; other times in an apparently insignificant way. Clearly we are not looking only for **identical cases**. What we must be trying to prove is that two (or more) cases are sufficiently similar to illustrate the same principle and so the doctrine of precedent can be applied. A comparison of facts will obviously help us achieve this. But we must also, and more importantly, try to see if the *reasoning* in the earlier case can be applied to the new set of facts in our case. It is worth remembering that lawyers cite cases in order to give authority to their argument. The question raised by the practitioner or academic is therefore: what is the principle of law for which that case is authority, and how does it relate to the case in hand? Or, to put it the other way: is there a case which is authority for the point I wish to make? This is the way that a busy practitioner is more likely to pose the question.

In the previous chapter we presented an exercise on fact-comparison:

- In *case (1)* a man driving a Ford Mondeo runs over an old lady who was lawfully using a zebra crossing. The man is held to be liable in negligence.
- In *case (2)* a woman driving a BMW runs over an old man who was crossing the road. Should she be found liable too?

We asked whether you might examine the facts more closely, or ask more questions, before deciding on the answer. Students new to legal studies (and others who should know better) tend to say that the woman in *case 2* is liable. If asked why this is so, the poor student tends to say: 'It's obvious'. Such students may have a shorter or less successful career in Law than they anticipated. Slightly better students say: 'The woman is liable because *case (2)* is the same as *case (1)*—no explanation; everything is apparently clarified in this one utterance. Still better students say: 'The woman may not be liable because the old lady in *case (1)* was on a zebra crossing, but that is not so in *case (2)*'. The best student will ask himself/herself: 'Why was the man liable in *case (1)*? Before I know that I cannot really say whether *case (2)* will follow *case (1)*.' For all we know there may be a law against driving Ford Mondeos.

Reading this you probably think this is a trite statement of the obvious. Don't! These examples of analysis (on a variety of facts) have all surfaced in seminars and tutorials, in different institutions, in different countries, spoken by LLB undergraduates, undergraduates in other degrees who study Law, and even post-graduates. Karl Llewellyn offered these words of advice (or admonition) in 1930 to American Law students:

> Now the first thing you are to do with [a case] is to read it. Does this sound commonplace? Does this amuse you? There is no reason why it should amuse you. You have already read past seventeen [legal] expressions of whose meaning you have no conception...The next thing is to get clear the actual decision, the judgment rendered...You can now turn to what you want peculiarly to know...what has the case decided, and what can you derive from it as to what will be decided later? (1960:41)

Any law lecturer will echo these words, but it is easy to forget as an academic or practitioner just how daunting reading cases for the first time can be. From the student perspective things look a little different, but the point we are making is still the same. To show you that you are not alone in the minefield of case law, consider these words written by Scott Turow (1988:28)—better known perhaps for his legal thrillers—detailing his experiences as a law postgraduate student at Harvard:

> OK. It was nine o'clock when I started reading. The case is four pages long and at 10:35 I finally finished. It was something like stirring concrete with my eyelashes. I had no idea what the words meant. I must have opened *Black's Law Dictionary* twenty-five times and I still can't understand many of the definitions.

Anyone who has ever studied law will have sympathy with these words. The aim of this chapter, therefore, is to emphasise that legal analysis is not just a question of comparing facts; of using a set of balancing-scales to see if the facts weigh about the same. The game is more complicated, more stimulating, and much more enjoyable than that.

6.2 Development of Case Law

Take a look at the following exercise. It sets out the facts of two well-known cases together with the result in each case. Ask yourself *why* the second case should be decided in the same way as the first.

EXERCISE 9   Dead snails and exploding underpants

Case 1: *Donoghue v Stevenson* [1932] AC 562

Bare Facts Mrs Donoghue and a friend went into a cafe in Paisley. The friend ordered ice-cream and ginger-beer for both of them. The shopkeeper poured out some of the ginger-beer over the ice-cream. Mrs Donoghue consumed some of the mixture. Her friend poured out the remainder of the ginger-beer for Mrs Donoghue and a decomposed snail fell out of the bottle. The bottle was of dark opaque glass so that the contents could not have been detected.

What was the claim? The claim was against the manufacturer of the ginger-beer (Stevenson) for negligently causing Mrs Donoghue to suffer gastro-enteritis and nervous shock; the negligence arising from the manufacture of the product. As you will see in the Contract Law course Mrs Donoghue could not claim against the cafe owner because she had no contract with him; nor had he been negligent.

What was the decision? Mrs Donoghue succeeded in her claim; the House of Lords holding Stevenson liable by a majority of 3:2. Lord Atkin, in the majority, said that a manufacturer of products will be liable for want of reasonable care if he sells them in a form which shows they are meant to reach the ultimate consumer in the same form as when they were manufactured (with no reasonable possibility of intermediate examination) and if he knows that the absence of reasonable care will cause injury.

Case 2: *Grant* v *Australian Knitting Mills* [1936] AC 85 (Privy Council)

Bare facts Grant purchased two pairs of underpants from a retailer in Australia. He contracted severe dermatitis (mainly around the ankles—they were 'long johns') owing to an excess of sulphites in the garments which should have been removed by the manufacturing process. He was ill for a year!

What was the claim? He sued the retailer for breach of contract; and brought a negligence action against the Australian Knitting Mills. This demonstrates that more than one claim can arise from one set of events. However, Grant would not be able to get damages twice: if Grant was successful then one claim would be off-set against the other.

What was the decision? Grant won the breach of contract action and the claim for negligence was also successful, following the principles laid down in *Donoghue* v *Stevenson*.

QUESTIONS

(a) Why do you think Grant was successful? Why should *Donoghue* v *Stevenson* apply to his case?

(b) What arguments would you have used if you had been representing the Australian Knitting Mills?

ANSWERS

(a) 'Exploding underpants' and dead snails are not the same thing. If you have thought carefully about the cases you will have experienced some problems in assessing why *Donoghue* v *Stevenson* was applied in *Grant* v *Australian Knitting Mills*. But remember, both sides in *Grant* thought they had convincing reasons why they should win. Neither side could simply say 'dead snails equal (or do not equal) underpants'. The Privy Council assessed the principle of *Donoghue* v *Stevenson* by quoting Lord Atkin:

A manufacturer of products, which he sells in such a form as to show that he intends them to reach the ultimate consumer in the form in which they left him with no reasonable possibility of intermediate examination, and with the knowledge that the absence of reasonable care in the preparation or putting up of the products will result in an injury to the consumer's life or property, owes a duty to the consumer to take that reasonable care.

The Privy Council stated that *Donoghue* v *Stevenson* could be applied only where the defect is hidden and unknown to the consumer; but that in *Grant* the chemical in the underpants represented a latent defect equivalent to the snail in the opaque bottle.

(b) *Grant* v *Australian Knitting Mills* raised a number of arguments. Amongst these were that: *Donoghue* v *Stevenson* only applied, at its widest, to cases of food and drink— that when Lord Atkin referred to 'products' he could only refer to the product in the case; the decision was not unanimous, especially as regards the interpretation of earlier cases; there had been no possibility of anyone tampering with the bottle, but the underpants were loosely packed (it was not alleged there had been any tampering); and that Grant should have washed the underpants before wearing them (which would have removed the danger).

So, however we try to compare the facts, we cannot answer the question whether the woman in our example should be liable for her negligent driving without first understanding *why* the man was liable in case (1). What were the issues on which the first case turned? Was it important that the old lady was using a pedestrian crossing? Was it important that she was an old lady? The question *why* liability was found is all-important, and a point often ignored by students who presume that if they have discovered two cases which are similar on their facts then that is enough. However, two cases may look similar but produce different results because of a different perception of the apparently similar facts or because of a vital distinction in the reasoning employed by the judges. In other words, cases may be *distinguished* on the material facts or the reasoning employed.

And if we are asking *why* the court decided one way we must equally be aware that cases do not exist in isolation—there is a whole history behind the issues involved in a case. All these previous cases will have affected the language used by the judges and the decisions they reached. The way that a word was legally defined in, say, 1850, may have an enormous impact on the reasoning of a judge in 1999.

Thus when we talk of a judge being bound by a precedent we mean something more than matching the facts of cases—we say that a judge is bound to follow the *ratio decidendi* (the reason for deciding—usually referred to as the *ratio*) of the earlier higher authority. The judge only has to follow the *ratio*. It is not only the facts of the earlier case which are important, but also how the judge expressed the law in relation to those facts— how the judge justified the decision in law. For as long as you study Law the *ratio* of any case will be vital to your investigations.

6.3 Trying to Define *Ratio Decidendi*

Difficulties still lie ahead. Various judges and academics have tried to define what we mean by *ratio decidendi*. It is a surprisingly difficult problem. One complication is that a judgment may last for two, ten, or fifty pages. Somewhere in there is an account of the facts as found, a discussion of legal principles, a comparison with earlier cases, and a decision on the facts as to who won. A judge may apparently formulate a *ratio* only to continue with his judgment and formulate the *ratio* again; this time with slightly different words, with slightly different emphasis. This can prove galling. It happens. And nowhere will you find a sentence saying: 'Here comes the *ratio*'.

Yet another complication is that a judge in a later case may perceive the principle (the *ratio*) that is to be derived from the earlier case as something different from that which the original judge intended. If this strikes you as particularly odd, just consider the following everyday example: you always go to the local mall rather than the town centre because you think the shopping is better there; your friend thinks you go there because the parking is easier. May be both are true, but there is a difference in perception and interpretation over a fairly simple decision. And even if you say your reason was the quality of shopping, your friend may accept that but still think the parking point (although unsaid) can be inferred from your decision.

A question frequently posed by students at this stage is: 'So, how do I spot the ratio?' The question is a fair one. If there is an answer, it is the rather unsatisfactory one that, for both the practitioner and academic, this is a matter of skill and interpretation built on experience. After years of reading cases one instinctively formulates an opinion on what a case means (the basic theories of legal method having long been forgotten). The word we wish to stress here, though, is 'opinion'; and opinions can always be wrong or at least open to argument. Further, saying that experience aids one's understanding does not provide any help to someone new to the study of law. Thus, in the text below we have attempted to take a practical line by trying to find the most understandable and useful starting point for analysing the *ratio* of a case.

There are a number of excellent articles and books which take this academic debate to its limits: see, e.g., MacCormick (1987); Montrose (1957); Goodhart (1959). However, our experience is that at the outset of legal studies such in-depth analysis tends to produce confusion rather than comfort. We are in some agreement with Twining and Miers that the intricacies of the debate can (at least with regard to students beginning their legal studies) be a 'long and rather sterile' one. Nevertheless, as you encounter a greater range of cases and gain in confidence you may then wish to explore the problem of defining *ratio* in more depth.

There is no set single test for defining what is meant by *ratio* or for establishing the *ratio* of a particular case. As Cross stated: 'It is impossible to devise formulae for determining the *ratio decidendi* of a case'. But before you lose heart altogether, Cross also stated that 'this does not mean it is impossible to give a tolerably accurate description of what lawyers mean when they use the expression' (1991:72). Like so many things in law this problem of identification is not unique to legal studies. Think of the plot to a book or a film. The facts are clear, the storyline can be described; but if a group of people were asked to say what the film etc. was *about* then opinions would vary. Some might see the film as nothing more than, say, an adventure film; others might see a social or political message in it; others might think the director was clearly paying tribute to an earlier famous director. And even if the writer or director was asked to spell out the meaning, the purpose, of the film (equivalent to reading the judgment of a case) the onlooker's reply could still be: 'You may have meant that, but you produced something different.'

Thus, to the student who asks 'how do I spot the *ratio*?' Twining and Miers would respond:

> Talk of *finding* the *ratio decidendi* of a case obscures the fact that the process of interpreting cases is not like a hunt for buried treasure, but typically involves an element of choice from a range of possibilities. (1999:335)

It is unwise, therefore, to presume that there is one and only one possible *ratio* to a case. There are many cases, usually older cases dealing with fundamental principles in a particular area, where lawyers have accepted a general formulation of the *ratio*. For instance, textbooks will normally say more or less the same thing about the nineteenth-century 'offer and acceptance' cases in Contract Law, but reading a case is an exercise in interpretation; an exercise in exploring the range of possibilities. This is why we stressed the word 'opinion' above. Consequently, there is nothing wrong in reading a case and thinking: 'That case is not really authority for the proposition stated in the textbook; or even that stated by a judge.' All you have to do then is prove you are right; but it is surprising how many times the cases cited in footnotes as authority for a legal proposition turn out to be nothing of the sort.

Now, one of the classic ways of 'defining' what *ratio* means is to say that it is the material facts of the case, plus the decision made in relation to those facts. We will discuss what is meant by 'material facts' below. For the moment we will take the term as meaning those facts which were important in the judge's formulation of his decision; and so, the formulation of a rule which proceeds an inch beyond those material facts is suspect. This approach was taken by Goodhart (1931:25). It has been criticised mainly on the ground that Goodhart focused on the way in which the original judge formulated the *ratio*; and this fails to recognise sufficiently the role played by later judges in interpreting and applying the earlier case. We can agree with this criticism but it does not weaken the proposition that there is advantage to be gained in concentrating on what facts were material in a case, provided that one does not lose sight of the fact that a case does not stand in splendid isolation. How the case in question relates to other cases plays an important part in assessing its implications.

6.4 Perception and *Ratio*

The points raised in the last few paragraphs frequently cause students problems. It is not illogical when first studying law to believe that, if cases form the basis for legal propositions, you should be able to read a case and say what authority it stands for. After all, if you look at a maths equation you would expect to apply it time and time again in the same way. Why should the same not apply to legal cases?

First of all, maths equations are not always as certain and unchanging as we believe. For most of the time most mathematical equations will hold true; but in extreme circumstances they have to be modified. Thus Newton's general laws of gravity stood the test of time until some modifications had to be made following Einstein's work on relativity. The same is true for law. Many basic principles are well established and safe; what you learn now will probably still be true in fifty years' time. But law, in particular, has two key problems to deal with. First, as new cases arise in a particular area they have to be set against the established principle; and it may be that the principle has to be modified to accommodate these new cases. Think of it this way. Begin with a simple rule, then start asking questions along the 'What if?' line of reasoning. For example:

Rule: A vehicle must never cross double white lines in the middle of the road

What if…?	Decision	Possible later alterations/additions to the original rule
Case 1: The road is blocked by a parked car?	The general rule should not apply strictly in such cases.	You must never cross double white lines in the middle of the road **unless your right of way is blocked by a car** *(or another vehicle).*
Case 2: The left-hand side of the road is flooded?	The alteration to the general rule seen in Case 1 should also apply here.	You must never cross double white lines in the middle of the road **unless your right of way is blocked by a car or passage is impossible because of an obstruction.**
Case 3: You are turning right into a driveway and this means you must cross the white lines?	This is no different from cases 1 & 2—an exception to the general rule.	You must never cross double white lines in the middle of the road **unless … or you are turning right into a driveway** *(and no other signs prevent you doing so).*
Case 3 again:	**OR, if the decision was that you cannot cross the white line in such cases.**	You must never cross double white lines in the middle of the road **even when you wish to turn right (into a driveway). This case in distinguishable from cases 1 & 2.**
Case 4: A police officer directs you to do so?	The instructions from the officer override the general rule.	You must never cross double white lines in the middle of the road **unless directed by a police officer** *(and no other danger is obvious).*
Case 5: The double white lines have been partially obliterated in some way?	Partial obliteration does not detract from the safety aspects of the general rule.	You must never cross double white lines in the middle of the road **even when they have been partially obliterated.**
Case 5 again:	**OR, if the decision was that partial obliteration means that it would be unfair to enforce the general rule.**	**… unless they have been partially obliterated** *(and no other signs warn you of the presence of restrictions).*

This is a very simple example and most of the answers are obvious, but the same principle applies here as with the comparison of previously-decided cases.

Secondly, lawyers have to use words to express the principles and concepts; and particular words do not always mean the same thing to different people. It is at this point that problems of *perception* arise.

We are used to problems of perception when they concern the senses. Optical illusions are probably the best example of different perceptions, though hearing (e.g., with music) and taste (e.g., foods) also show the range of subjective responses to standard data. Somehow with *words* we expect our interpretation to be both universally accepted and certain. Any level of experience tells us this is not so; but the sanctity we impart to words (especially our own utterances) seems to overcome our experience.

6.5 *Ratio* and interpretation

Imagine that we have a case concerning the law on the protection of confidential information; we shall call it *Park Ltd* v *Moloney*. The issue is whether an employee, on leaving the company, can disclose his former employer's confidential information to another company. The case is heard in the Court of Appeal and the leading judgment is given by Tomlinson LJ. He rules that the employee is free to use the information. Tomlinson LJ states:

> During his employment an employee must not disclose any of his employer's confidential information to a third party. But once that employment has ended an employee should be free to use information which he has come by in the course of his employment unless that information amounts to a trade secret. The information in this case is confidential but not so confidential as to amount to a trade secret. Therefore the employee cannot be restrained from making use of it on termination of the contract of employment.

How might judges in later cases react to this ratio? Here are some examples of how later judges might express their different perceptions of Tomlinson LJ's *ratio*:

- *Judge 1*: In *Park* v *Moloney* Tomlinson LJ clearly established the principle that an ex-employee is bound to observe his former employer's secrets only in very limited circumstances.

- *Judge 2*: In *Park* v *Moloney* Tomlinson LJ did not give ex-employees a free hand to disclose secrets on leaving employment. There are clear words of limitation in the phrase 'trade secrets'. All manner of things, in particular circumstances, may amount to a trade secret. We therefore need to explore what is meant by 'trade secret'.

- *Judge 3*: When Tomlinson LJ stated that an employee 'should be free to use information which he has come by in the course of his employment' he could not have meant this to apply where the employee has signed a contract specifically forbidding him from disclosing information once the contract has ended. The use of the word 'should' clearly shows that there are limits to this freedom.

- *Judge 4*: In *Park* v *Moloney* Tomlinson LJ clearly stated that an employee could use information which he has 'come by in the course of his employment'. The use of the words 'come by' is interesting. I doubt whether his Lordship meant his judgment to include cases where the employee has not 'come by' information by accident but has been specifically entrusted with the information by his employer.

Although the *Park* v *Moloney* case and the comments are fictitious they are based closely on real cases. They are simplified versions of how a judgment may be perceived by later judges, but they give you a taste of how a *ratio* is open to further interpretation.

6.6 Summary of points covered

Before looking at a short exercise on this idea of 'interpreting the *ratio*', we can summarise the points made above:

(a) Many cases do not give rise to much argument as to what they mean, what the *ratio* was.

(b) Every case is, however, open to some reinterpretation. As we noted in **Chapter 5** (and will return to in **Chapter 8**), this may prove to be a particularly significant point if the earlier case law is seen to be in conflict with principles of human rights as set out in the Human Rights Act 1998.

(c) The earlier cases will have dealt with specific facts. Later cases will deal with different specific facts.

(d) The need to interpret the *ratio* of these earlier cases arises when you try to apply that case to the new set of facts in front of you.

(e) The judge's formulation of the *ratio* in any particular case is not always clear.

(f) Whether it is clear or not, later judges have the right to interpret these words, to add an emphasis which the earlier judge may not have intended, or which the earlier judge would have intended had he or she been faced with the new set of facts in question.

(g) Every time a case is decided in a particular area it may:

    (i) apply;
    (ii) confirm;
    (iii) extend;
    (iv) reinterpret;
    (v) distinguish;
    (vi) criticise;
    (vii) narrow;
    (viii) modify;
    (ix) limit;
    (x) weaken;
    (xi) obliterate; or
    (xii) ignore

the principles established by the earlier cases.

EXERCISE 10 Things likely to do mischief

The case of *Rylands* v *Fletcher* (1868) LR 3 HL 330 is one of the more famous Tort cases in English law. It was heavily criticised when it first appeared because many perceived the judges as having invented a legal principle not previously found in the case law (perhaps reflected in the fact that the form of liability derived from the case is simply known as the Tort of *Rylands* v *Fletcher*). Nevertheless the case stood the test of time until recently.

In *Rylands* v *Fletcher*, the House of Lords had to consider whether Fletcher could recover damages against Rylands when a reservoir constructed by Rylands burst through some disused mine shafts on his land and flooded the mines of Fletcher, who was Rylands's neighbour. On the facts, Rylands had not been negligent in constructing the reservoir. In holding that Rylands was nevertheless liable for the damage caused, Lord Cairns cited the judgment of Blackburn J in the court below:

> We think that the true rule of law is, that the person who, for his own purposes, brings on his land and collects and keeps there anything likely to do mischief if it escapes, must keep it in at his peril; and if he does not do so, is *prima facie* answerable for all the damage which is the natural consequence of its escape.

QUESTIONS

(a) Do you think that this expresses a clear legal proposition which you could apply to other cases?

(b) Earlier in Lord Cairns's speech he referred to the 'non-natural' use of land. Should this be read in to the statement given above?

(c) Do you foresee difficulties with the words used? What do you think was meant by 'for his own purposes', 'brings on', 'escape', 'likely to do mischief'?

(d) Do you think a later judge might say that the principle was expressed wider than was necessary to decide the actual case?

(e) Would later judges be justified in applying or not applying the words used to situations with very different facts? For instance, how would you use the principle where a visitor to a munitions factory is injured by the explosion of a shell which is being manufactured in the factory (see *Read* v *J. Lyons & Co. Ltd* [1947] A C 156, [1946] 2 All ER 471).

COMMENT

The first and second questions help to illustrate that the *ratio* is not set in stone but is subject to interpretation. The fact that textbooks give you the *ratios* of many cases only means that this is the conclusion the author reached after doing the same exercise. However, if lawyers have been doing this for centuries then it is not an impossible art to master. For instance, quite often (as in *Rylands* v *Fletcher* itself) a fairly clear idea of the *ratio* can be found in one sentence or paragraph. It is also part of a lawyer's skill to gather the *ratio* from reading the whole judgment (or judgments). This may test one's ability to deal with concepts and linguistics, but it is not an insurmountable task. Although it is sacrilegious to say this, when starting out studying law a good idea of what most people will regard as being the *ratio* of a case is contained in the Headnote to the case. This is written by an experienced barrister and most practitioners would admit that, on many occasions, this is all they have read in a case. But this is a dangerous practice when used long-term. It gives only one interpretation, does not actually quote what the judges said, does not give any impression of key *obiter* points and, in some famous cases, may actually be wrong—even the most experienced barristers muck it up sometimes.

The third question illustrates the point that, even if the *ratio* is easy to spot, words do not always have a clear, single meaning. The word 'escape' was a major issue in the case of *Read* v *Lyons*, noted in question (e).

One question we did not pose, which can be dealt with only by reading the case itself is: what earlier authorities were cited by the court? We noted in the introduction to this exercise that *Rylands* v *Fletcher* was criticised for 'inventing law'. Nevertheless, the judges still referred to a number of cases; cases which they said were analogous to this situation. Hence our previous comment that cases do not stand in splendid isolation.

The fourth and fifth questions lead us into a discussion on another vital aspect of reading a case—the question of what constitutes a *material fact*. This question exemplifies the idea that the *ratio* of a case strictly relates only to the actual facts of that case, but is often expressed in wider terms. The fifth question asks you to decide whether changing a material fact (here, that *Read* was on the premises and not outside) might make such a difference that the original *ratio* should not be applied. But before analysing what is meant by the term *material fact* we will take the opportunity to note that not everything said by a judge when giving judgment can constitute a precedent. As Cross indicates (1991:39), the *ratio* can only relate to pronouncements of law, not the facts of the case; and then only those pronouncements which the judge considers necessary for his decision are said to form part of the *ratio*.

6.7 Obiter Dictum

Anything else said in the case that does not relate to the material facts is called *obiter dictum* (this means 'a thing said by the way'—the plural is *obiter dicta*). *Obiter dicta* statements are not binding on a later judge. MacCormick describes *obiter dicta* as 'statements of opinion upon the law and its values and principles in their bearing on the instant decision, statements which in some way go beyond the point or points necessary to be settled in deciding the case' (1987:156).

Obiter comments can arise in many ways—here are a few examples:

(a) Where the judge makes a hypothetical pronouncement, e.g., 'If the facts had been different (in some respect) then my decision would have been...'; or

(b) The judge might say what he would have decided had he not been bound by *stare decisis*; or

(c) The pronouncement by the judge might be entirely relevant to the material facts, but his or her judgment was in the minority. A minority judgment has its own *ratio*, but that cannot be the *ratio* of the case since that judge's view did not prevail.

(d) The judge may make a number of general comments on the topic of law under discussion. In *Donoghue* v *Stevenson*, for instance, Lord Atkin made a number of observations about liability for negligent acts. One observation was that one owed a duty of care not to injure one's 'neighbour'—a person so closely affected by one's acts that one must take reasonable care not to injure them. This is an *obiter* statement because it is not directly related to the facts; it proceeds far beyond that in its generality.

Most *obiter dicta* were never intended by the judge to be anything else. However, as you will see (especially in Exercise 11), a later court may always decide that what was said by a judge in the prior case was unnecessary to the decision and therefore not part of the *ratio*. This 'reassessment' is one of the devices used to overcome the binding element of precedent discussed in **Chapter 5**.

A judge can decline to follow anything that is not the *ratio*. This is why the classification is important. However, do not cast aside *obiter* comments. For one thing, if the *ratio* of a case is an arguable point you should not be too hasty in relegating a comment to the status of *obiter dictum*; one man's *obiter* may be the next man's *ratio* to a case. For another, *obiter* comments can turn out to be much more influential than the actual *ratio*. Lord Atkins's 'neighbour principle' was not an irrelevancy; far from it. Rather, it was used by later judges to form the basis upon which the law of negligence was to develop. From a case about dead snails the 'neighbour principle' has been extended to consumer items, industrial accidents, road accidents, misstatements, and many other areas.

Throughout the remainder of this chapter we concentrate on the two important aspects of analysing *ratio decidendi*: 'how precedents develop' and the 'material facts' of cases. These two topics are interwined and, in our experience, it would be ideal to consider them both simultaneously. Unfortunately, there is no simple way of doing this. Therefore, by way of explanation and introduction we will summarise the points to begin with:

(a) In the next section 'How Precedents Develop', we will seek to show that, from the starting point of a single case, a line of cases can arise with similar facts which can apply or modify the *ratio* found in the first case. This exercise is something like analysing the history of computers. Forty years ago it took a computer the size of a room a long time to produce fairly simple results. Working from the same principles as that early computer the next generation of computers were smaller and did the same job more quickly. The use of silicon chips changed the size again and brought about added refinements and advantages. The modern computer is the state of the art—but this will change yet again, so that although the basic principles have probably remained the same, the modern device is, in most respects, quite unlike its ancestors. What we will stress is that in law it is the *reasoning* employed in a case that is passed on for examination to the next generation, even though the facts change with each case.

(b) In the section 'Material Facts' we will attempt to explain which parts of the previous cases are considered vital to the decision. In other words, if the facts of each case are inevitably different to some degree, which facts do we consider material (vital) enough to say: 'That case was decided in a particular way and this case is sufficiently similar to it that it too should be decided in the same way'?

6.8 How Precedents Develop

6.8.1 Comparing the Reasoning in Cases

Once a case has been decided it falls to judges in later cases sitting in an inferior court to apply the case, or find reasons not to apply it. This much is demanded by the doctrine of *stare decisis*. Even if there is no binding element attached to the earlier decision, it will not simply be ignored (the persuasive nature of precedent should not be underestimated). The reality is that the later judge will (to a greater or lesser extent) formulate his own opinion as to the *ratio* of the earlier case. This may not be the same as the opinion held by the judge in that earlier case. There may be a difference of emphasis. It may be a wider *ratio* than the first judge intended; it may be narrower. It is rather like the writing and singing of a song: even when the same words are being sung the interpretation of different artists may be quite striking—consider the various versions of 'My Way' (e.g. that of Frank Sinatra and that of Sid Vicious).

A common mistake made by law students, however, is to ignore all this and, as we indicated above, to discover a similarity and take the analysis no further. A lawyer cannot rest like this. Various arguments might be presented regarding the similarities of cases, such as:

- 'This present case is on all fours with the previous case'; or
- 'The facts are dissimilar at first sight, but both cases illustrate the same principle'; or
- 'The present case is clearly distinguishable from the earlier case because one of the material facts of the earlier case is missing here'; or
- 'The present case is clearly distinguishable from the earlier case because there are additional material facts in this case which were not present in the earlier case'; or even
- 'When Lord Justice Bloggs formulated the principle in the earlier case he paid insufficient attention to fact (a) which he should have treated as material.'

There are therefore many ways in which one can try to use apparently dissimilar cases to argue your case; or argue that apparently similar cases are of little or no use at all. Remember, when you are arguing your client's case you are trying to persuade the judge to apply the *rationes* which are helpful to you and disapply the rest. It is a matter of legal ethics that you have a duty as an advocate to bring to the court's attention all relevant authorities, whether for you or against you; but that does not stop you arguing that the ones against you are worthless or distinguishable.

By way of illustration you will find below an example of how a case might develop. We shall use the example of the road accident first set out in **Chapter 5**. You may remember that the facts were: in *case (1)* a man driving a Ford Mondeo runs over an old lady who was lawfully using a zebra crossing. The man is held to be liable in negligence. In *Brenda's case* a woman driving a BMW runs over an old man who was crossing the road.

The question before the court is therefore: how does the decision in *case (1)* apply to the facts in *case (2)*? (We should state here that none of what follows is meant to be an accurate statement of the law—we have simplified many things to illustrate our general point.)

We shall start by assuming that in *case (1)* the driver (we shall call him Alfred) argued that he was not liable because the old lady stepped onto the zebra crossing so late that he could not stop. The court did not accept that this was a legitimate excuse and Alfred was found liable in negligence to the old lady for the injury he caused her. Alfred's appeal to the Court of Appeal failed. By looking at the judgment of the trial judge and taking the comments of the Court of Appeal, we can put together the following **material facts**:

(a) The weather conditions were excellent.

(b) The old lady was on a zebra crossing;

(c) The fact that she stepped onto the crossing late did not, in law or on the facts, excuse Alfred from liability because:

  (i) Alfred was speeding;

  (ii) Alfred's attention was distracted as he was using his mobile phone at the time.

We might say that the *ratio* of this case is: where a person is not paying adequate attention and is speeding, they will be liable for their negligence if they injure a pedestrian who is using a zebra crossing, even where the pedestrian steps onto the crossing late, if a careful driver (taking account of the weather conditions) could have still avoided causing injury.

The fact that Alfred is male, that the injured person is female or old, that the car was a Ford Mondeo, have not been held to be relevant as **material facts**. Now we have to apply this reasoning to *case (2)*—the woman (Brenda) driving a BMW, who hits an old man crossing a road. First we can make a simple comparison of (material) facts:

Material facts in Alfred's case	Facts in Brenda's case
Fact (a): use of a zebra crossing	Not present—this was a straight piece of open road
Fact (b): speeding	Brenda was also speeding
Fact (c): attention distracted by use of mobile phone	Similar—attention distracted by noisy child in the back seat
Fact (d): the old lady stepped onto the crossing late	Not present
Fact (e): weather conditions good	Same

We shall assume that the court in *Brenda's case* decides that the absence of facts (a) and (d) does not affect the general principle to be found in *Alfred's case*. This means that the judge believed that the fact the old lady in *Alfred's case* was injured whilst using a zebra crossing was not material to the *ratio* of *Alfred's case* when looked at in the light of the present case so that the same principle applies even where the injured person is crossing another part of the road. The judge will have fixed on the presence of facts (b), (c), and (e) in *Brenda's case* as the determining factors (even though they are not identical to *Alfred's case*)

The ratio of *Brenda's case* might then be: **where a person is not paying adequate attention and is speeding they will be liable for their negligence if they injure a pedestrian who is crossing the road, if a careful driver (taking account of the weather conditions), could have still avoided causing injury.**

Our perception of the legal principles relating to driving negligently has been widened, even if only slightly. Gone is the requirement for the presence of the zebra crossing, and the related fact of the person stepping onto it late. Also gone now is the basis for any argument which tried to limit the ratio of *Alfred's case* to inattention caused by the use of mobile phones. In other words, we are beginning to get a clearer picture of what is required for liability and what does not matter.

We can now introduce a final example. *Carol's case* involves a woman, Carol, driving a VW Golf, who runs over a student crossing the road (this time on a bend). The material facts this time are:

Material facts in Alfred's case	Material facts in Brenda's case	Material facts in Carol's case
Fact (a): use of a zebra crossing	Not present—this was a straight piece of open road	Not present—accident on the bend in a road
Fact (b): speeding	Brenda was also speeding	Carol was **not** speeding
Fact (c): attention distracted by use of mobile phone	Similar: Brenda was distracted by a noisy child in the back seat	Similar: Carol was distracted by a dog, not on a lead, wandering around the roadside
Fact (d): the old lady stepped onto the crossing late	Not present	Not present
Fact (e): weather conditions good	Same	Different: it was raining

You can see that the facts have moved on a little from both the first two cases. It is possible that this shift will mean that Carol is not liable. It is also possible that the judge may find that the differences are immaterial to the general principle so that she is liable. In any decision there is a point where a judgment has to be made and this is not a purely mechanical exercise (one reason why it is so difficult to invent a computer-based 'expert system' for deciding cases).

We shall say that Carol is also found to be liable. This means that the judge has confirmed that the principles of liability as originally set out in *Alfred's case*:

(a) are not limited to cases involving zebra crossings (though this probably came out of *Brenda's case* anyway);

(b) are not limited to accidents occurring on straight roads (as happened in *Brenda's case*);

(c) are not limited to cases where the driver is speeding (which was the position with both *Alfred* and *Brenda*);

(d) are not limited to cases where the weather conditions were good; and

(e) are not limited by the fact that Carol's attention was distracted by a genuine and understandable concern that a loose dog might run into the road. On this, we can now speculate that any excuse regarding lack of attention will be very limited in its scope.

The *ratio* for *Carol's case* might be: where a person is not paying adequate attention, even where there is an understandable reason for that lack of attention, they will be liable for their negligence if they injure a pedestrian who is crossing on the bend of a road, if a careful driver could have still avoided causing injury.

Compare the possible formulations of *ratio* in the three cases. How important are the minor differences?

Alfred's case	*Brenda's case*	*Carol's case*
Where a person is not paying adequate attention and is speeding, they will be liable for their negligence if they injure a pedestrian who is using a zebra crossing, even where the pedestrian steps onto the crossing late, if a careful driver (taking account of the weather conditions) could have still avoided causing injury.	Where a person is not paying adequate attention and is speeding, they will be liable for their negligence if they injure a pedestrian who is crossing the road, if a careful driver (taking account of the weather conditions) could have still avoided causing injury.	Where a person is not paying adequate attention, even where there is an understandable reason for that lack of attention, they will be liable for their negligence if they injure a pedestrian who is crossing on the bend of a road, if a careful driver could have still avoided causing injury.

This type of exercise is fine for examining decided cases—as you will do throughout your studies. But there is the practical 'prediction' aspect of law too. For instance, let us assume for a moment that you are a solicitor interviewing a client. The client, David, tells you that he injured a young man in a car accident. The man was crossing the road, at a junction, in a wheelchair. Can you say that the cases we have discussed will apply? Is the introduction of a new fact—that the injured person had been in a wheelchair—sufficiently different from the precedents that they may have no application?

One thing you would certainly have to do is to read the cases. We have simplified things. There are no statements here from judges as to *why* they reached these decisions. It might even be that there is an *obiter* comment in one of the cases where a judge said that had the injured person been in a wheelchair or similar device the decision would have been different. This *obiter* comment is not binding but it might be highly persuasive to a later judge; the judge in your case perhaps.

Remember, though, that when the material facts are found to be sufficiently similar then the later court is bound to follow the decision of the earlier *superior* court (and possibly that of a court of equal status): it must apply the principle of law pronounced in the earlier case. The only other alternative is to **distinguish** the case. By this we mean that the lawyer or judge will seek to show a significant difference in the material facts or the reasoning employed in the two cases such that the court should not feel obliged to follow the earlier case. It is almost impossible to define coherently when courts will or will not feel inclined to distinguish a case. But do not be put off by the difficulty of predicting when a judge will distinguish cases. The ability to argue differences in cases, to argue why a case should or should not apply, lies at the heart of the Common Law. This is what you are training to do. The fact that the judge finally disagrees with you may be annoying, but it's a fact of life. Sometimes your talents will be recognised even in the most hopeless of cases, as with Lord Donaldson's comment on David Pannick QC in *Attorney-General* v *Barker* [1990] 3 All ER 257 at 261e: 'My abiding impression of this case is that I have confirmed my admiration for counsel . . . as an advocate in his ability to dress up the wholly unarguable as if it had a scintilla of a basis of reason.'

Anyway you distinguish things every day. At its simplest level, you distinguish physical objects—a television from a video recorder for example. Their size, shape, and functions tell you that these objects are different. At a more complicated level, human beings share over 95 per cent of their DNA with chimpanzees and about 60 per cent with bananas, but, on the whole, we can tell the difference. More inexplicably we all distinguish the faces of billions of people, despite the fact that they are built of the same, limited number of component parts. We would submit that, saying *exactly* why Deb and Jane are not the same person might, in the end, be more difficult than distinguishing between *Alfred's case* and *Carol's case* in our examples above.

What the 'negligent driving' exercise tells us is that the analysis of the *ratio* of a case involves a high degree of interpretation—of applying the *principle* in one case to the different facts in another. The principles that emerge from a case can thus often be seen only in retrospect. Looking back at *Alfred's case*, knowing that later cases have expanded upon such things as the position of the pedestrian on the road, we tend to generalise. Our account of the *ratio* of *Alfred's case* is much more general than it would have been immediately after *Alfred's case* was reported. When the decision in *Alfred's case* was given you could not say with any certainty that the presence of the pedestrian crossing or the fact the driver was speeding would be irrelevant to liability. It might be that you now feel you could extract a wide principle from the three cases, e.g., that a driver who does not look where he or she is going, for any reason, is guilty of negligent driving. Perhaps this is accurate; but would you have been confident in saying this when *Alfred's case* was the only decided case?

It is like watching a game of chess where you have not been told all the rules. You might see a knight move and conclude that chess pieces move in an 'L' shape. Only in subsequent observations do you find that this principle applies to only one piece; and you may not have deduced yet that the knight has the ability to jump over other pieces. The real attributes of the knight—the first case—are seen only as things develop and by comparison with other events. This comparison was once used by the late Richard Feynman to describe the discovery of scientific principles; it applies equally here. And, as with Feynman's analogy, there is always the possibility that just when you think you understand everything about chess (or science, or legal principles) something totally unexpected happens, such as 'castling'.

For instance, assume that a new major case has just been reported. At this stage you cannot say with certainty how it will be used in the future. How will later judges apply it to different facts? Is the *ratio* going to be restricted to the particular facts of the case, or used in many other similar (but possibly only remotely similar) cases? In other words, how will judges in later cases use the precedent?

If we might borrow and adapt an example of this form of reasoning from Dworkin (1987:chap. 7) we can see that this twisting and turning of principles can apply outside the legal context too. Consider that Charles Dickens had never written *A Christmas Carol*. You have been commissioned to do so. In writing chapter 1 you have a completely free hand in deciding on the character of Scrooge and what will happen to him. Think of this as the first case in a line of precedents.

Now imagine that someone else is commissioned to write chapter 2. She takes your basic material, but place a different emphasis on it—maybe one you never intended. By the end of the novel (with even more authors having contributed) Scrooge, instead of being redeemed, is taught his lesson and still cast into hell. Your original idea has been changed out of all recognition, despite the fact that each chapter follows logically from the previous one.

6.8.2 Multiple and Inconclusive *Rationes*

It will not now come as a surprise that a case can be said to have different *rationes* in that there may be different interpretations of what is the proposition of law for which the case stands as authority. Equally, you need to be aware that: (i) even 'crystal clear' judgments occasionally contain more than one *ratio*; and (ii) that in some cases no one can find the *ratio*.

On the first point we have in mind the position where a judge says: 'I find for X for the following reasons...I would also say that there is another (unconnected) reason for which I find for X'. Which is the *ratio*? This occurred in the Court of Appeal case of *Turner* v *London Transport Executive* [1977] ICR 952. The traditional answer is that both statements are *ratio*. Later judges do not, however, follow a consistent line when dealing with such cases; they 'relegate' one of the statements to mere *obiter dictum*: see Lord Denning's comments on *Turner* in *Western Excavating* v *Sharp* [1978] ICR 221; [1978] 1 All ER 713 (also Court of Appeal).

This technique also even enables later judges in lower courts to re-assess the *ratio* of an earlier case. Thus, in *Great Peace Shipping Ltd* v *Tsavliris Salvage (International) Ltd* [2002] EWCA Civ 1407; [2002] 4 All E.R. 689 Lord Phillips of Worth Matravers, MR in the Court of Appeal re-assessed the words of Lord Atkin in the famous House of Lords contract law case of *Bell* v *Lever Bros* [1932] AC 161 and concluded that Lord Atkin had proposed two *rationes*, the first of which was based on very weak authority and so could be ignored in favour of the second *ratio*.

On the second point we have in mind a number of confusing cases which the lawyer usually relates as being 'an authority for any proposition of law for which you care to use it'. This will arise where the judges are agreed as to the decision (X won) but present their reasons in quite different formulations. *Bell* v *Lever Bros* (above) is one example.

Chaplin v *Boys* [1971] AC 356 has long been cited in this area as a case where their Lordships in the House of Lords agreed on the result but were faced with three possible grounds for reaching their decision; if one adds up the various opinions one discovers that each of the grounds was actually rejected by three of the five Law Lords. The High Court of Australia managed to do something similar in *Northern Sandblasting Pty Ltd* v *Harris*

(1997) 188 CLR 313. Nine-year-old Nicole Harris had been electrocuted and reduced to a vegetative state when water pipes had become live owing to the negligence of an electrician. Because the case involved rented accommodation the law on who was responsible had particular complications outside the scope of this text. In deciding to award substantial damages, two judges found for Nicole on what we shall call ground (a), but the other five judges rejected this reasoning; two found for Nicole on ground (b) but four of the remaining judges rejected this ground, the final judge not dealing with the issue.

Another contract case along the same lines is *Esso* v *Commissioners of Customs and Excise* [1976] 1 WLR 1; [1976] 1 All ER 117. The issue was quite simple. Esso had established a campaign whereby their garages were giving away free 'World Cup' coins (tokens bearing the faces of England's 1970 World Cup squad) with every four gallons of petrol. Customs and Excise claimed these coins were chargeable to purchase tax (the forerunner of VAT) because they were 'produced in quantity for general sale'. The customs officials placed a value on the coins and claimed £200,000.

The House of Lords held that Esso was not liable to purchase tax on the coins. But when one reads the judgments one finds that:

(a) Two Law Lords held that there was no intent to create legal relations as regards the coins: they were gifts (see Viscount Dilhorne and Lord Russell).

(b) Two Law Lords held that the advertisement on the garage forecourts was an offer which the customer accepted when he bought the petrol. However, the coins themselves were ancillary to the main contract and were transferred only when the motorist bought the petrol. Therefore the coins themselves were not produced for sale (Lord Simon and Lord Wilberforce).

(c) Lord Fraser dissented, finding that there was intent to form a contract and the coins were part of that contract.

This summary ignores the many *obiter* statements which add greater confusion.

These cases do not occur that often, but they do exist. They help to illustrate our overriding point that cases are not merely objects that remain fixed and unaltered every time you look at them. Moreover, even if they could be considered as objects they would be more like hi-fi systems than washing machines: the washing machine is a unit which does not change from purchase but the hi-fi system can be altered substantially (new cables, speakers, etc.), and though it still performs its original purpose it does so with very different results—and may even accommodate a completely new component such as the introduction of compact discs.

6.9 Answering Legal Questions on Precedent

In Exercise 11 we have drafted an problem on *ratio* and *stare decisis* based on both the information above and that in **Chapter 5**. Its aim is to reiterate some of the points made and to show you a general plan in answering legal questions. It also gives us an opportunity to note that in legal education, if not in practice, you will be asked to write essays relating to quotations as well as analyse problem situations.

EXERCISE 11 Precedent and the congenital idiot

Lord Asquith once recounted a joke told to him regarding *ratio* and *obiter* that: 'The rule is quite simple, if you agree with the other bloke you say [the statement] is part of the *ratio*; if you don't you say it is *obiter dictum*, with the implication that he is a congenital idiot.' *Discuss.*

ANSWER

This question asks you to analyse how a judge uses or avoids precedent: what do the terms *ratio decidendi* and *obiter dictum* mean; and is a judge really bound by the doctrine of *stare decisis*? Thus this is a specific question which demands a **specific** answer—not merely general comments. This style of question is one which is commonly found throughout all areas of law: a quotation questioning or denying the logic of a fundamental rule. For instance, the question might be: 'The formation of a contract is not based on assessing the parties' true intentions but on what the law defines as their intentions according to their conduct set against established case law. Discuss.' Or: 'When people talk of the United Kingdom losing its sovereignty since joining the EU they fail to recognise that sovereignty is an economic fact, not a political aspiration. Discuss.' You are asked to perform four tasks:

(1) **IDENTIFY THE AREA CONCERNED.** In this case this hardly presents a problem because of the introductory words. But a quotation on theft, or misrepresentation in contract, may have hidden points.

(2) **LIMIT YOURSELF TO THE TOPIC IN QUESTION.** In the context of this chapter, this again is not difficult; but when such a question appears at the end of a course the task becomes more difficult. It is vital to see at what limited area the question is aimed. Not all the topics that fall within 'legal method' are relevant to the question posed here. Thus the **poor student** will tend to do one of two things:

(a) Launch into a lengthy discussion of various or all aspects of precedent. This is known as the 'shotgun' approach: something has to hit the target. With a question on provocation in Criminal Law, for instance, nearly every defence under the sun will emerge at some time.

(b) Spend too much time on introductory matters such as describing the court structure in detail. This would not be the crux of the question. This might be even more obvious when one glances down the examination paper to discover a question asking for just this type of information. With a question on Contract Law, for instance, there may be a page introduction setting out as many aspects of contract formation as possible when the question is only concerned with one aspect of offer and acceptance.

(3) **STRUCTURE THE ANSWER.** Do not leap into a discussion of the topic without planning the development of the essay. An examiner has difficulty following an answer that constantly repeats itself, re-states points or arguments for no apparent reason, or makes sense from sentence to sentence but not from paragraph to paragraph. A safe bet is to begin

with some (we stress *some*) introductory words. *For example*:

'The doctrine of precedent is central to the development of Common Law. The doctrine of *stare decisis* provides the mechanism for the operation of judicial precedent. *Stare decisis* demands that where a decision has been made on a particular point of law then later inferior courts (or courts of equal status in many cases) must not be merely persuaded by the earlier decision, but are bound to follow it. In its strictest form, therefore, this approach promotes certainty. However, the doctrine does not mean that all judges are simply machines; applying fixed rules already laid down. If that were so then the two sides would probably not be arguing the point. The difficulty is that the doctrine demands that *like cases should be decided in the same way*. This always leaves room for deciding when two cases are sufficiently similar that the doctrine of *stare decisis* should be applied: i.e., cases can very often be distinguished on their facts and the key point of *stare decisis* rests in the analysis of the *ratio* and *obiter dicta* of the earlier case. It is the principle in the earlier case that must be followed, not merely the decision.'

You might then go on to explain the difference between *ratio decidendi* and *obiter dicta*.

(4) **REFER TO THE QUESTION.** To obtain the best marks you should try to relate your comments to the quotation. At various points in your answer review the relevance of parts of your answer to the quotation. Here is an example:

'We have said that the doctrine of *stare decisis* provides certainty. Thus we can say that the 'law' on a topic can be discovered, and *stare decisis*, in particular, narrows down the enquiry. But such an approach assumes that the principle of a case (its authority) is not open to interpretation itself. If, however, **as the question implies or at least suggests**, the judge has at some early stage decided which way the case should go then his task is one of showing how the authorities that he wishes to follow are very similar to the case before him; and how the other 'apparently' similar cases are based on entirely different facts. But even if one does not take such a cynical line, it is also true to say that the *ratio* of any case is not fixed and immutable. Different judges perceive cases as authority for differently stated principles.

(5) **REFER TO SOME CASES TO ILLUSTRATE YOUR ARGUMENTS.** Here you could use cases which distinguished other cases on seemingly minor points, for instance—or cases where a judge felt compelled to follow earlier cases even when he believed them to be wrong. You could choose cases from areas you have studied e.g., Contract Law or Criminal Law. Legal method, remember, is about how law is analysed; it is not a separate subject in itself.

Cases are cited in a number of ways. We shall take this opportunity to look at these methods of citation. Here are five general examples of alternative methods. The case is on employment law and the legal definition of 'dismissal'. Do not worry about understanding the legal issues. The key point is that if an employee resigns he may still claim, in law, that he was dismissed. The aim of this provision is to prevent employers forcing an employee to resign without any remedy; it is referred to as 'constructive dismissal'.

(a) In *Western Excavating* v *Sharp* an employee was short of money following disciplinary action by his employer. He asked for an advance of his pay but, in keeping with company regulations, this was refused. He resigned in order to obtain his holiday pay; and because he felt his employer was acting unreasonably. The question before the court was: did a resignation because of 'unreasonable' conduct on the part of the employer fall within the legal definition of dismissal? The Court of Appeal held that a resignation could constitute a dismissal only where the employer had committed a serious breach of contract, not just because he may have been acting unreasonably. Hence there was no 'dismissal' here. **N.B. if you have time to do this for each case you cite in an examination you can write more quickly than any student we know!** There is always a compromise to be drawn (even with coursework where there will be word limits) but the same is true in real cases where very often there are time limits to observe in making your submissions. So, the remaining examples make some form of compromise.

(b) The principle was established in *Western Excavating* v *Sharp* that an employee can resign but still claim he was dismissed if the employer has seriously breached the contract (**N.B. case names appear in italics in texts. In essays it is always best to emphasise case names for clarity**).

(c) The Court of Appeal in *Western Excavating* v *Sharp* stressed that the employer must be in serious breach of contract, not just acting unreasonably, before an employee can resign and still claim he was dismissed.

(d) A resignation cannot be classed as a dismissal unless the employer has seriously breached the contract: *Western Excavating* v *Sharp*.

(e) In the 1970s there existed much judicial disagreement on when a resignation might constitute a dismissal. One camp argued that if the employer acted unreasonably this would constitute a constructive dismissal. Others pressed the point that what was required was a serious breach of contract on the employer's part. The issue was apparently settled in *Western Excavating* v *Sharp* wherein the Court of Appeal pronounced in favour of the 'contract test'.

(6) **CONCLUDE.** The reality of the quotation is probably that some judges feel they must adhere to precedent at all cost because this promotes certainty; whilst others take a more creative standpoint. In the end it is probably true to say that judges do both things: they adhere to precedent and also use or adapt precedent to justify their decisions. The statement merely confirms that, despite our strict views of *stare decisis*, there exists the role of choice in our judicial process. Judges, after all, try to achieve 'fairness'. And if judges did not modify the law from one year to the next then, as Lord Goff comments in *Kleinwort Ltd* v *Lincoln Council*: 'the common law would be the same now as it was in the reign of Henry II ... [but it] is a living system of law, reacting to new events and new ideas...' The idea that judges merely 'declare' what existed in the common law all along and do not actively make law was also finally put to rest (if anyone ever believed it) by Lord Browne-Wilkinson in the same case.

The statement also recognises the interpretative element in describing the *ratio* of a case. The finer points of distinguishing cases, or showing how one case relates to others, can lead to a justifiable disagreement as to what is the *ratio* of a case.

6.10 Material Facts

The facts of a case are revealed in the documents, statements, and evidence produced. All these are relevant to a case, but they are not all relevant to the *ratio* of the case. In our case of negligent driving, the legal reasoning is unlikely to hinge on whether the claimant was called Alfred, or what make of car he drove, or the colour of the car. Whether he was speeding is more **likely** to be material.

There is no set hierarchy of facts which will always be important or irrelevant. Change the issue before the court and different questions have to be posed. Alfred's name could be important where he is claiming that *he* is the 'Alfred' cited in a millionaire's will; so too his height, nickname, and age. The colour of the car might be the whole issue at stake in a breach of contract action where Alfred has ordered a red car and is presented with a yellow car which he refuses to accept, but most likely irrelevant in a road traffic accident.

So one thing you need to be aware of is: what is the case about? What is the legal point at issue? Once you have established this, certain facts cannot be material. Secondly, be aware that facts can be viewed as 'narrow' or 'general'. This depends upon the level of **abstraction** with which one views the facts of a case; whether one takes only the literal facts as being relevant or one observes the facts as merely representing something wider. For instance, is a statement about the meaning of giving someone a red rose limited to red roses, indicative of all roses, all flowers, or representative of symbols of affection?

In the table below we show how abstraction of facts operates. The three columns, each representing a wider abstraction of facts, are based on the analysis by Stone (1959:597) of the case of *Donoghue* v *Stevenson*. We considered *Donoghue* v *Stevenson* in Exercise 9 in deciding why two cases should be decided the same way. To repeat the facts in brief: Mrs Donoghue and a friend went into a cafe in Paisley. The friend ordered ice-cream and ginger-beer for both of them. The shopkeeper poured out some of the ginger-beer over the ice-cream. Mrs Donoghue consumed some of the mixture. Her friend poured out the remainder of the ginger-beer for Mrs Donoghue and a decomposed snail fell out of the bottle. The bottle was of dark opaque glass so that the contents could not have been detected. Mrs Donoghue sued Stevenson (the manufacturer of the ginger-beer) for negligently causing her injury. She succeeded.

In the first column will appear a material fact that relates very closely to what happened. The next two columns go wider in their interpretation. Picture yourself as a judge and ask which level of generalisation you would adopt in a later case to see whether the decision in *Donoghue* v *Stevenson* should be applied. Our experience is that students are attracted to the 'widest interpretation of the facts' on points 1, 2, and 4; the 'wider facts' column tends to be preferred on points 3 and 5. You may feel differently.

The point of this experiment is that the wider you set your *abstraction* of the facts the easier it is to apply one decision concerning a particular set of facts to another case concerning different facts.

Abstraction of Facts

Narrow facts	Wider facts	Widest interpretation of facts
1. The case is only about dead snails	The case is about the presence of any animal	The case is concerned with liability for any foreign body
2. The material point is only about the sale of liquids	The material point is that the bottle was opaque; the liquid is irrelevant	The case is about articles in containers, not necessarily bottles
3. The defendant must be a manufacturer of ginger-beer	The defendant simply has to be a manufacturer of foodstuffs	Anyone dealing with an item for consumption is potentially liable
4. It is material that the plaintiff was a Scottish widow	It is material that the plaintiff was a woman	Any person may claim
5. A key point is that the snail was not visible.	The snail was not discoverable without damaging the container.	The defect must not be discoverable by anyone who could reasonably be expected to inspect the item.

Assessing whether facts are 'material' or not can therefore be a difficult exercise. There is no set formula because it depends upon how narrowly or widely you view each fact. The case of *Donoghue* v *Stevenson is* about dead snails, ginger-beer, and a Scottish widow, but if that was all it stood for as an authority we would wait centuries before those facts resurfaced in a new case. Meanwhile, the slightest difference in facts would mean that when your client asked you for advice and she was an English widow, the drink was milk, and a dead mouse had emerged you would be starting your argument afresh. Clearly you would abstract from *Donoghue* v *Stevenson* a slightly wider set of material facts.

In this light you might look again at *Grant* v *Australian Knitting Mills* in **Exercise 9** and consider whether the court took a narrow or wide view of the material facts in *Donoghue*. You can follow this up by looking at a textbook on torts to discover what has happened to the principles enunciated in a simple 1932 case about dead snails.

One method we have tried in discovering material facts, which has proved successful with students is to analyse the importance of facts by removing them from the description of the case in hand and ask whether this would have made a difference to the decision. If the reasoning would have been altered and the decision would consequently have been different, it seems highly likely that something hinged on the now-missing fact. Hence the removed fact would appear to be crucial to the formulation of the *ratio*.

6.10.1 Material Facts and the Question of 'What If [x] happened?'

We can attempt to put this into practice with one of the most famous cases in law: *Carlill* v *Carbolic Smoke Ball Co.* [1893] 1 QB 256. The defendants placed an advertisement in various newspapers relating to their product, 'The Carbolic Smoke Ball'. The advertisement claimed that by using the smoke ball properly the purchaser could avoid influenza, colds, and a whole variety of other complaints ranging from neuralgia to whooping cough. The claim was made that many thousands of these smoke balls had been sold and in no ascertained case was influenza contracted by those using the smoke ball. It was stated that a £100 reward would be paid to anyone who used the smoke ball properly and who still contracted these illnesses. The advertisement went on to say that, '£1,000 is deposited with the Alliance Bank, Regent Street, showing our sincerity in the matter'. Mrs Carlill read the advertisement, bought one of the smoke balls, used it as directed, and caught influenza. She claimed the £100 'reward'.

The issue was whether the advertisement constituted an offer which could be accepted, or whether it was only an 'advertising puff'. If it was an offer, and had been validly accepted by Mrs Carlill correctly using the smoke ball, there was a contract and she was entitled to the £100. One of the main arguments propounded by the defendants was that the vagueness of the document showed that no contract was ever intended.

When her claim came before the Court of Appeal she won her case. The question for us to address, then, is what should be the *ratio* of the case? For a true appreciation of this, of course, one would have to read the judgments. If you do read the case, note how Lindley and Bowen LJJ stress quite different matters in their judgments. Here, however, we are concerned only with the idea of 'material facts'. So, in formulating a *ratio*, which facts would be material? Under the test proposed above we will eliminate or alter some of the facts. If this alters the reasoning and result of the case we can regard that affected fact as material.

- **If the advertisement had appeared in a shop window only, would that have made a difference to either the result or the *ratio*?** Unlikely. The case acknowledges that the offer was made to the 'world at large'. A smaller audience is hardly relevant. However, the use of a newspaper might carry with it more credibility than a shop window and so exhibit a greater degree of seriousness.

- **If Mrs Carlill had not used the smoke ball as directed, would that have made a difference?** This must be material because Mrs Carlill would otherwise not, in law, have accepted the terms of the offer. Hence, whatever the status of the advertisement, there could have been no contract.

- **If the sums of money had been £10 and £100, would that have made a difference?** The usual response to this is that the amount is generally immaterial. However, some would argue that the large amount (for 1893) indicated a serious intent on the part of the defendant and so is material. For instance, one of our past students once argued persuasively that the converse was true: that the sums of £100 and £1,000 set against the cost of the smoke ball (ten shillings) showed that the tenor of the company's claim was so extravagant that it was only on the outer limit of being taken seriously. A smaller 'reward' might indicate sincerity more easily.

- **If the defendants had not deposited the £1,000, would that have made a difference?** Our experience in conducting this exercise is that this question causes a split in the student vote. Many feel that it is this element which lent intention to the defendants' claim. Others feel that the *promise* to deposit was the key point.

- **If the defendants had not promised that they had deposited a sum of money, would that have made a difference?** Most students draw the line here. The presence of the promise is seen as a vital factor in the case.

- **If Mrs Carlill had not known about the advertisement, but had bought the smoke ball anyway, would that have made a difference?** Here we enter the realms of the relevance of other case law. Other cases had tackled the problem as to whether one needs to know of an offer before performing an act in order to accept it legally. We put this question to reiterate that, though the analysis of material facts aids our understanding of the authority of a precedent, we must be aware that one case stands in relation to others, e.g., here *Williams* v *Carwardine* (1833) 5 C & P 566.

One final question, to show that legal analysis need not be merely an abstract exercise but relates to the society in which it operates.

- **Influenza, at the end of the century, was a more serious illness than it is now and large numbers of people died in the epidemics: so if the product claimed only to cure, say, bunions, do you think that that would have made a difference?** If you think there would have been a difference, is this because the question of seriousness and intent would have been affected; or might it be that the judicial attitude would have been different for reasons really unconnected with legal technicalities, i.e. the social setting?

One of our part-time degree students, a medical practitioner, once added a gloss to this: the smoke ball claimed to *prevent* an illness, whereas the 'bunion product' would be claiming to cure an illness. Thus, although concerned with a less serious topic, the bunion *cure* was less speculative and, as a *cure*, might be taken more seriously.

We have been doing what many judges in later cases do when reviewing earlier authorities. Later judges must assess the extent to which the facts of the original case fit the case before them. In doing this they interpret the *ratio* of the earlier case by evaluating the importance of the facts: placing them in a narrow or wide setting. What we have not the space to do, however, is to consider whether the order in which one removes the facts might matter, or the effect of removing groupings of facts. You might wish to consider this with *Carlill.*

6.11 What Can Happen to a Case?

There are seven main possibilities:

(a) The case may be followed in its strictest form, or applied, in later cases. As we noted in Chapter 5, under the doctrine of *stare decisis* the earlier case may be followed even though the later judges disagree with it.

(b) Sometimes the later court may be superior in status to the earlier court. If it follows the reasoning of the inferior court it is said to have *approved* the earlier case. Obviously it may equally disapprove of or overrule the earlier case. Disapproval may diminish the status of the earlier case. In the case of overruling, the earlier case ceases to be an authority of any sort (unless an even more superior court reinstates it at a later date). *Overruling* is not that common, at least where the principle has been established for some time; but it does happen. In *R v R* [1991] 3 WLR 767; [1991] 4 All ER 481, for instance, we saw in Chapter 5 that the House of Lords overruled a long line of case law on marital rape; in *Pepper (Inspector of Taxes) v Hart* [1992] 3 WLR 1032; [1993] 1 All ER 42 the House of Lords did the same in connection with the rules on statutory interpretation; in *Polkey v Dayton* [1987] AC 344; [1988] ICR 142 the House of Lords again overruled a decade's worth of Court of Appeal decisions on the question of determining fairness in an unfair dismissal.

(c) The term *overruling* tends to be applied when a court reviews previous precedents. However, if a court's decision is subject to an appeal the higher court obviously has to allow or dismiss the appeal. If the higher court reaches a different decision it is said to *overturn* or *reverse* the decision of the lower court. The higher court might not overturn the actual result of the lower court (i.e., X still wins) but may reformulate the law or approve of only part of the decision in the lower court.

(d) When the facts are found to be dissimilar the later court is said to *distinguish* the earlier case. The art of distinguishing cases is a major weapon used by advocates, especially when confronted with problems of *stare decisis* The attack is usually concentrated on showing a difference in the material facts of the two cases.

(e) The later case may decide that the decision in the earlier case was reached *per incuriam.*

(f) An Act of Parliament may change the law.

(g) The later case may state that the earlier case has no clear *ratio* and is therefore not binding. See on this *Esso* v *Commissioners of Customs and Excise,* detailed above.

EXERCISE 12 Tales from the grave

This exercise centres on the law of Succession, in particular the requirement for a testator to sign a will in order for it to be valid. The purpose of the exercise is to examine the possible ways you might attack an earlier precedent to show why it should not be applied in your case. Although we have used a particular case this is by way of illustration only. The techniques and questions raised here can be used in any exercise on Criminal Law, Torts, Contract, etc. where you are comparing cases.

The earlier precedent: In *Wood* v *Smith* [1992] 3 All ER 556 the testator made a will two days before he died which started, 'My will by Percy Winterborne...'. He did not sign his name at the foot of the will and when the witnesses pointed this out to him he replied that he had signed it at the top (referring to the opening statement) and that it could be signed anywhere. The will was contested on the ground that it was not validly executed. The Court of Appeal held that this was indeed a valid signature for the purposes of s. 9, Wills Act 1837 (as amended) so that the will was valid.

The relevant statute: Wills Act 1837, s. 9, states that no will shall be valid unless: '(a) it is in writing and signed by the testator... (b) it appears that the testator intended by his signature to give effect to the will; and (c) the signature is made or acknowledged by the testator in the presence of two or more witnesses present at the same time...'.

Your case: John Doe decided to make a will and purchased a 'will form' from a local shop. He started drafting it one day at work but was interrupted and did not complete the will until the following day. The first line of the will reads: 'John Doe—this is my last will and testament.' A witness pointed out to him that there was no signature on the will, but Doe said that this was all right since he had run out of space and provided wills were written on 'will forms' there was no need to sign them. The will was properly witnessed.

QUESTION

What devices (e.g. distinguishing the cases) could you use to argue that *Wood* v *Smith* does not apply to this case?

ANSWER

The best way to approach this exercise is to read *Wood* v *Smith* and all the cases it cites. You should concentrate on four things in particular:

(a) Which court are you in? This matters in relation to questions of *stare decisis.* Assume in this exercise that you are in the Court of Appeal.

(b) Exactly *why* did the Court of Appeal decide that the will was valid?

(c) What precise words did Scott LJ use to explain the decision?

(d) What differences in material facts can you find?

Whether or not you have had the opportunity to read the case, consider the following points in your argument:

Attack 1: Argue that the earlier case should not apply to the present one

(a) Is the case of *Doe* distinguishable on its facts from *Wood* v *Smith*?

(b) Is the case of *Doe* distinguishable as regards the issue of law raised in *Wood* v *Smith*?

Attack 2: If the case is not distinguishable, argue that *stare decisis* has no application

(c) Was there a clear *ratio* in *Wood* v *Smith*?

(d) Was the decision in *Wood* v *Smith* made *per incuriam*; or did it at least misinterpret the reasoning in earlier cases?

(e) When *Wood* v *Smith* had to decide matters that had not been raised in earlier cases, was the reasoning doubtful or unclear?

(f) Has *Wood* v *Smith* been doubted in other cases?

(g) Are there any decisions of the same level which conflict with *Wood* v *Smith*?

(h) Are there substantive conflicts in the reports of the case found in the All England Law Reports and the Weekly Law Reports?

(i) Were there any *obiter* statements which might help because they show that had the present facts arisen the court would have decided differently?

Attack 3: Argue that the case should be bypassed on more general grounds

(j) Has *Wood* v *Smith* been criticised by academic writers?

(k) Were the words used by Scott LJ clear as to why the will was valid; and were those words limited to the special circumstances of *Wood* v *Smith*?

(l) Have social conditions changed so radically that the earlier case should be doubted in a modern setting? (Not particularly useful in relation to *Wood* v *Smith* itself.)

One can see much of this at work in the cases flowing from *Donoghue* v *Stevenson*. However, by way of giving a different example we shall turn to the postal rules of acceptance in the Law of Contract to illustrate the development of a *ratio*.

6.12 The Postal Rule Cases

In **Chapter 5** we took some of the 'postal acceptance' cases as examples of how judges use earlier authorities. We attempted to show that the doctrine of judicial precedent is not simply a mechanical process of matching similarities and differences; cases can appear to be similar at first glance, without necessarily proving to be so. As promised, we return to these cases to illustrate the development of a rule.

The format for this part of the chapter is to combine a description of the development of a simple rule with some exercise-type questions. You should be able to formulate opinions on the information provided; but, as always, you might devise better answers if you read the cases themselves.

As we explained in **Chapter 5**, a contract is formed when there is an offer which is accepted, without the addition of new terms, by the other party. The general rule is that acceptance has to be communicated. If the offeree communicates by post, when does the acceptance take place? When the letter of acceptance is posted, or only when it arrives with the offeror?

The first 'postal acceptance' case (some would argue, the first case on what we now term the rules of 'offer and acceptance') was *Adams* v *Lindsell* (1818) 1 B & A 681. Here an offer was made by post to sell some wool. The letter was sent on 2 September, reply to be by return of post. The letter was mis-addressed and was not received until 5 September. It was accepted by post immediately. On 7 September the offeror had not received his reply by return of post and sold the wool elsewhere the day after. The letter of acceptance arrived on 9 September. Was there a contract established by these letters? If there was a contract then the seller was in breach because he had sold the wool to another person.

Held: There was a contract at the moment the offeree posted the letter of acceptance.

Questions:

• *How would you present the* ratio *of this case?*

• *Which facts should be seen as material; and how wide a description would you give to them?*

• *Should it be a material fact, for instance, that the offeror mis-addressed the offer letter, but that the letter of acceptance did eventually arrive?*

Possible Narrow *Ratio*: Where an offer to form a contract is sent by post but is late reaching its destination because the letter was mis-addressed by the offeror, the acceptance will be valid from the moment of posting provided the offeree complies with the relevant conditions of the offer and the acceptance eventually arrives.

Possible Wider *Ratio*: If the offeror chooses to use the post as a means of communicating an offer he must take the consequences. Thus, he will be bound by a postal acceptance from the moment the acceptance is posted.

Dunlop v *Higgins* (1848) 1 HLC 381; 9 ER 805 was the next case to deal with this problem, as we noted in **Chapter 5**. Dunlop wrote to Higgins offering to sell some iron; reply to be by return of post. The offer was accepted by Higgins in a letter but bad weather delayed the post. In the meantime there had been an increase in the price of iron. Dunlop maintained that because the reply had not been by return of post there was no contract—which would allow them to sell to other customers at the new price.

Held: The House of Lords decided that a contract existed when the letter of acceptance was posted.

Questions:

• *How would you present the* ratio *of this case?*

• *Which facts should be seen as material?*

• *Should it be a material fact that the parties were trading companies?*

• *How does this decision alter the original principle established in* Adams v Lindsell? *Is the 'postal rule' now (in 1848) wider or narrower? For instance, does it now matter that, in* Adams v Lindsell, *the offeror misaddressed the offer letter?*

Possible Narrow *Ratio*: Where an offer to form a contract is sent by post but the acceptance is late reaching its destination because of bad weather, the acceptance will be valid from the moment of posting provided there is a trade usage to use the post and the letter of acceptance is properly addressed.

Possible Wider *Ratio*: The use of the post is an exception to the rule that communication of acceptance must be effective. If the offeror chooses to use the post as a means of communicating an offer he must take the consequences. Thus, he will be bound by a postal acceptance from the moment it is posted provided the letter eventually arrives.

Effect on *Adams* v *Lindsell*: The narrow *ratio is* formulated differently and one would now (in 1848) need to ask whether the offeror's error in *Adams* v *Lindsell* is crucial to the point. The possible formulation of the wider *ratio* has not changed substantially. However, you will remember that in **Chapter 5** we saw that the judges in *Household Fire* v *Grant* (below) disagreed about the real meaning of *Dunlop* v *Higgins*.

In *Household Fire Insurance Co.* v *Grant* (1879) 4 Ex D 216 Grant made an application in writing to the company for shares. A deposit was paid, the remainder to be paid within twelve months. The company allotted shares to Grant and posted the allotment to him. The letter never arrived. The company later went into liquidation and the liquidator sought the balance of Grant's application which was still outstanding. Grant maintained he had no contract with the company because his offer had not been accepted. No contract would mean no liability to pay. The company maintained that the offer had been accepted when their letter of acceptance had been posted even though it never arrived.

Held: Grant was liable to pay the outstanding amount on the shares. The letter of acceptance was valid on posting even though it never arrived.

Questions:

• *How would you present the* ratio *of this case?*

• *Which facts should be seen as material?*

• *Should it be a material fact that the letter of acceptance never arrived?*

• *How does this decision alter the original principle established in* Adams *v* Lindsell? *Is the 'postal rule' now (in 1879) wider or narrower?*

Possible Narrow *Ratio*: Where an offer to form a contract is sent by post the acceptance will be valid from the moment of posting even though it never arrives, provided the letter of acceptance is properly addressed and the parties expressly or impliedly agree to the use of the post as a means of communication.

Possible Wider *Ratio*: If the offeror chooses to use the post as a means of communicating an offer he must take the consequences. The non-arrival of the letter of acceptance does not alter the general rule.

Effect on *Adams* v *Lindsell*: The narrow *ratio* is formulated differently and one would now (in 1879) need to ask whether the late arrival of the letter of acceptance in *Adams* v *Lindsell* was crucial to the point.

In *Henthorn* v *Fraser* [1892] 2 Ch 27 (CA) Henthorn visited Fraser's offices. Henthorn was given an option to purchase a house (i.e., an offer). Fraser withdrew the offer by letter, but not before Henthorn had accepted by post. So the letters crossed in the post. All letters arrived at their destinations on time.

Held: The acceptance was valid when posted. The rule was not limited to trade usage but, in the words of Lord Herschell, extended to: 'Where the circumstances are such that it [the use of the post] must have been within the contemplation of the parties'.

Questions:

• *How would you present the ratio of this case?*

• *Which facts should be seen as material?*

• *Should it be a material fact that Fraser was attempting to withdraw the offer by use of the post?*

• *How does this decision alter the original principle established in Adams v Lindsell? Is the 'postal rule' now (in 1892) wider or narrower? For instance, has the fact that the offer was not made by post made a difference?*

Possible Narrow *Ratio*: An acceptance which arrives at its destination will be valid from the moment of posting provided the letter of acceptance is properly addressed and the parties expressly or impliedly agree to the use of the post as a means of communication. This applies even where the offer was made in person and not by post.

Possible Wider *Ratio*: Where the circumstances allow for the use of the post as a means of communicating an acceptance the offeror must take the consequences. Where the parties live in different cities, there may be an indication that using the post is acceptable.

Effect on *Adams* v *Lindsell*: The narrow *ratio is* again formulated differently and one would now (in 1892) need to ask whether much of what actually happened in *Adams* v *Lindsell* is now regarded as crucial to the point.

Finally, for our purposes, we have the case of *Holwell Securities* v *Hughes* [1974] 1 WLR 155; [1974] 1 All ER 161. Here an offer of an option to purchase property was sent by post. It stated: 'The option shall be exercisable by notice in writing to the vendor within six months'. Holwell accepted the offer, properly addressing the letter; but the letter never arrived.

Held: There was no contract. The acceptance was not valid on posting. The specific wording of the offer letter showed that the acceptance was only valid when delivered to the offeror. The postal rules were held not to apply in all cases where there is postal acceptance: '[They] probably do not operate if their application would produce manifest inconvenience and absurdity'. *Adams* v *Lindsell* was distinguished.

Questions:

• *How would you present the ratio of this case?*

• *Which facts should be seen as material?*

• *How does this decision alter the original principle established in Adams v Lindsell? Is the 'postal rule' now (in 1974) wider or narrower? For instance, can we now say that the postal rules can be excluded? If so, do we know which other forms of wording will be effective?*

Possible Narrow *Ratio*: Where an option (offer) is granted in writing and specifies that the acceptance must be 'by notice in writing to the vendor' an acceptance which is never delivered will not be valid from the moment of posting.

Possible Wider *Ratio*: The language used in the offer may be such that the express terms override the postal rules. The postal rules are rules of convenience only.

We can now pose four questions to conclude this discussion:

(a) If you were writing a textbook on the Law of Contract how would you present a general principle which would summarise these cases and describe the 'postal rules of acceptance'?

(b) If the cases had occurred in a different sequence, do you think the rule might have been differently formulated?

(c) Should these rules, by analogy, be applied to other forms of communication, e.g. telex, fax, or messenger rider?

(d) *Adams* v *Lindsell* was the seminal case from which all the other cases cited are directly descended. Do you think the judges in *Adams* v *Lindsell* could have forecast how their judgment would be applied in those later cases? After all, much of what seemed to matter in 1818 has probably disappeared. So is the position analogous to Dr Jacob Bronowski's comment on the 'Ascent of Man': that the ancestor of man two million years ago would not recognise us today as his own descendant?

6.13 The 'Uncertainty Principle' of Cases

Our final comment on the development of case law brings us to a theory in physics known as the 'Heisenberg Uncertainty Principle'. One of the themes we have tried to develop throughout this chapter is that later cases often change our perceptions of earlier cases. This often causes students problems, but, as we have said, discerning the *ratio* of a case is not like a hunt for buried treasure; it is one of interpretation and argument.

The problem is not unique to legal studies. The German physicist, Werner Heisenberg, argued in 1927 that as soon as you set about investigating an object you alter its state. If, for instance, you try to measure the temperature of a hot bath then the introduction of the thermometer alters the temperature—however slightly. The same is true with reading legal cases: the supposed *ratio* of an earlier case is open to reinterpretation by lawyers in later cases. Once the earlier case is looked at in the light of a new set of facts the perception of the case may be altered. Further, the way you phrase your question as to the meaning of the earlier case has an impact—which facts you concentrate on; which judicial phrase you subject to scrutiny.

In *Adams* v *Lindsell*, for instance, there is a marked difference in asking: (1) is the case authority for the rule that acceptance does not always have to be communicated?; and (2) is the case authority for the proposition that an offeror must always accept the risk for any mistakes he makes in *his* communication? The question posed as to the relevance of

Adams v *Lindsell* will depend upon the facts of the case in front of you now and the issues thereby raised.

EXERCISE 13 **Parking tickets and jiffy bags**

Q1.   Please read the facts of *Thornton* v *Shoe Lane Parking* and formulate a *ratio* for the case.

Question 2 follows the case description. It would be best if you could read the actual reports of the cases. Failing that, however, we provide a short summary of the issues raised.

Thornton v Shoe Lane Parking
[1971] 2 QB 163; [1971] 1 All ER 686.

The plaintiff drove into the entrance to the defendant's automatic car park. A notice outside stated: 'All cars parked at owner's risk.' He took a ticket from the machine, the automatic barrier lifted, and he drove into the garage. He looked at the ticket to see the time printed on it. The plaintiff also noticed some printed words on the ticket which he did not read. When he went to collect the car an accident occurred in which he suffered personal injuries, partly through the negligence of the defendant garage.

The defendants admitted fault but relied on the ticket which contained the clause: '... *issued subject to the conditions of issue as displayed on the premises.*' These conditions were displayed on the back of the ticket; they were lengthy, and excluded liability on the part of the garage for loss or damage to customers' property, or personal injury, howsoever caused. These, said the defendant, were contractual clauses which bound the plaintiff.

Mocatta J held the defendants liable. They appealed.

Lord Denning reviewed the relevant cases, some of which are noted here:

• *Parker* v *South Eastern Railway* (1877) 2 CPD 416. The plaintiff deposited a bag in a railway cloak-room. He was handed a ticket on which were the words 'see back'; on the back there were printed conditions excluding liability for loss or damage. The bag was lost. The Court of Appeal held that the key questions were:

(a)   Did the plaintiff read the clause?

(b)   Did the railway company do what was reasonably sufficient to give the plaintiff notice of the clause?

• *Olley* v *Marlborough Court Ltd* [1949] 1 KB 532; [1949] 1 All ER 127. It was held that a notice in a hotel bedroom which excluded liability for damage to guests' luggage was not valid as the contract had been made in the lobby of the hotel so that notice of the clause came too late.

Lord Denning dismissed the appeal. He indicated that the 'ticket cases' such as *Parker* were based on the theory that the customer, on being handed the ticket, could refuse it and decline to enter the contract on those terms. However real that theory was, it could not apply to a ticket which was issued by an automatic machine: 'The customer pays his money and gets his ticket. He cannot get his money back. He may protest to the machine, even swear at it; but it will remain unmoved.'

Lord Denning applied the reasoning given in *Olley* v *Marlborough Court*. In *Thornton* the offer was contained in the notice at the entrance giving the charges for garaging and saying 'at owner's risk'. The acceptance took place when the customer put his money into the slot. The terms of the offer contained in the notice placed on or near the machine could be binding only if they were sufficiently brought to his notice before the contract was concluded. So, once the customer had accepted the offer, a contract was concluded on the terms known to exist which could not then be altered.

Parker v *South Eastern Railway* meant that, unless the customer knows that the ticket is issued subject to a clause to be found on the back of the ticket, or the company did what was reasonably sufficient to give him notice of it, the company cannot avoid liability by relying on the later exclusion clause.

Counsel for the defendants admitted here that the defendants did not do what was reasonably sufficient to give the plaintiff notice of the exempting condition. Lord Denning held that the exclusion clause was:

> so wide and so destructive of rights that the court should not hold any man bound by it unless it is drawn to his attention in the most explicit way ... In order to give sufficient notice, it would need to be printed in red ink with a red hand pointing to it, or something equally startling.

Megaw LJ also dismissed the appeal. He declined to comment on when the contract was concluded. As regards the other points, His Lordship was in general agreement with Lord Denning MR. Under the three conditions noted in *Parker*, he concluded that the plaintiff in *Thornton* did not know of any printing on the ticket or, therefore, there were any contractual conditions. As well as this, however, His Lordship laid stress on the fact that the conditions in this contract contained the sorts of restrictions that were unusual. Thus:

> at least where the particular condition relied on involves a sort of restriction that is not shown to be usual in that class of contract, a defendant must show that his intention to attach an unusual condition *of that particular nature* was fairly brought to the notice of the other party. (emphasis added)

Megaw LJ thus linked the type of clause in question (whether it was an unusual or usual clause in this type of contract) to the amount of effort needed on the defendant's part to bring the clause to the notice of the customer.

Sir Gordon Willmer agreed with Lord Denning and Megaw LJ, saying: 'any attempt to introduce conditions after the irrevocable step has been taken of causing the machine to operate must be doomed to failure'.

EXERCISE 13 Parking tickets and jiffy bags

Q2: Read this second case—*Interfoto Picture Library Ltd* v *Stiletto Visual Programmes Ltd* [1988] 1 All ER 348; [1988] 2 WLR 615—and:

(a) **decide whether the ratio of *Thornton* applies;**

(b) **reach a decision on the *Interfoto* case;**

(c) **formulate a *ratio* for your decision, either applying the *Thornton* ratio (in whole or part) or distinguishing *Thornton* on the facts.**

The defendant ordered certain photographic transparencies from the plaintiff. The photographs were consigned in a jiffy bag to the company messenger with the 'delivery note'. The defendant's manager ignored the note but, impressed by the contents of the bag, telephoned his acceptance.

There were a number of conditions contained in the delivery note. Condition 2 set the daily charge for retaining the transparencies beyond the stipulated date of return. These charges were exorbitant, representing a figure ten times higher than that charged by other comparable agencies. The central issue was whether condition 2 was enforceable by the plaintiffs.

We provide no answer for this exercise except to indicate one or two salient points. The first is that the *Interfoto* case is interesting because it posed the question whether the logic used for a number of years and in a number of cases regarding one type of clause—one which excluded liability—could be applied to a 'similar' type of clause: one which sought to impose onerous terms on the other party. The second is that if you read the case in full you will see that there were only two judges in the Court of Appeal. It is as well that they agreed with each other as to the outcome of the case.

The final point is that the judges did not fully agree with each other. The decision reached was the same: that condition 2 was not valid; but the reasoning employed by the judges differed greatly. Dillon LJ took a conventional line of arguing from precedents and drew a correlation between 'exclusion' clauses and 'onerous' clauses. Bingham LJ took a wider, more European, approach and looked to general notions of 'acting in good faith' to hold that the clause could not stand. This conceptual style of reasoning is very interesting; especially as there is no formula for defining 'good faith' in the English Law of Contract.

To see how academics reacted to this case we strongly recommend you to read the contrasting views seen in the following articles: Chandler and Holland, (1988) 104 LQR, 359; McLean, (1988) 47 CLJ, 172; MacDonald, (1988) LMCLQ, 294.

To see how the case has been employed in later cases, see *Circle Freight International Ltd v Medeast Gulf Exports Ltd* [1988] 2 Lloyd's Rep 427. This case involved two businesses which had frequently dealt with each other on standard terms. These terms, which included an exclusion clause, had never been read by the party who suffered loss. Were these terms effectively incorporated into the contract?

6.14 CONCLUSION

Discovering the *ratio* of a case and predicting how that *ratio* will be interpreted and applied in the future are some of the skills with which a lawyer must come to grips. There is no magic formula for acquiring these skills; they develop from practice. In turn, that practice must have some thought behind it. Reading a coaching text on your favourite sport will not, in itself, make you an Olympic athlete; and practising without analysing your play will get you only marginally further.

The key point we wish to make with this chapter is that there is nothing resembling a template that can be placed over a decision to highlight and reveal the *ratio* of the case. Whether it is a student, a practitioner, or a judge reading the case the exercise is still one of interpretation; and that form of exercise extends to persuasive precedents as well as binding ones.

Perhaps the most helpful thing we can offer is to address some of the most commonly-raised questions we have had from students over the years. In the table below we have listed these student questions in the left-hand column and their provided some short answers opposite.

Does each case have one defined *ratio*?	**No.** There is no "fixed" *ratio* to a case, though there may be a generally accepted one (e.g., to be found in textbooks or in later cases).
Can a case stand for more than one legal principle?	**Yes.** A case may contain more than one *ratio*. This depends on what part of the case you are examining and why you are analysing it.
What is the make-up of a *ratio*?	In general terms the *ratio* of a case is made up of a legal principle based on: (i) existing case law prior to the case in hand; (ii) the material facts of the case; (iii) the decision in the case.
Materiality: do judges make this obvious?	**No.** Judges sometimes expressly state that they regard particular facts as "material". But, most often, you have to work this out by inference from the judgment.
Can later courts re-assess the importance of facts?	**Yes.** Facts may not appear to be "material" until looked at later in comparison to a new case, i.e. even if a judge says that certain facts are material that does not determine the status of those facts forever. The status of those facts can (*sometimes*) be re-assessed in later cases (see the "negligent driving" example above and the development of "non-natural use" in *Rylands v. Fletcher*).
Can later courts promote other facts to the status of being classed as "material"?	**Yes.** other facts which did not appear that important at first sight in the earlier case might be seen to be material when that case is later analysed.
What is meant by "Abstraction of facts"?	Facts may be viewed as narrow or representative of something wider (see the "Scottish widow" or "dead snail" examples in *Donoghue v. Stevenson*). **This is the basis of arguing that an earlier case should be "applied" or "distinguished".**
Can you have different "levels" of *ratio*?	**Yes.** In the same way that one fact may be taken as a literal example (ginger-beer) or representational (drink) or more abstract (consumable item, or even any product), so too can the *ratio* of a case exist at different levels.
Who creates the "legal principles"?	Cases do not exist in a legal vacuum. It is very unlikely that the case you are examining was the first of its kind. There will be a whole history of similar cases before it. These have to be looked at, as the legal principle involved in those cases will have helped to determine the "materiality" of the facts in the case being examined. You need to know **why** facts were regarded as material and the extent to which *stare decisis* has influenced the judge's analysis in order to formulate a *ratio*.
Is it important *how* the judge expresses the legal principle?	**Vital:** The exact words used by a judge are important. The judge may have thought the words used were clear, but all words are open to interpretation.
What happens when you have more than one judgment in a case?	Each judge in a case may give a judgment (called an "opinion" in the House of Lords). Each judgment given will contain a *ratio*. The overall *ratio* of the case is derived from the *rationes* of the majority judgments. Thus, if there can be argument as to what the *ratio* of a single judge is, this is made even more a matter of interpretation and argument when trying to formulate a "general" *ratio* of the combined judgments. Differences in the *rationes* of judges (even those who agree on the overall result) often relate to different emphasis being placed on material facts or the use of particular words to describe the legal position.

REFERENCES

BINGHAM, T. (2000), *The Business of Judging: Selected Essays and Speeches* (Oxford: Oxford University Press).

*CROSS, R. (1991), *Precedent in English Law* (4th edn., Oxford: Clarendon Press).

DWORKIN, R. (1987), *Law's Empire* (London: Fontana).

GOODHART, A. (1931), *Essays in Jurisprudence and the Common Law* (Cambridge: Cambridge University Press).

—— (1959), 'The *Ratio Decidendi* of a Case', 22 *Modern Law Review* 117.

LLEWELLYN, K. (1960), *The Bramble Bush* (Chicago, Ill.: University of Chicago Press).

MACCORMICK, N. (1987), 'Why Cases have *Rationes* and What these Are', in L. Goldstein (ed.), *Precedent in Law* (Oxford: Clarendon Press).

MONTROSE, J. (1957), 'The *Ratio Decidendi* of a Case', 20 *Modern Law Review* 587.

STONE, J. (1959), 'Ratio of the *Ratio Decidendi*', 22 *Modern Law Review* 597.

TUROW, S. (1988), *One L: What They Really Teach You at Harvard Law School* (London: Sceptre).

TWINING, W., and MIERS, D. (1991) and (1999), *How to Do Things With Rules* (3rd and 4th edns., London: Weidenfeld Nicolson).

7
Making Sense of Statutes

7.1 Introduction

On the whole, statutes are not a fun read. Worse still, they are written in a style and format quite different from those of many other documents (though insurance documents and many credit card agreements are written in similarly dense styles). The language used is traditional (if not archaic) and often has a very flat-prose style and a dependence on complex phrasing and language (see Maughan & Webb, 1995:226–35). But, of course, an Act is not meant to be a piece of amusing literature; it is not designed to entertain but to declare the law on a particular topic.

The aim of this chapter, therefore, is to introduce you to the techniques and problems of analysing the **structure** of statutes. Making sense of statutes (or, at least, some statutes) can be a real problem for students, practitioners and judges alike. So, to being with, we need to look at how statutes are set out, what tricks are employed, what particular catch-phrases mean, and how to make sense of the opaque language often used. For an extremely good explanation of how we inherited the system we have today and also why 'The language of our legislation cannot be reduced to baby talk for consumption by the masses', see Hunt (2002, 24)

In **Chapter 3** we dealt with the basics of what statutes look like, e.g., how sections are organised and the use of subsections, schedules, long titles, etc. and in **Chapter 8** we will explore the techniques used to *interpret* words in a statute. But in this chapter we are concerned with finding the best way to read, understand and analyse the structure used—in other words, how to work your way through what is often a very complex layout. The problem arises because there are always many different ways of explaining even the simplest idea and what is an acceptable arrangement of the material to one person is confusion to another.

7.2 Drafting Styles

Imagine you have been given the job of drafting a rule defining when a ball (in whatever sport) is 'in' play or 'out of' play. First, you need instructions from the rules committee as to what it wants: does it want a ball which is 'on the line' to be in play or out of play? (it varies with different sports, e.g. in football and tennis the line is in play but it golf the line itself is out of bounds). Let us assume here that the line is 'in play'. So, how could we put this into rule form?

The simplest method must be something like: 'A ball is always in play until it has completely crossed the line'. Rule 22 of the Code of the International Tennis Federation puts it like this: 'A ball falling on a line is regarded as falling in the Court bounded by that line.' FIFA's rules for football (law 9) talk of a ball being in play until it has 'wholly crossed the [line]' but add 'whether on the ground or in the air'. But this still only provides us with a very simple formulation; it does not cover exceptions and does not add definitions. So a draftsman has to consider how these extra elements will be woven into the document. Should he or she start with a general point and then add variations,; or maybe begin with definitions and then go on to the rule itself; or deal with each individual aspect of the rule bit by bit?

It is often quite easy to explain rules to someone orally because you can keep going back over points of confusion, or put things in slightly different ways. In a written document such devices are not available. So, a draftsman has to spell out the idea as fully as possible.

Here is an example of how two different draftsmen might use quite dissimilar methods of drafting to convey the same message using (very nearly) the same words but arranging them quite differently.

First drafting style	Second drafting style
Section 1: Subject to sections 2 and 3 of this Act a ball is always in play until the whole of the ball has crossed the relevant line forming the border of the [playing field] [pitch] [court]	*Section 1:* A ball is always in play until the whole of the ball has crossed the relevant line forming the border of the [playing field] [pitch] [court] ....
Section 2: For the purposes of section 1, and subject to section 3(1), the whole of the ball has crossed the relevant line only when it has cleared the outside boundary of the relevant line.	*Section 2:* For the purposes of section 1 'whole of the ball' shall mean the full circumference of the ball, as would be evident if viewed directly from above.
Section 3: For the purposes of this Act: (1) 'ball' shall mean only the official measurements as authorised by [the governing];	*Section 3:* A ball will remain in play unless and until: (a) it has been propelled by a player across any line of the playing area; or (b) it has been struck by a player and rebounds from the referee so as to cross the line.
(2) 'line' shall mean only the official measurements as authorised by [the governing body], these being set out in Schedule 1 to this Act.	Provided always that the whole of the ball, as defined in section 4, has not cleared the outside boundary of the relevant line.
(3) any reference to the term 'whole of the ball' shall be construed as relating to the full circumference of the ball as would be evident if viewed directly from above.	
(4) a ball is: (a) in play unless and until it has been propelled by a player across any line of the playing area or it has been struck by a player and rebounds from the referee so as to cross the line; but (b) is out of play where the whole of the ball has crossed the line.	
	Section 4: For the purposes of this Act the words 'ball' and 'line' shall mean only the official measurements as authorised by [the governing body], these being set out in Schedule 1 to this Act.

Note that the first style uses phrases such as 'subject to...' in section 1 and both styles use 'for the purposes of...', together with cross-references to later sections or schedules in the Act. This is not everyday speech. Both versions also attempt to state general points and then move on to the specific definitions etc. The second version does this by avoiding using 'subject to...' and similar phrases, but it has still has to include cross-references and has also had to include an additional section. In the end, both these methods of explanation say the same thing and each of them uses techniques common in drafting statutes. You will encounter various forms of drafting throughout your studies and in practice and we therefore aim in this chapter to give you some clues as to how to recognise and utilise them.

A good place to start with real drafting practices is with a fairly straightforward statute, namely the Theft Act 1968. Section 1 is headed 'Basic Definition of Theft' and it reads as follows:

> (1) A person is guilty of theft if he dishonestly appropriates property belonging to another with the intention of permanently depriving the other of it; and 'thief' and 'steal' shall be construed accordingly.
>
> (2) It is immaterial whether the appropriation is made with a view to gain, or is made for the thief's own benefit.
>
> (3) The five following sections of this Act shall have effect as regards the interpretation and operation of this section (and, except as otherwise provided by this Act, shall apply only for purposes of this section).

The language used is not particularly complicated, but there are a number of technicalities and hidden depths. For instance, what is meant by 'dishonestly'? What does 'appropriation' mean? Where would you find the answers to these questions? In one sense these are matters of interpretation and therefore fall within the province of **Chapter 8**, but, in structural terms, the Theft Act 1968 is set out in a very helpful way, so that all the words in section 1 are expanded upon in subsequent sections. Therefore, to understand section 1 you need to 'read into' it all the definitions in sections 2–6.

For instance section 3 says that 'appropriation' means:

> (1) Any assumption by a person of the rights of an owner amounts to an appropriation, and this includes, where he has come by the properly (innocently or not) without stealing it, any later assumption of a right to it by keeping or dealing with it as owner....

Thus, this meaning of 'appropriation' has to be 'read into' the definition of theft in section 1(1). Equally, section 4 tells you what the word 'property' means in this context; section 5 deals with 'belonging to another'; and section 6 covers 'with the intention of permanently depriving the other of it'.

This is a common method of drafting statutes. Other, similar methods employ detailed explanations within the section itself, or specific definition sections elsewhere in the Act, or more detail in the schedules. Thus, in section 8 of the Theft Act 1968, when the section uses the word 'steal', then, without anything else appearing in the statute to the contrary, that word takes on the meaning given to it in section 1 above, even though there is no specific cross-reference. Section 8 states: 'A person is guilty of robbery if he steals, and immediately before or at the time of doing so, and in order to do so, he uses force on any person or puts or seeks to put any person in fear of being then and there subjected to force.'

We should also note that many draftsmen use words knowing that there is a body of case law which defines these words and upon which judges will rely, so no explanation is offered in the statute itself, e.g. where an Act uses the word 'offer' in a contractual setting the court will presume it bears the meaning derive from hundreds of years of case law (see the case of *Fisher* v *Bell* [1961] 1 QB 394; [1960] 3 All ER 731 as a good example—or *R* v *Collins* [1973] QB 100; [1972] 2 All ER 1105 on the word 'trespass' in section 9 of the Theft Act 1968, which concerns burglary).

One tends to be more sympathetic with the problems facing the draftsmen when one tries to draft a document oneself. It is worth spending a few minutes on the next exercise.

EXERCISE 14   The minimum speed limit

In this exercise you are a Parliamentary draftsman appointed to deal with the problems of slow-moving traffic. Assume that you have been instructed to draft legislation which will introduce a 'minimum speed limit' in country areas and on motorways. The purpose of this exercise is:

(a) to explore the style of wording you use—how many clauses; how concise the wording;

(b) to see how difficult it is to anticipate all the possible situations that may occur.

ANSWER

There is of course no single right answer to this problem. Instead here are a few situations which we think your legislation should allow for. Glancing through them you may feel your drafting covers them, more or less. Our experience is that it is a sobering (or exasperating) exercise to get a friend to compare the situations with your piece of draftsmanship. The chances are that at one stage (at least) you will find yourself saying: 'Yes, but I meant it to cover that...' or 'Of course it covers that'. But does it?

Consider whether your legislation covers: stopping at junctions or traffic lights; stopping at hazards such as temporary roadworks; breakdowns; having to slow down because of moving hazards such as tractors; separate criteria for tractors and other agricultural vehicles (if so, how do you define an agricultural vehicle?). For that matter, how did you define 'vehicle'? Did you have the same speed limits for different roads, e.g., the B4106, the A4018, and the M5? Did weather conditions come into the definition, such as fog or bad visibility?

We will examine some of the problems of structure in more depth shortly. Before that, however, it is worth noting one or two points on why statutes are drafted this way.

7.3 The Problems of Drafting Statutes in English Law

Although for constitutional purposes primary legislation is created by Parliament, the actual drafting of statutes is the province of civil servants. Most of the work is done by the various Government departments together with Parliamentary draftsmen in the Office of Parliamentary Counsel. There are only about thirty of these specialist draftsmen. Their job is to translate the political objectives behind a proposed Bill into the appropriate legal form, to assess its impact upon the existing law, and to make sure that changes to the existing law are effected properly. This is a demanding task.

So, how do the draftsmen approach that task? In a major article published some years ago Francis Bennion (1978), a former Parliamentary Counsel, identified nine targets of the draftsman's work; these he describes as:

(a) **legal effectiveness:** the draftsman must take sometimes very generalised political policy and convert that into a legal form without losing sight of its intended aims. This is not always straightforward, particularly as one Bill may reflect a range of intentions, not all of which may be equally practicable.

(b) **procedural legitimacy:** the Bill must comply with the formal procedures for creating legislation laid down by both Houses of Parliament.

(c) **timeliness:** the draftsmen are constrained by the fact that they must work within the time constraints created by the Parliamentary timetable. A Government wishing to push through large quantities of reforming legislation will inevitably impose considerable pressure on the draftsmen thereby. The difficulty is compounded by the fact that most people, including the draftsmen, are inclined to underestimate the amount of time it takes to draft an Act. The late Professor Driedger (1976, p. xix) cited one such incident in Canada where a government department requested a Bill within three weeks; gave public assurances that it would be ready on time, and then had to wait the eighteen months it took an experienced draftsman (working full-time) to prepare the Bill.

The lack of time may mean that there is not only an increased risk of making errors under pressure, but also more generally a lack of opportunity finally to review draft legislation with a view to tidying up its structure, or simplifying its language, with the result that Bills entering Parliament may be, as one Member of Parliament has put it, 'ill-formed, ugly or premature progeny': Rhys Williams (1987:138)

(d) **certainty:** (see below)

(e) **comprehensibility:** (see below)

(f) **acceptability:** the language of legislation has to be 'acceptable'. By this Bennion means that it must obey the rules traditionally prescribed. These were essentially laid down in the latter half of the nineteenth century, at the time the Office of Parliamentary Counsel was created. Bennion himself once drew considerable criticism from within the House of Commons for using the phrase 'tried his best' rather than the more conventional 'used his best endeavours'.

(g) **brevity:** one should not necessarily assume that brevity and clarity go hand in hand. One of the lessons we have already learned from attempts to develop 'plain English' styles of legal document drafting is that it may take *more* words, not fewer, to increase the clarity of legislation. However, as we shall argue below, in terms of brevity, there is little comparison between most English and Continental drafting. The latter seems frequently to achieve similar ends with notably less verbiage.

(h) debatability: legislation should ideally be framed in such a way that the general principles are debatable in Parliament. This requires Counsel to consider carefully both the complexity and even the order of clauses.

(i) legal compatibility: the draftsman must finally work out how the proposals fit in with the existing law. This apparently simple statement disguises a number of difficulties. First, the draftsman needs to know what the existing law actually says. In that respect, the briefings from the instructing department are often an essential starting point, but any draftsman would then engage in research to determine not just what the law says but *how* it says it. As a general principle, a draftsman ought to attempt to use the same form of wording as appears in other legislation covering the same subject matter. With old or already complex legislation, this principle may act as a further constraint on the draftsman, as he may be obliged to import the same archaic terminology or complex concepts into the amending Act. Secondly, the draftsman should also indicate the manner in which and extent to which existing legislation is amended by the proposed Bill. This often requires further, sometimes difficult, research.

Although we can describe points (a)–(i) as targets they are not all mutually compatible; as a result, drafting tends to be rather like negotiating a path through a maze of both political and technical legal constraints. All of these points are important but, for the purposes of this chapter, we will concentrate on 'certainty' and 'comprehensibility'.

7.3.1 Certainty

This is probably one of the most debatable points about English drafting. Although it is desirable that a provision should normally only have one clear meaning it is an ideal that is often difficult to achieve for a number of reasons

(a) As we sought to show in **Chapter 4** the English language itself is not always a very precise tool. This problem has to be confronted the draftsman who is required to make his meaning as clear and certain as possible. In achieving certainty the draftsman has to bear in mind the ordinary or, if necessary, technical meaning of the term he wishes to use. He must also be aware of the approach that the courts are likely to take when approaching questions of interpretation. Let us illustrate each of these points.

For instance, using a Thesaurus, look up any word, e.g. *invention*. The range of synonyms is: contraption, design, device, discovery, gadget, fabrication, development, fantasy, fiction, illusion, creativity, ingenuity, innovation, inventiveness, originality.

But if you perform the same exercise with one of the words in the above list, e.g., *fabrication* then you get a further list: falsehood, fib, lie prevarication, story, construction, manufacture, production.

A sentence in a statute that therefore reads:

An employee must surrender to his employer any *invention* made in the course of his employment is unlikely to mean

> An employee must surrender to his employer any *fantasy* made in the course of his employment

but it could mean

> An employee must surrender to his employer any *fabrication* made in the course of his employment

or

> An employee must surrender to his employer any *design* made in the course of his employment

A design and a fabrication are not, however, the same thing, even accepting that 'fabrication' does not mean 'lie' or 'fib' in this context. 'Design' and 'fabrication', for instance, would have a different meaning in the fashion industry from that in the computer industry when applied to any definition of 'invention'. Clearly, the context of the word in the statute and the problem before the court must affect the meaning and accuracy of the application of the word.

Anticipating the reaction of the courts is not always easy. The word, or wording, does not even have to be complicated to cause problems. The statute can be about a very simple topic, and yet lead to many odd cases. Consider, as an example, the Wills Act 1837, section 9. This section originally stated that the signature to a will must appear at 'the foot or end' of the will. But did this mean the physical positioning at the end of a document, or that the signature was the last thing written on the will, i.e. that the signature could appear anywhere as long as, in terms of time, it came at the end of making the will? Signatures appeared everywhere on wills because people always manage to do strange things. Some judges were lenient as to the physical positioning of the signatures; others were not (we will concentrate on how you can get variations in interpretation in the next chapter). In 1852 the Act had to be amended to read that the signature should come:

> At or after, or following, or under, or beside, or opposite to the end of the will, that it shall be apparent on the face of the will that the Testator intended to give effect to the will.

The wording to this section was changed again in 1982, by the Administration of Justice Act of that year. It became:

> No will shall be valid unless... it appears that the testator intended by his signature to give effect to the will...

This removed any reference to the position of the signature, so that should have resolved all the earlier problems. Nevertheless, the case of *Wood* v *Smith* [1993] Ch 90, [1992] 3 All ER 556, C.A. shows that, even with the amended wording, the judges can still manage to disagree about the effect of the section. In this case the deceased had signed his will at the top, then written out the various bequests, and finally had it signed by his witnesses. At first instance, the High Court held that it was not a valid will. It was the natural construction of the words of the Act that the maker should sign the will *after* making the various dispositions, not before. There has to be something in the nature of a disposition before a will exists and can be signed. The Court of Appeal took a rather different view of the issue. It decided that a signature did *not* have to be appended after the dispositive

provisions of the will had been written, provided that the writing of the will and its signing by the testator constituted 'one operation' (a concept which is barely defined by the
courts). So, on this point the High Court was overruled, since there was no doubt on the
facts that the testator had completed his will as a single operation. In its final version
Wood v *Smith* thus appears to have done what the legislation intended, and, for the majority of cases, the decision shifts the court's focus away from the position of the signature,
and on to the issue of testamentary intent

(b) The desire for certainty frequently leads to undue verbosity, precisely because the
draftsman is seeking to delineate meaning to such a high degree. That is why we find examples of such extremely dense prose as section 8.16(1) of the Social Security Act 1975:

> If a person is more than 5 years below pensionable age on the qualifying date in any period of inter-
> ruption of employment then, subject to the following provisions of this section, in respect of every day
> of that period in respect of which he is entitled to an invalidity pension, he shall also be entitled to an
> invalidity allowance at the appropriate weekly rate specified in relation thereto in Schedule 4, Part I,
> paragraph 3; and 'the qualifying date' means the first day in that period (whether before the coming
> into force of this section or later) which is a day of incapacity for work or such earlier day as may be
> prescribed.

It is not exactly light reading. If we look at what makes it so difficult, we can see a number
of factors. One is the cross-referencing to other technical issues, both implicit in the use of
terms such as 'pensionable age' or 'relevant amount', which are defined elsewhere in the
Act, and explicitly in the reference to Schedule 4. A second is the actual length of the sentence, and the number of dependent clauses it contains. By the time we reach the end there
is a real risk that we will have forgotten what the subsection first set out to do (i.e., define
entitlement to invalidity allowance). The third factor is the use of terms which would be
redundant in ordinary usage, but are used to emphasise the interrelationship between different parts of an Act. Here there are two such examples in the phrases 'subject to the following provisions of this section' (could we not work that out by reading it?) and 'specified
in relation thereto' (if it was not so specified, why mention it in the first place?)

The poor quality drafting of section 16 has been acknowledged, and when that provision was consolidated into the Social Security Contributions and Benefits Act 1992
(s. 34), it was amended to read:

> (1) If a person is more than 5 years below pensionable age on the qualifying date in any period of in-
> terruption of employment then, subject to the following provisions of this section, in respect of every
> day of that period in respect of which he is entitled to an invalidity pension, he shall also be entitled to
> an invalidity allowance at the appropriate weekly rate specified in Schedule 4, Part I, paragraph 3.
>
> (2) In this section 'the qualifying date' means the first day in the period of interruption of employment
> (whether that day falls before the coming into force of this section or later) which is a day of incapacity
> for work or such earlier day as may be prescribed.

Note the main changes that have been made. The language and structure still does not
make easy reading, but then this is a complex topic.

(c) Sometimes it may happen that a provision is left deliberately vague. As Bennion
points out this may well happen where the framers of the Act are themselves uncertain of

how to handle it. Cynically, one might say that the courts are simply burdened with the responsibility. The most common 'signs' for this can be seen in phrases imposing duties on people such as factory owners 'where reasonably practicable' or where matters of judgment are expressly left to 'the court's discretion'.

7.3.2 Comprehensibility

Despite what we have just said, draftsmen do aim for legislation that is understandable. However, in so doing they tend to have a specialist audience in mind, in that legislation is designed to be read first and foremost by lawyers. Ideally it should also be comprehensible to Members of Parliament, who may not share the same degree of expertise as a legal audience. How effectively it reaches the latter audience is certainly debatable (e.g. Rhys Williams, 1987:140). What is beyond doubt is that legislation is not drafted for lay people to read and understand with ease.

Comprehension also implies some degree of clarity and logical structure. We have already illustrated how linguistic problems affect clarity. However clarity can also be influenced by the overall structure of an Act, particularly in the way it is broken down into composite parts and sections. In our system, it is considered good practice that draftsmen should start with matters of general principle, before getting buried in consequential detail. Yet this principle seems to be frequently overlooked. Sir William Dale, one of the sterner critics of English drafting, has cited a number of examples of poor arrangement in an article published some twelve years ago. One of those Acts, the Unfair Contract Terms Act 1977 (UCTA), was briefly introduced in **Chapter 3**. According to Dale (1981:148–9) UCTA is drafted quite illogically. Section 1 of the Act is purely a definition section, which makes no sense at all until we have read the rest of the Act. Further, the key provisions, regarding exclusion and exemption of liability, are relegated to sections 2 and 3 (though even then section 2 commences with excluding liability in negligence, rather than contract). This is particularly curious given that the Act was based upon a draft Bill proposed by the Law Commission, which *began*, more logically, with exemption clauses in contract.

With all this in mind, therefore, it is worth looking at some examples of statutes to see how they are put together or, more importantly, what techniques you need to master in order to take them apart and apply them to factual situations (see also: Stark, 2002, on approaches to drafting statutes).

7.4 Examples of Drafting Practices and How to Approach Them

Students new to the study of law can sometimes be put off delving into statutes simply because the words or structure used are confusing. To show that, like all legal method techniques, this is not really a black art to be mastered by only the few, we have selected a few statutes below which show some of the different drafting techniques you will encounter in your studies. These examples are drawn from statutes which have caused our own students problems in the past. Our aim is simply to reveal the tricks used and how very often the most complicated-looking provision is really nothing of the sort.

We are still not yet concerned with how to *interpret* these (or any other) statutes; we are concerned only with how best to approach reading and understanding them. In particular, we are looking at how to deal with phrases such as 'subject to section 2...', or 'notwithstanding the duties laid out in section 2...', or 'Save as permitted by section 2...,.

The best way to set about this is for you to read the wording of the Act given in the left-hand column in each of the tables in Sections 7.4.1 to 7.4.5 below, and see what sense you can make of it; then have a look in the right-hand column and you will see suggestions as to how to approach the statute.

7.4.1 The Knives Act 1997

We start with a reasonably simple section. This extract from the Knives Act 1997 illustrates the basic rules of structure noted above—a general opening statement describing the offence followed by more specific 'definitional' matters. This statute was introduced following a public outcry when a headmaster was stabbed by a pupil outside his school. Legislation already existed prohibiting the carrying of offensive weapons: what society demanded was more legislation on the *sale* of knives. To outlaw the sale of all types of knife was obviously impracticable, so some other approach was needed-outlawing the marketing of knives which could be used as a weapon—the phrase eventually chosen being 'combat knives'.

Wording of Section	Commentary
Unlawful Marketing of Knives **1.** (1) A person is guilty of an offence if he markets a knife in a way which— (a) indicates, or suggests, that it is suitable for combat; or (b) is otherwise likely to stimulate or encourage violent behaviour involving the use of the knife as a weapon.	Section 1(1) sets up the offence, which has two disjunctive elements—(a) **or** (b). The use of the word 'or' creates two very different ways of committing the offence. Note, however, that it is the 'marketing' of the knife that is illegal, not the mere possession. At this stage in your reading of the statute you should also have been wondering what words such as 'markets', 'suitable for combat' or 'stimulate' mean. At first sight the Act appears unhelpful in that it does not tell you if these words are going to be defined (but they are, just a few subsections later). So, in reading the section, establish what you think is the basic offence; you can fill in details later.
(2) 'Suitable for combat' and 'violent behaviour' are defined in section 10.	Subsection (2) gives us a cross-reference to further definitions in section 10, where you will find a long list of definitions. Thus, in section 10 'suitable for combat' means "suitable for use as a weapon for inflicting injury on a person, or causing a person to fear injury". This definition is thus 'read into' section. 1.
(3) For the purposes of this Act, an indication or suggestion that a knife is suitable for combat may, in particular, be given or made by a name or description—	Another definition subsection (which applies to the whole Act —sometimes definitions only apply to particular sections or parts of Acts). Here, Subs (3) defines the rather vague terms of 'indication/suggestion' we first saw in section 1(1)(a).

Wording of Section	Commentary
(a) applied to the knife; (b) on the knife or on any packaging in which it is contained; or (c) included in any advertisement which, expressly or by implication, relates to the knife.	However, the wording of subsection (3) does not help much as you will notice that it has the term 'in particular' hidden half way along. This must mean that although points (a)–(c) are clear examples there may be others,
(4) For the purposes or this Act, a person markets a knife it— (a) he sells it or hires it; (b) he offers, or exposes, it for sale or hire; or (c) he has it in his possession for the purposes of sale or hire.	Finally we get the meaning of the word 'markets', so, again, this has to be read back into the original description of the offence. Note that 'possession' still has to relate to the sale or hire of the knife

7.4.2 The Wild Mammals (Protection) Act 1996

This next example looks like a mess on first reading. To start with it begins with the puzzling phrase 'If, save as permitted by this Act...' and then goes on to list a whole range of forbidden activities. But appearances can be deceptive: it is actually very straightforward. The phrase 'save as permitted...' appears quite often in statutes. It means that the actions listed in section 1 might still be lawful if made so elsewhere in the Act. You are not told where this 'saving' provision might be so it could appear anywhere in the Act and even arise from the context rather than specific wording.

Wording of Section	Commentary
1. Offences If, save as permitted by this Act, any person mutilates, kicks, beats, nails, or otherwise impales, stabs, burns, stones, crushes, drowns, drags, or asphyxiates any wild mammal with intent to inflict unnecessary suffering he shall be guilty of an offence. **2. ...(omitted here)** **3. Interpretation** In this Act 'wild mammal' means any mammal which is not a domestic or captive animal within the meaning of the Protection of Animals Act 1911....	A formidable list, but not that confusing when dealt with one at a time. Any other act of cruelty you can think of might still fall within this section if it is like the action listed. Note also the key point at the end that 'intent to inflict unnecessary suffering' is required. So, if someone impales or burns a mammal accidentally or for some good reason they will not have committed an offence under the Act. Section 3 gives definitions, but you need to refer to another Act to understand them. Such external source cross-referencing is very annoying.

7.4.3 The Copyright, etc and Trade Marks (Offences and Enforcement) Act 2002

As with the Wild Mammals Act example, this section sets up a general rule but tells you, right at the start, that rule has to be read with exceptions. This time, instead of using the phrase 'save as permitted', it uses the more direct phrase 'subject to ... [a particular sub-section],—so at least you know where to look this time. The trick here is to ignore the subject to ...' part until you have worked out clearly what the general rule is. Students often make the mistake of trying to read the subsection referred to before establishing the general rule. That way lies madness.

This extract deals with the situation where someone has breached another person's copyright and made illegal recordings of their material, e.g. pirated CDs. What should be done with those CDs?

Wording of Section	*Commentary*
Section 4 (8) **Subject to subsection** (9), where any illicit recordings are forfeited under this section they shall be destroyed in accordance with such directions as the court may give. (9) On making an order under this section the court may direct that the illicit recordings to which the order relates shall (instead of being destroyed) be forfeited to the person having the performers' rights or recording rights in question or dealt with in such other way as the court considers appropriate.	*Subsections (1) to (7) omitted here* A straightforward subsection which presents a **general** rule that illicit recordings which have been forfeited by the court will then be destroyed. Subsection (9) then sets out the exceptions referred to by the phrase 'subject to ...' in subsection (8). In this case, illicit recordings will be destroyed unless the court decides: (i) to allow them to be forfeited for the benefit of certain people involved in their creation or (ii) dealt with in another way. This latter point clearly allows the court a very wide discretion. So subsection (8) is the normal procedure, but it can be varied according to subsection (9)

7.4.4 The Churchwardens Measure Act 2001

There is nothing particularly complicated about this next Act, but it is useful because it illustrates two things: (a) how a statute can set up an elaborate system and then provide exceptions; (b) the use of the word 'notwithstanding', which draftsmen love using. The word 'notwithstanding' basically means 'despite'. It appears in sentences such as: 'Subsection (1) shall have effect **notwithstanding** any agreement to the contrary...'; and 'The acts and proceedings of any person appointed to be a member...of a Service Authority and acting in that office shall, **notwithstanding** his disqualification or want of qualification, be as valid and effectual as if he had been qualified.' Note how the word is used in this Act.

Word of section	*Commentary*
1 Number and qualifications of churchwardens *(1) and (2) omitted here*	This subsection lists who may be churchwardens.
(3) The churchwardens of every parish shall be chosen from persons who have been baptised and— (a) whose names are on the church electoral roll of the parish; (b) who are actual communicants; (c) who are 21 years of age or upwards; and (d) who are not disqualified under section 2 or 3 below.	Note the requirements are **cumulative** so if one condition is not met, the person cannot be a churchwarden. Requirements are often presented this way—we saw a list of requirements presented in the alternative in the Knives Act above.
(4) If it appears to the bishop, in the case of any particular person who is not qualified by virtue of paragraph (a), (b) or (c) of subsection (3) above, that there are exceptional circumstances which justify a departure from the requirements of those paragraphs the bishop may permit that person to hold the office of churchwarden **notwithstanding** that those requirements are not met. Any such permission shall apply only to the period of office next following the date on which the permission is given.	This subsection provides exceptions to subs (3). There must be 'exceptional circumstances' (not defined) before this operates. But note that the exception only applies where section (3)(a), (b) or (c) is/are missing. *It is easy to miss fact that if section.1(3)(d) applies then there is no exception to the general rule.* The bishop is given powers **'notwithstanding'** (i.e., 'even though') the requirements in subsection (3)(a), (b) or (c) are not met. So here, despite the apparently clear list of requirements, the bishop is still given a power to appoint in certain circumstances; though even here there is a time limitation on this power.

7.4.5 The Trustee Act 1925

We end this list of examples with this beauty—a section which always causes students problems. The law is not that complicated; it is the density of the material that is the problem—section 36(1) is actually all one sentence. However, though this looks daunting, it can be broken down into simpler elements (whether you use a flow chart approach or other device is a matter of preference). The key is to get the general picture of it first; later you can fill in the specific requirements and/or exceptions. If you can master this you are well on your way to handling the structure of statutes.

Word of section	*Commentary*
36 Power of appointing new or additional trustees (1) Where a trustee, either original or substituted, and whether appointed by a court or otherwise, is dead, or remains out of the United Kingdom for more than twelve months, or desires to be discharged from all or any of the trusts or powers reposed in or conferred on him, or refuses or is unfit to act	**STEP 1:** The heading is usually a good indication of what the section is about (though, very occasionally, it can be misleading). **STEP 2:** First, take the opening words of section 36(1)'**Where a trustee**...' The next few clauses merely make clear which trustees are covered so ignore them for the moment. **STEP 3:** The second key phrase is: '**is dead (or other things have happened)**' We are merely

Word of section	*Commentary*
therein, or is incapable of acting therein, or is an infant, then, subject to the restrictions imposed by this Act on the number of trustees— (a) the person or persons nominated for the purpose of appointing new trustees by the instrument, if any, creating the trust; or (b) if there is no such person, or no such person able and willing to act, then the surviving or continuing trustees or trustee for the time being, or the personal representatives of the last surviving or continuing trustee; may, by writing, appoint one or more other persons (whether or not being the persons exercising the power) to be a trustee or trustees in the place of the trustee so deceased remaining out of the United Kingdom, desiring to be discharged, refusing, or being unfit or being incapable, or being an infant, as aforesaid.	trying to find out what the general position is here, so do not get concerned yet about these **STEP 4:** The next key word is **'then…**, i.e. what is going to happen or be allowed? So, the gist so far is: **'Where a trustee is dead (or something else has happened) then…'** **STEP 5:** The phrase **'Subject to the restrictions…**, merely puts you on guard that the Act has other provisions covering the numbers of trustees which we will have to look at later. Ignore this for the moment. **STEP 6:** At first sight paragraphs (a) and (b) look like the 'then' noted in STEP 4, but in fact they merely describe who has the power to act when the trustee is dead etc. So, ignore this too for the moment. Annoying though this may be, this style of drafting is quite common (and, to be fair, it is difficult to set up such a rule without doing something like this). You need to look to the final paragraph to see exactly what is going on. **The essence of the section so far is that when a trustee is dead some people have the power to do certain things.** **STEP 7:** Finally we get to what these persons may do. We find that they may appoint others to be trustees in place of the trustee who died (etc). The only other point you have to note is that the appointment must be made 'by writing'. Amazingly straightforward in the end!

Statutes of course do not exist merely to provide exercises in analysis. They have to be applied in practice; so, having done your work on the wording of the Trustee Act 1925, you can now put that to use with a client's problem.

For example, say your client is a trustee of a charity and tells you that one of the other trustees has died and he wants to appoint a replacement.

- You know that section 36(1) is generally about this sort of situation.

- You can now look at the detail to see that the first requirement of the section is met (i.e. that an existing trustee has died).

- You would next have to ask: does such an appointment fall foul of the number of trustees allowed under the Act? You would therefore need to look elsewhere in the Act.

- If all is well, then you would need to see if your client falls within paragraphs (a) or (b), i.e. does he/she have the right to make the appointment or do we need to get someone else to do it?

If all these requirements have been met you would then advise that such an appointment has to be made in writing.

7.5 Amending Earlier Statutes

Another aspect of drafting practice you need to master arises when an Act (say, one passed in 2003) amends an earlier Act (say, one of 1990). The amendment may be wholesale: the earlier Act may be repealed and replaced by the later Act (or a whole string of Acts may be **consolidated** into the new Act). But, more commonly, the later Act will amend only parts of the earlier Act or Acts. It is quite common, therefore, for one Act to 'insert' new words or even new sections into an existing Act. There is nothing too puzzling about this and the new wording or section is simply referred to as if it had always been in the original Act; the real problem is that if you went and looked at the original Act you would not see the amendment (though you would in the electronic versions to be found on LEXIS and Westlaw). Laymen representing themselves in court often make the mistake of relying on the original wording of the statute without realising there has been an amendment. Lawyers are presumed to know better.

7.5.1 Inserting Words

We will use the Employment Act 2002 again to illustrate these points:

The original words to section 227(1) *Employment Rights Act 1996*	Schedule 7, Para 47 *Employment Act 2002 amends section 277.*	So, section.227 now reads (new wording in italics here) as follows, and many practitioners will amend their copy of the original statute to show this:
(1) For the purpose of calculating— (a) a basic award of compensation for unfair dismissal, (b) an additional award of compensation for unfair dismissal, or (c) a redundancy payment, the amount of a week's pay shall not exceed [£X].	(1) Section 227(1) (maximum amount of week's pay) is amended as follows. (2) Before paragraph (a) there is inserted— '(za) an award of compensation under section 80I (1)(b),'. (3) For 'or' at the end of paragraph (b) there is substituted— '(ba) an award under section 112(5), or'.	(1) For the purpose of calculating— (za) *an award of compensation under section 80I (1)(b)* (a) a basic award of compensation for unfair dismissal, (b) an additional award of compensation for unfair dismissal, (ba) *an award under section 112(5).* *or* (c) a redundancy payment, the amount of a week's pay shall not exceed [£X].
	Note the use of section 80I— a capital I—not a misprint for 'one' This means that between the original section 80 and section 81, numerous new sections have later been added by later Acts (see next example for how this is done)	**Note the use of '(za)' to make it clear it has been inserted before (a). The draftsman could have inserted '(ab)' after '(a)' in the same way that '(ba)' was inserted after '(b)' or he or she might even have re-written the section; but this was the method chosen.**

7.5.2 Inserting New Sections

Section 34 Employment Act 2002 inserts a new section (section 98A) into the Employment Rights Act 1996. The most usual method of inserting new sections is to put A or B etc after the old section number. The idea is that this saves having to re-number the whole Act. Most statutes do not get as far down the alphabet as the example we saw above, viz section 80I. In the table below one can see the wording of section 34 of the Employment Act 2002 in the left-hand column and, in the right-hand column, a commentary on how to read this.

---

34 Procedural fairness in unfair dismissal

(1) Part 10 of the Employment Rights Act 1996 (c.18) (unfair dismissal) is amended as follows. (2) After section 98 there is inserted— **98A Procedural fairness** (1) An employee who is dismissed shall be regarded for the purposes of this Part as unfairly dismissed if— (a) one of the procedures set out in Part 1 of Schedule 2 to the Employment Act 2002 (dismissal and disciplinary procedures) applies in relation to the dismissal, (b) the procedure has not been completed, and (c) the non-completion of the procedure is wholly or mainly attributable to failure by the employer to comply with its requirements.	This 'new' section (98A) defines when an employee will be deemed automatically unfairly dismissed. It directs you to a Schedule of the Act —the irony being that section 98A of an Act originally passed in 1996 now refers you to the schedule of an Act passed in 2002. The way to read this is to be clear about the general rule and then look at the conditions that have to be complied with. The first condition is that, one of the procedures detailed in that Schedule must apply. If it does, **and** (b) and (c) have not been followed, the dismissal is unfair, But the conditions are cumulative—if any one of them is missing then the dismissal will not be automatically unfair.

Amendments do not make a great deal of sense when read in isolation and 'textual amendments' (such as the insertion of words) are usually wholly meaningless out of context. They have the advantage of being short statements. However, they leave the reader with a lot of work to do, comparing the old and new text and often rewriting the text.

7.6 Other Points on Drafting

There is also an increasing problem in ensuring compatability with EC law. The drafting complexities created by Community membership are twofold:

• First there is a general obligation on Member States to avoid legislating in contravention of Community law. This adds a substantial body of rules to the existing law, which should be considered when domestic legislation is being proposed.

• Secondly, there is the further problem of implementing Community Directives. Implementation involves expressly translating a piece of Community legislation into the form of domestic law. Ideally, it should be achieved without misinterpreting the substance of the original legislative Act. The difference in styles between Community and UK or Irish legislation may make this problem more acute in Britain and the Republic of Ireland than elsewhere in the EC. The difference in style is a point to which we shall return in more detail later in this chapter. First, we should note one or two points on the different drafting style used on the Continent.

7.7 European Legislative Drafting

7.7.1 The Drafting Process

The English style of drafting is not universal. It can be directly contrasted with the somewhat different techniques adopted in the Civilian systems of continental Europe, which have also come to dominate the form of European Community law. Given that many areas of our law are now dominated by European-derived legislation, this is a topic we cannot ignore.

You will recall that in **Chapter 1** we made the point that the great majority of Civilian systems are built upon principle of codified law. That emphasis on codification has, of course, had an impact on the whole legal process, not just on the drafting of legislation. For that reason, before we focus on the specifics of drafting technique, it is worth thinking about the general characteristics of codified as opposed to uncodified law. We shall focus on five key features.

Coherence

One of the problems with the Common Law, it is said, is that it lacks coherence. It is fragmentary and dispersed through a variety of sources, with negative consequences for both the clarity and certainty of the law. Restatement in a codified form potentially overcomes this problem, by bringing the law together within a single document or coherent set of documents.

Comprehensiveness

To a greater or lesser extent, codes claim to be complete restatements of the area of law to which they apply. This is not always easy to achieve, and may require a degree of complexity that is ultimately undesirable—an extreme example of such was the *Allgemeines Landrecht* promulgated in Prussia in 1794 which ran to an unmanageable 17,000 articles. The extent to which codes are complete statements depends on a variety of factors; most notably the extent to which the code has been updated by subsequent codified and uncodified legislation. Codes are difficult to replace in their entirety (for one thing it is an extremely lengthy legislative process), and attempts to dismantle an established

Code may be politically sensitive. For example, the revolutionary roots of the French Civil Code give it a 'sanctity' which would make its repeal an extremely emotive issue. Such problems encourage a policy of tinkering, by amending the 'outdated' parts by new legislation.

Knowledgeability

In theory, codification has been seen as a means of democratising law by extending knowledge of the law to the ordinary citizen and curbing the power of the judiciary—the original French Civil Code, the *Code Napoléon*, is one example of codifying law passed with this aim in view. The extent to which the Common Law lacks knowledgeability is a long-standing criticism. Jeremy Bentham (1748–1832), one of the most influential English members of the codification movement, pointed to this in his famous statement that the Common Law was 'dog law': the pragmatic, case-by-case development of the Common Law meant that people were punished for their actions *ex post facto*, as you would beat a dog only after it had misbehaved. (For further discussion of Bentham and the movement for codification in nineteenth-century England, see Lobban, 1991.) However, a lack of knowledgeability is not a characteristic unique to the Common Law. As the range of human activities demanding regulation has expanded, knowledgeability has been the chief victim, and is one attribute that is not widely found in modern codified systems, other than as an idealised notion of how the law ought to be.

Clarity

Knowledgeability and clarity are obviously related concepts, since clarity of language and exposition can greatly influence the knowledgeability of the law. But clarity is also a relative concept; some codes may seek to achieve a very high degree of brevity and simplicity in their formulation, while others may settle for a more technical level of clarity. However, one aim of codification has always been the clarification of law by the removal of what Vanderlinden (1967) calls (to paraphrase) obscurity, doubt, and ambiguity in the formulation of legal rules. Most Common Law draftsmen share those aims. They are not easily achieved, and demand a high-quality drafting process. It is possible to argue that, in many instances, both Common and Civil Law systems have been tried and found wanting so far as clarity is concerned—see the discussion later in this chapter.

The absence of contradiction

The process of *redaction*—of converting uncodified law to a codified form—gives the lawmaker an opportunity to resolve contradictions which may be present in uncodified law—e.g. in conflicting customary or case law. On the positive side, it is thereby possible to create greater certainty, but it may involve the lawmaker in a more or less subjective choice of one formulation of a rule over another. This part of the codifying process will often prove controversial. Problems of this sort have arisen in the attempts to produce a Draft Criminal Code for England (see de Búrca & Gardner, 1990).

7.7.2 The Perceived Benefits of Codification

As the preceding discussion suggests, the benefits of codification are somewhat debatable. Before you make up your own mind, let us consider how these general principles (and problems) come to be reflected in the technicalities of continental drafting.

Once again, generalisation is a little difficult. Most European states have laws that are not fully codified; in Spain, for example, the Civil Code (*Código Civil*) is often of only subsidiary force in some of the regions where the *Fueros*, or local law can still hold greater sway. Similarly, some states have a federal system, or other form of subsidiary legislature capable of legislating in its own right—for example, the codification of the *Fueros* by some Spanish regional governments; or the legislative activities of the German *Länder*. The following comments are only really exemplary of the more 'conventional' systems of codified national laws.

The drafting process in many European countries is, in some senses, a less specialised activity than in England. The initial drafting is usually completed solely by lawyers within the relevant ministries, or else by external commissions set up both to review a problematic issue and propose a draft law upon it. The latter, of course, has its analogy with the English use of Royal Commissions or bodies like the Criminal Law Revision Committee, though in the European context the draft proposal seems less likely to be significantly tampered with than is the case in England.

After the initial drafting, the proposal will be revised. In France, this is the function of the *Conseil d'Etat*—a consultative as well as judicial body—which is empowered to propose detailed changes to the legislation, and though the government is not obliged to follow that advice, it generally does so (see Ducamin, 1981). A similar system exists in Italy and in The Netherlands, while in Germany that function is performed by the Ministry of Justice. In all these countries it is only after this first revision by legal experts that further revision before Parliament takes place: a significant variation on the British pattern of legislating.

In the EC itself, there is again no equivalent of the Parliamentary Counsel, with the actual drafting (of, say, European Directives) normally being undertaken by staff within the European Commission—one of the key law-making institutions of the Community. This is normally followed by a detailed consultation period involving committees of experts appointed from within the Member States, and the Legal Service of the Commission, which must ultimately approve the draft before it goes before the Commission itself. Once approved, the proposal is set before the Council of Ministers (the other body with direct law-making power); it may sometimes be placed simultaneously before the European Parliament. From there, the process becomes extremely complex, with procedures depending upon the nature of the legislation and the criteria laid down for its revision and implementation. In most cases, consultation with Parliament is required before the Council can adopt the proposal, though this is not always necessary; in other cases, under the Single European Act, the Parliament has been given greater power to propose amendments to legislation, though the Council retains the last word. Only when legislation has finally been adopted by the Council is it signed by the President and thus capable of having the force of law. The roles of these institutions in the legal process will be discussed further in **Chapter 10**.

7.7.3 The Style of Drafting

In most codified systems much of the basic legal structure is now firmly established, and drafting styles broadly reflect the forms adopted by the eighteenth- or nineteenth-century authors of their codes. To a lawyer trained in any other tradition, English legislation comes as something of a shock; as a Bulgarian commentator has suggested:

> It is a challenging and arduous task to find one's way through the intricacies of English law when, as a translator, or professionally as a continental lawyer, one has to acquire a working knowledge of this uncommon law. (Dodova, 1989:69)

In this section we shall therefore try to identify the key distinguishing features of Civilian forms of drafting, then look at some of the specific drafting issues surrounding EC law. There is a distinct contrast between Common Law and Civil styles, summed up quite neatly in the description of the Common law style as 'fussy' and the Civil style as 'fuzzy': Campbell (1996).

Structure

We have already said that one of the arguable failings of English drafting is its poor arrangement—for example, the lack of rational distinction between points of principle and of detail, or its tendency towards centrifugence. By comparison, Civilian law often shows a far greater concern to establish a rational overall structure. One of the clearest examples of this is the German Civil Code—*Bürgerliches Gesetzbuch* (BGB).

The BGB consists of five books and approaching 2,500 paragraphs. The five books reflect the main conceptual divisions of the German Civil Law, which tend to follow the classical 'institutional' divisions of the French Civil Code. Thus, Book One is the General Part; Book Two covers the Law of Obligations; Book Three, Property; Book Four is on Family Law; and Book Five contains the Law of Succession. The provision of a General Part carries an explicit message about the purpose of those provisions. It denotes a high degree of conceptual abstraction, whereby the rules of Book One are of widespread application and are not tied to a specific institution.

This movement *from the general to the particular* is a common feature of codified laws and greatly aids interpretation by allowing us to establish general rules clearly before we look for exceptions. Thus, the General Part of the BGB contains the rules governing the legal personality of individuals and corporations; and more specific principles governing, e.g., avoidance powers in cases where legal intent is lacking; or provisions concerning the capacity of parties to act (i.e. by reason of age, mental capacity, etc.). Such a structure can also help us in interpreting the legislative purpose behind particular rules, and also sometimes ease the process of actually *finding* specific principles (though some commentators would argue that some divisions within the BGB are so abstract that it is not as easy to use as many later codes). The structure of the BGB can be contrasted with English law, where often general rules either do not exist, or lack a unified legislative source, or appear illogically ordered within the Act (e.g. UCTA as above).

Linguistic simplicity

Here, there is perhaps much greater practical variation in style between continental systems. The Swiss Civil Code of 1907 and the original Napoleonic Code of France are frequently cited as good examples of legislative simplicity, whereby principles are expressed in clear, naturalistic language. This ideal is not always sought, let alone achieved, even within a codified system. The BGB, for example, is noted for its technical language, though it still maintains a high degree of clarity for all that, and some of the later French Codes are similarly of greater complexity than the *Code Napoléon*—perhaps not least because they are dealing with modern legal phenomena such as social security rights, which are not as amenable as some areas of law to (relatively) simple exposition.

Brevity

Connected with our second point, we can often see in Civilian legislation an attempt to keep legal statements brief and to the point. English proponents of the 'European approach' to drafting (e.g. Dale, 1981) often cite this as a key difference between English and continental styles.

Both these differences can be seen more clearly by comparing the following extracts from the Sale of Goods Act 1979 and the French Civil Code (taken from Smith, 1980).

Sale of Goods Act	*French Civil Code*
41(1) Subject to the provisions of this Act the unpaid seller of goods who is in possession of them is entitled to retain possession of them until payment or tender of the price in the following cases, namely: (a) where the goods have been sold without any stipulation as to credit; (b) where the goods have been sold on credit, but the term of credit has expired; (c) where the buyer becomes insolvent. (2) The seller may exercise his right of lien notwithstanding that he is in possession of the goods as agent or bailee.	1612. The seller is not bound to deliver the property if the buyer does not pay the price for it, unless the seller has granted him time for payment. 1613. He shall also have no duty of delivery, even if he shall have granted time for payment, if after the sale the buyer has become bankrupt or insolvent so that the seller is in imminent danger of losing the price, unless the buyer gives him security for payment on the due date.

A fairly quick scan of the wording tells us that each of these provisions is doing essentially the same thing: defining the rights of an unpaid seller in respect of both cash and credit sales. There are comparatively few differences in terms of content, the main exception being that the Code contains no equivalent to subsection (2) of the Act.

The French text is obviously simpler, even though Article 1613 is rather verbose by the standards of the Civil Code. So, what is it about the Code which makes it seem so much more approachable than the Act?

First, it is a question of the language used—technical terms like 'lien' and 'bailee' are notable for their absence in the French text. Also, European drafting techniques place less emphasis on explicit definition. This reflects a general determination to use ordinary words in an ordinary way wherever possible. An absence of lengthy definitions can substantially simplify and shorten legislation. It is hardly surprising, therefore, that one common difference that has been much commented upon is the relative length of English and continental legislation. Dale provides a graphic example by a comparison of various national copyright laws. He concludes:

> All these copyright laws give effect to common international obligations, and ... are much the same in substance. The United Kingdom Act is twice as long as the German, more than three times as long as the French, and five times as long as the Swedish. (1981:145)

English lawyers argue that a lack of definition actually creates uncertainty. As we have seen, certainty has always been the great virtue claimed by the English for their legislation. But if it is so certain, why do our courts spend so many hours arguing over questions of construction? In part, the answer to that has been given in **Chapter 4**—it is a question of shades of meaning and, to that extent, exactly the same problems arise in Europe (see also **Chapter 8**). However, one can argue that the English make a further rod for their own backs by attempting to produce lengthy and 'exhaustive' definitions, both of specific words and of situations in which the Act is to apply. As Sir William Dale has long argued, however, definition does not make for certainty; his own position (which we support) is to agree with the Italian jurist Calamandrei that 'The statutes cannot foresee all the cases that reality, much richer than the most fervid imagination, brings before the judge' (1981:159). In other words definition can often cause, as much as alleviate, uncertainty by creating doubt whether certain fact situations are covered.

Secondly, approachability is also a matter of the form into which those words are put. The two Articles from the French Civil Code in the table above cited represent a more 'normal' narrative form than the sections of the 1979 Act. English legislation does not reflect the way people talk or think. We do not normally have to break concepts down into highly structured, itemised, lists. Why do we do it for legislation? The answer seems to lie in the density of the language used. The verbosity of English statutes is a throwback to the style of drafting which existed prior to the 1860s. Then sections were very densely written, with minimal punctuation (resulting in sentences that could run to many lines), and virtually no attempt to separate criteria within sections. Compared with this the highly technical structure of modern English statutes provides far more clarity, but the form of language is not wholly dissimilar.

Before we jump to the conclusion that Civilian drafting styles are *always* superior, we should remember that Civilian lawyers today are facing many of the same legislative problems as their English counterparts. As Jean-Eric Schoettl, a member of the French *Conseil d'Etat* explains:

> In France the situation is far from being satisfactory ... the main reasons for this are well known. The first is the rapidity with which changes take place under the pressure of events, or under the imperious pressure of political will. We can be very hasty in the way we prepare provisions. They are superimposed

one on another without clearly fitting with previous law. The chief draftsman at the Ministry of the Interior, M. Latournerie, calls this 'panic' legislation.

The second reason is the fact that legal language is no longer reserved for a small circle of people brought up in the same nursery. All branches of human activity are involved. Technical government departments, independent administrative authorities, local authorities, trade unions, employers—all these people take a part in drafting, and they have not necessarily had the same intellectual preparations. They come to law in different ways, and they have very different concerns. The result of this is what M. Latournerie calls 'legal babel'—the law is expressed in a multitude of dialects. (Dale, 1986:36)

Plus ça change, plus c'est la même chose?

7.8 The Style of Community Legislation

Not surprisingly, the structure of EC legislation more closely reflects Civil as opposed to Common Law style. For example the important equal pay Directive 75/117 states in Article 1:

The principle of equal pay for men and women outlined in Article 119 of the Treaty, hereinafter called 'principle of equal pay', means, for the same work or for work to which equal value is attributed, the elimination of all discrimination on grounds of sex with regard to all aspects and conditions of remuneration.

In particular, where a job classification system is used for determining pay, it must be based on the same criteria for men and women and so drawn up as to exclude any discrimination on grounds of sex.

Again, it is apparent that the Article concentrates heavily upon general principle. The Directive as a whole is also silent on technical detail, such as the matter of proof which creates some of the greatest difficulties in this area (particularly the question of *how* we evaluate 'work of equal value'). This is the kind of detail that is left to the courts to fill in— see on this point Case 61/81 *European Commission* v *United Kingdom* [1982] ECR 2601 and Case 237/85 *Rummler* v *Dato-Druck GmbH* [1986] ECR 2102; [1987] 3 CMLR 127.

This lack of technical detail is not a consistent feature of all EC legislation; some Directives and Regulations can be highly detailed and technical *where the subject matter so requires*—for example, Directive 82/501 on health and safety at work, which lays down a fairly complex notification scheme for certain hazardous industries. But even there the layout and language of the provisions are less dense than in much English legislation.

There are two further, special, dimensions to EC law which make questions of drafting/ interpretation rather interesting.

7.8.1 Languages in the Community

Language (or languages) can be a problem in the Community. In respect of the Treaties, 'authentic' (i.e. fully official) versions do not exist in all Community languages. Before its demise the European Coal and Steel Community Treaty had only the original French version as authentic; the Treaty of Rome is authentic in German, French, Italian, and Dutch, though the Treaty of Accession does, of course, have an authentic English version. Other

EC legislation has to be translated from the language in which it was originally drafted (which may be any of the Community languages, depending upon the preference of the team engaged in drafting) into all Community languages. In both cases, this can create an element of doubt. Can we be sure that translation effectively carries the legislative intent of an act across the linguistic divide?

This is not solely a problem within the EC, but afflicts any state where legislation is enacted in more than one language. Canada provides a good comparative example, where, since 1982, all legislation has been enacted in both English and French. McEvoy (1986) illustrates the problem by reference to section 8 of the Canadian Charter of Rights and Freedoms, which reads:

> Everyone has the right to be secure against unreasonable search or seizure.
> Chacun a droit à la protection contre les fouilles, les perquisitions ou les saisies abusives.

One assumes that the legislature intended these to be equivalent provisions. Certainly, both cover seizures ('*les saisies*' in French) and searches, though the French is actually more precise than the English as '*les fouilles*' and '*les perquisitions*' clearly cover searches of both persons and property. The difficulty arises in the apparent equation of 'unreasonable' and '*abusive*'. *Abusive* in French denotes something which is excessive or unauthorised. As McEvoy argues, therefore, 'it is not a true cognate' (1986:158) of the English 'unreasonable'; though there is clearly an area in which the terms overlap (something which is excessive is surely unreasonable), the fit is not exact: is something unreasonable necessarily unauthorised? This may seem to be a (semantic) storm in a teacup, and may be a lesser problem in countries where the lawyers are less inclined towards literalism than the Common Law-orientated Canadians. Even so, as McEvoy shows, there is a case for saying that courts dealing with bilingual enactments should not just *assume* linguistic equivalence.

In the EC, this seems to have been acknowledged. There are many cases where the Court's attention has been drawn to linguistic differences as part of the interpretative process; see, e.g., Case C–372/88 *Milk Marketing Board* v *Cricket St Thomas Estate* [1990] ECR I–1345; [1990] 2 CMLR 800 (a comparison of French and German versions of the Treaty with the English version). Sometimes the nuances may be so fine as to make no practical difference in the context; though occasionally the Court of Justice has found conflicting versions, and been forced to adopt a version which seems to accord either with the majority of the texts, or with the presumed legislative intent. For example, in Case 13/61 *de Geus* v *Bosch* [1962] ECR 45, the Court was faced with a provision in the Treaty of Rome where all four authentic texts conveyed a different meaning. Advocate General Lagrange submitted that the Court was free to decide the issue according to the spirit of the text. Certainly no single language is treated as having primacy in interpretation.

7.8.2 Directives

A further problem in EC law arises out of the use of Directives. We mentioned in **Chapter 1** that a Directive becomes fully effective in a Member State only once implemented by domestic law. In the United Kingdom alone, implementation requires a major transition of style. There is as yet little evidence that the Westminster draftsmen are adopting different stylistic techniques in respect of EC-based as opposed to 'home-grown' legislation. This means that we still have the problem of how effectively a broadly drafted Directive can be converted into the form and language of a British Act or Statutory Instrument. We will return to this in **Chapter 10**.

7.9 CONCLUSION

Perfecting any legislation is a very difficult task. The balancing of clarity, generality, conciseness, precision, and the avoidance of excess verbiage to achieve a satisfactory statute requires a great deal of skill. Further, certain words are, as we saw in **Chapter 4**, probably beyond universally applicable definition—words such as 'reasonable' or 'practicable'.

Which of the English and European styles is ultimately the more effective? In some cases that is possibly debatable, but it would be a hardened Anglophile who would support the case of English drafting without hesitation.

In terms of structure, the way in which an English Act is put together can, at best, aid interpretation by clarifying the relative degree of dependency that sections, sub-sections, and paragraphs have on each other. Sometimes, however, the structure imposed by the English draftsman can seemingly obscure that very same relationship. Much depends upon the quality of the drafting which, as we have seen, may be affected by a number of variables.

In terms of the detailed language used, there seems to be much in English legislation that is redundant, or redolent of a formalised language that is largely unrecognisable to the majority of the community. The greater emphasis on detail and definition in English legislation certainly does not make legislation any more litigation-proof. One suspects that what it does do is to shift the level of judicial debate from a consideration of the purpose and effect of legislation to a dispute over semantic detail. The reasons for this can be briefly explained.

Once a question of interpretation arises, European judges are normally given substantial discretionary powers. For example, Article 1 of the Swiss Civil Code entitles the judge, in the absence of clear statutory authority, to decide an issue 'in accordance with the rule he would establish as legislator'. In this sense, Civilian systems imply a partnership between Parliament and court, whereby the latter is there (to paraphrase Lord Denning) 'to fill the gaps and iron out the creases' left by the former. It is often expressed as a power to interpret legislation according to its objectives, or the intention of its authors. This power may be explicit in the legislation itself, or in the jurisprudence of the court—see, e.g., paragraph 133 of the BGB; also the decision of the Court of Justice of the European Community in Case 22/70 *European Commission* v *Council of the European Community* [1971] ECR 263.

In England judges also seek to implement the will of Parliament. But unlike the codified approach seen on the Continent, English judges have not (at least until recently) shown much inclination to claim extensive powers to look at the general purpose of the Act. For the most part they will therefore adhere to the plain meaning of the words, so far as that proves possible. The way in which they go about these tasks forms the subject of the next chapter.

REFERENCES

*BENNION, F. (1978), 'Statute Law Obscurity and the Drafting Parameters', 5 *British Journal of Law and Society* 235.

CAMPBELL, L. (1996), 'Drafting Styles: Fuzzy?' 3 *Murdoch University Electronic Journal of Law* No. 2.

DALE, W. (1977), *Legislative Drafting—A New Approach* (London: Butterworths).

—— (1981), 'Statutory Reform: The Draftsman and The Judge', *International and Comparative Law Quarterly* 141.

—— (ed.) (1986), *British and French Statutory Drafting* (London: Institute of Advanced Legal Studies).

DE BÚRCA, G., and GARDNER, S. (1990), 'The Codification of the Criminal Law', 10 *Oxford Journal of Legal Studies* 559.

*DODOVA, L. (1989), 'A Translator Looks at English Law', *Statute Law Review* 69.

DRIEDGER, E. (1976), *The Composition of Legislation* (2nd edn. Ottawa: Department of Justice).

DUCAMIN, B. (1981), 'The Role of the *Conseil d'Etat* in Drafting Legislation', 30 *International and Comparative Law Quarterly*, 882.

HANSARD SOCIETY (1992), *Making the Law* (London: The Hansard Society).

HODGES, C. (1998), 'Development Risks: Unanswered Questions', 61 *Modern Law Review* 560.

HUNT, B. (2002), 'Plain Language in Legislative Drafting: Is it Really the Answer?', *Statute Law Review* 24.

HUTTON, N. (1979), 'Legislative Drafting in the United Kingdom', *The Parliamentarian*, no. 253, 100.

LOBBAN, M. (1991), *The Common Law and English Jurisprudence, 1760–1850* (Oxford: Clarendon Press).

McEVOY, J. (1986), 'The Charter as a Bilingual Instrument', 64 *Canadian Bar Review* 155.

MAUGHAN, C., and WEBB, J. (1995), *Lawyering Skills and the Legal Process* (London: Butterworths).

*RENTON COMMITTEE (1975), *The Preparation of Legislation*, Cmnd. 6053 (London: HMSO).

RHYS WILLIAMS, B. (1987), 'Legislation and Parliament', *Statute Law Review* 38.

SMITH, J. (1980), 'Legislative Drafting: English and Continental', *Statute Law Review* 14.

STARK, J. (2002), 'Learning from Samuel Johnson about Drafting Statutes', 23 *Statute Law Review* 227.

VANDERLINDEN, J. (1967), *Le Concept de Code en Europe Occidentale de XIIIe au XIXe Siècle* (Brussels: Editions de l'Institut de Sociologie, Université Libre de Bruxelles).

8

Interpreting Statutes

8.1 Introduction

Most people are willing to believe that case law can present problems because facts are never precisely repeated; at the same time most people also believe that statutes are precise and accurate so that anyone can 'look up' the law in a statute. For the most part the implementation of statutory provisions will indeed be a routine matter, but this is not universally true. Once words appear in a statute they are open to all manner of argument and interpretation. Those arguments may be about the meaning of the language used in the statute (a sort of translation exercise), or about the application of the language to the facts (application exercise), or about both.

By a 'translation' exercise we mean the court having to deal with phrases such as: 'equipment includes any plant and machinery, vehicle, aircraft, and clothing'. So, does the word 'equipment' include a ship? The first question to ask here is whether the word 'includes' means that the subsequent items fall within the definition of 'equipment' and everything else is excluded; or whether 'includes' means that the list is not closed, i.e. that vehicles etc are included, but other things may also be included. This problem arose in *Coltman* v *Bibby Tankers Ltd* [1988] AC 276; [1987] 3 All ER 1068. We will return to this case later. The 'translation' was that the list was not closed—other items than those specifically mentioned could be 'included'. The House of Lords then had to consider whether the phrase, as translated, applied to ships: the application exercise.

The same problems arise, of course, in ordinary life with insurance policies, contracts, and even the rules of games. We saw this in **Chapter 7** as regards the structure of statutes, and the same applies here when interpreting the words used. Take a look, for instance, at the rules of 'Monopoly'. Under the heading *Landing on 'Chance' or 'Community Chest'* the rules state: 'A player takes the top card from the pack indicated and after following the instructions thereon, returns the card face down to the bottom of the pack'. Let's say you land on 'Chance'. You know (because you have been concentrating) that the only card still to come is a property repairs card; a fact which will cause you severe problems. Do you have to take the card? What arguments could you use not to? Do you have to show the card to anyone? Would the type of argument be the same as when you argued (but presumably lost) that you did not have to take the card at all?

When you look at any document the meaning attached to words is often influenced both by the fact that you wish your interpretation to be accepted and also by your general approach to life. What we mean by this last point is that some people are by nature apt to take words at their literal meaning—'it says X so it should mean X' (or, the Monopoly rules say 'take the card' so you must take the card)—whilst others naturally find themselves looking for the purpose behind the words—'what are these words trying to do?' (or what is the point in having cards marked 'Chance' if they leave you no choice whether to take them or not; surely there is a difference between 'Chance' and 'Community Chest'?).

Statutes are designed in the same way as the rules of a game or the rules of a committee. They seek to tell you what you can do, what you cannot do, and perhaps how you are meant to do it. Equally, as we have seen in the previous chapter, they need to be drafted very carefully. Written words are not like conversation: there is no inflexion, no stress, no sense of irony; no opportunity to ask 'what do you mean?'; the lifeblood of everyday speech is missing. The reader therefore has to give life to the words by interpreting what they mean and how they are meant to apply to particular situations. This is what is meant by statutory interpretation. The problem is: how do you interpret statutes? What rules do you use? When do you know you have found the *correct* meaning?

8.2 The So-called Rules of Interpretation

If you look in textbooks and cases written over the last five centuries, especially those on Land Law or the Law of Succession or the Law of Contract, you will see that lawyers have classified the basic means of reading documents under three headings:

- *The Literal Rule* (take only the plain, literal meaning of the words used because those are the words the draftsman chose to employ);
- *The Golden (or Purposive) Rule* (try to ascertain what the draftsman intended by these words by looking at the general purpose of the section and the social, economic or political context); and
- *The Mischief Rule* (which directs you to look to the history of the Act (or other document) to see what was wrong with the law (what was the mischief?) that the draftsman sought to remedy).

These are rather crude labels for describing a complex mechanism, i.e. making sense of what someone else has written. The labels are in common use, but they are dangerous. For a start, they use the word 'rule', and this gives the impression that if you follow a particular pattern you will not go wrong. They also have an aura of scientific authenticity about them when the reality is (as Lord Templeman says in the Foreword to this book) that interpreting any document is more of an art than a science.

Generations of lawyers have had problems applying these 'rules'. It is almost impossible to resist believing that if you know what the 'rules' mean you can apply them universally in understanding a section, a statute, or any document. One of the great writers on statutory interpretation, Rupert Cross, experienced this problem as a student; and when he became a lecturer at Oxford he found that his students shared his dilemma (Cross, 1995: Preface):

> Each and every pupil told me there were three rules—the literal rule, the golden rule and the mischief rule, and that the courts invoke whichever of them is believed to do justice in the particular case.

I had, and still have, my doubts, but what was most disconcerting was the fact that whatever question I put to pupils or examinees elicited the same reply. Even if the question was What is meant by 'the intention of parliament'? or What are the principal extrinsic aids to interpretation? back came the answer as of yore: 'There are three rules of interpretation—the literal rule...'

In the text below we will explain these 'rules' in some more depth and will give some examples of their operation. The fact that we have chosen to do this seems almost hypocritical, given what we have just said above. But we do so only because no matter what is written by commentators on statutory interpretation, lawyers and judges persist in using these terms because they are well-understood shorthand labels.

8.2.1 Why Do We Still Refer to the 'Rules'?

In continuing to refer to these 'rules' we have, along with other writers, been accused of perpetuating an outdated approach to interpretation (Cross, 1995:198). But, surprisingly, coming from such a distinguished text, this criticism misses the point we have made since the first edition of this book: no lawyer believes that by merely saying 'we should adopt a literal (or purposive) approach' one has *interpreted* the statute or constructed an argument, but the terms appear in judgments and in textbooks on Contract, Torts, etc., so you need to be aware of their usage. Put another way: merely because a map has recognised routes on it does not mean you have to follow them slavishly; but being ignorant of these routes is negligent, and trying to cut loose across country where there are no roads is unlikely to get you to your destination. The labels, the 'rules', are useful as map signs (especially when you are just starting your legal studies) but they do not tell you *how* to drive.

The one *caveat* we would make at this point is that the 'purposive' approach is not a licence for invention or a substitute for that time-honoured student phrase, 'But it's not fair'. Both your client and you (or any other combination) may well feel that the wording of a piece of legislation is 'unfair'. But this is not an argument in itself, and no lawyer can afford to depart from the wording of a statute merely because it does not suit his or her client's case or his or her own sense of justice. Each interpretation offered has to have reasoning behind it and must actually bear some relevance to the words as they appear. And remember, what is fair or unfair is a question of opinion, not fact.

Perhaps the main difficulty with these 'rules' lies in the fact that, in order to see them in operation, one invariably looks at the reasoning given by the judge. Thus, you come across phrases such as 'If we apply the literal rule to these words we can see that...'. To analyse the 'rules' by looking at which one a particular judge chose to apply in any given case is a bit like looking at the results of a horse race and then pretending the outcome was clear all along, because it now seems so obvious. Looking at a judgment, or at a results sheet, means that you are looking at a **conclusion**; what is omitted is why the conclusion was reached or why that particular horse won. The problem with reading statements like the one above is that an impression is gained that there was a *correct* analysis and that if only you looked for it more carefully you could have found it. Instead, you need to think of these 'rules' as *approaches* to interpretation, as tools of argument.

Very often, one lawyer will try to argue a literal interpretation ('the words say this and nothing more'), whilst the other seeks to use a more purposive approach ('the words may say this but they cannot be taken so literally when you look at the purpose behind the section'). The essence of statutory interpretation is the construction of arguments which favour your client's case. The judgment reflects whether you were successful; and this depends on a whole host of things such as how well you and your opponent presented your arguments, whether the judge was by nature more inclined to accept one approach, and whether there were any precedents that helped or hindered you.

8.2.2 How Do We Use these 'Rules' in Legal Argument?

General textbooks which present the rules of statutory interpretation as though they are fixed and adhered to in an unchanging logical form are misleading. Here, we certainly agree with Cross. The reality is much less certain, because these 'rules' are really nothing more than techniques of reading a document, and may be used singularly or in any combination. There is nothing wrong, for instance, in an argument which runs:

1. 'The plain meaning of these words show that my client's actions conformed with the requirements of the section (*a literal approach to the wording*).

2. Further, if we look at the purpose behind this section we find that it was designed to remedy the very problem for which my client seeks redress (*a purposive argument*).

3. And indeed, if we look at why this Act came about the history of this area shows that the Act was necessary to overcome the problems with previous cases in this field' (*use of the mischief rule*).'

In *Oliver Ashworth (Holdings) Ltd* v *Ballard (Kent) Ltd* [1999] 2 All ER 791, Laws LJ explained the reality of these 'rules' (at 805): '[I]t is now misleading—and perhaps it always was—to seek to draw a rigid distinction between literal and purposive approaches . . . frequently there will be no opposition between the two, and then no difficulty arises. Where there is a potential clash, the conventional English approach has been to give at least very great and often decisive weight to the literal meaning of the enacting words. This is a tradition which I think is weakening . . .'.

So do not get too worried about these rules for now. You must know what they are seeking to do, but only as a tool for the way you argue your case; and so that you can make some guess at how the judge might decide the issue. Instead of thinking about statutory interpretation as just another legal topic—like homicide, theft, or offer and acceptance—you should think about the ideas outlined below and try to make use of them, either in academic discussion or in practice, across the whole range of legal subjects.

But we must emphasise again that these are not fixed rules of law; for the most part they are examples of the use of language generally. Cross, for instance, refers to cases which decided such awe-inspiring questions as 'Is a bicycle a "carriage"? Is a goldfish an "article"?' and concludes:

> Conundrums of this sort are part of the daily bread of judges and practitioners. In solving them the courts usually pay due regard to the context, but, in many instances, the answer must . . . be treated as a matter of common sense. (1995:75)

Understanding the 'rules' of statutory interpretation is important, therefore, because:

(a) Judges are not robots; their personality affects the way they will approach a problem of interpretation. Judges do not follow a 'critical path' analysis, progressing from one rule of interpretation to another in a logical fashion. If they did, we would have far more 'expert systems' available where people could just answer a series of questions generated by a computer and obtain an answer at the end. You need to be aware, therefore, what range of analytical options are open to a judge.

(b) When arguing your case, or analysing the advantages and disadvantages of pursuing that case, you need to know the framework in which you are operating. It is often said that a bad workman always blames his tools; a workman who does not even know which tools exist deserves all he gets.

(c) It helps if you can combine (a) and (b), but that means you need to know how the judge is likely to react to the approach you have chosen. An argument based on the grand purpose of a statute delivered to a judge who believes firmly in a literal inter- pretation of words will fall on stony ground. You will discover from reading cases which senior judges favour which approach. This may not help on your first appear- ance in court before an unknown junior judge—which is why point (b) is important.

8.3 Examples of the 'Rules' in Action

These traditional 'rules' may be explained as follows.

8.3.1 The Literal Rule

The 'literal rule' is founded on the assumption that the words chosen by Parliament in the Act clearly show its intentions in passing that Act. The rule demands that one looks at what was said, not at what it *might* mean; that one is concerned with linguistics rather than considerations of the purpose of the Act or the wider context in which the statute was enacted. To do otherwise, as was said in *Duport Steel* v *Sirs* [1980] 1 WLR 142; [1980] 1 All ER 529, 541, might mean that the court is not interpreting the Act but really making law. There, Lord Diplock said:

> Where the meaning of the statutory words is plain and unambiguous it is not for the judges to invent fancied ambiguities as an excuse for failing to give effect to its plain meaning because they consider the consequences of doing so would be inexpedient, or even unjust or immoral.

Presented in this way the rule is seen as a safe bet — judges simply apply what is there. Safe bet or not, it is not a true reflection of reality. If the words were that clear nobody would have brought the case in the first place. The literalist is prepared for this challenge. What the liter- alist would be looking for is the *primary* or most *obvious* meaning of the word, not any *gen- eral* or *secondary* meaning. And he will usually do this by looking at the way the word or sentence fits into the rest of the section or even the Act as a whole (see Summers & Marshall, 1992:213). The literal rule at its most extreme echoes the approach of a fundamentalist:

consideration of the word or phrase as written is sacrosanct. The rule does not demand that the word be viewed in isolation from the rest of the sentence or section; but demands steadfastly that the investigation as to meaning does not stray beyond this point.

Thus the literal rule does not call upon a judge to consider the consequences of the interpretation. Sometimes this can still lead to what appear to be pretty odd results. The literal rule does not always generate a feeling that justice has been done even though it may be linguistically precise. Nor does it bear mathematical precision. As Willis stated:

> it is quite possible for all the members of the court to agree that the meaning of a section is so plain that it cannot be controlled by the context and yet to disagree as to what the plain meaning is. (1938:2)

Many examples can be given of judges relying upon the literal rule. But if we listed 100 cases all we would see is 100 different examples of the rule being used. The examples would not necessarily tell us how to interpret the next case. However, here are two examples that might help to give a flavour of literal interpretation in action.

In *R* v *Harris* (1836) 7 C & P 446 a statute made it an offence to 'stab, cut or wound' another person. Harris bit off her friend's nose in a fight—and then the policeman's finger. Was she guilty under the statute? The answer was no. The words in the statute pointed towards the use of a *weapon*. Teeth (even false?) are not a weapon. This conclusion was given further force by the fact that elsewhere in the section were references to the use of weapons, such as the word 'shooting'. You may think she should be guilty of something, but she was not guilty as charged. See also *R* v *Munks* [1964] 1 QB 304; [1963] 3 All ER 757 in a similar vein on the meaning of the word 'engine'.

In *Fisher* v *Bell* [1961] 1 QB 394; [1960] 3 All ER 731, an Act of 1959 made it an offence to 'sell or hire or offer for sale or hire' certain offensive weapons such as flick-knives. Bell placed a flick-knife in his Bristol shop window with a price-tag on it. Was he guilty of the offence? Again the answer was no. As you will see in the Law of Contract, placing an item on display is not the same thing as 'offering it for sale'. If the statute had used the phrase 'expose for sale' the answer would, on this analysis, have been different.

EXERCISE 15 **Are we still on strike?**

Take a look at the following case summary. We pose a few questions at the end of the account.

Stock v Frank Jones (Tipton) Ltd
[1978] 1 WLR 231; [1978] 1All ER 948

This concerned the dismissal of employees who were on strike. Under the Trade Union and Labour Relations Act 1974 (TULRA) an employee who was dismissed for striking could not claim unfair dismissal unless 'one or more of the employees, who also took part in that [strike], were not dismissed for taking part'. So all employees taking part in the strike had to be treated the same way. If one employee, e.g., the shop steward, was victimised by being the only person dismissed, he could claim that the dismissal was unfair (which would be decided on the facts). In this case the employees were on strike and, following fairly normal industrial relations tactics, the employer threatened them with dismissal if they did not return to work. Some did return. The employer dismissed those who did not return and they claimed unfair dismissal.

(a) Using the literal rule, what do you think the words 'employees who took part in that [strike]' mean? Do they mean:

   (i) all the employees who originally took part in the [strike]? or

   (ii) those employees who were still taking part in the [strike] when some of the others had returned to work following the threat?

(b) What are the consequences of choosing each option?

ANSWER

Under the then law the House of Lords decided that 'employees who took part in the [strike]' could only refer to those employees who were participating in the strike **when the strike began**. Thus, when some employees returned and were not dismissed they still counted in the number of those who 'took part in the [strike]'. The employees who had been dismissed had therefore been 'victimised' and could claim unfair dismissal.

If the House of Lords had taken the second and less literal option then, provided all those who stayed out on strike had been dismissed (which had happened) the employer would have been protected against any claim for unfair dismissal. After this case employers argued that this made nonsense of industrial relations for if the employer threatened to dismiss anyone not returning to work and one person out of a thousand did return the employer would either have to dismiss no one or dismiss everyone, including the one who returned! As a consequence the law was changed soon afterwards, but it has changed considerably on many occasions since and is still under debate.

It is often said that the literal rule will not be used when it would lead to inconsistency or absurdity. This must not be taken too widely. Many people would disagree with the above cases; this is not the same thing as saying that relying on a literal approach produced an absurd result. So, when will judges deem the literal rule inappropriate?

8.3.2 The Golden (or Purposive) Rule

The golden rule can be best described as an *adaptation* of the literal rule. We use this form of interpretation every day when reading signs such as 'Stop Children'; hardly an instruction to act like Herod! The context aids the interpretation. The classic exposition of the rule is to be found in *River Wear Commissioners* v *Adamson* (1876–77) 2 App Cas 743 at 764–5, *per* Lord Blackburn:

> I believe that it is not disputed that what Lord Wensleydale used to call the golden rule is right, viz, that we are to take the whole statute together and construe it all together, giving the words their ordinary signification unless when so applied they produce an inconsistency, or an absurdity or inconvenience so great as to convince the court that the intention could not have been to use them in their ordinary signification and to justify the court in putting on them some other signification which, though less proper, is one which the court thinks the words will bear.

Sadly, his Lordship did not offer us much assistance on **how** the interpretation is to proceed once we have discovered the absurdity. We can overcome this by arguing that the only logical way to deal with an absurd interpretation is to correct it by assessing what Parliament was trying to do. We can do this by looking at the *purpose* of the Act. For that reason it is sometimes called a 'purposive approach'—though some care is required when employing that term because the judiciary have been highly inconsistent in their use of it, as we shall see below.

In *Stock* v *Frank Jones (Tipton) Ltd* [1978] ICR 347; [1978] 1 All ER 948 Lord Simon advocated departure from the literal rule only when:

(a) there is a clear and gross anomaly;

(b) Parliament could not have envisaged the anomaly and would not have accepted its presence;

(c) the anomaly can be obviated without detriment to the legislative intent; and

(d) the language of the statute allows for such modification.

This is in keeping with the tenor of statements made by judges in the nineteenth century, particularly Lord Wensleydale in *Grey* v *Pearson* (1857) 6 HL Cas 61, which linked the idea of absurdity with the situation where a literal meaning would prove repugnant or inconsistent with the rest of the section or Act (the *internal* context). The emphasis is laid on establishing that the literal meaning is a nonsense when the rest of the statute is considered; it clearly does not mean that an absurdity can be said to arise merely because a literal meaning might offend one's sense of justice.

Viewed this way the golden rule can be seen as an accessory to, or shadow of, the literal rule. It does not exist independently of the literal rule but comes into play only as a back-up when the literal rule has failed; usually focusing on the range of secondary meanings of the word or phrase in question. The literal rule will be departed from mainly where there is confusion *within* the Act—that a clear interpretation is not possible because of surrounding words and sections. It is interesting to note, however, that many of the cases which developed the golden rule were in fact cases on the interpretation of another type of document: testators' wills. And even a cursory study of the interpretation of wills in the law of succession reveals that there has always been a major conflict of judicial attitude here: do you follow only what the testator wrote, or do you look for other evidence of his intentions? The law of succession has had the same problems as seen in statutory interpretation. It has not produced a satisfactory answer. Even Lord Wensleydale, the sometime father of the golden rule, was known to adopt a strong literal approach when interpreting wills (see, for instance *Abbott* v *Middleton* (1858) 7 HLC 68).

It is respectfully submitted that Lord Simon's guidelines are useful, although they still leave us with the one major problem with the golden rule: how do we know when something is an anomaly, an ambiguity, or absurd? This is a question most frequently avoided by commentators. Cross, however, does make a number of helpful points on this problem (1995:81–92).

First, the primary meaning cannot be abandoned, 'simply because it produces a result which [the judge] believes is contrary to the purpose of the Act. No judge can decline to apply a statutory provision because it seems to him to lead to absurd results.' Equally, however, judicial treatment of the topic does not lend itself to simply saying judges are concerned

only with the *internal* context of the words. Cross is forced to conclude that judicial applications of the rule tend to show that 'absurdity' 'does mean something wider than irreconcil-
ability with the rest of the instrument' (1995:89). In other words, some judges at least will go
beyond merely examining the words of the section etc., and probe into the purpose of the
Act. Discovering whether something is absurd when matched against the purpose of the Act
may involve examining the wider legal, and even social, setting of the Act. That is to say,
judges, to a greater or lesser extent, will look to the *external context* of the statute.

Indeed, it is fair to say that the *purposive approach* is becoming the dominant judicial
interpretation technique. Like all things there are trends and, in law, the modern trend is
towards a more purposive approach to statutory interpretation. Judges may not ignore
the words written in statutes, but they are more inclined to adopt a purposive interpretation whenever possible. This is partly due to the effects of EC legislation which, as we will
see, works on the basis that a purposive interpretation will be given to the wording. It may
also be related to the questionable standard of drafting seen in modern statutes.

Again there are many cases which illustrate the rule, but that is all they do—*illustrate*.
As a lawyer you are concerned with using the rule to argue—it is of little value citing a
case which simply proves that the courts do occasionally use the rule if the case cited has
nothing to do with your argument.

Here, however, are two famous examples of the golden rule in operation: *R v Allen*
(1872) LR 1 CCR 367: Allen, who was already married, married a woman called Harriet
Crouch. The statute in question said: 'whosoever being married shall marry any other
person during the lifetime of his spouse' shall commit bigamy. Now, Harriet was in fact
closely related to Allen so this apparently bigamous marriage was actually void. Thus
Allen argued that he had not married Harriet (because at law this was impossible) and so
had not committed bigamy. He argued that the second marriage had to be a legal marriage before bigamy could be committed. But this would of course produce an absurdity
because logically no bigamous marriage is lawful by its own definition; so, if Allen's argument was accepted, the judges would have had to pretend that the section was meaningless. Therefore they took a more purposive approach and read the words in the section
'shall marry' as meaning 'going through the ceremony'.

Re Sigsworth [1935] Ch 89; [1934] All ER Rep 113: Mrs Sigsworth was found dead. An
inquest found that she had been murdered by her son, who was also found dead. Mrs
Sigsworth's will left everything to her son. However, old rules of public policy dictated
that the son (and therefore his estate) could not inherit in these circumstances. Therefore
Mrs Sigsworth died intestate. But, under the Administration of Estates Act 1925, section 46,
the person entitled on intestacy was her son and, through him, his estate. The money had
gone round in a circle; and the statute dealing with intestacy said nothing about murderers
being barred from inheriting.

The court held that the statute could not have been intended to allow murderers to
inherit, despite being silent on the point. The old rule which applied to inheriting under
a will was applied to intestacy on the grounds that cases such as *Sigsworth* would be
'obnoxious' to that old principle and must be read as being subject to it.

EXERCISE 16 Not all there; or, present and correct?

Please read the following case summary. We pose only one question at the end of the account.

Under the Statute of Frauds 1677 it was a requirement that a will had to be signed by the testator 'in the presence' of witnesses.

In *Casson* v *Dade* (1781) 28 ER 1010 Miss Honora Jenkins went to her attorney's office to execute her will. She signed the will but then felt faint and was taken outside to sit in her carriage with her maid. The witnesses to the will remained in the office and gave their signatures to the will. The maid gave evidence that at the moment the witnesses were signing the carriage horses reared up, causing the carriage to move into a line of sight with the office window. The maid stated that, had Miss Jenkins looked through the window she would have seen the witnesses sign.

Was the will validly witnessed?

ANSWER

The court held that the will had been properly witnessed. Miss Jenkins was 'in the presence' of the witnesses even though she was not physically present in the same room. The fact that she was in the line of sight of the witnesses and could have seen them sign had she looked was enough. For, as had been said in the 1687 case of *Shires* v *Glascock* 21 ER 1134, to demand otherwise would mean that 'if a man should but turn his back, or look off, it would vitiate the will'. In modern parlance, it would be absurd to hold otherwise!

8.3.3 The Mischief Rule

Akin to the golden rule is a much older aid to interpretation called the mischief rule, or the rule in *Heydon's Case* (1584) 3 Co Rep 7a, 7b.

Like the golden rule, the mischief rule stresses the need to interpret an enactment in such a way as to give effect to its objectives. However, the mischief rule is, formally, of narrower application, in that the approach is located purely in the context of an identifiable common law status quo which existed prior to the Act. Thus the courts are required to consider four things:

1. What was the common law before the Act?

2. What was the 'defect or mischief' for which the common law did not provide?

3. What remedy did Parliament intend to provide?

4. What was the true reason for that remedy?

Great care must be taken when relying upon this rule in argument:

First, when *Heydon's Case* was determined the mischief could in fact be discovered within the Act itself because the reason for the Act's existence was always stated in the **preamble**. Thus a judge did not have to go beyond the bounds of the Act to discover the mischief it sought to remedy. The *internal* context was sufficient. A classic example of the use of preambles comes in the **Charitable Uses Act 1601** which states:

> WHEREAS Lands, Tenements, Rents, Annuities... have been heretofore given, limited, appointed and assigned, as well by the Queen's most excellent Majesty, and her most noble Progenitors, as by sundry other well disposed Persons; some for Relief of aged, impotent and poor People, some for Mainte-nance of sick and maimed Soldiers... which Lands, Tenements, Rents, Annuities... nevertheless have not been employed according to the charitable Intent of the givers and Founders thereof by reasons of Frauds, Breaches of Trust, and Negligence in those that should pay, deliver and employ the same: For Redress and Remedy whereof Be it enacted...

Lord Diplock recognised this in *Black-Clawson International Ltd* v *Papierwerke Waldhof-Aschaffenburg Aktiengesellschaft* [1975] AC 591; [1975] 1 All ER 810 when he said:

> So, when it was laid down, the 'mischief rule' did not require the court to travel beyond the actual words of the statute itself to identify the 'mischief and defect for which the Common Law did not pro-vide'... the mischief rule must be used with caution to justify any reference to extraneous documents for this purpose.

The point concerning 'extraneous documents' is significant. As we will see below, judges have not, traditionally, been allowed to look at any and every source in order to discover the mischief. Recently this approach has altered.

Secondly, 'mischief' itself can be difficult to define. All Acts came about for **some** rea-son, be it social, economic, political, or because of some technical legal defect. This last reason is a reasonably safe basis upon which to attach the tag 'mischief'. One can easily find out what the law was before the Act came into effect; and thereby see the apparent changes the Act sought to make in the law. The other means of identifying the mischief are fraught with danger because they clearly involve making value judgements.

Thirdly, as was noted most recently by Lord Bingham in *R* v *Secretary of State, ex parte Spath Holme* [2001] 1 All ER 195 (HL), an Act may have more than one mischief and the interrelationship between these may affect the question of interpretation. Two good examples of the mischief rule in operation are the cases of *Gorris* v *Scott* (1874) LR 9 Ex 125, and *Smith* v *Hughes* [1960] 1 WLR 830; [1960] 2 All ER 859. In *Gorris* v *Scott*, Scott con-tracted to transport some sheep by sea. The sheep were swept overboard because they had not been fenced in. Orders in Council made under the Contagious Diseases (Animals) Act 1869 required that the sheep should have been put in pens. Gorris thus claimed that Scott was in breach of the Act. The Court of Exchequer held that the purpose of the Act (which was clear from the preamble) was to prevent the spread of diseases amongst sheep or cattle en route to Britain; not to give a right to claimants like Gorris.

In *Smith* v *Hughes*, section 1 of the Street Offences Act 1959 stated: 'It shall be an offence for a common prostitute to loiter or solicit in a street or public place for the pur-poses of prostitution.' Prostitutes began trying to attract customers by signalling to the men from balconies or from windows. The report notes that the prostitutes would indic-ate the price by raising three fingers—and that on one occasion they received a counter-offer of two raised fingers! The Divisional Court of the Queen's Bench Division (on an appeal by way of case stated) decided that the mischief of the Act was to 'clean up the streets'. The words of section 1 did not indicate **who** had to be in the street; and so an offence had been committed under the section.

It is probably fair to say that, today, the distinction between the mischief and golden rules is, in the minds of some judges, so fine as to be virtually non-existent. It could even be argued that both rules have become subsumed within a general purposive approach. An example of such thinking can be seen in Lord Diplock's approach to the Abortion Act 1967 in *Royal College of Nursing* v *DHSS* [1981] AC 800; [1981] 1 All ER 545. His lordship began by defining his method for discovering the purpose of the Act:

> one starts by considering what was the state of the law relating to abortion before the passing of the Act, what was the mischief that required amendment, and in what respect was the existing law unclear.

He continued his analysis by looking at the whole context of the abortion problem—its social and economic aspects, as well as its legal history. He then concluded that:

> the wording and structure of the section are far from elegant, but the policy of the Act, it seems to me, is clear. There are two aspects to it: the first is to broaden the grounds upon which abortions may be lawfully obtained; the second is to ensure that the abortion is carried out with all proper skill and in hygienic conditions.

Be careful, however, not to assume that, in discovering the 'purpose' of an Act the judges are dealing with some sort of absolute, clearly definable, objective. Discovering the purpose of a rule is often an act of creative interpretation by the judge. Purposes and reasons for legislating are at least as indeterminate as the rules themselves.

8.4 Secondary Aids to Construction

The three 'Canons of Construction' so far considered are sometimes called **primary** aids to interpretation. It is now necessary to consider a set of secondary rules that can be employed within the framework of the primary aids to facilitate interpretation. These relate either to the use that can be made of parts of the statute itself, or to external (*extrinsic*) materials. Many of the rules noted below are simply rules of grammar which are not unique to legal terminology. For instance, to borrow part of the exercise we set at the end of this chapter, consider the following list: *cats, dogs, horses, cattle, sheep, pigs, and snakes or insects common to the British Isles*. Is it only snakes and insects that have to be common to the British Isles?

8.4.1 The Title of the Act

It is very tempting to point to the long or short title in order to show the purpose of the Act. It should be stressed that the long title is rarely used for this purpose and the short title is practically irrelevant. A classic example of this is the case of *R* v *Galvin* [1987] QB 862; [1987] 2 All ER 851. Galvin acquired 'restricted' Ministry of Defence documents. When Galvin was charged under the Official Secrets Act 1911 he argued that the documents had ceased to be secret and had never actually been 'official'—which, he said, is what the title of the Act demanded. Nevertheless he was found guilty because the section referred only to 'documents' and the title, being merely a label, had to give way to the words actually used in the section. The conviction, however, was quashed on other grounds.

On the use of the long title, see *Vacher* v *London Society of Compositors* [1913] AC 107. Note also that special rules will apply to the use of the Schedules that often appear at the end of an Act: see *Buchanan & Co. Ltd* v *Babco Forwarding & Shipping Ltd* [1978] AC 141; [1977] 3 All ER 1048.

8.4.2 Inclusory Words and Lists

A word which often arises in a statute is 'include': thus you find a section which might read:

> For the purposes of this Act references to sending include delivering, causing to be sent or delivered, transferring and posting.

The question would then be whether the word 'include' meant all the subsequent terms were included **and everything else was excluded** or that the subsequent terms were examples only, so that other terms might also be included. For instance, should 'distributing' or 'handing out' be included? Again, think of an everyday example: if you say that the Football Association Premiership includes Manchester United, Liverpool, and Arsenal, does this mean that there is no other team in the league? On the other hand, if you say that the Grand Slam tournaments in golf include the US Masters, the British Open, the US Open, and the US PGA, there are in fact no others, so this list has 'included' everything.

As we noted above, this problem was considered in *Coltman* v *Bibby Tankers* [1988] AC 276; [1987] 3 All ER 1068. The House of Lords solved the problem by looking at other sections in the Act which listed things. These other lists were very specific when not introduced by the word 'include'. This tended to indicate that when the word 'include' did occur it was merely stating examples, so that items not stated in the list might still fall within the definition of 'equipment' in the Act. Thus a ship was 'included' in the definition of equipment when that definition read: 'equipment includes any plant and machinery, vehicle, aircraft, and clothing.' Lord Oliver stated at 1073a:

> The key word in the definition is the word 'any' and it underlines, in my judgment, what I would in any event have supposed to be the case, having regard to the purpose of the Act, that is to say that it [the subsection] should be widely construed so as to embrace every article of whatever kind furnished by the employer for the purposes of his business.

Thus the mere fact that a list is introduced by the word 'includes' does not automatically mean that the list is open-ended. Much more needs to be considered. Indeed, we strongly recommend you to read this case as it encompasses many of the techniques of statutory interpretation discussed in this chapter—including a reference to the long title of the Act which is introduced without excuse or explanation (showing how judges—if not students—can bend the rules when they so wish).

Legal maxims (there are more to come and many we do not cover) used to be the lifeblood of any lawyer; today they are looked on with some disdain, especially as they are often contained in Latin phrases. But this loses sight of the history by which they came about (we are not the first generation of lawyers to struggle making sense of a document) and the fact that they are still useful grammatical tools. As long as we do not regard ourselves as slaves to these maxims, they can still help a great deal (see also Graham, 2001). Nevertheless, we know from bitter experience that students do not like dealing with these maxims (not least because of the problems of pronunciation).

8.4.3 *Expressio Unius est Exclusio Alterius*

Closely connected to the problem of what is meant by 'include' is the position where a simple list of words appears. Can other words be added to the list? As always there is a Latin maxim to cover this: *expressio unius est exclusio alterius* (the expression of one thing also known as inclusion to others or exclusion *alterius*–the inclusion of one thing is the exclusion of others). Using this maxim one can argue that if the legislature produces a list of items then it is logical that all other items were specifically excluded. Thus one might use this rule to decide whether a faith healer fell within 'clairvoyant, fortuneteller or diviner'. This maxim might have applied in *Coltman* had it not been for the presence of the word 'include'.

8.4.4 *Eiusdem Generis*

What should happen when an Act employs a generic but non-exhaustive list? For example, an Act may state that a licence is required to keep 'dogs, cats, budgerigars and **other animals**'. Would you consider that a cow could be included on that basis? Obviously it is difficult to say without more information about the context in which those words appear. We can, however, identify a specific legal method of dealing with such a problem by saying that where general words follow a list of specific words then the general words must be read according to the *genus* (i.e. type or group) of the preceding specific words. It is the legal equivalent of explaining what one means by 'etcetera'. Thus, we must discover the *genus* which our named categories have in common and then interpret the general words ('other animals') so that they do not conflict with the specific words ('dogs' etc.). This is called the *eiusdem generis* rule.

   Although this is a very useful rule of grammar, that is all it is; one still has to persuade the court that the *genus* of the preceding words is what you say it is. A good example of the arguments that may surround this rule arose in *Massey* v *Boulden* [2002] EWCA Civ 1634, where the Court of Appeal had to decide whether a person had the right to drive a vehicle along a track which ran across a village green, owned by another person, in order to gain access to his home. The owner of the land submitted that the use of the track contravened section 34(1)(a) of the Road Traffic Act 1988 which states that a person commits an offence if 'without lawful authority [they drive] a mechanically propelled vehicle—(a) on to or upon any common land, moorland or land of any other description, not being land forming part of a road...'. The Court held that it was quite difficult to identify what the *genus* might be here but a village green would certainly fall within its scope (other types of land might be more difficult to decide upon). The use of the track therefore contravened section 34.

In our example concerning the phrase 'or other animals' we could therefore argue, depending upon context, that 'other animals' could refer to any commonly domesticated animal, or to **any** commonly domesticated animal normally **kept as a pet**. Either interpretation might be feasible, which is why it is important to remember that such rules are secondary aids—and therefore used only within the context of our understanding of the provision as a whole.

See, for examples of this rule in operation, *Powell* v *Kempton Park Racecourse* [1899] AC 143 on whether Tattersall's Ring fell within 'other place' in the phrase 'house, office, room or other place'—it did not; *R* v *Staniforth, R* v *Jordan* [1976] 3 WLR 887; [1976] 3 All ER 775 on whether pornographic material could fall outside the definition of obscene material under the Obscene Publications Act 1959 as being 'in the interests of science, literature, art or learning, or of other objects of general concern'. The argument was that the obscene material had psychotherapeutic value, so falling within the definition. That argument failed in the House of Lords.

8.4.5 *Noscitur a Sociis*

Linked with the *eiusdem generis* approach is the maxim *noscitur a sociis*—a word is known by its associates. The meaning of a word is affected by the surrounding words and should be interpreted accordingly. This rule is similar to the *eiusdem generis* rule and students often confuse the two. The *eiusdem generis* rule comes into effect only when dealing with general words at the end of a list. Thus if we take the Wills Act 1837, section 20 as an example, one of the ways of revoking a will is by 'burning, tearing, or otherwise destroying'. The *eiusdem generis* rule tells us that 'or otherwise destroying' is to be read in the light of burning and tearing; the cases showing us that this requires an act of physical violence rather than, say, amending the text or crossing things out. The *noscitur a sociis* rule cannot be used here. It could only apply if the section read: 'burning, tearing, mutilating, or defacing.' Then one would ask: what if the will had been partially destroyed by fire? How should you read the word 'burning'? Does the burning have to be complete before the will is revoked, or is partial burning enough? From the surrounding words, especially 'mutilating' and 'defacing', it seems that this act does not have to be complete—that burning could be read as including partial burning.

To take one final example of the *noscitur a sociis* rule: the rule would be useful in ascertaining what *type* of fortune-teller would be covered in the list: 'clairvoyant, fortune-teller or diviner.' Would a palmist be covered?

We should emphasise, however, that all these are merely rules of grammar. A judge does not have to apply these rules if he or she believes the wording of the Act does not justify their use.

8.4.6 *Ignorantia Leges non Excusat*

Perhaps the most famous maxim of all: ignorance of the law is no defence (though this is in fact derived from Roman Law and was a maxim created when laws were fewer and more widely published, though not necessarily simpler).

8.4.7 Other Statutes

Provided statutes are *in pari materia* a word in an Act can be given the same meaning it had in an earlier Act. *In pari materia* means concerning the same matter. Thus the way the word 'horse' was interpreted in an Act concerning breeding rights could not be used readily to interpret the same word in an Act pertaining to the definition of a dangerous animal.

See, for instance, *R* v *Wheatley* [1979] 1 WLR 144; [1979] 1 All ER 954 on whether 'explosive substance' in the Explosive Substances Act 1883, section 4, included a pyrotechnic device. The 1883 Act gave no definition, but the Explosives Act 1875 dealt with the same subject matter and encompassed pyrotechnic devices in the term 'explosive'. Note also *British Amusement Catering Trades Association* v *Westminster City Council* [1988] 2 WLR 485; [1988] 1 All ER 740, in which, in order to decide whether video games in an amusement arcade fell within the meaning of 'exhibition of moving pictures' in the Cinematograph Act 1982, the court considered every occurrence of this phrase within the long line of Cinematograph Acts dating from 1909 and the Cinemas Act 1985.

Linked with the idea of *in pari materia interpretation* is what is sometimes referred to as the 'Barras principle'. It is taken from the speech of Viscount Buckmaster in *Barras* v *Aberdeen Steam Trawling and Fishing Co Ltd* [1933] All ER Rep 402, 411: 'It has long been a well established principle to be applied in the consideration of Acts of Parliament that where a word of doubtful meaning has received a clear judicial interpretation, the subsequent statute which incorporates the same word or the same phrase in a similar context, must be construed so that the word or phrase is interpreted according to the meaning that has previously been assigned to it.' One would have to say, however, that this is not really a principle of interpretation, more a useful starting point or presumption. It should be used with great caution (as was stated by the other Law Lords in *Barras* itself and again *per* Lords Scarman, Roskill, and Templeman in *R* v *Chard* [1984] AC 279; [1983] 3 All ER 637).

8.4.8 The Interpretation Act 1978

You should be aware of the existence of this Act, but it is not as helpful as it first sounds. The Act simply states that certain words will have a standard meaning unless specifically changed.

Thus 'month' means a calendar month and not 30 days; 'he' is read as including 'she'; singular words include the plural, and so on.

8.4.9 Punctuation

The modern view is that punctuation can be used as an aid to interpretation. Traditionally, however, this is not true of headings and marginal notes in a statute, though occasional references can be found to headings in particular if they help to resolve an ambiguity: see *Dixon* v *British Broadcasting Corporation* [1979] ICR 281; [1979] 2 All ER 112.

8.4.10 Dictionaries

Dictionaries can be used by judges where a word has no specific legal meaning. One must be careful here, however, as words can change meaning by dint of time, usage, and context.

One example of a court using dictionaries to interpret sections arose in *Flack* v *Baldry* [1988] 1 WLR 393; [1988] 1 All ER 412. The case concerned the legality of possessing a 'stun gun' which could administer an electric shock of 46,000 volts. Did this offend against the Firearms Act 1968 as a 'weapon designed for the **discharge** of any noxious liquid, gas, or other thing'? The court found that 'discharge' had a dictionary meaning of 'emit' rather than 'physical ejection', so that the stun gun was caught by the Act.

One has to tread carefully here, though. Different dictionaries often give different slants to the meaning of words. For instance, in one exercise we give to our students a key question arises whether a person has committed an act of 'violence' when he has been found guilty of causing criminal damage to a snack bar. Depending upon which dictionary is used you tend to get definitions which will stress either that 'violence' relates only to causing injury to people, or that it includes damage to property as well as injury to people.

8.4.11 *Travaux Préparatoires*

This translates literally as 'preparatory works'. In the English context it refers to the consideration of public materials by the courts in order to discern the purpose of the legislation. A common example is the reports or working papers (though not the recommendations) of law reform bodies such as the Law Commission or Criminal Law Revision Committee. The question as to whether White Papers may be referred to in aid of interpretation has been inconclusively mooted by the Court of Appeal in *Thomas* v *Chief Adjudication Officer and Secretary of State for Social Security* [1990] IRLR 436; [1990] 3 CMLR 611; but for earlier contrary authority see *Katikiro of Buganda* v *Attorney-General* [1961] 1 WLR 119.

In the European context, the willingness to consider *travaux préparatoires* has traditionally been greater. EC case law, for instance, thus includes references to the use of legislative proposals as published in the *Official Journal*; parliamentary debates in Member States, though never to the deliberations of the Council or Commission. Similarly, in the Commonwealth, the (English) exclusionary rules have gradually been relaxed across most jurisdictions since the early 1980s: see Zander (1994:159–61) for examples.

8.5 The Use of Hansard

In contrast to what we have just said about the use of *travaux préparatoires* in European courts, the English courts have until recently taken a restrictive view of the range of documents which may be so used. For instance, all Parliamentary debates in the House of Commons and House of Lords are recorded in a text called *Hansard*. Traditionally, *Hansard* could not be referred to explicitly by a court in order to gauge Parliament's intention (although some judges have admitted over the years to looking at the debates anyway). In the international context, such as dealing with the interpretation of international treaties, the English courts have taken a more relaxed attitude: see *Fothergill* v *Monarch Airlines* [1981] AC 251; [1980] 2 All ER 696. And, in the European context, as more and more legislation has owed its origins to the European Community the House of Lords has referred to Hansard on several occasions and moved more towards harmonisation with European methods of interpretation in the use of *travaux préparatoires:* see *Pickstone* v *Freemans* [1988] 3 WLR 265; [1988] 2 All ER 803; *Litster* v *Forth Dry Dock* [1990] AC 546; [1989] 1 All ER 1134 and *R* v *Secretary of State for Transport, ex parte Factortame Ltd* [1990] 2 AC 85; [1989] 2 All ER 692.

8.5.1 *Pepper* v *Hart*

In 1992 the House of Lords delivered a blockbuster in the case of *Pepper (Inspector of Taxes)* v *Hart* [1992] 3 WLR 1032; [1993] 1 All ER 42. By a six to one majority (Lord Mackay LC dissenting) the House of Lords decided to allow reference to be made to *Hansard* in limited circumstances. Reference to Parliamentary materials will therefore be allowed where:

(a) legislation is ambiguous or obscure, or leads to an absurdity;

(b) the material relied upon consists of one or more statements by a minister or other promotor of the Bill, together if necessary with such other Parliamentary material as is necessary to understand such statements and their effect;

(c) the statements relied upon are clear.

In this case, the effect of permitting reference to Hansard was that the literal meaning of the statute in question was not followed.

Some comments by their Lordships are worth noting here. Lord Bridge stated (at 1039H, WLR) that:

> It should, in my opinion, only be in rare cases where the very issue of interpretation which the courts are called on to resolve has been addressed in Parliamentary debate and where the promoter of the legislation has made a clear statement directed to that very issue, that reference to Hansard should be permitted.

Lord Oliver commented (1042H, WLR):

> It can apply only where the expression of the legislative intention is genuinely ambiguous or obscure or where a literal or prima facie construction leads to a manifest absurdity...

Lord Mackay (dissenting) observed:

> I believe that practically every question of *statutory* construction that comes before the courts will involve an argument... [on (a) to confirm the meaning of a provision as conveyed by the text, its object and purpose; (b) to determine a meaning where the provision is ambiguous or obscure; or (c) to determine the meaning where the ordinary meaning is manifestly absurd or unreasonable]... It follows that the parties' legal advisors will require to study *Hansard* in practically every such case to see whether or not there is any help to be gained from it. I believe this is an objection of real substance. It is a practical objection not one of principle... (1037G, WLR)

> Such an approach appears to me to involve the possibility at least of an immense increase in the cost of litigation in which statutory construction is involved. (1038B, WLR)

Lord Bridge further commented on the issue of additional costs (1039H, WLR):

> Provided the relaxation of the previous exclusionary rule is so limited, I find it difficult to suppose that the additional cost of litigation or any other ground of objection can justify the court continuing to wear blinkers which, in such a case as this, conceal the vital clue to the intended meaning of an enactment... [W]here *Hansard* does provide the answer, it should be so clear to both parties that they will avoid the cost of litigation.

8.5.2 The Rise and 'Fall' of *Pepper* v *Hart*

Despite Lord Bridge's reassurances, *Pepper* v *Hart* initially cut major inroads into the traditional methods of statutory interpretation. In the six months immediately following the decision the House of Lords itself had made express use of *Hansard* in no fewer than three important cases: *Chief Adjudication Officer* v *Foster* [1992] 2 WLR 292; [1993] 1 All ER 705, *Stubbings* v *Webb* [1993] 2 WLR 120; [1993] 1 All ER 322, *R* v *Warwickshire County Council, ex parte Johnson* [1993] 2 WLR 1; [1993] 1 All ER 1022. In the last case, for instance, a question arose on the interpretation of Consumer Protection Act 1987, sections 20, 39, and 40. A shop had displayed a misleading 'price promise'. The problem was: could an employee who refused to honour the advertised price be guilty under the Act or was this limited to the employer/owner? The case hinged on the meaning of the rather curious and ambiguous phrase that liability rested on such notices appearing in 'any business of his'. Reference to *Hansard* showed that it had been clearly intended that only the employer should be liable.

In contrast to this, however, reservations or scepticism concerning this new-found research source began to emerge. Thus in *Sheppard* v *Commissioners of Inland Revenue*, 23 February 1993 (LEXIS transcript), Aldous J expressed concern regarding the problem of determining what is an ambiguity for the purposes of reference to Hansard and on the level of clarity required in a Minister's statement specifically on the issue in question. Indeed in *Melluish (Inspector of Taxes)* v *BMI (No. 3)* [1995] 3 WLR 630, the House of Lords itself expressed reservations on the over-use of *Pepper* v *Hart* (e.g. *per* Lord Browne-Wilkinson, who had been one of the Law Lords in *Pepper* v *Hart* itself, that the statement by the appropriate minister must be 'directed to the very point in question in the litigation').

However, before that, the full potential of *Pepper* v *Hart* was realised in *Thomas Witter Ltd* v *TBP Industries Ltd* [1996] 2 All ER 573. This case neatly illustrates the true width of the problem: the potential ambiguity of *any* statutory provision and the fragility of our existing understanding of established areas of the law. This case involved examining section 2(2) of the Misrepresentation Act 1967. Jacob J considered this subsection to be ambiguously drafted and, relying on the support of *Pepper* v *Hart*, decided to examine the relevant extracts from *Hansard*. His Lordship concluded that these extracts were sufficient to establish that the accepted meaning of the subsection was incorrect. This of course meant that the previous understanding of the great majority of academic writers (endorsed by judicial *obiter* comments) and practitioners since the inception of the Act was erroneous.

Such a reassessment of an area of law has occurred before, on many occasions and in many different ways—the flexibility of case law depends upon such changes. Nevertheless, it is worrying that *all* long-established principles built up using the pre-*Pepper* v *Hart* methods of interpretation are potentially open to re-examination. It gets even more worrying when one examines the quality of analysis and debate seen in Hansard regarding this section. It would not win prizes from Mr Spock. One wonders (especially as regards a Parliamentary debate that occurred in the pre-*Pepper* v *Hart* era) whether, for instance, the Solicitor-General knew when he responded to his few remaining colleagues at 3.30 a.m. on 20 February 1967 (some of them clearly keen to discuss another issue) that his comments would have the force of law, and be subjected to a level of analysis that would normally demand an opportunity for considered forethought and painstaking preparation? For further comment on this case, see Chandler and Holland (1995:503).

After all this initial confusion and enthusiasm things have settled down. A trawl through the cases shows an increasing reluctance to rely on extracts from *Hansard* unless the guidelines noted above have been shown to justify the search.

It is not surprising, therefore, to find more and more decisions where the courts are reluctant to allow references to Hansard without a fair bit of persuasion. For instance, in *Regina* v *Richmond upon Thames London Borough Council, ex parte Watson* [2001] QB 370; [2001] 1 All ER 436, the Court of Appeal was faced with the question whether section 117 of the Mental Health Act 1983 (as amended) required local authorities to provide and pay for certain 'after-care services' or whether it merely operated as a 'gateway' section to trigger provisions under other statutory provisions which they would not have to pay for. Counsel had submitted that words such as 'after-care services' were ambiguous and therefore triggered a reference to *Hansard*. The Court rejected this Otton LJ stating:

> The local authorities point to the lack of 'tightness' in the wording of the provision and the absence of regulations governing the exercise of the section 117 duty. Although there is a positive duty to provide the after-care services there is clearly a discretion as to the level at which those services should be provided . . . This discretion cannot be said to introduce ambiguity into the section. Similarly, the absence of any definition of 'after-care services' does not render the provision ambiguous. The absence of a definition simply points to the discretion accorded to the authorities in the appropriateness of the provision for each individual patient.

The case clearly demonstrates that merely because a particular interpretation is arguable or may lead to a perceived injustice against your client does not mean that the word or section is ambiguous or absurd so as to trigger a reference to Hansard. The court must be persuaded that such a reference is justified. One way to do this is to show internal inconsistencies within the Act, or to demonstrate the logical consequences of following only one line of interpretation, or to show that case law on this area has already been divided on the topic, as was the case in *Mirvahedy* v *Henley* [2001] EWCA 1749; [2002] QB 769. Equally, it should be stressed that the mere discovery of a ministerial statement does not mean anything in itself. Not only must that statement be clear but (as was illustrated in *Hone* v *Going Places Leisure Travel Ltd* [2001] EWCA Civ 947) one must also have regard to the context in which the statement was made: in this case it was clear that, looking at the full text of the speech, the minister had not been purporting to construe the relevant legislation at all.

These are real obstacles to making use of Hansard reports. However, sometimes you may persuade a court to look at Hansard *de bene esse.*

8.5.3 The *De Bene Esse* Approach

This means 'For what it's worth'. To take a point *de bene esse* is to allow it to be argued for the present but to make no ruling on whether, once things have been more fully argued, it will be accepted. In other words, to overcome the rather circular arguments that can arise over whether there is an absurdity and what Parliament really meant to do, judges sometimes allow the lawyer to refer them to *Hansard* but this does not mean that, in doing so, they accept that what is said in *Hansard* determines the point. Here is an example of its use by the Court of Appeal in *Shipley's Application*:

> Both parties pray in aid various extracts from *Hansard*...Although *de bene esse,* I considered the parliamentary statements relied upon by both sides. To my mind neither satisfies the stringent tests laid down in *Pepper* v *Hart*...

This can be seen in action in the Court of Appeal decision in *R* v *Deegan* [1998] 2 Cr App Rep 121. This concerned section 139 of the Criminal Justice Act 1998. Deegan had been found in possession of a folding pocket-knife which was capable of being locked into an open position. Section 139 made it an offence to have in a public place 'any article which has a blade or is sharply pointed except a folding pocket-knife'. Previous case-law had held that a knife which locked open was not a *folding* pocket-knife for the section 139 exemption. It was argued that a reference to Hansard under the *Pepper* v *Hart* rule would reveal statements showing that the type of knife being carried by Deegan was intended to be excluded from the section. The Court looked at these extracts *de bene esse.* After expressing the view that this was not an easy case, Waller LJ stated:

> Although in one sense the statements made in Parliament were clear, in that they undoubtedly thought they were excluding from this section not just pocket-knives that fitted the previous case law's interpretation of 'folding', but some which 'locked' when the blades were open, we think that in the sense required by *Pepper* v *Hart*, they were not clear. They were not clear because 'locking pocket-knives' is itself an ambiguous phrase. If in answer to that point it were said that the court could attempt to define the phrase by for example saying that it should only include 'locking pocket-knives' that were manually locked and manually unlocked...that would be asking the court to go beyond its proper function. It would no longer be interpreting the intention of Parliament, it would be writing the legislation it thought was reasonable. In those circumstances we do not think that the conditions of *Pepper* v *Hart* are fulfilled...

The *de bene esse* approach was evident again (though not specifically referred to) in two recent House of Lords' decisions which dealt with the problems of *Pepper* v *Hart*. The first case was that of *R* v *Hinks* [2000] 4 All ER 833 (a case dealing with the meaning of 'appropriates' in section 1 of the Theft Act 1968). Lord Steyn quoted a famous statement by Lord Reid in the *Black-Clawson* case (see above) that: 'We often say that we are looking for the intention of Parliament, but that is not quite accurate. We are seeking the meaning of the words which Parliament used. We are seeking not what Parliament meant but the true meaning of what they said.' Lord Steyn used this as the basis for his refusal to allow counsel to submit (supposedly under the rule in *Pepper* v *Hart*) a memorandum written by the drafter of the Theft Act to the Larceny Sub-Committee of the Criminal Law Revision Committee, explaining what he had thought he had meant by the term 'appropriates'. This is perhaps not too surprising, as it really was pushing the boundaries to argue that such a memorandum fell within the *Pepper* v *Hart* guidelines.

A short time later the House of Lords commented on a number of important statutory interpretation points in *R* v *Secretary of State, ex parte Spath Holme* [2001] 1 All ER 195. One of those points was the admissibility of *Hansard*. All the Lordships were clear that the guidelines laid down in *Pepper* v *Hart* should be adhered to strictly. On the facts their Lordships held that, as the words in question were not ambiguous, reference to *Hansard* was not permissible. However, the key area of disagreement in this case ironically concerned what was meant by 'an ambiguity'. Their Lordships were clear that if the words in the statute were ambiguous then *Hansard* could obviously now be referred to. However, what if the words themselves were clear but there was some 'ambiguity' as to what the words were meant to do: what was the policy or purpose behind the statute? Could this type of ambiguity trigger a reference to *Hansard*?

The issue in *Spath Holme* was whether a minister could issue an order capping rent increases for certain types of tenants. The words were clear as to the minister's powers; the argument was as to when he could exercise those powers. The history of the relevant statutes showed that such a power was first introduced because of massive problems of inflation in the 1970s, but updating and consolidating legislation had since been added, when no such inflation existed. All the Acts were silent as to whether the policy or purpose was limited to introducing capping only where there were problems of inflation or on wider grounds, but there were some statements to be found in *Hansard*. So, was the ministerial power limited to interfering only when there was high inflation, or could it be invoked for other reasons?

Lords Bingham, Hope, and Hutton felt that *Pepper* v *Hart* was never designed to allow reference to *Hansard* in order to ascertain what the Executive (the Government) had in mind as their policy. Their Lordships felt that this was extending the decision in *Pepper* v *Hart* well beyond its limits, and one which usurped the power of Parliament and the courts. However, Lords Bingham and Hope thought there might be rare instances where this would be permissible. As Lord Bingham stated: 'Only if a minister were, improbably, to give a categorical assurance to Parliament that a power would not be used in a given situation, such that Parliament could be taken to have legislated on that basis, does it seem to me that a Parliamentary statement on the scope of a power would be properly admissible' (at 212a). However, Lords Nicholls and Cooke took the opposite line and felt that *Pepper* v *Hart* 'ambiguities' *could* extend to matters of policy: 'The purpose for which a statutory power is conferred is just as much a question of interpretation of the statutory provision as is the meaning of a particular word or phrase' (*per* Lord Nicholls at 218b). Though Lord Cooke also noted that 'Government statements, however they are made and however explicit they may be, cannot control the meaning of an Act of Parliament...it is for the court...to decide how much importance, or weight, if any, should be attached to a government statement'. (at 218h).

8.5.4 The Practice Direction

To help deal with the real and practical difficulties of referring to *Hansard* material, there is now a practice statement relating to the use of *Hansard*: *Supreme Court Practice Direction (Hansard: Citation)* [1995] 1 WLR 192. This demands, for instance, that anyone wishing to rely on *Hansard* must serve copies of the extract on the court and other parties, together with a brief summary of argument, not less than five working days before the hearing.

8.5.5 Views on *Pepper* v *Hart*

There is some division in the legal world as to the efficacy of *Pepper* v *Hart*. Indeed, there is some division between the authors of this book. There are certainly undoubted advantages in making use of all relevant materials to interpret a statute, and the cases to date have generally allowed perceived justice to win over technicalities. The rule was being eroded anyway, in practice if not in law. Equally, Lord Mackay's words as to the extra level of research and costs involved in litigation should not be disposed of lightly. Possibly more pertinent to this book is the fact that practitioners, academics, and law students will now have to come to terms with a new source of material in their research. Despite the appearance of *Hansard* on CD-Rom (and its limited introduction on the Internet), such research can prove difficult. The CD-Rom and Internet access relates only to recent years; for any other research one has to overcome the appalling indexing for *Hansard*. Moreover, reports on the Committee stage are held in only a handful of libraries across the country—and yet this is where many important amendments are recorded. All this is in addition to the fact that when you start you can never be sure you will find anything at all—a point which your paying client will only be too happy to appreciate.

On a wider scale, however, one of the objections to *Pepper* v *Hart* might be that it encourages (perhaps even obliges) the courts to adopt an assumption of ministerial infallibility when describing the meaning or purpose of statutory language. The problem is well illustrated by the debate on the effect of the Criminal Appeal Act 1995 below.

8.5.6 Example of *Pepper* v *Hart* in Action

Section 2 of the 1995 Act amended section 2(1) of the Criminal Appeal Act 1968, which governs the grounds for appeals against conviction to the Court of Appeal. The original section 2(1) stated:

(1) Except as provided by this Act, the Court of Appeal shall allow an appeal against conviction if they think—
  (a) that the verdict of the jury should be set aside on the ground that under all the circumstances of the case it is unsafe or unsatisfactory; or
  (b) that the judgment of the court of trial should be set aside on the ground of a wrong decision of any question of law; or

(c) that there was a material irregularity in the course of the trial, and in any other case shall dismiss the appeal:

Provided that the Court may, notwithstanding that they are of opinion that the point raised in the appeal might be decided in favour of the appellant, dismiss the appeal if they consider that no miscarriage of justice has actually occurred.

The section had been widely criticised for its complexity and lack of precision, which had arguably contributed to a number of miscarriages of justice. By contrast, the new provision states:

Subject to the provisions of this Act, the Court of Appeal—
(a) shall allow an appeal against conviction if they think that the conviction is unsafe; and
(b) shall dismiss an appeal in any other case.

Do you think the new section increases or curtails the powers of the Court of Appeal? This is where the debate begins. During the passage of the Criminal Appeal Bill, the Home Secretary and his Minister of State affirmed that the new clause essentially *restated* existing practice under the 1968 Act in a more comprehensible form: a view which Professor Sir John Smith (1995:924) has described as 'the most remarkable feat of "restatement" in history. It takes over 50 pages of *Archbold* to deal with the present practice of the Court of Appeal'.

Although it was well-recognised that there were substantial areas of overlap between the three grounds in the 1968 Act, there is a substantial amount of case law which shows that everything after 'unsafe' was not just meaningless verbiage. This must support a counter-argument (as Smith notes at 1995:927) that the grounds of appeal have actually been *narrowed* by the 1995 Act.

The view represented in Hansard is at odds therefore both with the desires of the Royal Commission to increase the powers of the Court and with a more literal analysis of the legislative history. In reality the Court of Appeal will almost certainly adopt the Parliamentary view, though whether by stealth or direct reference to Hansard remains to be seen. One might argue this is the most 'democratic' solution, since it means that the Act is being interpreted according to the will of Parliament rather than the whim of unelected judges. Nevertheless, you may consider that this example offers such a cavalier approach to the language of law reform that it is quite breathtaking. Hypothetically, it would be possible for the judges to turn round and interpret the section more narrowly than Parliament intended, by reference perhaps only to former case law on 'unsafe [and unsatisfactory]' on the basis that there is no linguistic ambiguity or obscurity in the new section 2. The ambiguity (in intent) arguably becomes apparent only through reading Hansard. For Parliament not just to adopt the Humpty Dumpty approach to language ('words mean what I say they mean') but to expand it to say that 'words imply all that I say they imply' seems a somewhat dangerous and uncertain practice. Moreover, one wonders, would Parliament have taken such an apparently sanguine view of the Minister's assurances without *Pepper v Hart*?

8.5.7 Recent Views on *Pepper v Hart*

Some problems have already begun to surface in the case law, the main one being that the courts often do not adhere to the principles stated in *Pepper v Hart* (but then neither did their Lordships do so in *Pepper* v *Hart* itself anyway). Inconsistency is not helpful, but one of the most interesting references to *Hansard* so far arose in the Court of Appeal decision in *R* v *Secretary of State for the Home Department, ex parte Hickey (No. 1)* [1995] 1 All ER 479. Here, between the decision of the Divisional Court and the appeal to the Court of Appeal, the Secretary of State was asked a question regarding the meaning of the Act in question. The Court of Appeal made specific reference to the question and answer as reported in *Hansard* ([1995] 1 All ER, 485c). Leaving aside the problem of a statement made between hearing and appeal being referred to, the statement by the Secretary of State clearly post-dates the Act being examined. If Ministers can make statements *after* the passing of an Act to explain its meaning, which may be taken as authoritative by the courts, this is even more dangerous than the opponents of *Pepper* v *Hart* most feared. One hopes that this is an isolated incident, but it does illustrate the range of uses to which the *Pepper* v *Hart* decision has been put.

It is worth noting here the article by Summers and Marshall (1992:213) advocating the interpretation of statutes based on using the 'ordinary' meaning of words as opposed to wide purposive or teleological methods and applauding English law for not falling for the same loose approach to interpretation seen in the USA—an article published just before *Pepper* v *Hart* appeared. For a fascinating and critical analysis of *Pepper* v *Hart* by the Law Lord, Lord Steyn (speaking extra-judicially), which calls for a review of the case, we would recommend you read his article entitled '*Pepper* v *Hart*; A Re-examination' (Steyn: 2001)

Two final comments: first, given this sea change in interpretation techniques, we cannot state categorically that the 'rules' noted above concerning matters such as the bars on reference to the long and short titles to statutes are still sacrosanct. Secondly, once again we are instructed to refer to material extraneous to the statute only when the words are 'ambiguous' or 'obscure'. Do you feel you have heard these terms before? These are classic terms for preferring a purposive to a literal approach. But, as we commented earlier, there is a problem in defining these terms in the first place (see the very interesting account of the meaning of the term 'ambiguous' by Lord Cooke in *R* v *Secretary of State, ex parte Spath Holme* [2001] 1 All ER 195 at 219j).

One should therefore be very wary of using the rule in *Pepper* v *Hart* as if the finding of any statement which backs your interpretation automatically solves your problem or will be allowed as part of your argument. It is clear from their Lordships' speeches in *Spath Holme* that the criteria laid down in *Pepper* v *Hart* should now be viewed very strictly; further, that it is rare for such parliamentary material to prove helpful. As Lord Cooke said: 'Reference to *Hansard* does not often help the courts with issues of statutory interpretation, but experience has shown that it does so occasionally. . . . A practice of constant citation is unacceptable to the court.'

8.6 From Rules to Reality

The question posed by all students at some stage is: in what order will the rules be applied? The analysis of statutory interpretation found in many textbooks begs the same question. Most of them fail to answer it. The reality is that not only is there no answer; it is the wrong question to ask.

The right question is: how do judges choose to explain the construction they have placed on the statute? Posed this way the question recognises, as Willis put it, that there is not 'one great sun of a *principle*, "the plain meaning rule", around which revolves in planetary order a series of minor rules of construction.... Any one of these approaches may be selected by your court' (1938:1). There is no rule that says a judge must look at the literal meaning of words first. The fact that many judges do this is simply the recognition that most English judges do not want to be seen to be *creating* law, and a logical starting point in reading any document is to see what has actually been written. By examining the literal meaning of the words judges appear to take a logical and safe line. However, if they wish then to rely on a more purposive argument they will do so by finding absurdity or inconsistency; they have at least guarded against some criticism.

8.6.1 Styles of Interpretation

We would suggest that interpretation is a question of *style*, not rules. By emphasising the *style* of judging we would draw a parallel with Llewellyn's analysis of how judges use case law. In 1960 Llewellyn drew attention to two different approaches used by judges; he termed these 'grand' and 'formal'. The 'grand' style reflects a judicial willingness to base a decision on public policy and to take a creative or flexible approach to precedent. Conversely, the 'formal' style demands rigid adherence to traditional doctrine and the denial of a creative judicial function.

So too, we submit, is this the case with statutory interpretation. Judges who employ the 'grand' style place substantial emphasis on the external context of the statute. They place less weight on the dictionary meaning of words, preferring to seek out the sense of the provision in question. One who adopts the 'formal' style, however, is more concerned with the form the statute takes, the internal context, and the perceived hierarchy of the rules.

The formalist will, therefore, frequently seek to find a safe embarkation point in a literal approach. This does not prevent the formalist then making use of the golden and mischief rules; but this method of 'follow the pathways' analysis provides appropriate justification for departing from a strictly literal interpretation. Such 'formalism' can be seen extensively in the House of Lords' decision in *Duport Steel* v *Sirs* (cited above).

On the other hand, the 'grand' style will encompass those judges who will tend to move much more easily to reliance on the external context for interpretation. Such can be seen in *Royal College of Nursing* v *DHSS*; but equally its ranks will also be filled by judges prepared to go beyond this point to using a 'teleological' approach. A teleological approach is a rather grandiose name for an interpretation which is based on the purpose or object of the text confronting the judge. It goes beyond the inquiry as to the external context of the Act; examining instead the broader social, economic, perhaps political reasons behind the Act. It thereby attempts to give the fullest effect to the grand design of the law. It is, in the end, not really different from a purposive approach; it is more an extreme method of discovering that purpose and surfaces more in the analytical styles of European judges than in English Law.

The hallmark of the 'grand' style is often that the approach is extremely credible from a commonsense viewpoint: the authority for such (often) sweeping statements is less clear.

8.6.2 Example of the Use of Different Styles

In support of the above analysis any examples are inevitably somewhat selective. However, we suggest that a good illustration of these styles in action is a case we first mentioned in **Chapter 5** concerning *stare decisis: Davis* v *Johnson* [1979] AC 264; [1978] 1 All ER 841 (CA) and 1132 (HL).

Jennifer Davis and Nehemiah Johnson were joint tenants of a council flat. Davis was subjected to extreme violence by Johnson and eventually fled the flat with her infant child. She applied to the county court, under the Domestic Violence and Matrimonial Proceedings Act 1976 (DVA), section 1, for an injunction restraining Johnson from assaulting or molesting her or the child and ordering him to vacate the flat and not return. At first the injunction was granted and then withdrawn. We are concerned with the case in the Court of Appeal and the House of Lords. The case illustrates the points we have been making because, even when the various judges were agreed as to the outcome, their approaches to the question of interpretation differed extensively.

The case is dealt with in texts mainly as regards the issue of *stare decisis* raised by the Court of Appeal's judgment. We will not dwell on that aspect of the case in this analysis. However, the case is a fine example of the areas of judicial precedent and statutory interpretation overlapping; and this is an aspect of statutory interpretation that is worth noting. As with judicial precedent, cases concerning statutory interpretation do not exist in isolation. When a court is considering the meaning of a statute it will frequently have to interpret it in the light of previously decided cases.

Returning to *Davis* v *Johnson*: in the Court of Appeal Lord Denning MR, Sir George Baker P, and Shaw LJ found in favour of Ms Davis and the injunction was granted. Goff and Cumming-Bruce LJJ dissented. The House of Lords unanimously dismissed Johnson's further appeal. These are three points we need to examine here:

(a) what was the question of interpretation?

(b) how did the judges in the Court of Appeal set about the question of interpreting the statute? and

(c) how did the House of Lords interpret the statute?

We shall now consider each of these.

(a) What Was the Question of Interpretation?

Section 1 of the DVA stated:

(1) Without prejudice to the jurisdiction of the High Court, on an application by a party to a marriage a county court shall have jurisdiction to grant an injunction containing... [(a) and (b) are irrelevant here] ... (c) a provision excluding the other party from the matrimonial home...

(2) Subsection (1) above shall apply to a man and a woman who are living with each other in the same household as husband and wife as it applies to the parties to a marriage and any reference to the matrimonial home shall be construed accordingly.

So, did this section apply to the case in hand? It was argued that section 1 was procedural in its effect; it had not changed the existing law on property rights and could not have been meant to do away with these rights. In other words, if the man had property rights in the home (e.g. as a joint tenant, as was the case here) he could not be excluded from the property.

The *stare decisis* point (see **Chapter 5**) was that there were two binding Court of Appeal decisions where similar applicants to Davis had failed: *B* v *B* [1978] Fam 26; [1978] 1 All ER 821, and *Cantliff* v *Jenkins* [1978] 2 WLR 177n; [1978] 1 All ER 836.

(b) How Did the Judges in the Court of Appeal Set About the Question of Interpreting the Statute?

Lord Denning began by recounting the history of the Act—an Act designed to protect 'battered wives'. He then commented that 'No one, I would have thought, could possibly dispute that those plain words [section 1 above] by themselves cover this very case.' One sees here a reliance on the literal reading of the section (though without full explanation) and hence the 'formal' style in operation.

In reviewing the two earlier Court of Appeal decisions, Lord Denning set about proving they had inadequately interpreted the section. If *B* v *B* was right, he argued, the only woman who could obtain an injunction would be one who owned the property solely. Thus, he said, 'In order to give s. 1 any effect at all, the court must be allowed to override the property rights of the man' (849b). Even when faced with House of Lords authority which appeared to give preference to the protection of property rights, Lord Denning reacted: 'Social justice requires that personal rights should, in a proper case, be given priority over rights of property . . . I prefer to go by the principles underlying the legislative enactments rather than the out-dated notions of the past' (849e–f). This is a purposive approach in the 'grand' style. The term 'social justice' looks like a logical and analytical argument, but in fact it has appeared from nowhere. Try to look up 'social justice' as a legal term of art: you will have difficulty.

Lord Denning then returned to the history of the Act and investigated Reports of Select Committees and statements made in Parliament. This was more than simple reliance on the 'mischief rule' and again demonstrates a 'grand' style purposive approach.

Sir George Baker P began by discerning the 'mischief' on which the DVA centred by reference to legal history and the long title of the Act. There is nothing apparently unconventional in this. On the whole this is still a 'formal' approach; though it moves away from the strict canons of interpretation by its premature use of the long title. That mischief was the protection of family partners (married or unmarried) from violence. His analysis continued on a 'formal' basis: he rejected the idea that only a woman who was a sole owner could bring such an action. This interpretation he justified on the grounds that any other interpretation would deprive the Act of any practical meaning or purpose. Although Sir George Baker talks of 'purpose' the style of the judgment is still 'formal'. He had to make the point as to 'purpose' in order to overcome the decision in *B* v *B*. What he is actually saying is that:

(a) a literal reading of section 1 produces this solution; it gives the woman a right to have the violent male excluded; it does not even mention a limit to be placed on this; and

(b) it was the earlier cases which had gone beyond this literal reading by importing into the wording the sanctity of property rights and, in doing so, had not implemented the purpose of the Act. He is therefore arguing that it is the use of a 'formal' style which produces the real purpose and not the 'grand' style.

Shaw LJ first considered that the meaning of the section was plain: nothing in the wording took account of the 'other party's' property rights so it could not have intended this to be relevant. He reviewed the arguments to the contrary, and, though attracted by them, concluded that the 'section would be utterly stultified' if nobody but a sole owner could gain the injunction. The general theme of the section was to subordinate property rights to the need to protect the victim of violence. Shaw LJ's decision thus has a strong 'formalist' feel about it, though there are odd hints of a wider approach such as: 'The construction of a statute dealing with a morbid aspect of society must, it seems to me, be pursued in the practical context of the evil sought to be remedied rather than with analytical detachment' (876a).

Goff LJ (dissenting) dwelt on the *stare decisis* aspect and felt bound by the earlier decisions although he expressly did not agree with them. However, he made some comment on the interpretation of the section. He reiterated the point that a woman should not have to be sole owner of the home in order to make the application, for this would deprive the section of all effect. Goff LJ continued in a classic 'formalist' vein by analysing the relationship of section 1 to other parts of the Act. He concluded that, if he were free of binding precedent, he would adopt a 'liberal approach' and grant the injunction because:

> the strict construction ... virtually strikes the power of eviction in s. 1(1)(c) ... since where the (woman) is sole owner of the property she does not need it ... yet where she is not sole owner and so the Act is needed to protect her from just the same evil, it is held inapplicable. (874:d)

His Lordship was prepared to make reference to the mischief of the Act, but only by discovering that mischief on the accepted (limited) grounds. The meaning of Parliament, he said, must still be found in the words used in the Act.

Cumming-Bruce LJ (also dissenting) agreed with the decision in *B* v *B* and, for the most part, with Goff LJ; but concentrated his reasoning on points of precedent. The tenor of his judgment is in the 'formal' style. This is particularly noticeable in his references to the mischief rule and his consequent disapproval of using debates in Parliament to assess the purpose behind the Act on which he says (at 885):

> The task of this court is to decide what the words of the Act mean. The subject should be able, as in the past, to read the words of an Act and decide its meaning without hunting through Hansard to see whether the Act has a different meaning from that which is to be collected by application of the subtle principles of construction that this court has worked out over the last three centuries.

(c) How Did the House of Lords Interpret the Statute?

The House of Lords unanimously dismissed Johnson's appeal but the Law Lords were not of one mind in their reasoning.

Lord Diplock stated a preference for a narrow 'formal' approach to the interpretation of section 1, to which he added adverse comment on the practice of looking at reports on

Parliamentary debate to discern the meaning of a statute. This latter point was treated in the same way by the other Law Lords.

Viscount Dilhorne stated (at 1145) that the 'language is clear and unambiguous and Parliament's intention apparent'. To differentiate between married and non-married women would 'frustrate the intention of Parliament'. At first sight this appears to be a 'formal' style; but it is difficult to see from where Viscount Dilhorne derives his conclusions apart from the line (at 1145): 'Subsection (1) is not concerned with property rights.'

Lord Kilbrandon took a literal approach to the section; expressly agreeing with Lord Salmon and Lord Scarman.

Lord Salmon adopted a 'formal' style, moving from a literal reading ('It has been said that its [section 1] meaning is as plain as a pikestaff. I agree') to a more purposive stance based on an examination of the legal history of the Act and the mischief it sought to remedy.

Finally, Lord Scarman also looked to the mischief the Act was designed to remedy. Out of this Lord Scarman identified the purpose of the Act and had no difficulty extending this purpose to allow an unmarried woman with no property rights to be, nevertheless, granted the injunction. His Lordship's speech lies between the 'formal' and 'grand' styles. Lord Scarman concentrates on the mischief. There are wide statements of purpose (at 1156): 'I would expect Parliament, when dealing with the mischief of domestic violence, to legislate in such a way that property rights would not be allowed to undermine or diminish the protection being afforded.' But, having said that, the tenor of the speech is that of a formalist. He refuses, for instance, to look at *Hansard* to determine either mischief or purpose; and the other pillar to his decision is effectively that Parliament has stated a right clearly so if it affects property rights by a side wind, so be it.

Thus when one just adds up the decisions of all the judges (merely who won and who lost) in this case as well as *B* v *B* and *Cantliff* v *Jenkins* one finds seven Lords Justices on one side and the Master of the Rolls, the President of the Family Division, and two Lords Justices, together with five Law Lords on the other. And, as we have shown, this simple arithmetic does not reveal the diversity of approach.

As to the styles adopted: we have made some comment as to 'formal' or 'grand', but it must be admitted that we were occasionally in some healthy disagreement about which side of the line the judge's approach fell: and this is the very point we wish to emphasise. There are gradations even within these approaches; there can be no fixed formula. To the extent, for instance, that nearly every judge examined the mischief of the Act one could classify these remarks as being in the 'grand' style. But this does not always follow. Their approach may have been a standard example of turning to the literal meaning first, and only then falling back on the mischief. One needs (in good literalist fashion?) to read what they actually said. With this in mind we have been conservative in classifying every purposive approach as 'grand style'. In the end we would prefer you to make up your own mind and then ask: is the classification absolutely vital? And to this we would reply 'No', because our classification has only been designed to underscore our wider point that it is *styles* of interpretation that matter, not the rules.

Even where the judges are in agreement as to the outcome, the route they followed in getting there is not always shared by others. And one judge does not always maintain a consistent style. You may recall that Lord Denning, in *Davis* v *Johnson*, relies on a literal reading of the section at one stage, only to turn to the purpose of the Act later. He was not alone. There was, for instance, another problem with section 1: subsection (2) speaks of the woman having the right to claim the injunction if the parties are a man and a woman 'who *are living* with each other in the same household'. A literalist view would be that once she left she was no longer 'living' with the other party. Thus she could not bring her application.

Some judges who commented on this, e.g., Sir George Baker and Cumming-Bruce LJ stated that this could not mean that once the woman left (once 'the door shuts behind her') she lost her right to apply. Since most women faced with violence would have fled the home, such a literal interpretation would be a nonsense. Thus whilst one major point in the case is, on the whole, decided by using the 'formal' style, this second point could be said to have been decided: (a) in the 'formal' style (effectively the absurdity triggering the golden rule); or (b) in the 'grand' style—never mind the words, look at the purpose of the Act.

8.6.3 Criticisms of the Styles of Interpretation

Two final points need to be made here. First, it is very tempting to criticise those who adopt the 'grand' or purposive style as inventing reasons to fit decisions they have already reached. But on closer examination, when a judge adopts a more 'formal' style it is still often difficult to understand exactly where *the purpose* to which he refers came from, as we can see with the treatment of the phrase 'living with each other' above. The 'formal' style, ranging from literalism through to a more purposive approach, is not automatically entitled to be termed logical.

Secondly, if you approach the problems of interpretation by only asking 'which rule will be used?', you will miss the point. To adapt the chess analogy we used in **Chapter 6**: knowing that your opponent *can* 'castle' does not tell you that he *will* 'castle'. There is no set moment when your opponent will 'castle'—if at all. And if you are playing chess and do not know what 'castling' is, and when it may be used, you are at a serious disadvantage. Thus the rules describe the limits of what *may* happen; and they tell you what will *not* happen. Your opponent cannot move his pawn as if it were a knight, for instance. Equally there are limitations placed, by convention and common sense, on even the most purposive of judges. The rules may tell you *what* will happen in terms of basic structure; they cannot tell you *how* the game will progress. Each player has his own style.

We agree, therefore, with Twining and Miers that 'We do not believe that there is one right answer in hard cases or that problems of interpretation can be solved primarily by rules' (1991:376) and with Zander that 'The rules and principles of interpretation therefore do little or nothing to solve problems. They simply justify solutions usually reached on other grounds' (1994). It is not unfair for a student new to legal studies to ask which rule will be used; it is unfair, however, for us to pretend there is a 'right' answer.

However, most of your academic life will be spent presenting an argument for one side (the same will be true if you go on to practise law). Your problem does not therefore lie in which approach you should use to *determine* a case: that will not be your function.

Instead, your problem lies in determining which approach to adopt so that your argument is at its most convincing. Consequently, if you can master the types of reasoning available to you described above and learn to judge when one style is more applicable than another then you will have done all you can in presenting your argument professionally. The fact then that there is no single correct way to read a statute becomes a less daunting prospect.

8.7 Interpretation and the European Community

The influence of the European Community and the Civil Law's more 'purposive' approach to interpretation has begun to produce changes in judicial technique, even as regards legislation unconnected with the Community.

We have seen throughout this book that the Civil Law tradition is different from ours as regards case law. Here we must recognise that European legislation is structured in a manner that is also very different from English Acts of Parliament. The former follows the *Civilian* tradition in emphasising simplicity of drafting and a high degree of abstraction which is quite different from the exhaustive approach adopted by common law draftsmen. This means that a wide-ranging purposive approach (a teleological approach) is even more central to the interpretive process in the context of European Community legislation. Here, questions of broad economic or social aims are regularly considered by the courts, in a way that could be attacked in the English courts as a 'naked usurpation of the legislative function'.

This difference in approach has increasingly been recognised by the English judges when considering Community legislation, or even when considering English legislation that has been passed to fulfil an obligation under European Community law. Indeed the House of Lords completely (and openly) ditched the literal approach in *Litster* v *Forth Dry Dock* [1990] AC 546; [1989] 1 All ER 1134, where the statute in question was derived from a Directive of the European Community. Instead of the literal approach the Lords adopted a very wide purposive approach in line with European judges.

There have been inconsistencies of approach: the decision in *Litster* can be compared with that of a differently constituted House of Lords in *Duke* v *GEC Reliance (formerly Reliance Systems)* [1988] AC 618; [1988] 1 All ER 626, which took a far more traditional (i.e. narrow) approach to a related problem of interpretation. And few English judges have followed the line taken by Lord Denning in *Bulmer* v *Bollinger* [1974] Ch 401; [1974] 2 All ER 1226, to argue that the English courts should generally adopt a broad purposive approach, akin to the European style, in *all* cases. However, one can detect an increasing tendency towards this approach: see *R* v *Registrar-General ex parte Smith* [1991] 2 QB 393; [1991] 2 All ER 88. It is probably fair to say that the purposive approach is now the favoured method, both as regards Community-derived legislation and more 'home-grown' material.

We have left describing the methods utilised by European judges and lawyers to interpret legislation until **Chapter 10**.

8.8 Interpretation and the Human Rights Act 1998

In the next chapter we will deal with the topic of human rights at some length. For the moment we can note the following:

- The HRA 1998 came into effect on 2 October 2000.
- The HRA 1998 selectively incorporates elements of the European Convention on Human Rights by giving them a special legal status as 'Convention rights' under section 1 of the Act.
- The HRA 1998 requires judges to interpret legislation, so far as possible, consistently with Convention rights, and where consistency cannot be achieved, to declare such laws incompatible with Convention rights.

Thus, there is the potential that courts may be presented with arguments which require the judges to embark upon a radical re-think of all legislation that comes before them, whenever that legislation was enacted. And this will be on an even more significant scale than has occurred with the decision of *Pepper* v *Hart*.

8.9 Interpreting Secondary Legislation

When looking at the rules of statutory interpretation, it is easy to forget that much legislation is not created by statute but by statutory instrument or by-law. You will recall that we considered the growth, and importance, of this whole area of 'secondary legislation' in **Chapter 1**. We now need to consider the principles of interpretation that apply to secondary, or delegated, legislation.

As a starting point, we can say that generally the same rules do apply; which is a relief. The courts will look at the words used in a regulation, and interpret them according to their immediate linguistic context, only straying beyond this point in cases where the judge finds some absurdity or ambiguity demanding a more purposive approach. However, within this framework there are a number of substantive differences which reflect the fact that delegated legislation is, ultimately, a different creature from primary legislation.

This is because delegated legislation does not stand alone, in the way that an Act of Parliament does; it forms part of a legislative 'package' which includes the parent Act, and possibly other sets of regulations, which may affect our assessment of meaning. It is also because the courts are less constrained by problems of sovereignty when dealing with secondary as opposed to primary legislation.

These various differences can be explored in relation to two issues: the way in which we define the context of secondary legislation; and the way in which the courts handle questions of validity.

8.9.1 Defining the Context

As we have said, delegated legislation is to be read within a potentially wider context than statute law. The meaning of a particular provision is to be ascertained from the whole body of regulations of which it forms part, the parent Act and the Common Law. Exceptionally, the environment within which the regulations operate may also be considered as part of the context. The part played by each of these will be considered.

The regulations

The principle here is the same as that applied to statute. Just as you would not take one section of an Act out of context, so you should not consider a regulation outside its instrument. This may be particularly important if a reading of the parent Act offers alternative interpretations.

The parent Act

This is of central importance in defining meaning. This is emphasised by the fact that section 11 of the Interpretation Act 1978 requires words used in secondary legislation to be read as having the same meaning as in the parent Act, unless a contrary intention appears. This is fine, of course, so long as the meaning in the empowering legislation is clear! If it is not the court has to work it out for itself, from possibly a variety of competing explanations. Where there are doubts about the meaning of a word used within the parent Act, then it seems permissible for the court to look at both the parent Act and the regulations in assessing meaning: see *Nurse* v *Morganite Crucible Ltd* [1989] AC 692; [1989] 1 All ER 113.

The Common Law

This can also be of significance. The courts will be reluctant to interpret any delegated legislation in such a way that it conflicts with an established and fundamental principle of Common Law. For example, in *R* v *Secretary of State for the Home Department ex parte Anderson* [1984] QB 778; [1984] 1 All ER 920, the court had to assess the validity of order 5A(34) made by the Secretary of State under powers contained within the Prison Rules 1964, which were themselves made under the authority of section 47(1) of the Prison Act 1952. The order sought to prevent prisoners from obtaining visits from their legal advisers regarding complaints about their treatment in prison. Section 47(1) was silent in respect of such rights of access, so the court resorted to the Common Law. As a result it held that the fundamental right of access to the courts was wide enough to include a prisoner's right of access to legal advice. Parliament could not be deemed to have legislated against that right purely by implication, so order 5A(34) was held invalid. The courts' powers to declare secondary legislation invalid is a point to which we shall return.

8.9.2 The Principle of Validity

We noted in **Chapter 1** that the courts have the power to declare secondary legislation invalid where it involves an exercise of power exceeding that granted by Parliament. The decision to invalidate is thus dependent upon a question of interpreting, first, the scope of the powers contained within the delegated legislation and, secondly, the scope of the grant within the parent Act. In dealing with these situations, the courts have developed a number of principles.

First, in some specific instances, they have ruled that delegated legislation may only do certain things if there is express authorisation within the parent statute. There are two particularly significant situations where this applies:

(a) The courts apply a presumption against retrospectivity to prevent instruments having an effect on events which precede their introduction. The presumption may be used to require not only that the possibility of retrospective effect is specifically alluded to within the instrument, but that it was also within the ambit of the original grant of power by Parliament—see, e.g., *Marshall's Township Syndicate Ltd* v *Johannesburg Consolidated Investment Co. Ltd* [1920] AC 420, *Webb* v *Ipswich Borough Council* (1989) 21 HLR 325.

(b) Parliament will not be presumed to have authorised the amendment of primary by secondary legislation without clear authority within the parent Act. Thus, in the case of *McKiernan* v *Secretary of State, Guardian,* 28 October 1989, the Court of Appeal refused to imply that social security regulations modified an otherwise mandatory condition laid down under the parent Act in the absence of express authority. Even where such powers have been granted, the courts have tended to construe them narrowly. However, in *R* v *Secretary of State for Social Security ex parte Britnell* [1991] 1 WLR 198; [1991] 1 All ER 726, the House of Lords appeared significantly to depart from such a restrictive interpretation. In this case, their Lordships determined that a transitional provision in social security regulations could properly modify the parent Act so as to allow the Department of Social Security to recover an overpayment of supplementary benefit made some fifteen years earlier. This was despite the fact that such a conclusion required the court to find that what was, in reality, a radical policy innovation towards overpayments constituted no more than a 'modification' of the parent Act. The *Britnell* decision is, it is submitted, a worrying development, for as Professor David Feldman (1992:212 at 217) has argued:

> [i]f the courts are prepared to adjust principles of interpretation in order to legitimate a questionable exercise of delegated legislative power, this creates a threat to the principle of legality and, by implication, to the legislative supremacy of Parliament.

Secondly, the courts have, as we suggested at the beginning of this section, shown a marked reluctance to allow secondary legislation to be invalidated purely because of problems of ambiguity or uncertainty—*Percy* v *Hall* [1996] 4 All ER 523. The courts have used the maxim *ut res magis valeat quam pereat* ('it is better for a thing to have effect than to be void') to justify whichever of competing interpretations would be a valid exercise of power. This principle has become widely used in Common Law jurisdictions to avoid treating delegated legislation as *ultra vires*. Strictly speaking, it should not be adopted in cases where the meaning of the regulation is clear from the face of the document, or where its application would require a virtual rewriting of the legislation. In that respect it is no more than a manifestation of the rules against ambiguity.

Thirdly, in cases where delegated legislation is only partially invalid, the courts recognise that they have a power of 'severance'. Severance is a process whereby invalid portions of a document may be separated from those which are valid, leaving those valid parts still standing: see *DPP* v *Hutchinson, DPP* v *Smith* [1990] 2 AC 783; [1990] 3 WLR 196. As such, it can be seen as a derivative of the principle of validity. This point has been emphasised by a couple of more recent cases, which support the view that severance can apply in any situation where 'a law is held to be in part inconsistent with a higher law' (*per* Lord Goff in *Commissioner of Police* v *Davies* [1994] 1 AC 283 at 298) and not just to 'secondary legislation' as we have defined it so far. Thus, in the *Davis* case, the Privy Council held that part of section 28(8) of the (Bahamian) Dangerous Drugs Act 1988, which empowered a magistrate in certain contexts to commit a convicted person to the Supreme Court for sentencing with the possibility of life imprisonment, was void and unconstitutional. This was because it prevented an accused from exercising the right to jury trial for serious offences contained in the Bahamian Constitution. The Privy Council also held that this provision was severable from other, valid parts of the subsection. Moreover, in *British Sky Broadcasting* v *David Lyons* [1995] FSR 357, the English High Court appears to suggest, *obiter*, that *Hutchinson* severance could be applied to provisions of an Act of Parliament that are contrary to applicable EC law. The mechanics of 'severance' are extremely complex and we do not recommend that you consider them in any greater detail.

8.10 Illustration of How to Analyse a Case on Statutory Interpretation

The following case illustrates a number of these points on statutory interpretation. After the headnote etc., the judgment is noted in the left-hand column, with notes on legal method aspects appearing in the right-hand column. The case contains many of the aspects discussed throughout this book and highlighted above—the notable exceptions, because of the specific issues and the date the case was heard, being that of any European Community law or human rights references.

Director of Public Prosecutions v *Bull*
[1994] 3 WLR 1196
[QUEEN'S BENCH DIVISION]

1994 March 28: Mann LJ and Laws J
May 5

CATCHWORDS

Crime—Sexual offences—Soliciting—Man charged as common prostitute—Whether 'common prostitute' applying exclusively to women—Street Offences Act 1959 (c. 57) ss. 1(1), 2(1)

HEADNOTE

The term 'common prostitute' in section 1(1) of the Street Offences Act 1959 applies exclusively to female prostitutes. Where, therefore, a stipendiary magistrate accepted a submission of no case to answer to a charge that a male respondent, being a common prostitute, loitered in a street or public place for the purpose of prostitution, contrary to section 1(1) of the Act of 1959, and the prosecution appealed:

Held, dismissing the appeal, that the submission of no case to answer had been rightly accepted (post, p. 1201C–D, G).

CITATIONS

The following cases are referred to in the judgment of Mann LJ:

Fothergill v *Monarch Airlines Ltd* [1981] AC 251; [1980] 3 WLR 209; [1980] 2 All ER 696, HL(E)
Pepper v *Hart* [1993] AC 593; [1992] 3 WLR 1032; [1993] 1 All ER 42, HL(E)
R v *De Munck* [1918] 1 KB 635, CCA
R v *McFarlane* [1994] QB 419; [1994] 2 WLR 494; [1994] 2 All ER 283, CA
Wicks v *Firth* [1983] 2 AC 214; [1983] 2 WLR 34; [1983] 1 All ER 151, HL(E)

The following additional cases were cited in argument:

Dale v *Smith* [1967] 1 WLR 700; [1967] 2 All ER 1133, DC
R v *Ford (Graham)* [1977] 1 WLR 1083; [1978] 1 All ER 1129, CA
R v *Gray* (1981) 74 Cr App R 324, CA
R v *Kirkup* [1993] 1 WLR 774; [1993] 2 All ER 802, CA
R v *Webb* [1964] 1 QB 357; 3 WLR 638; [1963] 3 All ER 177, CCA

FACTS

Case Stated by the Wells Street Metropolitan Stipendiary Magistrate.
(*Statement of facts as appears in the report omitted. Facts are stated in the judgment below.*)

COUNSEL

Jeremy Carter-Manning QC and John McGuinness for the applicant.
Adrian Fulford for the respondent.

Cur. adv. vult.

COMMENTS ON THE TEXT

JUDGMENT

5th May

Mann LJ read the following judgment: There is before the court an appeal by way of case stated. The appellant is the Director of Public Prosecutions and the respondent is Andrew John Bull. The case has been stated by Mr Ian Michael Baker, metropolitan stipendiary magistrate for the Inner London commission area, in respect of his adjudication as a magistrates' court sitting at Wells Street Magistrates' Court, London, W1, on 27 April 1993.

§ *History of the case*

§ *A stipendiary magistrate is now called a District Judge (Criminal)*

On that day Mr Baker had before him a charge against the respondent to the effect that on 4 December 1992 he, being a common prostitute, did loiter in a street or public place for the purpose of prostitution contrary to section 1(1) of the Street Offences Act 1959. At the conclusion of the prosecution case counsel for the respondent submitted that there was no case to answer on the basis that section 1(1) applies only to female prostitutes. This

§ *Outline of facts and arguments*

submission was upheld by the magistrate, who has now posed this question for the opinion of the court:

> Whether I was correct in construing section 1(1) of the Street Offences Act 1959 so as to limit it to the activities of female prostitutes and to exclude from its scope the activities of male prostitutes.

§ *Phrasing of the Case Stated by the magistrate for consideration in the High Court*

The magistrate made certain findings of fact to which I think it unnecessary to refer. Suffice to say that he remarks in paragraph 7 of the case stated that had the submission not been accepted he would have held that there was a case to answer. So far as is material, the long title to the Act of 1959 is:

> An Act to make, as respects England and Wales, further provision against loitering or soliciting in public places for the purpose of prostitution...

§ *Indeterminate reference made to long title*

The further provision is to be found in sections 1 and 2. The material subsections of section 1 are subsections (1), (2) (as substituted by the Criminal Justice Act 1982, section 71) and (3):

§ *Key aspects of section 1 highlighted*

§ *Wording of the Act (as later amended)*

(1) It shall be an offence for a common prostitute to loiter or solicit in a street or public place for the purpose of prostitution.

(2) A person guilty of an offence under this section shall be liable on summary conviction to a fine of an amount not exceeding level 2 on the standard scale...or, for an offence committed after a previous conviction, to a fine of an amount not exceeding level 3 on that scale.

(3) A constable may arrest without warrant anyone he finds in a street or public place and suspects, with reasonable cause, to be committing an offence under this section.

The material subsection of section 2 is subsection (1), which provides:

> Where a woman is cautioned by a constable, in respect of her conduct in a street or public place, that if she persists in such conduct it may result in her being charged with an offence under section 1 of this Act, she may not later than 14 clear days afterwards apply to a magistrates' court for an order directing that there is to be no entry made in respect of that caution in any record maintained by the police of those so cautioned and that any such entry already made is to be expunged; and the court shall make the order unless satisfied that on the occasion when she was cautioned she was loitering or soliciting in a street or public place for the purpose of prostitution.

§ *Reference to a related section in the Act*

The other legislative provision which is material is the earlier section 32 of the Sexual Offences Act 1956, which provides: 'It is an offence for a man persistently to solicit or importune in a public place for immoral purposes.'

§ *Reference to a related Statute (of three years earlier)*

As Mr Jeremy Carter-Manning for the appellant pointed out, there are differences between the components of an offence under section 32 of the Act of 1956 and those of an offence under section 1(1) of the Act of 1959. Thus (i) section 32 requires actual soliciting *or importuning*; section 1(1) requires either actual solic-iting *or loitering*, (ii) section 32 requires *persistence*; section 1(1) does not, and (iii) section 32 requires *an immoral purpose*; section 1(1) requires a *prostitutional purpose*.

§ *Key differences in the working of the two Acts observed*

The submission for the appellant was that section 1(1) of the Act of 1959 is unambiguous and is not gender specific. Our atten-tion was drawn to the following factors which were relied upon: (i) The phrase in section 1(1) 'a common prostitute' was linguisti-cally capable of including a male person. The *Oxford English Dictionary*, 2nd ed. (1989), includes within the possibilities for 'prostitute,' 'a man who undertakes male homosexual acts for payment'.

§ *Reference to the arguments put to the court*

§ *Linguistic argument*

§ *Use of dictionary*

(ii) Lord Taylor of Gosforth CJ has recently said in *R v McFarlane* [1994] QB 419 424D that 'both the dictionary definitions and the cases show that the crucial feature in defining prostitution is the making of an offer of sexual service for reward'. I do not regard this factor as of significance. Lord Taylor CJ was speaking in a case which concerned a woman who had been clipping.

§ *Case quoted but distinguished ('clipping' means offering sexual services for reward, being paid in advance, but never intending to provide the service)*

(iii) Section 1(2) and 1(3) of the Act of 1959 refer respectively to 'a person' and 'anyone'.

§ *Wording or related section and subsections analysed*

(iv) In contrast section 2(1) refers specifically to 'a woman'. The reason for this is conjectured by Mr Carter-Manning to be that until the Sexual Offences Act 1967 homosexual acts between men were criminal offences and thus cautioning was inappropriate.

§ *Historical analysis*

(v) Since 1967 male prostitution has been in certain circum-stances not unlawful and accordingly in the new environment it is open to the court to interpret section 1(1) of the Act of 1959 as being applicable to prostitutes who are male 'even if this was not the original intent of the provision'. This in my opinion is a bold submission.

§ *Response to Counsel's invitation to read present law and social attitudes into the Act*

It was based upon observations by Lord Bridge of Harwich in *Wicks v Firth* [1983] 2 AC 214, 230C-E, but Lord Bridge was dealing with a situation where an enactment has been re-enacted in a new context.

§ *Use of earlier case rejected on the grounds it is distinguishable*

(vi) Where Parliament intends to deal with gender specific prostitution it uses specifically the word 'woman', 'girl', or 'her' as in sections 22, 28, 29, 30 and 31 of the Sexual Offences Act 1956. See also section 5 of the Sexual Offences 1967 as regards a 'woman' living on male prostitution.

§ *Analysis of terms in other Acts in pari materia*

It is to be observed, for completeness, that Mr Carter-Manning recognised he could obtain no assistance from the gender

§ *Application of section 6 Interpretation act 1978—which*

provisions of section 6 of the Interpretation Act 1978 because the provision that words importing the feminine gender, as does ordinarily the phrase 'common prostitute', include the masculine is inapplicable to enactments such as the Act of 1959 (see Part I of Schedule 2 to the Act of 1978). Mr Adrian Fulford, who appeared for the respondent, submitted that the phrase 'common prostitute' was for many years before 1959, and is now, regarded as a term of art which had the meaning formulated by Darling J when delivering the judgment of the Court of Criminal Appeal in *R v De Munck* [1918] 1 KB 635. He said, at pp. 637–638: 'The court is of opinion that the term "common prostitute" in the statute is not limited so as to mean only one who permits acts of lewdness with all and sundry, or with such as hire her, when such acts are in the nature of ordinary sexual connection. We are of opinion that prostitution is proved if it be shown that a woman offers her body commonly for lewdness for payment in return.'

The statute referred to was section 2(2) of the Criminal Law Amendment Act 1885 (48 & 49 Vict. c. 69) which however was gender specific for it spoke of 'women or girls'. Although the decision was in that context, I believe there to be great force in Mr Fulford's submission that 'common authority prostitute' is ordinarily regarded as signifying a woman. The statute was referring to a common law concept. Mr Fulford drew our attention to the only textbook which appears to deal with the problem, Rook and Ward, *Sexual Offences* (1990), where at para. 8.12 the authors state: 'The better view is that the offence under section 1(1) may be committed as principal only by a woman.'

However, Mr Fulford's main submission was that the court should avail itself of the report which led to the Act of 1959 and of the parliamentary debate upon the Bill for the Act *Pepper v Hart* [1993] AC 593. The availability of a report which led to an Act as an aid to interpretation is discussed in Bennion, *Statutory Interpretation*, 2nd ed. (1992), p. 450. He cites *Fothergill v Monarch Airlines* Ltd [1981] AC 251, 281, where Lord Diplock said:

> Where the Act has been preceded by a report of some official commission or committee that has been laid before Parliament and the legislation is introduced in consequence of that report, the report itself may be looked at by the court for the limited purpose of identifying the 'mischief' that the Act was intended to remedy, and for such assistance as is derivable from this knowledge in giving the right purposive construction to the Act.

Section 1(1) of the Act was a result of a recommendation in paragraph 256 of the Report of the Departmental Committee on Homosexual Offences and Prostitution (1957) (Cmnd. 247) ('the Wolfenden committee'). The relevant chapters of the report are Chapters VIII and IX and a perusal of them leaves me in no doubt

states that 'In any Act, unless the contrary intention appears,—(b) words importing the feminine gender include the masculine'— rejected because later parts of the 1978 Act state that these words do not apply here.

§ *Reference to case law to show what might have been the draftsman's presumptions in using the terms and comment on an earlier related Act.*

§ *Statutory history of the area*

§ *Reference to an Academic text*

§ *Reference to* Pepper v Hart

§ *Reference to a practitioners' text*

§ *Discussion of methods of identifying the mischief*

§ *Analysis of mischief as recounted by the report of the investigating committee*

that the committee was concerned only with the female prostitute. Thus, and for example:

> 223. It would have taken us beyond our terms of reference
> to investigate in detail the prevalence of prostitution or
> the reasons which lead women to adopt this manner of
> life....

> 261. ... The problem of the prostitute is, in terms of numbers,
> far greater than that of the male importuner and, for that
> matter, far more of a public nuisance. In any event, we
> think it would be too easy to evade the formula by a game
> of 'general post' in which an individual prostitute would
> not loiter in a particular place though the number of pros-
> titutes in that place at a given time might be constant.

> 262. Our second difficulty related to the criteria which would
> enable the police to infer that a person was loitering 'for
> the purposes of prostitution'. We have in mind the possi-
> bility that any woman might, from ignorance or indiscre-
> tion, put herself in a position in which she might be said to
> be loitering, and by conduct which was quite innocent give
> rise to a suspicion in the mind of an observant policeman
> that she was loitering for the purposes of prostitution.

It is plain that the 'mischief' that the Act was intended to remedy
was a mischief created by women. The assistance which I derive
from the report confirms my strong impression that, notwithstanding the use of 'a person' and 'anyone' in subsections (2) and (3),
section 1(1) of the Act of 1959 is confined to women. The term
'common prostitute' is ordinarily regarded as applying to a
woman and, importantly, it seems improbable that Parliament
intended to create a new male offence which was but subtly different from the extant section 32 of the Sexual Offences Act 1956.

§ *Conclusion on the mischief and a return to the analysis of the wording in the Act*

Accordingly I would dismiss this appeal and answer the magistrate's question in the affirmative.

§ *Decision*

I add this. I have not sought to avail myself of the doctrine in
Pepper v *Hart* [1993] AC 593 because in my judgment and with the
confirmation afforded by the Wolfenden committee report
the legislation is neither ambiguous, obscure nor productive of
absurdity.

§ *Further comments on the rejection of use of* Pepper v Hart

However, I must remark that a curious feature of this appeal
was Mr Carter-Manning's voluntary and frank concession, both in
opening and in reply, that if the court was to look at the parliamentary debates it would become plain that section 1(1) of the
Act of 1959 was intended to be applicable only to women.

§ *Recognition of the duty of counsel to cite all matters for and against him*

Had I concluded as a matter of interpretation that section 1(1)
applied to male prostitutes, then a curious situation would have
arisen. The judicially ascertained expressed intention of Parliament
would have been at variance with what the court had been told

§ *Obiter comment on the use of* Pepper v Hart

was the actual intention of the promoters. The ensuant problems may have to be addressed if concessions of the type made here are repeated on another occasion.

Laws J: I agree.

ORDER

Costs out of central funds.

§ *Other judgment in the case*
§ *Appeal dismissed.*
§ *Someone has to pay the costs and an order always has to be made (though not always reported).*

8.11 CONCLUSION

By way of conclusion we would like to suggest a rough guide on how you might approach the problem of interpreting a statute and then end with a short exercise on answering problems in this area.

8.11.1 Checklist for reading a Statute

The following table contains a checklist of research points you need to consider when reading a statute. The left-hand column sets out the general headings you should bear in mind, and the right-hand column explains these in more detail.

1. Read the section(s) carefully.	This may include: (1) noting any technical legal terms. For example, words such as 'property'; 'possession'; 'dismissal'; 'recklessness' all have technical legal meanings. In particular, check whether the word is covered by the Interpretation Act 1978. (2) noting any other technical terms relating to trade or industry. The Act (e.g. a Finance Act) may well have been drafted with these in mind. (3) checking dictionaries. (4) referring to any related sections in the Act. (5) checking the schedules to the Act. (6) checking for interpretations in the section and/or later interpretation sections. (7) checking related statutes which are *in pari materia* with this Act.
2. Research academic texts which will provide general guidance on the meaning of the section and point you to other authorities.	(1) textbooks (2) articles and case notes in legal journals (3) monographs (4) practitioners' texts (5) the internet
3. Understand the mischief of the Act	(1) refer to any annotations, e.g. in 'Current Statutes Annotated' (2) check for any Law Commission Reports (3) look at social, economic or political background (4) check whether you have found the mischief or whether there are multiple mischiefs (5) check *Hansard* under the rules in *Pepper* v *Hart*

(6) check the long title of the act: *Vacher* v. *London Society of Compositors.*

4. Check for any European derivation

Does the Act in question derive from a Treaty, Regulation or Directive? If so, refer to Chapter 10 for the implications.

5. Research existing or related case law.

(1) Are you sure your legal research has unearthed all the authorities?
  • English case law?
  • possibly decisions of the Judicial Committee of the Privy Council?
  • Relevant cases in foreign jurisdictions?
  • European case law at the ECJ or as applied in the UK?
(2) How will you present the *ratio* of each case?
(3) How will you deal with *obiter dicta*?
(4) You must decide how you are going to argue the relevance of helpful cases and distinguish unhelpful authority.

6. Are there any Human Rights Act 1998 implications?

(1) direct reference to human rights on basis that any case will be taken against a public authority?
(2) possible 'horizontal' use of Human Rights Act 1998?

7. Be aware of any technical rules of grammar.

For example, the *eiusdem generis* rule.

8. Be aware of judicial trends in methods of interpretation.

Are judges now more purposive in their approach? How will this affect your argument?

9. Be aware from which perspective you are viewing the problem and adopt the appropriate style of argument.

Are you acting as an advocate? Are you arguing the general possibilities? Answering an examination problem is quite different from acting as an advocate in a moot, for example. Even in real-life advocacy or the provision of legal advice, you must decide how to pitch your case in terms of emphasis on literal or purposive approaches.

10. Decide how to marshal your authorities to substantiate your approach.

For example, what degree of emphasis will you put on each case or other relevant material? Good arguments emphasise the key points, not every single point.

8.11.2 Exercise on Application

EXERCISE 17 Perilous poodles and rabid fish

This very short exercise explores the basic methods of interpreting statutes.

PROBLEM

It is to be assumed that, as a result of a recent outbreak of rabies (and following a consequent Law Commission recommendation) the **Rabies and Dangerous Animals Act 1993** has been passed. It states:

Section 1: It is an offence to leave animals unattended in any hotel, public house, restaurant or other public place.

Section 2: The keeping of any animal, other than a domesticated one, without an appropriate licence, is an offence. The form and cost of such a licence will be determined by orders issued from time to time by the Minister. A domesticated animal is one so defined by Schedule 9 of this Act.

Section 3: Private dwelling houses are exempted from the provisions of this Act.

Schedule 9: For the purposes of this Act a 'domesticated animal' includes cats, dogs, horses, cattle, sheep, pigs, and snakes or insects common to the British Isles.

Using the rules of statutory interpretation that have been developed, present arguments **AS IF YOU WERE COUNSEL FOR THE DEFENCE** in the following cases.

(1) *R v Alfred*

Alfred left his poodle in the changing rooms at his local tennis club while he played tennis. He is charged with contravening section 1 of the Act.

(2) *R v Bert*

Bert keeps piranha fish in a pond in his front garden. The garden is unfenced. He is charged with not having the appropriate licence under section 2.

Points to note in this exercise:

1. Alfred

Start any problem of this nature by breaking down the constituent elements of the section(as) involved. What is required for conviction here?

- there must be an animal (not a problem here)

- that animal must be left unattended

- in any hotel, public house, restaurant or other public place.

However simplistic this may seem it really is not (especially if the section is more complicated). You will find in seminars that many of your colleagues, when asked to analyse a problem like this, 'jump in' all over the place commenting on different aspects of the offence (or saying 'this is nonsense'). Structure matters and wins hands down over a disorganised argument. Here, remember, if the Crown fails to prove any one of the constituent elements of the offence, there can be no conviction.

Next, make sure there are no other parts of the Act which have to be taken into account e.g., a definitions section. Here, the only one that could be of relevance to Alfred is section 3.

From this we can say that the defence may rest on three grounds.

(a) The Act refers to 'hotel, public house, restaurant or other public place'. Does a tennis club, therefore, come within that last, general, category? The phrase 'or other public place' could be read *eiusdem generis* to restrict the general words to the genus of the preceding specific words. What is the genus of the preceding words? The prosecution will argue that these words show that the tenor of the section is to prevent animals being left in a place to which the public have general access. The defence could argue that the words indicate a place restricted to food and drink establishments. Further, if the tennis club is private (or has a limited membership) there might be a defence here. The express exclusion of private dwellings under section 3 could also be cited in support of this interpretation (since we are entitled to look at the effect of the **whole** Act). This is a weak point but could be used by ignoring the problematic word 'dwelling' and concentrating on the privacy element.

(b) In the alternative, the defence could argue that the above phrase is not sufficiently specific to create a genus, and that therefore, since a literal interpretation of such general words is virtually meaningless, the court should enquire into the purpose of the Act. A formal style of discovering 'purpose' would be to analyse the Act mainly by referring to the internal context. The short title of the Act is the Rabies and Dangerous Animals Act. This cannot itself be used, unlike the long title, as an aid to construction: *R* v *Galvin*. However, it does suggest that the Act is particularly concerned with the threat of dangerous animals (note the exclusion of domesticated animals by section 2 and schedule 9). This argument could be used to deny the application of the section to pet dogs, and the long title of the Act (if it has one) could be cited in support (if it offers that support—the question is silent on this). See *R* v *Galvin*, where it was stressed that the long title could be used as a minor aid to construction, provided it did not contradict the express language of the Act.

Seeking the purpose in the 'grand' style one can move away from the Act itself to matters such as social conditions. Similarly, the Law Commission's report could also be used in support, if that was the case (*Black-Clawson*), and even Hansard might prove useful on this point.

(c) Finally, one could argue that 'unattended' does not mean the animal always has to be in the owner's presence (or that 'presence' simply means 'in the line of sight' as in *Casson* v *Dade*).

2. Bert

Use the same structure as with Alfred. Here, the relevant section is section 2. What is required for conviction here?

- an animal must be involved (will a fish be included?)
- the Act does not apply to domesticated ones
- there must be no appropriate licence.

Again, make sure there are no other parts of the Act which have to be taken into account e.g., a definitions section. Here, there are two: section 3. (exempting private dwelling houses) and Schedule 9 (defining domesticated animals).

The first point to note is that you may have to do some research on what is an 'animal' (see various dictionaries, biology books, etc.). It comes as a surprise to many that fish are animals and so will require a licence unless Schedule 9 exempts them.

The defence is threefold:

(a) The most obvious line of attack is the purposive argument that, although fish may be animals, they are incapable (to the best of the authors' knowledge) of carrying rabies. The prosecution may well point out that the Act is concerned with both rabid *and* dangerous animals; a dangerous fish falls within the provisions of the Act. However, the purpose of the Act, as exemplified perhaps in the long title (not provided here) and gained through an examination of the social setting for the Act, would probably demonstrate that the two ideas were connected.

(b) The offence created by section 2 is absolute, save for the exclusion of domesticated animals in Schedule 9. Though a literal approach apparently catches Bert he might be able to utilise section 3. One must argue an extended meaning to 'private dwelling houses'. Land is usually included in such terms.

Bert could try to argue that as the fish are kept in his garden they should be excluded under section 3. This could be argued on the basis that the purpose of the Act is only to protect the public in places to which they normally have resort. As such, there is an argument that an individual's garden is as much his private property as his house, and that any wider meaning could create absurd results. One might try to find other statutes which have defined the term in an acceptable way for the defence. Finding one *in pari materia* might be more difficult. One such possible example might be the Dangerous Dogs Act 1991. And, indeed, the very question whether a garden path constituted a 'public place' under section 10 of the Act arose in *Fellowes* v *DPP, The Times*, 1 February 1993. Fellowes was convicted of having a dog which was dangerously out of control in a public place contrary to the Dangerous Dogs Act 1991 section 3(1), after his dog bit a paper boy who was delivering a newspaper to the house. The Queens Bench Division Divisional Court held that this was not a public place because of the purpose of the Act and that people entered the private premises only as visitors, not as general members of the public. Again, the same court has decided that a dangerous dog in a private car in a public car park had to be muzzled because, although a car is not in and of itself a public place, when the car is in a public place everything inside the car is deemed to be in a public place for the purposes of the Act (*Bates* v *DPP, The Times*, 8 March 1993; (1993) 157 JP 1004). Further, if the mischief in our fictitious Act is perceived as relating to 'danger', the unfenced pond is still a problem in our argument.

(c) The categories of animals referred to in Schedule 9 are wide; wider, perhaps, than a literal reading of the word 'domesticated' would lead us to expect; although it is presented as an inclusive definition. The case of *Coltman* v *Bibby Tankers* [1988] AC 276 considered the dual meaning that can be given to 'inclusive' definitions. The list might be either exemplary or exhaustive. It is notable that fish are excluded, and so if the definition is exhaustive, the prosecution might seek to argue the principle *expressio unius est exclusio alterius*. This would be difficult to counter, and the defence's only response, it is submitted, might be to argue that the definition is exemplary; that 'domesticated' here is sufficiently wide to include all animals that are in fact kept as 'pets'. Whether piranhas are on that basis common to the British Isles might nonetheless be a difficult point to argue!

REFERENCES

*CHANDLER, A., and HOLLAND, J. (1995), 'Pepper v Hart: Unearthing the Meaning of Rescission', *Journal of Business Law* 503.

*CROSS, R. (1995), *Cross: Statutory Interpretation*, 3rd edn., (by Bell, J. & Engle, G.), London: Butterworths.

FELDMAN, D. (1992), 'Commencement, Transition and Retrospective Legislation', 108 *Law Quarterly Review*, 212.

GRAHAM R.N. (2001), 'In Defence of Maxims', 22 *Statute Law Review* 45.

LLEWELLYN, K. (1960), *The Common Law Tradition* (Boston, Mass.: Little Brown).

SMITH, J. C. (1995), 'The Criminal Appeals Act 1995: (1) Appeals Against Conviction', *Criminal Law Review* 920.

STEYN, J. (2001) '*Pepper* v *Hart*: A Re-examination', 21 *Oxford Journal of Legal Studies* 59.

SULLIVAN, R. (2001) 'Some Implications of Plain Language Drafting', 22 *Statute Law Review* 175.

*SUMMERS, R., and MARSHALL, G. (1992), 'The Argument from Ordinary Meaning in Statutory Interpretation', 43 *Northern Ireland Legal Quarterly* 213.

*TWINING, W., and MIERS, D. (1991), *How To Do Things with Rules* (3rd edn., London: Weidenfeld & Nicolson).

*WILLIS, J. (1938), 'Statute Interpretation in a Nutshell', XVI *Canadian Bar Review* 1.

*ZANDER, M. (1994), *The Law-Making Process* (4th edn., London: Butterworths).

9

'Bringing Rights Home': Legal Method and the Convention Rights

9.1 Introduction

In **Chapter 1** we introduced the idea that English Law has increasingly become subject to two powerful pan-European legal forces. The most significant to date has, of course, been the influence of European Community Law. However, we now have another 'incoming tide' to deal with following the partial incorporation of the European Convention on Human Rights (ECHR) by the Human Rights Act (HRA) 1998, and by the legislation governing devolution in Scotland and Wales.

The HRA 1998 came into force in the UK on 2 October 2000. However, because the devolution Acts had to be drafted so that the Scottish Parliament and the Welsh Assembly cannot do anything which is incompatible with the ECHR, and those Acts came into force before the HRA 1998, this meant effectively that the HRA operated in Scotland and Wales prior to October 2000. Thus there was some case law on the incorporation of human rights principles even before the Act came fully into force across the United Kingdom.

In outline, the HRA 1998 is designed to work in nine main ways:

1. It makes it unlawful for a public authority to act in a way that is incompatible with the human rights set out in the HRA (called *Convention rights*). Where it is alleged that a public authority has breached a person's Convention rights, the claimant now has a new and distinct cause of action against that public authority for breach of those rights. The term 'public authority' has not been defined in the Act but will obviously include bodies such as local authorities.

2. The Act does not create a new cause of action for one individual or company to sue another individual or company for an alleged breach of Convention rights. Some commentators have argued that the HRA does indeed create such new rights (especially as regards freedom of expression), but the prevailing view is that only public authorities can be liable directly for breach of Convention rights.

3. A person may nevertheless rely on the rights contained in the HRA in actions against people who are not public authorities, but only to 'back up' existing legal rights, i.e., they cannot sue for a breach of human rights *per se* but can sue for, say, breach of

contract and then ask the court to interpret or apply the law so as to comply with the rights set out in the HRA and ECHR. This is because, as the courts fall within the definition of 'public authority' in the HRA, any decision they reach must comply with Convention rights.

4. Courts must therefore apply common law precedent so as to comply with Convention rights.

5. Courts must now interpret *all* legislation, so far as it is possible to do so within the rules of statutory interpretation, to comply with Convention rights.

6. All courts and tribunals must take into account the jurisprudence of the Convention, which means all the decisions of the European Court of Human Rights (also abbreviated to ECtHR), whenever a Convention right arises (HRA 1998, s. 2). However, UK courts are not **bound** to apply the decisions of the ECHR.

7. Courts have limited powers to disapply subordinate legislation which is found to contravene Convention rights.

8. The higher courts may declare primary legislation incompatible with Convention rights (HRA 1998, s.3—though they cannot disapply it) so that Parliament may choose to use a new fast-track procedure for amending it.

9. A person may still take a case to the European Court of Human Rights at Strasbourg, but only after having exhausted all domestic remedies.

In this chapter we shall expand on these summary points by outlining the scope of the ECHR, explaining the process of incorporation of the ECHR through the HRA, and by exploring the likely impact of the HRA 1998 on Legal Method. Two websites are very useful in this area: the first is that of the Court of Human Rights at www.echr.coe.int/; and the second is a special unit set up by the Home Office at www.homeoffice.gov.uk/hract/. The text of the Convention itself can be found at www.conventions.coe.int/.

9.2 The European Convention on Human Rights

9.2.1 What is the ECHR?

The ECHR is an international treaty which was signed in Rome on 4 November 1950, and came into force on 3 September 1953. It sets out basic civil and political rights. The ECHR was the first major convention to be created under the auspices of a body called the Council of Europe. Although a number of other treaties have followed, the ECHR remains probably the most significant.

The Council itself was established by treaty in 1949, largely as a reaction to the failures of democracy and ethics that accompanied the rise of fascism in inter-war Europe. It exists as a political association of European states committed to advancing European unity, social and economic progress, and human rights. Although, historically speaking, it shares certain common roots with the EU, it is institutionally and politically quite separate. There has, of course, been significant overlap in membership of the Council of

Europe and the EEC/EU, though the Council has always tended to be the larger body. There were ten original members of the Council (as compared with the EEC's six), namely the Benelux states together with Denmark, France, Italy, Ireland, Norway, Sweden, and the UK; the Council today has forty-one members, with a growing number of former Eastern bloc states having joined since 1989.

Not all members of the Council have ratified the ECHR, either at all or in its entirety. Britain, for example, has not formally ratified three of the substantive Protocols (see below). States signing up to the Convention have also been allowed to enter reservations to or derogations from particular provisions of the ECHR. A *reservation* is a statement made by a signatory, at the time of signing, that it recognises and reserves a position in which its laws are (to some specified extent) inconsistent with the Convention. For example, Britain has entered its only reservation to Article 2 of the First Protocol, which concerns the right of parents to have their children educated in conformity with their religious or other beliefs. A *derogation*, on the other hand, is a statement whereby a state notifies the Council that it is suspending certain rights under the Convention 'in time of war or other public emergency threatening the life of the nation' (Article 15 ECHR). This is a fairly elastic concept, though there are certain Convention rights from which it is not possible to derogate (under Articles 2, 3, 4, and 7). The UK has entered a derogation to Article 5(2) (the right to liberty) in respect of the extended detention powers exercised over terrorist suspects under successive Prevention of Terrorism Acts. Initially derogation was said to be justified primarily by the Northern Irish situation. The latest derogation follows the events of 11 September 2001 and the introduction of new powers intended to combat the threat of international terrorism— see Human Rights Act (Designated Derogation) Order 2001 (SI 2001/3644).

9.2.2 The Scope of the ECHR

The ECHR is concerned with the identification and protection of what are often called fundamental human rights and freedoms (see generally Jacobs & White, 1996; Gearty (ed.), 1997). These are prescribed in quite broad terms in the various substantive sections or 'Articles' of the Convention. They include the right to life itself (Article 2), the right not to suffer torture or inhuman or degrading treatment (Article 3), the right against slavery (Article 4), the right to liberty (Article 5), the right to a fair trial (Article 6), a right not to be punished retrospectively (Article 7), the right to protection of private life (sometimes rather optimistically called the right to privacy—Article 8), rights to freedom of conscience and religion (Article 9), freedom of expression (Article 10), and association (Article 11), and certain rights of non-discrimination (Article 14). There are also eleven 'Protocols' which constitute additions to the Convention since it was originally drafted. Some of these Protocols are substantive, such as the Sixth Protocol which committed the signatories to the Convention (called in the jargon of international law the 'High Contracting Parties') to abolition of the death penalty, whereas others are procedural, such as the Eleventh Protocol, discussed below. Given the potentially wide scope of such rights and their consequent impact on social governance, many of these are restricted or qualified from within the Convention itself. For example, freedom of expression may be curtailed (provided it is in a manner 'prescribed by law' and 'necessary in a democratic society') in the interests of national security, or for the protection of health or morals, or to prevent disclosure of confidential information, etc.

9.2.3 Enforcement

The Convention created its own enforcement procedures, separate from any measures taken by individual contracting states. Under Convention procedures, complaints about breaches of the ECHR may be brought by a High Contracting Party or, in some circumstances, by an individual petitioner. The enactment of the HRA 1998 has not altered the right for a person to take a case to the European Court of Human Rights (ECtHR).

An action can be brought only against (in effect) the government allegedly in breach; there is generally no possibility of one individual suing another before the ECtHR. It follows also that an individual may complain only if the respondent country (i.e., the one complained of) recognises the right of individual petition. This is not a condition of ratifying the Convention; Britain, for instance, agreed to the right of individual petition only in 1966—nearly thirteen years after ratifying the ECHR.

Originally, complaints were dealt with by a two-stage process. First, a body called the European Commission of Human Rights had to judge whether the complaint was admissible under the terms of the Convention. This required proof, amongst other things, that there were no available domestic remedies to deal with the complaint, or that such remedies had been exhausted. If the case was admissible then the Commission was empowered to try to broker a friendly settlement between the parties. If this failed the case would then be remitted to the ECtHR, for a hearing. If the Court established that there had been a breach of Convention rights then it could grant individual complainants compensation under Article 50 ECHR.

This whole process was increasingly criticised as unduly complex and time-consuming, causing unnecessary delays in what is an expanding jurisdiction. Indeed, one estimate suggested that, having gone through the domestic system, it took an average of a further five years and cost £30,000 for cases to be settled at Strasbourg (Home Office, 1997). Accordingly, an Eleventh Protocol to the Convention was agreed on 1 November 1998, abolishing the old Commission and Court and replacing them with a single new Court. This is based, like the old institutions and the Council of Ministers, in Strasbourg. Under the new procedures a party must still have exhausted all domestic remedies before petitioning the ECtHR, but admissibility is determined in a preliminary hearing before a three-judge panel of the Court, which must be unanimous if the case is to proceed to a hearing. If the case does proceed, it will normally be heard by a chamber of seven judges. The Court also has the power to sit in a Grand Chamber of seventeen judges where a case raises a particularly important question of interpretation of Convention rights. The remedies available to the Court remain unchanged. Note that one practical consequence of the Eleventh Protocol has been virtually to re-write large parts of ECHR. Be very careful that you do not refer to old versions of the Convention. Copies of the amended text can be found, for example, on the Council of Europe web site.

9.3 Incorporation under the Human Rights Act 1998

The purpose of the HRA 1998 was, as we have said, to achieve the partial incorporation of the Convention into English law. The method chosen for incorporation involves a fairly typical piece of British pragmatism. One of the great arguments against incorporation has been the damage that it could cause to Parliamentary sovereignty by increasing the powers of unelected judges—both by ceding authority directly to the European Court of Human Rights, and by giving greater constitutional power to the British judiciary. The HRA 1998, its supporters claim, has maintained a balance between enabling judicial protection of human rights and protecting the sovereignty of Parliament. At the heart of this balancing act are three features of the 1998 Act.

1. The Act has not simply declared the ECHR to be part of English law, it has, rather, selectively incorporated elements of the Convention by giving them a special legal status as '**Convention rights**' under section 1 of the HRA.
2. Secondly, the HRA 1998 has given domestic judges two significant legal powers. One of these is the duty to interpret legislation, so far as possible, consistently with Convention rights, and the other, where consistency cannot be achieved, is to declare such laws incompatible with Convention rights.
3. The third point flows from this: any action to deal with incompatibility of primary legislation rests with Parliament, not the courts. Breach of Convention rights cannot, unlike fundamental breaches of EC Law, post-*Factortame*, empower the courts to disapply an Act of Parliament.

In the remainder of this section we will look at the substantive elements of the HRA 1998 in a little more detail, before moving on to consider the impact of the devolution Acts, and then the significance of all of this for legal method.

9.3.1 The Convention Rights

Unlike the European Communities Act 1972, which simply incorporated EC Law wholesale into English Law, the HRA 1998 has selectively identified Articles 2–12 and 14 of the ECHR, together with Articles 1–3 of the First Protocol and Articles 1 and 2 of the Sixth Protocol (see schedule 1 to the HRA 1998). This in fact encompasses all of the major substantive rights under the ECHR, subject to the existing derogations and reservations entered by the UK Government (section 1(2), HRA 1998). The significant exceptions therefore are Articles 1 and 13 ECHR.

The exclusion of Article 1 may actually not be that significant, since this primarily imposes a duty on signatory states to ensure that those within their jurisdiction can enjoy the rights and freedoms guaranteed by the Convention. Arguably this is the purpose of the HRA 1998, and should not be an enforceable Convention right in itself. However, there is a view among human rights lawyers that Article 1 has some remedial significance in giving an element of 'horizontal effect' to the Convention (see Bamforth, 1999, and below). This may mean that the omission of Article 1 may yet cause substantive difficulties in the application of the 1998 Act.

The exclusion of Article 13 of the Convention, which guarantees citizens whose fundamental rights are violated an effective remedy before a national authority, was the subject of much debate in Parliament, where the Lord Chancellor argued that it was intended to restrict the creation of new judicial remedies. Finally, however, he was forced to concede that the courts would be entitled to take note of Article 13 and its associated case law and not just the remedial sections in the HRA 1998 itself (see *Hansard*, House of Lords, vol. 583, cols. 475–7, 18 November 1997). This principle, however, still does not appear on the face of the Act, thereby, as Ewing (1999:85) notes, raising the prospect of *Pepper* v *Hart*-influenced debate over the courts' powers to grant remedies under the HRA 1998. So far, however, this does not appear to have happened.

Many of the rights in the ECHR are expressed in absolute terms (e.g. 'No one shall be subjected to torture or to inhuman or degrading treatment or punishment': Article 3). But some of the Convention rights are not absolute rights: there are balances to be taken into account. For example, the right to freedom of assembly and association in Article 11 also notes that 'No restriction shall be placed on the exercise of these rights other than such as are prescribed by law and are necessary in a democratic society in the interest of national security or public safety...'; similar wording appears in Article 9 regarding freedom of thought, conscience, and religion. Equally, although some articles appear to create absolute rights, the jurisprudence of the ECHR shows that principles of interpretation, such as 'the margin of appreciation', may affect how the rights are observed. Similarly, even absolute rights may be restricted in so far as the courts consider that such restrictions are consistent with the absolute nature of the right. This is achieved by reference to the 'principle of proportionality', which is extremely important as a general principle of Human Rights law, and also arises as part of the jurisprudence of the ECJ (see further **Chapter 10**). It has already been relied on by the British courts in discussing the operation of Convention rights under the HRA. Thus, it has been held that where a Convention right is absolute, any interference with that right should be allowed only in so far as it is a proportionate and necessary curb on the freedom which it entails—see *per* Lord Steyn in *R* v *A* [2001] UKHL 25; [2001] 2 AC 45 at [38]. Where a court is considering whether a restriction on a Convention right is legitimate, the test of proportionality requires it to ask three questions, *per* Lord Clyde in *de Freitas* v *Permanent Secretary of the Ministry of Agriculture, Fisheries, Lands and Housing* [1999] 1 AC 69:

> whether: (i) the legislative objective is sufficiently important to justify limiting a fundamental right; (ii) the measures designed to meet the legislative objective are rationally connected to it; and (iii) the means used to impair the right or freedom are no more than is necessary to accomplish the objective.

The distinction between absolute and qualified rights has implications for legal method, and we will return to it briefly in section 9.6.1, below.

9.3.2 The Declaration of Incompatibility

The powers under sections 3 and 4 of the HRA to declare legislation incompatible with a Convention right were based by the draftsman on similar powers contained in the New Zealand Bill of Rights Act 1990. Section 6 of the New Zealand legislation imposed a duty on the courts in that country to interpret legislation consistently with the rights and obligations of the International Covenant on Civil and Political Rights. This has been interpreted (albeit somewhat controversially) by the New Zealand Court of Appeal as giving it a power to declare legislation 'inconsistent'—see, e.g., *R v Poumako* [2000] 2 NZLR 695—though no such power is contained in the Act itself. The UK approach has been both to impose a stronger duty to achieve a consistent interpretation *and* to give the domestic courts a *statutory* power to declare legislation incompatible. Where a court determines in any proceedings that a piece of primary legislation cannot, under section 3, be construed consistently with Convention rights, the court can issue a 'declaration of incompatibility' under section 4. This is, in effect, simply a statement that the legislation is not 'Convention compliant', and it serves to put the government on notice of that fact. A declaration does not in any way affect the validity of the Act in question. It remains law unless and until Parliament deals with the incompatibility. Thus, the court must still apply the legislation as it stands and the parties to the actual case are unaffected by the declaration: the declaration has no legal effect and the parties neither gain nor lose by it.

There is no legal duty on the government to repeal or amend incompatible legislation, though the political or moral pressure to do so could be considerable in some cases. As Greer (1999:15–16) points out, the declaration process is somewhat unsatisfactory as it must create uncertainty about how public authorities will deal with incompatible but not (yet) amended legislation. To try and minimise the problem there is a 'fast-track' procedure under section 10 of the HRA 1998, whereby ministers can amend non-compliant legislation by 'remedial order'—provided the minister concerned finds 'compelling reasons' (undefined by the Act!) for doing so. 'Fast track' is, of course, a relative term, and it is perfectly legitimate for the minister to await the exhaustion of the normal appeals process before taking any action. This could of itself add significant delays to the process and, possibly in some cases, hardship to litigants. See, for example, *Car Crash Line Ltd* v *Branton Edwards (a firm)* [2002] EWCA Civ 634, where more than a little legal uncertainty seems to have been generated while the declaration of incompatibility made in *Wilson* v *First County Trust* (discussed later in this section) is appealed to the House of Lords.

Secondary legislation may be declared incompatible under section 4; it may also be struck down by the normal process of judicial review in the Administrative Court. The way this would happen is that the secondary legislation would be declared *ultra vires* its parent Act. This use of judicial review is not restricted to issues of human rights and applied long before the introduction of the HRA 1998. It might be used in human rights cases where the parent Act is re-interpreted in such a way as to be Convention compliant, but as a consequence the powers conveyed under the Act are narrowed and the relevant subordinate legislation falls foul of this effect.

This does not give the courts a universal power to strike down secondary legislation. Because the **validity** of primary legislation is beyond judicial control, secondary legislation which appears to fall foul of Convention rights may still have to be applied by the courts if the failure stems from the parent Act and that Act cannot be reinterpreted to be Convention complaint. Only if the breach of human rights is **not** inevitable because of the primary legislation may the court quash or disapply the secondary legislation (or make a declaration of incompatibility). For these purposes primary legislation includes commencement orders and orders which amend primary legislation: HRA 1998, section 21(1).

Only certain courts have the power to make a declaration of incompatibility: in England and Wales these are the High Court, the Court of Appeal, the House of Lords, the Judicial Committee of the Privy Council, and the Courts Martial Appeal Court. In Scotland, the power can be exercised by the Court of Session and the High Court of Justiciary, in addition, of course, to the House of Lords.

A number of declarations of incompatibility have already been issued by the courts. The first was made in *R v Secretary of State for the Environment, Transport and the Regions, ex parte Holding and Barnes plc and others, The Times*, 24 January 2001. Here, the (then) Divisional Court of the Queen's Bench Division held that the processes by which the Secretary of State made decisions under the Town and Court Planning Act 1990 (and orders under related Acts) were incompatible with Article 6 ECHR as they did not provide applicants with a fair and public hearing by an independent and impartial tribunal—though this decision was later overturned by the House of Lords (see *R v Secretary of State for the Environment, Transport and the Regions, ex parte Alconbury Development and Others* [2001] UKHL 23; [2001] 2 WLR 1389). We will also mention two others, which, incidently, serve to give some flavour of the range of laws potentially at risk under the fair trial rights of Article 6. The first is *Wilson v First County Trust (No 2)* [2002] QB 74, in which the Court of Appeal declared that section 127(3) of the Consumer Credit Act 1974, which rendered certain credit agreements unenforceable, was a disproportionate restriction upon a lender's right to have an agreement enforced, and hence incompatible with Article 6(1) ECHR (an appeal in this case is pending before the House of Lords). The second case is *R v Secretary of State for the Home Department, ex parte Anderson* [2002] UKHL 46; [2002] 4 All ER 1089. Here the House of Lords overruled the Court of Appeal and held that the power of the Home Secretary to determine the tariff for mandatory life sentences in England and Wales is, following the reasoning of the European Court of Human Rights in *Stafford v United Kingdom* [2002] All ER (D) 422, also incompatible with Article 6. Nevertheless, we think it will remain relatively unusual for the courts to have recourse to declarations of incompatibility. The real impact of the HRA 1998 will lie with problems of interpretation and application.

9.3.3 Making a Claim

Only persons who are 'victims' within the meaning of Article 34 ECHR can bring a claim under the HRA 1998. There is no particular magic to the word 'victim' in this context, it simply means a person (or group) whose Convention rights have allegedly been infringed, though this does prevent the Act being used by non-victims to bring 'public interest' or 'test' cases purely as a matter of principle. Claims can be brought only against a 'public authority' (s. 6(1), HRA 1998). As a consequence, this creates a distinction akin to that in EC law between horizontal and vertical effect. The HRA 1998 has vertical effect, so that an individual can sue the state or a 'state-like' body, but it does not have horizontal effect, which would have allowed direct enforcement of rights between individuals.

'Public authority', however, is not defined in the Act, and its meaning is likely to be a source of litigation in itself. Although there is an obvious core of organisations that fall into the public description, such as central government departments, local authorities, regulatory bodies (like the Securities and Futures Authority, or the Law Society), the police, and, interestingly, the courts too, there will be others whose status as public or private bodies is debatable. The HRA 1998 tries to deal with this by recognising that the public/private distinction is not so much about status or ownership of the organisation, but rather about its functions. Thus the Act recognises that there will be 'hybrid bodies' (private organisations to whom the state has contracted out public functions, e.g. privatised utilities and professional bodies) which exercise both private and public functions. In relation to these hybrid bodies, exactly when they are acting within their 'public' responsibility is not clear. Certainly, where a body such as *National Rail* is conducting its normal business in operating the rail network that will be a public responsibility. Whether other actions (e.g. being an employer) are public or private functions is debatable and section 6(5), HRA 1998 states that 'a person is not a public authority by virtue of subsection (3)(b) if the nature of the act is private'. It was confirmed in Parliamentary debates that a 'public authority', such as local government, will be caught by the Act in *all* circumstances, but we do not know where the line will be drawn with the hybrid organisations.

We noted above that private individuals cannot be sued directly for breaching Convention rights, that there is no 'horizontal effect' contained in the Act. But this does not necessarily mean that individuals cannot ever recover compensation for breaches of their Convention rights by other individuals.

First, an individual may, in any proceedings, cite a Convention right to aid the argument. This is because section 6(1) of the HRA states that it is unlawful for a public authority to act in a way which is incompatible with a Convention right and section 6(3) states that 'public authority' includes courts and tribunals. Thus a court must take account of all aspects of Convention rights when reaching its decision. However, there is no distinct cause of action for breach of a Convention right unless the defendant is a public authority. Private individuals cannot sue another individual or company simply because they believe their human rights have been infringed; they must first establish a separate and recognised cause of action (e.g. breach of contract, negligence, defamation); only then, during the course of the legal argument, may they tag onto that argument a point on breach of human rights designed to augment their claim. They are still only suing for, say, breach of contract; it is just that another dimension has been added to the claim. Modifications to the court forms used for starting an action now asks for advance notice that such arguments will be presented.

Secondly, there is a significant body of authority within the case law of the European Court of Human Rights which holds the state responsible for its citizens' breaches of the Convention. For example, in *X and Y v The Netherlands*, Series A, No. 91, the Court held that, where an alleged sex offender escaped prosecution because under Dutch law the apparent victim (who was mentally handicapped) was not competent to initiate the prosecution, this was a breach of the victim's rights under Article 8. The state's obligation to protect the private lives of its citizens could extend to a positive duty on that state to adopt laws that would secure respect for private life '*even in the sphere of the relations of individuals between themselves*' (para. 23 of the judgment; our emphasis). In other words, the Court may be prepared to give the Convention a kind of *indirect* horizontal effect by making the state liable for ensuring that private rights between individuals are consistent with the ECHR. Given the free-standing basis of incorporation under the HRA 1998, there is of course no guarantee that this approach will be adopted by the British courts, but the point is clearly an arguable one.

Claims under the Act can be brought in any proceedings (s. 7(1)(b), HRA 1998), and so will encompass first-instance hearings before a court or tribunal, appeals, and judicial review in the Administrative Court. Claims against the courts themselves, however, can be brought only by means of judicial review, appeal, or any other procedure specifically created for that purpose by rules of court (see further Bamforth, 1999:164–5).

9.3.4 Remedies

Where a public body is found in breach of Convention rights, the court (or tribunal) can make whatever order it considers appropriate within its powers (s. 8(1), HRA 1998). This may include damages (compensation), provided this is within the powers of the court (it would not be within the powers of many tribunals), or alternative orders, such as injunctions (which may be used to prevent public authorities continuing actions which breach the Convention) and the public law orders attached to *certiorari* or *habeas corpus*. Moreover, the courts have accepted that, exceptionally, a citizen may bring an action prospectively (i.e. before the event) against the Crown, and the court may make a declaration that the applicant's proposed conduct is lawful (or not) under the HRA: *R* v *Director for Public Prosecutions, ex parte Pretty* [2001] UKHL 61; [2002] 1 All ER 1; also *Rushbridger* v *Attorney-General*, unreported, 22 June 2001. This is a wider power than simply the power of a court to declare legislation incompatible under section 3 HRA.

The HRA 1998 also specifically states that, in awarding compensation, the courts should take into account the principles applied by the European Court of Human Rights under Article 41 ECHR. Article 41 is significant because it makes an award of damages *discretionary* (damages are more often, though not always, awarded as of right under English law); the practice of the Court also tends to indicate that the scale of awards is relatively low.

9.4 Incorporation under the Devolution Acts

As we noted in the introduction to this chapter, Convention rights are also built into the legislation which created the Welsh Assembly and the Scottish Parliament. So, let us now consider what this involves, and its implications.

Devolution of limited government powers to the Welsh Assembly and Scottish Parliament was achieved primarily through two Acts of the UK Parliament: the Government of

Wales Act 1998 and the Scotland Act 1998. An important feature of the legislation is that both bodies are statutorily obliged to legislate in accordance with Convention rights (s. 107(1), Government of Wales Act 1998 and s. 29(2)(d), Scotland Act 1998). For these purposes 'Convention rights' are defined purely by reference to the HRA 1998 (see s. 107(5) and s. 126(1) of the respective Acts). Since each assembly has rather different legislative powers, however, the mechanics of the process are also different, as we shall now explain.

The Welsh Assembly has the power to create only subordinate legislation, and this explains the absence of any explicit enforcement powers in respect of breaches of Convention rights by the Assembly. To put it simply, any Assembly legislation will be treated like any other form of secondary legislation. Thus, if legislation is in breach of Convention rights contrary to section 107(1), it will be *ultra vires* (i.e. beyond the powers of the Assembly) and accordingly capable of being struck down by judicial review in the usual way. *Locus standi*, that is the right of an individual to bring an action, is, as with the HRA 1998 itself, explicitly limited, by section 107(2), to individuals who are 'victims' within the meaning of Article 34 of the ECHR. An identical limitation is imposed in Scotland by the Scotland Act 1998, section 100(1).

By contrast, the Scottish Parliament, as we have seen in **Chapter 2**, has the power to create primary as well as subordinate legislation, so specific rules have had to be built into the Scotland Act to deal with any Acts of the Scottish Parliament that may breach Convention rights. The first thing to note is that, unlike Acts of the Westminster Parliament, Acts of the Scottish Parliament which breach Convention rights are, in so far as they breach those rights, invalid (s. 29(1) and (2)(d), Scotland Act 1988). This seems to envisage severance of the invalid parts, where possible, rather than the automatic striking down of the whole Act. However, the Scotland Act tries to prevent the question of validity arising after the event by creating a three-stage process (see ss. 31–3) to stop invalid Acts from reaching the statute book in the first place. First, all Bills presented to the Scottish Parliament must be certified by their sponsoring minister as being within the 'legislative competence' of the Parliament, as defined by section 29 of the Scotland Act. Secondly, the 'Presiding Officer' of the Parliament must then also satisfy himself/herself that the Bill is within the legislative competence of the Parliament and make a statement accordingly. Lastly, any one of three Law Officers—the Advocate General for Scotland, the Lord Advocate, or the Attorney-General—may refer the question whether a Bill is within the Parliament's legislative competence to the Judicial Committee of the Privy Council for a ruling. A Bill cannot receive the Royal Assent until that process is complete and, if necessary, the Bill has been amended. This process does not seem to preclude a later challenge to an Act's validity by way of judicial review, though clearly such claims are likely to face an uphill task, particularly if a section 33 reference has been made to the Privy Council. Subordinate legislation will, of course, be challengeable in the same way as for Wales.

The inclusion of Convention rights in these Acts is an extremely important measure, since the Scottish and Welsh assemblies now take overall responsibility in their jurisdictions for many activities, such as public child care laws, primary and secondary (and, in Scotland, higher) education, planning, etc., which in England remain the primary responsibility of local government (which is caught explicitly by the HRA 1998). Since the devolution Act came into force before the HRA 1998, these were the first bodies in the UK to have to take direct account of the ECHR, and proved to be the test-bed for the judiciary's new powers to enforce Convention rights.

9.5 The Developing Case Law

All law subjects are now open to a human rights analysis, and the next few years will see the application of these principles tested to the full (three of the most widely affected will be criminal law, family law, and arguments on privacy, though areas of commercial law are also likely to be affected—for example the regulation of financial services—see *R v SFA and the Disciplinary Tribunal of the SFA, ex parte Fleurose*, unreported, 26 April 2001). Many cases to date have received widespread (and often inaccurate) publicity. Thus, we have seen cases on whether a motorist should have to declare who was driving a car when questioned in relation to alleged traffic offences (involving problems of self-incrimination and right to a fair trial under Article 6: *Brown v Stott (Procurator Fiscal, Dunfermline)* [2001] 2 WLR 817 (PC)); whether part-time judges (e.g. Deputy District Judges) were 'independent', given that their appointments were for a renewable fixed period (again, involving Article 6)—this one led to a change in the rules governing tenure of part-time judges: *Smith v Secretary of State for Trade and Industry, The Times*, 11 October 1999; that a company has human rights for the purposes of Article 6: *County Properties Ltd v The Scottish Ministers, The Times*, 25 July 2000 (Court of Session, Outer House), and privacy rights for the purposes of Article 8: *R v Broadcasting Standards Commission, ex parte BBC* [2000] 3 All ER 989. Moreover, in a case that generated considerable publicity, on whether the new identities and whereabouts of the then-child killers of toddler James Bulger could be revealed on their release from prison, the court had to consider the balancing of Article 10 on freedom of expression—here regarding the press—with the Article 2 (right to life), Article 3 (prohibition on torture), and Article 8 (respect for private and family life) rights of Venables and Thompson—see *Venables and Thompson v News Group Newspapers Ltd and others* [2001] 2 All ER 908.

The range of cases is ever-increasing as these new principles are tested. The details of how each area of law deals with these problems are outside the scope of this book and will be covered by the tutors in your specific subjects. It is worth commenting at this stage that many of the cases demonstrate a wide range of verbal gymnastics as the judges struggle to decide that the Convention rights are already present in the Common Law so that major changes are not required. However, we do note below a two cases which illustrate the operation of the HRA 1998.

9.5.1 *MacDonald v Ministry of Defence*

The first example illustrates how established case law on the meaning of a word in a statute might be revisited in the light of decisions on the application of the Convention. Under the Sex Discrimination Act 1975 (as amended) it is unlawful for an employer to treat an individual less favourably than it would treat a person of the opposite sex. The UK case law had established that 'sex' did not include sexual orientation, so that discriminating against someone because she was, say, a lesbian, did not fall foul of the Act if a male homosexual would have been treated in the same way; although discriminating against the lesbian because she was a woman would be caught.

In *Smith and Grady* v *United Kingdom* [1999] IRLR 734 (ECtHR), however, the ECtHR held that investigations by the Ministry of Defence into the sexual orientation of two employees violated their right to private life under Article 8 of the Convention. Again, in *Salgueira da Silva* v *Portugal*, App. No. 33290/96, 21 December 1999 (ECtHR), the ECtHR had held that discrimination on the grounds of sexual orientation was contrary to Article 14 of the Convention. The question posed to the Employment Appeal Tribunal in *MacDonald* v *Ministry of Defence* [2000] IRLR 748 therefore was: had these decisions on the application of the Convention affected the meaning of the word 'sex' in the Sex Discrimination Act 1975? Should the word be given a wider meaning than the case law had previously set to make it compliant with Convention rights? The Employment Appeal Tribunal decided that, in the light of Article 8 and its case law, the word 'sex' could be given a wider meaning to include sexual orientation.

9.5.2 *Douglas and others* v *Hello! Ltd*

The second example concerns how areas of law may develop more radically under the influence of (sometimes competing) Convention rights. One area that has caused English law a great deal of difficulty is that of privacy. English law has long recognised that privacy needs protection, but had done this through torts such as defamation or through the equitable doctrine of breach of confidence. What the English Common Law had not done was to take this further and create a specific **right** of privacy. However, Article 8 ECHR states that everyone has the right to respect for his or her private and family life, home, and correspondence. This is sometimes viewed as creating a right to privacy in general. On the other hand, Article 10 deals with the right to freedom of expression, which includes publication.

In *Douglas and others* v *Hello! Ltd* [2001] 2 WLR 992; [2001] QB 967 exclusive rights to publish photographs of the wedding of actors Michael Douglas and Catherine Zeta Jones were granted to *OK!* magazine. *Hello!* magazine intended to publish photographs taken surreptitiously at the wedding. The question was whether such photographs would be a breach of confidence so that *Hello!* should be restrained from publishing them. The case therefore concerned whether an interim injunction should be granted to *OK!* to prevent *Hello!* from publishing its photographs.

The Court of Appeal decided that, when considering whether to grant any relief which might affect the exercise of the right to freedom of expression by restraining publication before trial, a court would have to take into account any relevant rights under the ECHR, as scheduled to the Human Rights Act 1998. Sedley LJ, in particular, noted that section 12(4) of the HRA required the court to 'have particular regard to the importance of the Convention right to freedom of expression' which was protected by Article 10. However, he also seemed to imply that the qualifications in Article 10(2) which qualified the right to freedom of expression in favour of the reputation and rights of others and the protection of information received in confidence, were to be given equal consideration to the right they qualified. Keene LJ noted that Convention jurisprudence acknowledged different degrees of privacy. In *Dudgeon* v *United Kingdom* (1981) 4 EHRR 149 the ECtHR had ruled that the more intimate the aspect of private life being interfered with, the more serious must be the reasons for interference. His Lordship acknowledged that here the claimants had lessened the degree of privacy by allowing widespread publicity to be given to their wedding in *OK!* and that, in reality, the case centred on a battle between two commercial organisations.

In the end, the Court of Appeal refused the injunction, partly on the reasoning noted above and also on the ground that where, in an application for an interim injunction, damages at full trial would be a suitable remedy the court will not usually impose an injunction.

These cases illustrate the type of questions that will emerge over the next few years as lawyers struggle to find the boundaries of the conflict (if any) between UK law and the ECHR. Moreover, they also show the extent to which the English courts, in their own decisions, are not just referring to but actively applying the decisions and jurisprudence of the ECtHR. In *Douglas* v *Hello! Ltd*, in particular, Sedley LJ's interpretation of section 12(4) cound be explained by a concern that the balancing exercise between the two rights was determined by Strasbourg jurisprudence rather than a British reinterpretation, and hence distortion, of those principles. Interestingly, however, in the more recent case of *A* v *B and C* [2002] EWCA Civ 337, the Court of Appeal has allowed free expression to prevail over a claimant's privacy rights, on the basis that section 12(4) has emphasised the importance at Common Law of free speech over countervailing privacy rights. Doubtless this is one of those legal debates that will continue.

9.6 The Consequences for Legal Method (1): Statutory Interpretation

To understand the impact of the HRA 1998 on our legal methods, it is essential first to remember the distinctive basis on which incorporation is to be achieved. The 1998 Act, you will recall, has *not* made the ECHR, with the attendant jurisprudence of the Court, 'lock, stock and barrel' part of English law. Rather it has involved what Jaconelli (1996:8) has called the adoption of a 'free-standing' model of incorporation. This leaves British judges relatively free to arrive at their own version of Convention rights, guided, but not bound, by the approach and meanings adopted by the European Court of Human Rights. We will now consider the implications of this, first, for methods of interpretation and, in the following section, for precedent.

9.6.1 Interpreting UK Legislation

The primary role of the national courts under the HRA 1998 is an interpretative one; they must interpret UK legislation in the light of the Convention rights, and this in turn means that they must interpret the scope and meaning of the Convention rights themselves. How will they go about these processes?

The key provision in the HRA 1998, for our purposes, is section 3(1). As we have already noted, this imposes a statutory duty on all courts and tribunals to interpret primary and subordinate legislation in a manner consistent with the Convention rights.

The obligation to achieve interpretive consistency is not a wholly novel one. The courts are already required to do this in a number of contexts. First, it is a matter of general principle that the courts will aim to interpret UK legislation in a manner consistent with our international treaty obligations. However, it is a matter of some contention whether that duty is a general one or applicable only where the domestic legislation is clearly ambiguous—compare the judgments of Scarman LJ (as he then was) in *Ahmad* v *ILEA* [1977] ICR 490 and Lord Lowry in *R* v *Brown* [1994] 1 AC 212. Secondly, there is a specific duty to ensure consistency with EC law under the principle of compatibility contained (coincidentally) in section 3 of the European Communities Act 1972.

The duty under section 3 of the HRA, however, differs from both the above in some particulars. Thus, unlike the rule in international law, it is clear that section 3 of the HRA is *not* limited to cases of ambiguity—see, e.g., *per* Lord Hoffmann in *R* v *Secretary of State for the Home Department, ex parte Simms* [2002] 2 AC 115 at 132. Moreover, unlike section 3 of the European Communities Act, the HRA 1998 expressly requires the courts to achieve compatibility only *in so far as it is possible to do so*. Clearly the impact of such words is likely to prove crucial to the way the courts approach the interpretative task, and, not surprisingly, section 3(1) has already been the subject of academic debate. There are essentially two alternative ways of looking at the effect of this proviso.

On the one hand, we might suggest that the courts should use it restrictively. This argument has been advanced by Marshall (1998), who suggests that section 3(1) obliges the courts to find consistency only where that is achievable within the bounds of recognised principles of statutory interpretation. In other words, the courts should not artificially strain the meaning of statutory language to make it fit the Convention. This is also, arguably, consistent with the strong emphasis on Parliamentary sovereignty implicit in the whole structuring of the Act, and particularly the procedures for a declaration of incompatibility.

Alternatively, it might be possible to argue that the intention of section 3 is to impose a stronger duty on the courts, akin, as Hunt (1999:97–8) suggests, to the *Marleasing* obligation in EC law, which, by virtue of similar language to that of section 3(1) of the HRA 1998, has been taken to oblige courts to achieve consistency except where that is manifestly impossible on the language of the legislation (see further: Case C–106/89 *Marleasing SA* v *La Comercial Internacional de Alimentación SA* [1990] ECR I–4135, detailed in **Chapter 10**). This position too has other elements in its support (see also Ewing, 1999:87; Bennion, 2000). It is surely logical to suggest that the standard for achieving consistency post-incorporation should be significantly higher than that pre-incorporation. That pre-incorporation standard applied only to legislation which was passed *after* the 1950 Convention and was ambiguous (*R* v *Brown*, above); by contrast, the post-incorporation standard clearly encompasses pre-Convention legislation (see s. 3(2)(a), HRA 1998), and, so should impose a duty that applies in all situations, not just in cases of ambiguity on the face of the Act. Moreover, the Lord Chancellor also expressed the view in debate on the Human Rights Bill that the courts should apply the declaration of incompatibility only where it is *impossible* to construe legislation consistently with Convention rights (HL Debs., vol. 583, col. 535, 18 November 1997). The difficulty this argument faces lies in the very ambiguity of words such as 'so far as possible'. Not only does this make a *Pepper* v *Hart* reference to the Lord Chancellor's views more difficult (though compare the extra-judicial comments of Lord Steyn, 2001), it begs the possibility that the language of section 3(1) of the HRA 1998 may as readily be used to support as to deny the 'Marshall interpretation'. That said, the evidence to date is that the courts are inclining away from a narrow interpretation of their powers under section 3. As Lord Cooke of Thornden has pointed out (extra-judicially):

> Section 3(1) will require a very different approach to interpretation from that to which the United Kingdom courts are accustomed. Traditionally the search has been for the true meaning, now it will be for a possible meaning that will prevent the making of a declaration of incompatibility (cited by Butler-Sloss P stated in *Re K (a child) (secure accommodation order: right to liberty)*, CA, 15 November 2000, Smith Bernal Transcript).

This has been accepted to be the effect of section 3 in a growing number of cases, and notably in the House of Lords decision in *R* v *Director of Public Prosecutions, ex parte Kebilene* [1999] 4 All ER 801; [2000] 2 AC 326, *R* v *A* [2001] UKHL 25; [2001] 2 AC 45, and *In Re S and Others* [2002] UKHL 10. However, the actual process of interpretation seems to differ to a degree, depending on whether the legislation being interpreted was passed before or after the HRA.

Interpreting pre-HRA Acts

It is clear that section 3 HRA has a retrospective effect. The duty of the courts is therefore to interpret pre-HRA legislation in a way consistent with the Convention rights. As Lord Nicholls of Birkenhead has pointed out, '[it] is a powerful tool whose use is obligatory. It is not an optional canon of construction'—*In re S and Others* at [37]. It follows that the courts are no longer bound by pre-HRA authority on the meaning of any given statutory language—see also *per* Lord Hope of Craighead in *R* v *Lambert* [2001] UKHL 37; [2001] 3 All ER 577 at [81], and, perhaps even more importantly, legislative intent is no longer the decisive factor in construction. Consequently, we suggest the interpretative process can properly be seen as involving the following stages (Figure 9.1; see similarly Bennion, 2000).

Post-HRA legislation

So, the question that now arises is, what happens where the Act under consideration was passed after the HRA? So far there have been very few instances of this, however the recent decision of the House of Lords in *R* v *A* [2001] UKHL 25; [2001] 2 AC 45 is instructive in indicating how the courts are likely to approach problems of incompatibility in post-HRA Acts.

The issue for the House of Lords in *R* v *A* was whether the provisions of section 41 of the Youth Justice and Criminal Evidence Act 1999 were consistent with an accused's right to a fair trial under Article 6 ECHR. The accused in this case had been charged with rape

- the interpreter must determine, first, in the light of all the surrounding circumstances, whether there is a real doubt about the meaning of the statute
- if there is, that doubt must be resolved by reference to all the available principles and canons of construction
- in Convention cases involving pre-HRA legislation, the generally applied principles of statutory interpretation are modified in the following ways:
  - Parliament's intention is no longer the primary guide to establishing statutory meaning
  - Section 3(1) HRA creates a new canon of construction, imposing a strong obligation on courts to achieve a consistent construction between the statute and the Convention rights.
  - In so doing, the court must consider adopting the kind of 'teleological' (i.e. purposive) approach consistent with the jurisprudence of the ECtHR (see further 9.6.2).
  - In particular, the courts should seek to apply a construction which gives full effect to the fundamental rights and freedoms contained in the Convention—see *per* Lord Hope *Kebilene* [1999] 4 All ER 801 at 838–9, what constitutes a 'full effect' may depend to some degree on whether the Convention right is absolute or qualified—see 9.3.1, above.

Figure 9.1   Interpreting pre-HRA legislation

and wished to adduce evidence of previous consensual sexual relations with the complainant as part of his defence. This, he alleged, he was prevented from doing by virtue of Section 41 of the 1999 Act. Section 41(1), which is subject to only limited exceptions, reads:

(1) If at a trial a person is charged with a sexual offence, then, except with the leave of the court—

   (a) no evidence may be adduced, and

   (b) no question may be asked in examination by or on behalf of any accused at the trial, about any sexual behaviour of the complainant.

Clearly this imposes *prima facie* ban on calling the kind of evidence the defendant sought to use in *R* v *A*. This was presumably its intent. There has been a longstanding procedural problem with criminal defendants and their counsel abusing the right to use evidence of a complainant's previous sexual experience so that it establishes only what the Canadian Supreme Court (*per* McLachlin J in *R* v *Seaboyer* (1991) 83 DLR(4d) 193 at 278) has called the 'twin myths': that 'unchaste women were more likely to consent to intercourse and, in any event, were less worthy of belief'. In England, the Sexual Offences (Amendment) Act 1976, section 2, had sought, with only limited success, to restrict the calling of evidence about the complainant's previous sexual experience with a third party. But section 2 had not even attempted to restrict evidence of previous sexual relations between a complainant and defendant. Thus, the introduction of section 41 marked a considerable sea-change, since it did not make any such distinction.

The problem is, that while it was almost universally accepted that a better 'rape shield' law was needed, it was argued very early on that section 41 may have gone too far in protecting the victim (see, e.g., Birch, 2000), precisely because it did not distinguish between sexual history with the defendant and sexual history with third parties. While evidence of a sexual history with third parties might universally be seen as unduly prejudicial to the complainant, the same could not (at least in the view of a majority of commentators) necessarily be said for past conduct with the defendant. In *R* v *A*, Lord Steyn summarised the argument thus (para. 31):

> As a matter of common sense, a prior sexual relationship between the complainant and the accused may, depending on the circumstances, be relevant to the issue of consent. It is a species of prospectant evidence, which may throw light on the complainant's state of mind. It cannot, of course, prove that she consented on the occasion in question. Relevance and sufficiency of proof are different things... It is true that each decision to engage in sexual activity is always made afresh ... [but] a prior relationship may sometimes be relevant to what decision was made on a particular occasion ...

Consequently, by failing to make this distinction section 41, it was argued on behalf of the defendant and accepted by their Lordships, involved a denial of due process under Article 6.

In what is clearly the leading judgment Lord Steyn takes us through a number of steps. These are instructive in terms of approach. First, he starts with an extensive review of the content and legislative history leading up to the passing of section 41. He then explores the scope of section 41 itself, drawing extensively on both academic commentary and the Canadian 'rape shield' laws that were influential in shaping section 41, and also considering proposals from the New South Wales and New Zealand Law Commissions. On this basis he concludes that section 41 is too widely drafted and makes an 'excessive inroad into the right to a fair trial' (para. 36). His third step is to explore the interpretive options open to the complainant in the light of section 3(1) HRA, *if* 'ordinary methods of purposive and contextual interpretation' (para. 39) fail. Using these options, his Lordship rejects a number of ways of restricting the breadth of section 41 as impossible under both ordinary rules and section 3(1) HRA. Finally, his Lordship focuses on two of the statutory exceptions built into section 41. These give a judge discretion to admit evidence of a complainant's sexual history where:

- behaviour is relevant to the issue of consent and the relevant behaviour either took place at or about the same time as the event out of which the complaint came: section 41(3)(b), or
- it was so strikingly similar to the behaviour of the complainant at or about the time complained of, that it ought to be admitted: section 41(3)(c).

Having ruled out any possibility of using sub-section (3)(b) in this case (because too much time had elapsed between any previous sexual activity and the event complained of), the court focused on section 41(3)(c). Lord Steyn argued that, although the sub-section was not sufficient under ordinary methods of statutory interpretation to cure the problem, it was possible, by using section 3(1) of the HRA 'to subordinate the niceties of language' (para. 45) to interpret the provision to take account of 'modern considerations of relevance judged by logical and common sense criteria of time and circumstances' (ibid). Consequently, the House of Lords argued that the test of admissibility under section 41(3)(c) in such cases becomes whether, 'due regard always being paid to the importance of seeking to protect the complainant from indignity and humiliating questions... the evidence... is nevertheless so relevant to the issues of consent that to exclude it would endanger the fairness of the trial under article 6 of the convention' (para. 46).

Now, whatever the House of Lords may call it, this involves a quite breathtaking disregard of statutory language—to the extent that one of their Lordships, Lord Hope, was clearly uncomfortable with what was being done. A narrow exception, concerned only to admit what in the jargon we call 'similar fact' evidence, has been re-written as a much more generalised test of relevance. (Indeed, the full implications of this have yet to be tested by defence lawyers and the courts, so it is possible that the House of Lords may have re-opened the very 'Pandora's box' that section 41 was trying to keep closed—though that is a matter beyond the scope of this book.)

So what does this tell us about the legal method being adopted? From Lord Steyn's analysis it seems that the starting point (once it becomes clear that there is interference with a convention right) *is* the presumed legislative intent. Significantly, this is assessed in *R v A* by reference to the *mischief* that section 41 was intended to address and by purposive references to the experience of constructing 'rape shields' in other Common Law jurisdictions. This seems to be a logical prerequisite to using section 3(1) of the HRA to override the plain meaning of the offending provision. As their Lordships acknowledged in this case, section 3 is ultimately a rule of construction, it does not give judges the power to legislate (though, given the extent to which the House of Lords in this case has moved beyond the wording of section 41, this begins to look like a very fine distinction). Consequently, they must first be satisfied that Parliament has not either expressly or impliedly intended to legislate contrary to the ECHR, and this analysis of legislative intent does just that. It enables the court to show that the draftsman got it wrong, and to remedy the defect, using section 3(1) to justify the remedial nature of the surgery.

Consequently, on the basis of the reasoning in *R v A*, we suggest that the interpretative process for post-HRA legislation goes broadly as summarised in Figure 9.2.

- Is there a *prima facie* incompatibility between the Act and (a) Convention right(s)?
- If so, can that incompatibility be avoided by reference to legislative intent using mischief and/or purposive approaches or *Pepper v Hart*?
- If conventional methods of interpretation are insufficient to resolve the incompatibility, but there is no evidence of intent to legislate contrary to the HRA, then the Act must be read in accordance with section 3(1) HRA, to make it convention compliant. (An intent to legislate contrary to the HRA will not, it seems, be inferred from an incompatibility on the face of the Act)

Figure 9.2 Principles for Interpreting Post-HRA Legislation

So, in conclusion, how far are the courts prepared to go to achieve compatibility? Our review of the case law to date suggests a very long way indeed. The courts seem to be accepting three particular interpretive techniques as legitimate. First, courts may 'read down' (see Clayton & Tomlinson, 2000:168) words to achieve compatibility by giving them a *narrower* meaning than an ordinary construction would suggest. Secondly, they may 'read in' additional words to achieve a compatible meaning. Neither of these techniques is unknown to the pre-HRA Common Law, and they may be thought of as relatively unremarkable forms of purposive interpretation. Thirdly, however, the courts may engage in what Lord Hope has, in the context of pre-HRA legislation, called a process of 'translation' (*R v Lambert*, above, at [81]) in which incompatible words are to be read *as if* they were compatible. Lord Steyn has candidly acknowledged that this kind of approach takes section 3 well beyond our conventional understanding of purposiveness. Section 3 is thus 'more radical in its effect . . . a declaration of incompatibility is a measure of last resort. It must be avoided unless it is plainly impossible to do so'. Accordingly, at least in respect of post-HRA legalisation, it may be necessary to go even further, to quote Lord Steyn again: 'the techniques to be used will not only involve the reading down of express language in a statute but also the implication of provisions' (see *R* v *A* [2001] UKHL 25 at [44]). Again, reliance on such a 'strained interpretation' is by no means unknown to the pre-HRA law (see, e.g., *Connelly* v *RTZ Corp plc* [1997] 4 All ER 335), but it has conventionally been viewed as a largely exceptional approach. This, it seems, is much less the case where the issue is the HRA compliance of legislation. The courts, it seems, must consider doing pretty much whatever is necessary to achieve a compatible construction, short, but perhaps only just short, of re-writing the Act in question.

9.6.2 Interpreting the Convention Rights

The second point we need to explore is the courts' approach to interpreting the Convention rights themselves. There is of course already a substantial 'bank' of interpretive material in the jurisprudence of the European Court of Human Rights. However, one consequence of the 'free-standing' model of incorporation is that the English courts are not obliged to follow the interpretations laid down by the Court, though they are expected to have some regard to the decisions of that body (see the next section for more detail on this). Accordingly, it is conceivable that the English courts could develop a distinctive human rights jurisprudence which deviates significantly from the approach of the Court. One thing that possibly militates against that is the fact that the HRA 1998 does not oust the jurisdiction of the Human Rights Court (though it does make the journey to Strasbourg rather longer). Claimants who fail to establish a breach of Convention rights before the UK courts are still entitled to appeal to Strasbourg for redress. If they win, under Article 52 ECHR, the UK government is obliged to apply the decision of the European Court of Human Rights (unless it has entered a derogation), thereby overriding the inconsistent approach of the domestic courts. Commonsense thus suggests that too much independence on the part of the British courts would be counter-productive if it simply generated more appeals to Strasbourg than the present system. At the same time, this does not mean that the English and European Courts should necessarily proceed in absolute tandem. The Human Rights Court itself recognises that scope may exist for local variation in the application of the Convention and, regardless of whether a state has incorporated the Convention or not, allows a 'margin of appreciation'. This rather technical doctrine means that, in assessing compliance, the Court will in some respects defer to the appreciation of a problem by the national authorities, including the courts, thereby giving them some element of discretion (Jaconelli, 1996:11; Merrills, 1993: chap. 7).

Related to this is the question of what interpretative principles the domestic courts will bring to their analysis of Convention rights. We have already pointed out that the Convention rights are not necessarily capable of the kind of precise and detailed exposition that characterises a lot of domestic legislation. While the Convention may specify that we have a right to life and a right to privacy, the potential boundaries of these rights are difficult to define in the abstract, or in the detail often expected of legislation; similarly, problems will arise in defining the boundaries between competing rights. For example, is the practice of abortion to be protected because it constitutes an integral part of the woman's right to privacy, or challenged as a violation of the foetus's right to life? At what point may one right supersede the other? Resolving such problems requires not just analysis of the text, but a sensitivity to the 'spirit' of the Convention and to the social and ethical issues that such problems raise. Arguments about human rights often do not lend themselves to the narrower brands of legal literalism. In theory this should not be an insurmountable problem. British judges today are, given the EC context, far more familiar with broader, principles-based drafting and purposive styles of interpretation than they were thirty years ago, and generally more prepared for the kind of judicial activism that the ECHR demands. But the EC law analogy gives rise to a further question: should British judges consciously adopt the style of analysis used by the European Court of Human Rights? This is in some respects distinctive, reflecting both the special character of the ECHR and the general principles of interpretation developed under the Vienna Convention on the Law of Treaties (1969). The interpretive style of the Court is thereby characterised by three key elements: the 'textuality principle'; a 'teleological' approach to interpretation; and a capacity to supplement the express terms of the Convention by the recognition of 'implied terms' (see Merrills, 1993: chap. 4).

The **textuality principle** describes the Court's starting point, which, in common with all widely accepted traditions of interpretation, demands respect for the text of the Convention. As Article 31(1) of the Vienna Convention puts it: 'A treaty shall be interpreted in good faith in accordance with the ordinary meaning to be given to the terms of the treaty in their context and in the light of its object and purpose'. It is an approach, therefore, which avoids the extremes of literalism by accepting that the ordinary meaning is in large part determined by the context—both textual and social. This is reinforced by an expectation that the Court will look at the meaning of words or provisions within the context of the Convention as a whole. This has created some interesting problems, because the Court has sometimes found areas of overlap between different provisions of the ECHR, rather than, say, assuming that the express inclusion of one right in one part of the Convention precludes its implicit inclusion in another Article. For example, in *Rasmussen*, Series A, No. 87, a question arose as to Danish paternity law. Denmark had ratified the Convention but not the Seventh Protocol, which, in Article 5, expressly defined the rights of parents with regard to their children, and the Danish government therefore sought to argue that the case was not justiciable. The Court rejected this argument by finding that, despite the omission of the Seventh Protocol, the case could also be considered under Article 8 ECHR. In theory at least this could raise interesting questions in the British context, given that the Protocols not ratified by Britain are excluded from the Convention rights within the HRA 1998.

The idea of a **teleological approach** is primarily a very European way of describing purposiveness (cf. our discussion of European Community methods in **Chapter 10**). The

European Court of Human Rights has adopted a fairly cautious approach in this regard, seeking to tread a fine line between possibly excessive interference with the domestic jurisdiction and powers of individual states, and the need to give full effect to the aims and objectives of the Convention in securing individual rights and freedoms. Consequently, the Court has established a number of basic guidelines (see Merrills, 1993:77ff). For example:

(a) Where an Article limits or qualifies an individual right, such limits are normally to be interpreted narrowly.

(b) The Convention should be read as a 'living instrument', that is, by reference to current values and conditions, not those that existed when the Convention was adopted in the 1950s.

(c) Closely related to the above, following Article 31(3)(b) of the Vienna Convention, the interpreter is entitled to take account of the subsequent practice of the state in the application of the treaty. The precise scope and meaning of subsequent practice is, however, a contested and somewhat thorny issue, beyond the scope of our present concerns.

(d) In addition the Court has recourse to a number of *general principles*, notably, the 'margin of appreciation' (discussed above) and the principles of proportionality (see 9.3.1, above) and legal certainty (self-explanatory!), which it will use to determine the limits of state liability and individual rights. This approach is again one with which British judges have become more familiar through EC law, though it has been argued that both the courts and Parliament have underestimated the extent to which it could force judges further into the political arena when interpreting the HRA 1998 (cf. Lord Lester, 1998).

Lastly, the Court has also followed the general practice in the Law of Treaties of acknowledging that it is sometimes necessary to find **'implied terms'** when construing the Convention. The justification is often made by analogy with the law of contract, in which it is similarly often impossible to predict, at the time the agreement is made, all the situations that may arise during the performance of those obligations. Implied terms may be either implied rights or implied limitations. Often the same circumstances that lead the European Court of Human Rights to find implied rights will also lead it to consider the need for implied limitations. For example, in *Mathieu-Mohin and Clerfayt*, Series A, No. 113, the Court recognised that the right to hold free elections under Article 3 of the First Protocol itself implied a number of rights necessary to achieving that end. Since Article 3 did not spell out these rights, there must also be room for implied limitations. This approach could prove something of a novelty for British judges.

9.7 The Consequences for Legal Method (2): Precedent

In looking at the impact of Convention rights and the HRA 1998 on precedent there are essentially two questions: what is the likely impact of the 1998 Act on the doctrine of precedent, and what is the status of decisions of the Human Rights Court under the HRA 1998?

As regards the first of these points, all Common Law rules and precedents that are incompatible with Convention rights are potentially open to challenge. This principle, we suggest, extends *expressly* to those precedents which are interpretations of statutory provisions, since, if inconsistent with Convention rights, they will be caught explicitly by section 3 of the HRA 1998 (above), and *implicitly* to all Common Law rules *per se*. This argument is based on the fact that all courts and tribunals are, as we have seen, themselves 'public authorities' under the Act. As such they are obliged to achieve consistency with the Convention in respect of the substantive and procedural rules they have made. The correctness of this view appears to be supported by Lord Hope in *R v Lambert* [2001] UKHL 37; [2001] 3 All ER 577 at [114], where he expressly took the view that both a court's duty to construe legislation consistently with the Convention under section 3(1) and to decide cases on Common Law principles were 'acts' within the meaning of section 6(1) of the HRA. The interesting technical question will be how the courts face that particular challenge.

There is clearly some expectation with regard to previous (inconsistent) interpretations of legislation caught by section 3 that all courts/tribunals will be required to disregard such precedents, though this is implicit in section 3 rather than expressly spelled out in the Act (but see Home Office, 1997, para. 2.8, where the point is made explicit), nor is any such principle expressly established in respect of Common Law rules more generally. In this latter context, since all courts and tribunals are caught by the duties contained in section 6 of the HRA 1998, there is clearly some basis for saying that the duty to override inconsistent precedents *in general* lies with all courts and tribunals, regardless of the status or authority of the precedent involved. Of course, this may be a fine argument in principle, but still somewhat unattractive to the tribunal chair or district judge actually facing a House of Lords decision which he or she believes is incompatible with the HRA 1998. The inherent respect for precedent that is so much part of English legal culture may mean that the courts will disapply precedents only in so far as this is within their express powers under the doctrine of *stare decisis*. In other words, the inferior courts may well leave it to the superior courts expressly to overrule incompatible precedents. If this happens, the development of compatibility may be relatively haphazard and slow, as it will primarily depend upon claimants having the resources, willingness, and opportunity to appeal.

As regards the status of decisions of the European Court of Human Rights, section 2(1) of the HRA 1998 expressly requires the British courts to *take into account*, among other things, the judgments, decisions, and advisory opinions of the Court and opinions and decisions of the (now defunct) European Commission. This was interpreted by the Court of Appeal in *Barclays Bank plc v Ellis*, The Times, 24 October 2000 to mean that lawyers had to bring to the court's attention *all* the relevant case law of the ECtHR. Mere reference to the Convention, it was said, did not help the court and was not sufficient.

However this is an obligation only to consider; there is no express statutory duty to **follow** the established European case law on the ECHR. This is consistent with the freestanding model adopted by the UK, though different from the 'European' model of incorporation in which decisions of the Court are treated in effect as binding and hence more or less determinative (this is also the approach taken by the Court itself—see *Borges v Belgium*, Series A, No. 214–B). It also differs from the UK's obligations as regards decisions of the ECJ under section 2 of the European Communities Act. That said, the overwhelming evidence to date suggests that the courts are treating themselves as ordinarily obliged to adopt a consistent interpretation. In *Alconbury* (above), for example, the majority of the Law Lords undoubtedly treated the Strasbourg jurisprudence as *prima facie* binding, even if only for pragmatic reasons. In Lord Slynn's words:

> [i]n the absence of some special circumstances it seems to me that the [UK] court should follow any clear and constant jurisprudence of the European Court of Human Rights. If it does not do so there is at least a possibility that the case will go to that court, which is likely in the ordinary case to follow its own constant jurisprudence. (para. 26)

Of course, even Lord Slynn's language does not preclude the possibility that the British courts could 'go it alone' on specific issues, in 'special circumstances'. Indeed, in the same *Alconbury* decision Lord Hoffmann (at para. 76) hinted at his own reluctance to apply Strasbourg jurisprudence if to do so would compel a conclusion fundamentally inconsistent with the distribution of powers under the UK's established constitutional arrangements. So far, however, we have found no decisions where a judge has been so inclined.

9.8 Legal Research and Argumentation

The HRA 1998 raises a number of important practical and conceptual issues around legal research and argumentation.

First, it creates an obligation on all British lawyers (rather than just the human rights specialists) to become familiar with new sources of law. This is not a small task. There is not just the matter of developing a familiarity with the Convention itself (one probably needs to understand the Convention as a whole, not just the Convention rights enacted in the HRA 1998, for the reasons of interpretation already considered), there is also the slight matter of about fifty years'-worth of case law. Decisions of the Human Rights Court and Commission can be found in separate official series of reports published by the Council of Europe—the Court is identified by the 'Series A' and case number references you have seen in this chapter. Decisions can also be accessed in full-text version from the Council of Europe's web site (above), though not all decisions there are published in English. The most commonly accessible English-language version of European Court (and Commission) decisions is the *European Human Rights Reports* (EHRR), published by Sweet & Maxwell. Selected decisions of the Court also appear in English in the *International Law Reports*, published by Grotius, Cambridge. These law reports are not widely available outside academic and specialist libraries, and some series are not always available in those. There are also some specialist journals, notably the *European Human Rights Law Review*, though there has also been substantial coverage of incorporation issues in the more generalist journals, particularly *Public Law* and the *Criminal Law Review*.

Reading decisions of the European Court of Human Rights is also a somewhat distinctive process. The judgments are drafted as something of a compromise between the

Common Law and Civil Law styles we saw in **Chapter 3**. Until 1968, decisions of the Court adopted very much the continental style still used in modified form by the ECJ, with numbered paragraphs giving the Court's reasoning followed by a short judgment. This has been abandoned for a more flowing, narrative, style of analysis, with reference to its own earlier authorities as required (as we have briefly seen, the Court does abide by its own system of precedent, albeit not with the full rigour of the English model of *stare decisis*). Like the British courts, the Court requires decisions to be made by at least a majority rather than expecting unanimity. Judges may also, therefore, in Common Law fashion, offer separate opinions. This is clearly different from the collegial approach of the ECJ. In practice, it is relatively rare for judges of the Court to deliver separate opinions. Judges appear to have been very cautious in their use, and aware of the risk of undermining the authority of the Court by extensive divisions of opinion. Consequently, when the power has been used it is generally to deliver a dissent from the majority view, rather than a concurring judgment giving some distinctive reasoning. Joint dissenting opinions may also be delivered.

At a deeper level, as Hunt (1999) points out, the HRA 1998 will, more than ever, force lawyers to confront matters of morality and fundamental values, and this itself has implications for the form and content of legal argumentation. The traditional 'positivistic' conception of law has tended to keep law and morality separate. This is not to say that law is routinely assumed to have no moral content or foundation, but it does mean that legal and moral principles and reasoning have generally been treated as distinct species, with the courts being primarily concerned with the enforcement of law, not morals. By blurring that distinction the 1998 Act is likely to oblige lawyers, including the judges, to take account of a wider range of resources and forms of argument. This may involve both a wider academic literature, including the ethical and philosophical, not just the legal. As Lord Steyn has recognised, instead of trawling through endless *dicta* on *Wednesbury* unreasonableness, 'it may be more helpful to dip into Isaiah Berlin' (cited in Hunt, 1999:99). Comparative material, particularly from other Common Law jurisdictions that have adopted a culture of positive rights, such as Canada, South Africa, New Zealand, and the USA, is also likely to become relevant. Indeed, much of the HRA case law already cited in this chapter seems to support this assumption.

9.9 CONCLUSION

It seems reasonable to conclude that the HRA 1998 is bound to have at least some significant impact not just on the substantive law, but on how British lawyers construct, present, and determine cases before the courts. It would be wrong to present this as a total revolution. As we have seen, the ECHR was an interpretative source even before the 1998 Act, though the obligation to take account of Convention rights will inevitably be far stronger now that the Act is in force.

We would go so far as to suggest that the HRA 1998 is likely to have some impact on what we have previously called 'judicial style'. The shift from the traditional permissive approach of civil liberties, characterised by the idea that we are free to do anything which is not explicitly unlawful, to the positive rights of the HRA 1998 is likely to be difficult to ignore. At the very least, we suggest that it will curb some of the more pragmatic and unprincipled (in the sense of being without an underlying 'deep' rationale) decision-making that has frequently substituted for a more sophisticated discourse of rights in the English courts.

Attractive and sensible though such changes may be, we must acknowledge that they too add to the burden of lawyering at the beginning of the twenty-first century. New forms of argumentation require new skills. Lawyers arguing points under the HRA 1998 need to master the jurisprudence of the European Court of Human Rights, perhaps the human rights jurisprudence of other jurisdictions too, and develop the facility for philosophical analysis. These are not tasks that will be accomplished overnight. Indeed, the lead-up to the 1998 Act generated a flurry of judicial training and continuing education in the professions; this is likely to continue. The impact will also be felt in academic and vocational legal education in the universities and colleges. In this light, the call for a greater emphasis on education in ethics and values by the Lord Chancellor's Advisory Committee's *First Report on Legal Education and Training* (1996; see Webb, 1998:135–6) looks remarkably prescient.

EXERCISE 18 Concept check

The following is simply a short comprehension exercise designed to assist you to become more comfortable with concepts used in this chapter. After reading the chapter, try to complete the following without referring back; then check your answers. Repeat the process of reading, answering and checking until you are satisfied that you *understand* the material. Alternatively you can do this as a group task by swapping answers and checking each other's. If you find you have different answers, consider why? Sometimes this may bring out important differences in understanding.

What do the following concepts mean? Try to define them in your own words:

free-standing model of incorporation	margin of appreciation
declaration of incompatibility	textuality principle
right of individual petition	victim
principle of proportionality	Convention rights
legislative competence	implied terms

REFERENCES

BAMFORTH, N. (1999), 'The Application of the Human Rights Act 1998 to Public Authorities and Private Bodies', *Cambridge Law Journal* 159.

*BENNION, F. (2000), 'What Interpretation is "Possible" under s. 3(1) of the Human Rights Act 1998', *Public Law* 77.

BIRCH, D. (2000), 'A Better Deal for Vulnerable Witnesses?', *Criminal Law Review* 223.

CLAYTON, R. and TOMLINSON, H. (2000), *The Law of Human Rights* (Oxford: Oxford University Press).

EWING, K. D. (1999), 'The Human Rights Act and Parliamentary Democracy', 62 *Modern Law Review* 79.

GEARTY, C. (ed.) (1997), *European Civil Liberties and the European Convention on Human Rights* (The Hague: Kluwer).

*GREER, S. (1999), 'A Guide to the Human Rights Act 1998', 24 *European Law Review* 2.

HOME OFFICE (1997), *Rights Brought Home: The Human Rights Bill*, Cm. 3782 (London: The Stationery Office).

HUNT, M. (1999), 'The Human Rights Act and Legal Culture: The Judiciary and the Legal Profession', 26 *Journal of Law & Society* 86.

*JACOBS, F. G. and WHITE, R. C. (1996), *The European Convention on Human Rights* (Oxford: Clarendon Press).

JACONELLI, J. (1996), 'Incorporating the European Convention on Human Rights: A Critical Guide to the Issues', Faculty of Law Working Paper No. 22 (Manchester: University of Manchester).

LESTER, LORD, OF HERNE HILL (1998), 'The Impact of the Human Rights Act on Public Law' in J. Beatson, C. Forsyth, and I. Hare (eds.), *Constitutional Reform in the United Kingdom: Principles and Practice* (Oxford: Hart Publishing).

*MARSHALL, G. (1998), 'Interpreting Interpretation in the Human Rights Bill', *Public Law* 167.

MERRILLS, J. G. (1993), *The Development of International Law by the European Court of Human Rights* (2nd edn., Manchester: Manchester University Press).

STEYN, J. (2001), '*Pepper* v *Hart*: A Re-Examination', 21 *Oxford Journal of Legal Studies* 59.

WEBB, J. (1998), 'Ethics for Lawyers or Ethics for Citizens? New Directions for Legal Education', 25 *Journal of Law & Society* 134.

10

European Legal Method

Britain's membership of the European Community has meant that the English Legal System is increasingly having to take account of the European dimension. As we have noted before, and shall explore in this chapter, Community law takes precedence over national law and can even take precedence over legislation. Not only does this mean that some of the law affecting us is created by institutions of the European Community rather than by our national Parliament and courts, it also involves us in a different way of thinking. We have touched upon these matters throughout the book but, as the role of the Community tends to run parallel with English law rather than fit clearly into the hierarchy, we felt that too much detail on Community law in the earlier chapters might lead to confusion. This chapter therefore explores the topics of Community institutions and legal method in greater depth.

Section 10.1 details the **Sources** of European Union law. **Section 10.2** sets out the **Institutions** of the EU and their increasingly important role in our law-making, and **Section 10.3** lists the **Analytical Techniques** employed by European lawyers. **Section 10.4** describes the **Legal Method** employed in the Court of Justice and the effect of EC Law on the **Drafting and Interpretation** of UK Legislation.

10.1 The Sources of Community Law

In the simplest of outlines, Community law is made up from the originating and amending Treaties of the Community (what might be seen as the Community's foundations), the 'Acts' of the various Community institutions (sometimes referred to as secondary sources), and the judgments of the Court of Justice.

10.1.1 The Treaties

The European Economic Community began life in 1957 under the Treaty of Rome, signed by France, Germany, Italy, Belgium, Luxembourg, and The Netherlands. The same six states had already created the European Coal and Steel Community in 1951; and added the European Atomic Energy Community to the list on the same day as the EEC itself was formed. The aims of the signatories were not limited to economics—a fact becoming more evident today. The Court of Justice of the European Communities and the Parliament (originally called the Assembly) were the only institutions that these

Communities shared until 1965, at which date the institutions with overlapping functions in the different Communities effectively merged.

The United Kingdom joined the Communities in 1973. As Treaties are not automatically part of our law, the United Kingdom Parliament passed the European Communities Act in 1972 to incorporate the Treaty provisions. In 1986 the Member States signed the Single European Act with its aim of removing trade barriers by 1992 and providing a framework for political unity. This European provision was incorporated into UK law by the European Communities (Amendment) Act 1986.

The Treaty of European Union 1992—(the Maastricht Treaty)—was the next piece in the jigsaw. The Maastricht Treaty sought to extend the sphere of the Community's interests beyond that of economic cooperation towards political, social, and cultural integration—the creation of a 'Union'. Such wide aims had indeed always been present as goals of the EEC, but now they have become more prominent. Thus, the aim to create a common currency, to establish a floor of rights for European Union citizens, to create a common foreign and defence policy, to create common employment law rights, and even the change in name itself—from European Economic Community to European Community and now to European Union—all display the overriding aims of many of the Member States (though for reasons explained in the Preface, we will refer to *Community* or *EC* law in this chapter).

On 1 May 1999 another treaty (the Treaty of Amsterdam) came into force. The changes brought about by the Amsterdam Treaty were mainly political or administrative ones, though there are legislative changes regarding matters such as social policy and discrimination. The latest in the line is the Treaty of Nice which came into effect on 1 February 2003 and deals mainly with the practical issues of how the great expansion in the number of EU Member States over the next few years is to be handled (matters such as how many members of the European Parliament there should be and how the voting system will operate in the European Council—which is the real decision-making body of the EU). Discussion is under way on how to consolidate all the various treaties into one single Treaty.

The Nice Treaty also proclaimed the Charter of Fundamental Rights of the European Union. This is based on the fundamental rights established in the European Convention for Human Rights but goes wider in setting out the civil, political, economic, and social rights of European citizens. It does not yet have the force of law and, in reality, is a restatement of existing rights.

Any student of EC law will need to be aware of these changes, but they are outside the scope of this book. What can be seen from these recent treaties since that of Maastricht, however, is the continuing divergence of aims held by Member States: on the one hand, there are those who favour a much more federal Europe, on the other there are those who see it as an economic community held together by sovereign Member States. The Nice Treaty makes such divergence easier to facilitate.

The aims set out in the original Treaty and its modifying Treaties are, with some exceptions, expressed in general terms and broad principles. Each 'section' of the Treaties is referred to as an *Article*. Thus Article 3 of the Treaty of Rome lists the activities of the Community, such as finance, trade, social welfare, and politics. When we refer to an Article it will relate to the EC Treaty unless otherwise stated. As noted in **Chapter 1**, however, there is one matter in the Treaty of Amsterdam which affected this text substantially: as a result of that Treaty most of the Article numbers in the original 1957 Treaty of Rome were re-numbered. Thus, Article 177 became Article 234 of the new EC Treaty. In this edition we have cited all Articles of the EC Treaty under their new numbers.

To these general aims set out in the amended Treaty are added various powers by which the European Community can give detail and definition to the general requirements. Under Article 249 the institutions of the Community, therefore, have powers to create law under the Treaties; officially styled 'Acts' of the institutions.

10.1.2 The Acts of the Institutions

Clearly someone has to have the power to make law within the Community on a year-by-year basis. That power falls to two bodies, termed *The Council of Ministers* and *The Commission*. We will deal with these two institutions below.

As we first mentioned in **Chapter 1**, the Community produces different forms of legislation and these are termed:

(a) Regulations;

(b) Directives; and

(c) Decisions.

Regulations and Directives are sometimes referred to as secondary sources of legislation. However, we prefer to adopt the view taken by Brown and Kennedy (1994) that the Acts of the institutions are too fundamental and broad to be relegated to a 'secondary' tag; they are, along with the Treaties, 'Community legislation'. You need to be aware what the difference is between these forms of legislation:

• A *Regulation* has a general application. Like the Treaty itself, the Regulation applies to all Member States and individuals, and is binding without further action on the part of the Member States. Regulations must be published in the *Official Journal* of the Community.

• A *Directive* also has general application in that it is binding on Member States as to the **result** to be achieved, but leaves open to each state the **form and method** of implementation. This enables the Community to establish the legal principle whilst allowing Member States to incorporate that principle within their own national legislation in the way they see fit. As we will see below, this idea can lead to problems when the wordings of the Directive and the national legislation do not correspond. Member States are invariably given a time limit for implementation. A Directive has no effect in law until it is implemented by the state (unless the time limit for implementation has passed), and the method of implementation will vary from state to state according to their own special conditions. The general aim must, however, be satisfied and must also be published.

• A *Decision* is not something of judicial origin, though it sounds as if it should be. Instead it is a binding 'order' issued by an institution of the Community and addressed to an individual or state. These frequently arise in competition law cases, with the Commission determining the legality of agreements.

To these three binding legal provisions we can also add *Recommendations* and *Opinions* which will be of persuasive authority (these are technical matters best left until you study EU law later in your course).

10.1.3 The Court of Justice of the European Communities

The Court is the supreme authority on the law relating to the European Community. **It deals only with the interpretation and validity of Community-generated law**. It is modelled on European systems, and most of its procedure and legal method bears little relationship to the Common Law world. The composition of the Court was noted earlier in **Chapter 3** and Article 220 deals with the jurisdiction of the Court. It states: 'The Court of Justice shall ensure that in the interpretation and application of (the Treaties) the law is observed'.

A key point to note is that it is the national courts and tribunals in each Member State which apply the interpretations handed down by the Court of Justice. The ECJ does not determine the cases themselves i.e. it makes no findings of fact, nor does it apply the law to the facts: it makes rulings on interpretation, not decisions on who wins or loses the case. On most issues, therefore, the Court of Justice is a court of **reference**, not a court of appeal. It assists the national court in making its decision but it does not make the decision for the national court in the actual case. When you hear news bulletins etc., speaking of the ECJ *deciding* a particular case or *hearing an appeal* from a UK court, these reports are simply incorrect—and reflect many of the misconceptions popularly held about the EU generally. This was commented upon most recently by Laddie J in *Arsenal Football Club plc v Reed (No. 2)* [2002] EWHC 2695;[2003] 1 All ER 137 in holding that where the ECJ had disagreed with the conclusions of fact reached at the trial the ECJ had exceeded its jurisdiction and the national court was not bound by its conclusion.

The Court has a wide jurisdiction given to it under the Treaties. Here are a few examples:

(a) it exercises judicial control over the institutions of the Community such as the Commission;

(b) it exercises powers of judicial review on the validity of Community legislation such as Regulations and Directives—in other words it can annul Community legislation;

(c) it hears cases brought by Member States or Community institutions against other Member States regarding violations of the Treaties;

(d) it decides whether international agreements entered into by the Community are compatible with the provisions of the Treaties; and

(e) it gives *preliminary rulings* under Article 234 when asked to do so by a court of a Member State concerning the interpretation of Community legislation.

Since 1989 it has also acted as an appeal court to a new court, the *Court of First Instance*, which deals with, amongst other things, cases relating to the staff of the Community. The Treaty of Nice has also addressed how the ECJ will be affected by the expansion in Member States and has begun the Job of sharing tasks between the ECJ and the Court of First

Instance more effectively. The Treaty also allows for the creation of specialist Chambers according to particular areas of law.

As this is just one chapter of a book concerned with legal method, and we cannot hope to do more than to show the impact and influence of Community law on our system, we will concentrate most of our attention in this chapter on (e) *Preliminary Rulings* and will return to the Court of Justice in the next section to describe how such cases come before the court.

10.2 The Institutions

There are five major institutions of the European Union:

* The Council of the Union (composed of the governments of the Member States);
* The European Commission (which is the driving force and executive body);
* The Court of Justice (the court which ensures compliance with EC law);
* The European Parliament (the body elected by the peoples of the Member States);
* The Court of Auditors (a body which oversees the sound and lawful management of the EU budget).

All institutions are equal, at least on a formal basis. In this book we shall not deal with the Court of Auditors or some of the other institutions, such as the Economic and Social Committee.

10.2.1 The Council of the Union

Article 202 of the Treaty states that the Council will ensure that the objectives set out in the Treaty are attained.

The Council is based in Brussels and is a political body which has the final say on nearly all legislative matters. The parliaments of the Member States do not create Community legislation; nor is Community legislation subject to the approval of the national parliaments. The responsibility of the national parliaments is merely to implement the Regulations, Directives, and Decisions of the Community.

However, power is not given up so easily. The Council is effectively the sovereign body of the Community and is made up of one ministerial representative appointed by each Member State. The representative sent by each state varies according to the issue at hand; economic matters will draw the Chancellors, other matters will require the appropriate minister. At the highest level the Heads of State will meet—indeed they are required to meet twice a year. When this occurs the Council is referred to as the European Council, or more informally as a 'summit'.

The Council does not itself generate legislation. That function, as we shall see, rests with the Commission. The importance of the Council, however, is that it decides whether proposals from the Commission shall take effect. The Council is not a fixed body, it is not in permanent session, and the ministerial representatives change frequently in 'reshuffles'.

In order to work effectively, therefore, there exists the full-time Committee of Permanent Representatives (COREPER), as well as a system of Management Committees. COREPER comprises state representatives of ambassadorial rank, and their function is to examine the Commission's proposals and sift through them to decide on the level of controversy they may generate when they come before the Council. Those issues which receive unanimous approval from COREPER are put on one list for the Council to 'rubber stamp'. The Council can then dwell on discussing, or disagreeing on, the more contentious issues.

Voting on issues is a complicated business in the Community. Some matters require a unanimous vote in the Council (e.g. fiscal measures); and in some cases of vital national interest one state may insist on a unanimous vote even though the Treaty does not demand this, i.e., the state may exercise a veto. Other issues can be carried by a simple majority or by a qualified majority. The phrase 'qualified majority' relates to the fact that voting takes place on a weighting system so that the larger states (e.g. UK, Germany, and France) have more votes than the smaller ones such as Luxembourg. Exactly which issues should be decided by unanimous voting (and therefore subject to veto by one or more states) and which should be decided by qualified majority has been argued over by the Member States for years. The trend, as seen in all the recent treaties, has been to expand the number of issues which can be decided by qualified majority, or even to allow some states to pursue one policy and allow others to opt out (e.g. the single currency).

10.2.2 The Commission

The Commission is based in Brussels and is the driving force in the legislative process. The head of the Commission is called the President. The Commission consists of nationals drawn from each Member State (presently with weighting for the larger states, but moving to one member per state to a maximum of twenty-seven as from 2005). They are not representatives, and are supposed to act independently of their national governments. Each Commissioner is allocated a special task. The Commission plays a vital role in the legislative process of the Community. It has three responsibilities:

(a) to act as an initiator of legislation;

(b) to safeguard the objectives of the Treaty; and

(c) to act as the Community's executive.

Initiator

The Council may have the final say on nearly all matters of legislation, but it is the Commission which formulates and proposes that legislation. Thus, instead of legislation being simply a list of state interests, the Commission is designed to act with the separate and distinct interest of the Community in mind. The Council of course then applies the nationalistic political factor. Under the original Treaty the Commission's proposals took effect only if the Council agreed to them unanimously. Since the Single European Act came into effect this is no longer necessary on all issues, a point which effectively increases the powers of the Commission.

The Commission prepares its proposals after consultation, to varying degrees, with national governments and experts. Political and economic reality plays a part, however, in that the Commission knows that ultimately the proposal has to prove agreeable to the Council members.

Watchdog

The Commission, under Article 226 of the Treaty, has the power to investigate and take proceedings in the Court of Justice against Member States infringing Community law. The term 'state' here includes the legislature, the executive, and the judiciary. The Commission will first issue an opinion on the failure by the state. Only if the state does not comply with the opinion will action be taken. However, even if the action proves successful no punitive measures will be levied by the Court of Justice, though it is rare for a state not to comply at this stage.

One such action occurred in one of the *Factortame* cases. The issues underlying the *Factortame* cases are complex (for fuller details of the background, see Gravells (1989:569–73)). At the centre of a lot of legal activity was a challenge to the legality of section 14 of the Merchant Shipping Act 1988 by a number of Spanish nationals affected by the changes. It was alleged that section 14 effectively prevented other EC nationals from registering fishing boats as British vessels (and hence entitled to greater fishing rights in British territorial waters) unless those vessels were at least 75 per cent British owned, and British managed. This, the Spanish fishermen argued, constituted unlawful discrimination against other EC nationals under Article 7 of the EEC Treaty.

The challenge to the Act was mounted first in the English courts, where the case went as far as the House of Lords, which then made a reference to the ECJ under the then Article 177 (now Article 234) (see *R v Secretary of State for Transport, ex parte Factortame* [1989] 2 WLR 997). In the meantime, the European Commission itself began proceedings against the UK under what is now Article 226. In May 1989, the Commission issued an opinion, to the effect that the Act was inconsistent with Community law. The British government disagreed, so, in October 1989, the ECJ, using its power to grant interim relief, ordered the British government to suspend the operation of section 14; see Case 246/89R *European Commission v United Kingdom* [1989] ECR 3125. One might have thought that was the end of the matter; but it was only the beginning. Since that time the case has been flying back and forth between Luxembourg and London like the proverbial shuttlecock. The main point of concern has been: if the Act contravened EC law, should the affected parties be compensated by the UK government? The ECJ would eventually rule that compensation was due to a party where a Member State had failed to implement EC law properly. This emerged through the *Factortame* litigation (joined with another case, Case C–46/93 *Brasserie du Pêcheur SA v Federal Republic of Germany* [1996] 1 CMLR 889) and the case of *Francovich* [1991] ECR I–5357; [1993] 2 CMLR 66. The next question was: how should damages be assessed? This in turn spawned extensive litigation, the latest chapter of which is the Court of Appeal's decision: *In the Matter of Application for Judicial Review, R v Secretary of State for Transport, ex parte Factortame and Others* [1998] 3 CMLR 192; [1999] 2 All ER 640. This judgment provides a clear explanation of the details of the entire history of this litigation.

The Commission itself can also take action against individuals in relation to breaches of Community competition law.

Executive

The Commission is largely subject to the political control of the Council. However, the detail of legislation is the work of the Commission, and certain matters such as competition law and the rules on agriculture are decided on by the Commission.

10.2.3 The Parliament

This body sits in Strasbourg, though many of its activities are carried out in Luxembourg (its administration) and Brussels (its committees). It was originally called the Assembly and its members were drawn from national parliaments. It was not a directly elected democratic body until 1979. Consequently it never was a legislative body in the way we would understand the term 'Parliament'. Rather it had the function of supervising and advising. This is still largely true today, despite the introduction of direct elections. In most respects it is a body exerting influence rather than power.

Despite being restricted to a debating forum, the Council must consult (though not negotiate with) the Parliament on important issues. Failure by the Council to do so can render legislation ineffective; and there are other procedural brakes that the Parliament can put on the actions of the Council or Commission. Further, the Commission must report to the Parliament, and this includes answering questions. Ultimately, the Parliament may dismiss the Commission collectively or force individual members of the Commission to resign. This has never happened, though the Parliament did effectively force a mass resignation following the corruption scandal of 1998–9. The Council likewise reports to the Parliament on a formal basis, though the Parliament exercises no control over the Council. Finally, the Parliament can bring an action in the Court of Justice against the Council or Commission for failure to act under Article 232.

10.2.4 The Court of Justice of the European Communities

The Court of Justice sits in Luxembourg and pre-dates the Economic Community. It was created when the European Coal and Steel Community was founded under the Treaty of Paris 1951. The Court is usually referred to as the European Court of Justice or (as in the European Communities Act 1972) the European Court. The Court deals with Community law only; it is not some supreme European court of appeal.

How does a Case come before the ECJ?

The most common way that a case will come before the Court of Justice is where a reference is made to the court *by a national court* for a *preliminary ruling* under Article 234 of the EC Treaty.

It is possible for actions to be taken against Member States (e.g. by the Commission) and for action to be taken against Community institutions but shall concentrate on Article 234 because it is this procedure that is generally most pertinent to the practising English law lawyer or student. Through the use of Article 234 we get a chance to see how our courts regard the Community and its institutions. To a great extent one can leave specialist Community law to the European law expert; but the impact of Community law is wider than the individual pieces of legislation.

It is the duty of each court in Member States to apply Community law; and remember that Community law takes precedence over national law. The interpretation of Community law may be a straightforward matter, but where authoritative interpretation is needed then that can be supplied only by the Court of Justice. Under Article 234 any country's domestic courts or tribunals can ask the Court of Justice for a ruling on Community law; but it is that domestic court or tribunal which implements the decision.

Thus, once a national court or tribunal is faced with a problem involving the application of Community law it may ask the Court of Justice for an authoritative interpretation of the Treaty Article or, for instance, a Community Directive. It does this by posing questions in the abstract; it does not ask for the solution to the particular case. The case is now lodged with the Court of Justice—and joins the backlog! A reference to the Court of Justice is, in this procedure, a step in the action before the national court; it is not an appeal because the case in the national court has simply been adjourned pending the opinion of the Court of Justice. Thus, although we call it a 'preliminary ruling' this is a little misleading: the reference to the Court of Justice is made **during** the case before the national court, not before the case has started. The closest thing to this in our system is probably the appeal by way of case stated.

In **Chapter 3** we looked at the structure of a ECJ judgment and identified the various personnel involved in determining the case. The basic pattern by which a case reaches that stage can be outlined as follows:

1. The national court decides to make the reference.

2. The court, with the aid of the parties, sets about formulating the relevant question(s) and establishing a statement of facts and law which will accompany the reference.

3. The reference is translated by the ECJ into the working languages of the EC and published. Written submissions may be made by interested parties, e.g. other Member States.

4. The case is assigned to a specific Judge-Rapporteur and an Advocate General.

5. The Judge Rapporteur produces an initial report and advises on the forum (e.g. to be heard in a chamber or in plenary) and whether further inquiries of fact or law are necessary. He or she summarises the legal background to the case and the observations of the parties submitted in the first, written phase of the procedure. In the light of the conclusions of the Advocate General appointed to the case, the Judge-Rapporteur draws up a draft ruling which is submitted to the other members of the Court.

6. The parties prepare for the hearing.

7. The oral hearing takes place.

8. The Advocate General gives an opinion on the case (the Judge Rapporteur may also provide an opinion, especially if disagreeing with the Advocate General).

9. The Court discusses the case and goes into deliberation.

10. The Court produces a judgment in French, which is then translated.

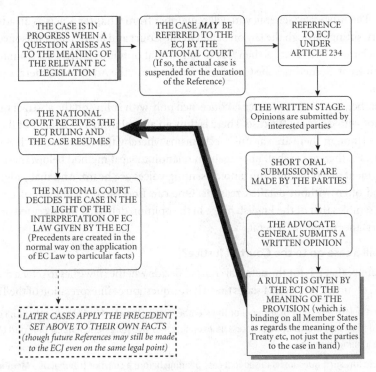

Figure 10.1 Preliminary Rulings in the ECJ

This procedure will take well over a year to complete, before the case is then taken up again at the national court. This procedure is illustrated in **Figure 10.1**.

Once the case comes before the Court we see a difference in approach from the Common Law system. As we argued in **Chapter 4**, English law still bears some relation to its roots in 'trial by battle'. The champion is now replaced by the solicitor or barrister, the swords replaced by words; but the basic plot is the same. Our system concentrates on the adversarial approach and depends greatly on oral argument. The continental approach depends far more on an inquisitorial procedure and written argument (though note that our own courts are increasingly demanding written submissions in advance of oral argument—called 'skeleton arguments'). Indeed, if the case is concerned with a *preliminary ruling* there are, strictly speaking, no parties involved—the national court has sought an opinion, not a fight. Significantly, notes issued by the Court of Justice ask counsel, if making any oral statement, not to exceed thirty minutes. In a court of English law it sometimes seems it takes this long for Counsel to say good morning.

All documents are sent by the Court of Justice's Registry to the parties in the national court, Member States, the Commission, and (possibly) the Council. All these parties have a right to make submissions on the case. For instance, in a case concerning part-time workers in Germany (Case 171/88 *Rinner-Kühn* v *FWW Spezial Gebäudereinigung GmbH and Co. KG* [1989] ECR 2743; [1989] IRLR 493) a number of Member States (recognising that the case was of great importance) made submissions to the Court even though they were not directly involved. The next major difference lies in the presence of the Advocate

General. The Advocate General, you will remember from **Chapter 3**, acts as an adviser to the Court, sifting through the law on behalf of the Court and producing a reasoned opinion in each case. The Court is then free to follow that opinion or derogate from it in any way it thinks fit. Sometimes the Court will simply adopt the Advocate-General's opinion wholesale.

Remember, the Court of Justice is concerned only with ruling on the abstract question of law, not with deciding the case. There is thus no appeal from a judgment of the Court of Justice (though there are various mechanisms whereby the Court can review its own decision). Further, as we shall note again in relation to legal method below, there is only one judgment given by the Court; no dissenting voices are heard. And that judgment is short and often without detailed reasons. One can find the presentation of reasoning which resembles that of the English judge in the opinion delivered by (accepted or not by the Court) the Advocate General.

When will a case go to the Court of Justice?

We said above that it is for the national court to decide whether it wishes to refer a matter to the Court of Justice. Article 234 states that where a question of interpretation of the Treaties:

> is raised before any court or tribunal of the Member State, that court or tribunal *may*, if it considers that a decision on the question is necessary to enable it to give judgment, request the Court of Justice to give a ruling thereon.
>
> Where any such question is raised in a case pending before a court or tribunal of a Member State, against whose decisions there is no judicial remedy under national law, that court or tribunal *shall* bring the matter before the Court of Justice. (emphasis added)

It has to be said that any perusal of the Reports (CMLR or ECR) reveals some of the most boring questions and issues ever encountered in legal texts (usually concerned with import duties, VAT, and regulations concerning agricultural matters). The range of topics that can be covered is nevertheless very extensive and getting wider by the day. There are glimmers, therefore, of real-life questions. Most of these centre on employment issues such as sex discrimination and equal pay. Some take on more expansive parameters, such as the case of Case C–415/93 *Union Royale Belge des Sociétés de Football Association (ASBL)* v *Bosman* [1995] ECR I–4921 [1996] 1 CMLR 645, for instance, which set the soccer world alight when it declared that certain transfer fees were in breach of Article 48 of the Treaty of Rome, which is now Article 39 EC Treaty. The case of Case C–235/94 *R* v *Bird* [1995] ECR I–3933; [1996] 1 CMLR 543 equally saw the ECJ tackling a knotty little problem. Mr Bird had been convicted of offences involving rest periods for lorry drivers, his actions being in breach of a Council Regulation. In his appeal to Bolton Crown Court he argued that Article 12 of the Regulation allowed drivers to depart from the strict hours limitations in order to ensure safety on the road. The only problem here was that Mr Bird was intent on departing from the strict hours even before he set off. Bolton Crown Court therefore posed the question whether Article 12 applied even in these circumstances. The ECJ ruled against Mr Bird—ingenious but futile.

On most EC law matters, any court or tribunal may refer a case to the ECJ; the court does not require permission from any higher court. National rules of precedent have no effect on a court's power to refer a matter to the ECJ. Under Article 68 (introduced by the Amsterdam Treaty), however, only the final appeal court (usually that will mean the House of Lords) may make a reference to the ECJ as regards certain matters relating to the maintenance of law and order or internal security. Linked with this is the idea (which has always been present in EC law) that, if a court is dealing with any question of EC law and that court is the final appeal court, it *must* refer the point to the ECJ. Thus the House of Lords should be bound to refer all cases to the Court of Justice which involve a problem of Community law. Further, there are rare instances where a case reaches a court from which there is no further appeal and that court is not the House of Lords. If this happens then that final court of appeal, for that case, must refer the matter to the Court of Justice. There is no clear ECJ ruling on what happens when a litigant effectively reaches the end of the road, e.g., on being refused leave to appeal. If, for example, the Court of Appeal rules on a point concerning EC law and then refuses one of the litigants leave to appeal to the House of Lords, has that Court of Appeal, for all practical purposes, become the final court in the process? In theory it is not the final court as the House of Lords stands above it; but the litigant has been refused leave to go there. Thus, is the Court of Appeal now bound to refer any question on the Community Law to the ECJ?

The House of Lords and other final appeal courts do not, however, refer all relevant cases to the Court of Justice anyway. The key word in Article 234, applied to both the discretionary reference relating to all courts and the mandatory reference, is 'necessary'.

What does 'necessary' mean? Article 234 states that the national court need make a reference only where it considers that such a reference is necessary to enable it to give judgment. If the same question was decided upon by the Court of Justice last week, for instance, then making a reference would seem pointless.

A major point to establish, then, is that the decision to refer lies with the national court alone. This was decided early in the Court's life in Case 6/64 *Costa* v *ENEL* [1964] ECR 585. It cannot be restricted by any national system of precedent, nor does it matter whether the parties request such a reference to be made.

In Case 283/81 *CILFIT Srl* v *Ministro della Sanit* [1982] ECR 3415; [1983] X CMLR 472 the Court of Justice ruled that a reference is **not necessary** if:

(a) the question of Community law is irrelevant; or

(b) the provision has already been interpreted by the Court of Justice; or

(c) the correct application is obvious.

Steiner and Woods (2000:477) draw the parallel with this formulation and the French Administrative Law doctrine of *acte clair*, in which there can be no question of needing to interpret a provision if the meaning is clear. As Steiner and Woods point out, this is a deceptively simple idea, because what is clear to one person is not necessarily clear to another, as we saw in the chapters on statutory interpretation. Indeed this was illustrated in *R* v *Henn* [1978] 1 WLR 1031; [1978] 3 All ER 1190, where the Court of Appeal did not ask for a preliminary ruling on the ground of *acte clair*; the House of Lords did not find the matter so obvious and pursued a reference (*DPP* v *Henn and Darby* [1980] 2 CMLR 229).

Equally, as we noted before, the Court of Justice is not bound by *stare decisis* and so is free to change its mind on a matter.

Taken to an extreme the notion of *acte clair* could spell disaster for the Court of Justice because there is no mechanism to force a national court to make a reference. But with one or two exceptional bursts of chauvinism from national courts the spirit of cooperation and collaboration has prevailed.

A reference is made in the form of a question. The Court of Justice is keen to convert any question which seeks an answer on how to *apply* the law into a more abstract question on what the Treaty or other provision *means* or whether the provision is valid. There is no set formula for putting these questions. The following is an extract taken from a House of Lords Reference to the ECJ in *R v Secretary of State for Employment, ex parte Seymour-Smith and Perez* [1997] ICR 371 (it reads remarkably like a set of examination questions):

1. Does an award of compensation for breach of the right not to be unfairly dismissed under national legislation such as the Employment Protection (Consolidation) Act 1978 constitute 'pay' within the meaning of Article 119 of the EC Treaty?

2. If the answer to question 1 is 'yes', do the conditions determining whether a worker has the right not to be unfairly dismissed fall within the scope of Article 119 or that of Directive 76/207?

3. What is the legal test for establishing whether a measure adopted by a Member State has such a degree of disparate effect as between men and women as to amount to indirect discrimination for the purposes of Article 119 of the EC Treaty unless shown to be based upon objectively justified factors other than sex?

10.3 Analytical Techniques Employed by European Lawyers

In the text above we have attempted to give a very brief description of the workings of the EC institutions. We will return to this topic later when we examine the specific legal method employed by the ECJ. To understand better the ECJ's techniques of legal analysis, however, we must first explain how it is that European lawyers approach legal problems in a quite different way from Common Law lawyers.

Traditionally the English lawyer has a distrust of theory and principle and places his faith in pragmatism. The development of the Common Law has been the work of practitioners, not philosophers. The Civil Law tradition, on the other hand, is different; here case law is an application of deduction from established and more abstract principles. An attempt is made to rationalise and arrange fundamental principles by way of legislation; known as a Code. From these principles contained in the Codes the whole law can, it is hoped, be deduced. French judges, for instances, are expressly forbidden to create general and regulatory principles; they must decide the case before them only and their decisions relate to the text of the Code. It is the Code, therefore, that is ultimately authoritative, not the case law; though this does not mean at all that case decisions are irrelevant to the Civil lawyer.

10.3.1 A Comparison of Concepts

It is interesting, for instance, to compare the different treatment rendered to one concept—that of 'good faith'—in English, French, and German law. We will confine our very brief remarks to the law of contract. The aim is to sketch the different approaches, not to analyse contract law. Most people instinctively know what 'acting in good/bad faith' is. It should be said, however, that no legal system has ever constructed a succinct legal definition of the term. This is why we chose it.

The notion of 'good faith' centres on principles of fair dealing. Traditionally, in English law, the search for a theory of 'good faith' offers little reward. It is, however, possible to unearth the odd clue and the occasional judicial or statutory reference to the requirement to act in 'good faith'. This is especially true of those cases or statutes owing their origin to mercantile law; but then the development of mercantile law owes a heavy debt to Continental influences. Allusions to elements of 'good faith' such as 'honesty', 'fair dealing', and 'reasonableness' can therefore emerge through the cases; but there is no overriding principle to be applied.

Consequently, the term sometimes emerges as an endorsement of other ideas, but it rarely stands on its own as justifying a decision. If a judge wishes to rely on such an indefinable notion as 'good faith' he will wrap it up, disguise it, with references to more orthodox, technical, conventional terminology such as terms being *implied* into a contract. Bowen LJ utilised the concept this way on a number of occasions in the late nineteenth century. One of the authors of this text once described this process as 'judges trying to pummel equitable notions such as good faith into a contractual setting like a Victorian belle being prised into her whale-bone corset'.

Sometimes however judges can surprise us. Such was the case with Bingham LJ's judgment in *Interfoto Picture Library Ltd* v *Stiletto Visual Programmes Ltd* [1988] 1 All ER 348; [1988] 2 WLR 615 to which we referred in **Chapter 6**. There, Bingham LJ recognised that English law has often supported the principles of good faith by the device of *ad hoc* solutions (though it has not lent support to the concept itself) when he said (at [1988] 1 All ER 352, 353):

> In many civil law systems, and perhaps in most legal systems outside the common law world, the law of obligations recognises and enforces an overriding principle that in making and carrying out contracts parties should act in good faith . . . English law has, characteristically, committed itself to no such overriding principle but has developed piecemeal solutions in response to demonstrated problems of unfairness . . . Thus equity has intervened to strike down unconscionable bargains.

There is no theory of 'good faith' evident here, nor the acknowledgment of any overriding principle; but there is a more outright recognition of an underlying theme in the law of contract. This is an exception. On the whole we are still governed by the idea of contract as an economic exchange; by the notion of *caveat emptor* (let the buyer beware) and the limitation of being bound primarily by express terms regarding performance of the contract.

The French regard their contract law as part of a theory of Obligations. This last word demonstrates quite a difference of approach. Accordingly, in France we find express reference to the concept of 'good faith' in the *Code civil*. Contracts must be performed in good faith: *Code civil* (1804) article 1134(3). Thus, as regards **pre-contractual dealings** (such as negotiations), Nicholas (1992) states that, 'the wider context is more favourable in French law to the importation of ideas of good faith or fair dealing (*loyauté*)' and 'there is a greater disposition to seeing silence (as to a fact which determined the other party's consent) as reprehensible'. However, Nicholas also notes that when it comes to analysing whether the **performance** of the contract has been fair, 'The French courts have made very little express use of Article 1134... It may be that, like the English courts, they are reluctant to set loose such a wide-ranging principle'.

Harris and Tallon, however, paint a slightly different picture. Whereas French law insists on exact performance of contractual obligations, the Anglo-American attitude presents a choice between performance and paying damages. 'It follows that French law resorts to issues of morality, such as fraud, serious fault, or good faith, more readily than does English law' they conclude (1989:386). Indeed, under Article 2268 of the *Code civil*, good faith is presumed, and it is for the party who alleges bad faith to prove it.

A description of the German approach proves interesting here. Sections 138, 157, and 242 of the *Bürgerliches Gesetzbuch* (BGB, which is the German Civil Code relating to private law) all contain references to the principle of good faith. Section 138 creates obligations of a general nature, rendering a legal transaction void if it conflicts with good morals. Section 157 deals with the construction of contracts and relates that contracts are to be construed as good faith requires. Most important of all, perhaps, is the apparently innocuous section 242 which states: 'The debtor is obliged to effect performance in such a manner as good faith requires, regard being paid to general practice.' This section regulates the manner in which contracts are performed. Horn, Kötz, and Leser (1982:135) describe this so:

> Unimpressive though it looks, s. 242 BGB is one of the most astonishing phenomena in the Code... a statutory enactment of a general requirement of good faith, a 'principle of legal ethics', which dominates the entire legal system.

The discussion which follows this quotation is well worth reading. However, Cohn's comments are also noteworthy: 'Section 242 has... considerably increased the freedom of the courts in interpreting contracts. No similar liberty is enjoyed by English courts' (1968:154). The strength of section 242 can be seen in the case law. Horn *et al.* comment: 'The numerous [contractual] duties that have been created... include duties of care, duties to supervise the manner and form of the principal performance, duties to assure performance, duties of cooperation, and duties of information and explanation' (1982:139). Good faith has even been used (in 1923) to revalue debts during times of hyperinflation. Debts incurred before inflation set in could be paid off easily once the effects of that inflation had made the currency practically worthless. The German courts revalued these debts by expressing them in the equivalent new currency to match the orig-inal sum. This was done even where the debt had already been paid off.

Finally, to complete this brief comparative survey, it is worth noting the approach adopted in the United States. Here we see the Common Law system in action. Yet we also find that the vague concept of 'good faith' is embraced in the case law through reference to the Uniform Commercial Code (UCC). Now this is not a *code* in the pure Civil Law sense. It is more like the original English Sale of Goods Act 1893, whereby the case law has been pulled together into a more systematic general restatement. The UCC is law in most jurisdictions in the USA by virtue of local (rather than federal) enactment.

In the UCC we find Articles 1§201, 1§203, and 2§–103, along with many others, give a general definition of good faith. Article 1§201 states that good faith means honesty in fact in the conduct or transaction concerned. Article 1§–203 imposes a general obligation of good faith performance and enforcement; and Article 2§103 says that, in the case of a merchant, it means honesty in fact and the observance of reasonable commercial stand-ards of fair dealing in the trade. These provisions have given rise to varied judicial and academic debate; not least as to whether there is a requirement for objective good faith to be found ('reasonableness', 'fair dealing') or only a subjective test—what has been referred to as the 'pure heart and empty head test'. Here we see that the Common Law still cannot rid itself of its fixation with the need to define terms through the cases. It is unable to cope easily with pure conceptual thinking.

It may be, therefore, that the conventional contrast between the two traditions—experience and pragmatism on the one hand, concept and doctrine on the other—is not always as clear-cut as it seems. The German system *should* be systematic as per the usual perception of a Civil Code system; but it is not. Case law *should not* play a creative role of law-making; but it does. The French system *should* allow for greater use of the concept of 'good faith' than the English system; but this is not guaranteed. The American system *should* pay as little heed to such an indefinable concept as we do; but it does so through a 'code'. And it is quite possible for all these systems, through different explanations, to ar-rive at the same conclusion, e.g. on the construction of the contract. This demonstrates the difficulty in finding even a common starting point for lawyers in the two systems. Szladits and Germain (1985:ix) describe the problems thus:

> Because of a different training, of a different 'legal method', there is an unavoidable inclination on the part of the Anglo-American lawyer to evaluate the importance of code provisions, of decisions of a higher court or of writings and comments in the light of his own background knowledge. He may attach undue importance to some decisions 'as precedents', and underrate the value of treatises or commentaries... He may also underrate the importance of cases and attach too exclusive force to code provisions. The continental lawyer, in contrast, will usually find himself at a loss among the innumerable precedents which are binding, but yet can be distinguished out of existence... and will vainly look for precise concepts among the legal synonyms, loosely phrased decisions and unsystematic textbooks...

In the first edition of this book (in 1991) we chose the idea of 'good faith' for comparison of approaches because it was an interesting topic, and one with which all jurisdictions have experienced difficulty. Since that time, further developments have occurred. In

1994, the Council Directive on Unfair Terms in Consumer Contracts (93/13/EEC) finally made its appearance in English law via the Unfair Terms in Consumer Contracts Regulations, SI 3159/1994, and then through the latest version: SI 2083/1999. This has far-reaching consequences in English Contract Law, one of which is the specific introduction of the concept of 'good faith' dealing in certain situations. So, for instance, under regulation 4 of the Regulations, an 'unfair term' means any term which, contrary to the requirement of *good faith*, causes a significant imbalance in the parties' rights and obligations under the contract to the detriment of the consumer (see the ECJ Cases C–204/98 to 244/98 *Oceano Groupo Editorial SA* v *Rocio Musciano Quantiro* [2000] ECR I–4941). 'Good faith' itself is defined more particularly in Schedule 2 to the Regulations and, as you will see in your study of Contract Law, this is slowly but surely being developed through litigation (e.g. *Director General of Fair Trading* v *First National Bank plc* [2001] UKHL 52; [2002] 1 AC 481; [2002] 1 All ER 97): that, of course, is when the Common Law lawyer feels most at ease—wading through a wealth of case law.

10.3.2 The Use of Precedent in European Legal Method

We have already seen in **Chapter 5** that a major distinction between how Civil lawyers (and courts) reason and the reasoning of Common Law lawyers is the use of *stare decisis*. As the quotation from Szladits and Germain indicates, however, it is wrong to say that case law is unimportant to the Civil Law lawyer. Reference to case law and a loose idea of precedent clearly exists in the Civil Law tradition. David and Brierley (1985:133) point out that statements which flatly exclude cases as a source of law in the Civil system:

> are somewhat ridiculous when used in countries such as France or Germany, where cases have been of primary importance in the evolution of some branches of law.

Cases are a source of law, in that a line of cases demonstrates a consistent pattern of thought. But whereas the Common Law judge draws openly on case law for his analysis, the Civil Law lawyer often hides behind the veil of 'interpretation' of legislation. The cases provide guidance on legal rules; but the rules do not carry with them any sense of obligation. Judges are not compelled to analyse earlier cases or justify departure from them. Indeed, in France, judges may not simply cite earlier authorities to support their decisions. This does not mean that the judges are unaware of the case law; though the structure of French judicial decisions is generally terse and fairly uninformative as to reasoning (to the English lawyer's eye). Equally, decisions of the French supreme courts are likely to be followed in practice, as are those of the *Cour de cassation*, which deals with judicial matters such as contract law, and those of the *Conseil d'Etat* which deals with administrative matters. In fact, 'There can be little doubt that the [case law] of the *Conseil d'Etat* is a true source of law, since most of the *general* principles and rules of administrative law have been created by its decisions' (David & Brierley, 1985:30).

Furthermore, as David and Brierley (1985:144–5) also note, though a general principle of Civil Law may be that case law is descriptive rather than prescriptive, there are instances where the notion of *binding* precedent is not alien to Civil Law jurisdictions either. Thus,

> it may on occasion happen that a judge must observe a judicial precedent or a line of previously decided cases. The authority of binding precedent is attributed in Federal Germany to the decisions of the federal Constitutional Court... The creative role of decided cases is officially recognised in Spanish law by the concept of *doctrina legal* (a judicial practice based on several decisions of the Supreme Court).

10.3.3 Legal Method in the Court of Justice

The Court of Justice of the European Communities was created by Civil Law lawyers. It therefore bears the hallmarks of the points noted above.

These hallmarks are important in a number of ways:

(a) first, as to whether the Court of Justice really regards every question as being open to re-examination;

(b) secondly, in investigating how our national courts should approach the status of preliminary rulings;

(c) thirdly, as to the future role of precedent in our courts; and

(d) finally, in examining the other sources of law used by Civil lawyers to analyse legal problems.

We shall deal with these issues in turn.

Does the Court of Justice really regard every question as being open to re-examination?

As we noted in **Chapters 5** and **6**, the absence of any *ratio decidendi* in the decision rather destroys the essence of precedent as we know it. The judgments are short, even terse, and bear little relationship to those of our courts, not least because they are given as a collegiate decision. By this we mean that, whether the court was unanimous or there was only a bare majority, only one decision is delivered. There is no record of dissent; no variant judgments dispensed.

The Court of Justice does, however, allude to earlier judgments and prefers to follow those decisions. But the Court is quite free to change its mind, develop principles, and create conflicting precedents as between Chambers. Part of this may be due to the fact that the Court sees its role as 'filling the gaps' in Community legislation. It is therefore openly creative and plays an active part in the law-making of the Community.

The Advocate General in a case will more frequently cite earlier cases; and the Advocate-General's opinion will be of persuasive authority in later cases, even where the Court did not follow it (you may notice, as a piece of absolute trivia, that there is no hyphen in 'Advocate General' except when referring to the possessive case).

The answer, therefore, to the question posed is that *every* question is open to re-examination; nothing precludes a national court, for instance, from seeking a further ruling on exactly the same point discussed in an earlier case (see Case 28/62 *Da Costa en Schaake* [1963] ECR 31 and Case 26/62 *NV Algemene Transport–en Expeditie Orderneming*

Van Gend en Loos v. *Inspecteur der Invoerrechten en Accijnzen, Veulo (10852T)* (*Tariefcommissie* (*NL*)) [1963] ECR 1). The notion of *acte clair* is not *stare decisis* in another form.

In practice, of course, there is a strong tendency to try to establish and maintain a coherent, or settled, jurisprudence, which does require some reference to precedent. Indeed there seems to be some evidence to suggest that direct reference to case law is a growing judicial practice—for example, in Case C–229/89 *European Commission* v *Belgium* [1991] ECR I–2205; [1991] IRLR 393, the Court went to some lengths to justify its decision by reference to the earlier cases of Case 30/85 *Teuling* [1987] ECR 2497, which had decided a closely analogous point of law, and Case C–171/88 *Rinner-Kühn* v *FWW Spezial Gebäudereinigung GmbH and Co. KG* [1989] ECR 2743; [1989] IRLR 493. However, this still does not mean that the Court regards itself as strictly bound by its own earlier decisions.

How should our courts approach the status of preliminary rulings?

Two points arise here: first, if the Court of Justice is simply interpreting Community law, is any decision retroactive? That is to say, is the interpretation to be applied from the date of judgment onwards (as with our system), or does it also have effect from the date the provision originally came into force? Secondly, how binding is a decision of the Court of Justice?

- **On the first point:** in general, the ruling will take effect from the date the legislation was brought into force—a retroactive approach. The Court is declaring what already existed. The Court may however choose not to do this (only the Court can decide this) on grounds of, say, the need for legal certainty. It did this in relation to equal pay rulings in Case 43/75 *Defrenne* v *SABENA* [1976] ECR 455 and regarding equal pay and pension rights in Case C–262/88 *Barber* v *Guardian Royal Exchange Assurance Group* [1990] ECR I–1889; [1991] 1 QB 344; [1990] 2 All ER 660. This idea of retroactive decisions has always been a controversial matter. So much so that, because of the ruling in *Barber* v *Guardian Royal Exchange* a Protocol to the *Maastricht Treaty* created a broad principle of non-retroactivity in relation to pension rights.

- **On the second point**: given that a national court can always ask the Court of Justice for a ruling (even on matters previously decided) the Court of Justice's decisions are not binding as such. They are binding, however, in as much as the national court must either apply them or seek a new ruling; it cannot simply ignore the Court of Justice. This point is reinforced by European Communities Act 1972, section 3(1).

There is no hierarchical system as *between* the various courts in Member States. What is decided in the national courts of Germany or France has no binding effect (though it may have a persuasive one) on our courts. As the Court of Justice is the only authority which can interpret provisions anyway, this should cause no problems. What should also be noted, however, is that if a question is posed to the ECJ on EC law by, say, Spain, the ruling given will, in most cases, apply as much to any other EC country as to Spain. The ECJ gives judgment on the interpretation of EC law, so it is irrelevant which country asks the question.

What will this mean for the future role of precedent in our courts?

First, much of our law still has no relationship with Community law. To this end the line of precedents on what constitutes an 'offer' or an 'invitation to treat' will continue to carry the same significance as fifty or more years ago. Where Community law is concerned it is clear that the higher courts in our system can no longer bind the lower courts on the meaning of EC legislation; only the Court of Justice can make authoritative rulings. The Court of Appeal, for instance, is not bound by a decision of the House of Lords on the *interpretation* of Community law. It may, however, be bound by a decision on the *application* of Community law to particular facts.

All this is unlikely to bring about the abandonment of *stare decisis* and all its intricacies. Thus we now have two systems of precedent. In practice the presence of Community cases can lead to some doubt as regards advising clients. We are not yet adept at treating wide statements of principle as having just as much effect as seventy pages of judgment by the House of Lords. For instance, in Employment Law we were faced with the decision of the Court of Justice in Case C–171/88 *Rinner-Kühn* v *FWW Spezial Gebäudereinigung GmbH and Co. KG* [1989] ECR 2743; [1989] IRLR 493. The case concerned what is now Article 141 of the EEC Treaty and Equal Pay Directive 75/117 and arose from a preliminary ruling given to a German labour court in relation to the right of part-time workers to receive sick pay.

The specific details on employment rights varied at that time (and still do in many cases) across the different Member States. Generally, however, employees qualified for rights such as unfair dismissal compensation only if they worked for a minimum number of hours per week; in the UK that number was sixteen. In the *Rinner-Kühn* case, Frau Rinner-Kühn argued that since a considerably smaller number of women than men could comply with the equivalent German restriction, this form of limitation was indirectly discriminatory. The Court of Justice decided that the Treaty should be interpreted as precluding legislation which had such an effect.

The decision was clear; the problem arose (and arises with so many decisions of the ECJ) whether this ruling applied to other rights which also depended on 'time qualifications'. In particular, the English lawyer immediately and instinctively seeks to apply, compare, or distinguish the decision to see what the ramifications will be. Should the comments of the ECJ on German sick pay legislation apply to UK unfair dismissal and redundancy rights, for instance?

The next chapter took some time in coming; indeed, between 1989 and 1993 many academic texts did not even present the *Rinner-Kühn* decision as a problem for UK employment lawyers. Most practitioners closed their eyes to the case and waited for someone else's client to spend money examining the law. But the Equal Opportunities Commission (the EOC) finally tested the water by bringing an application in the English courts for judicial review against the Secretary of State for Employment, requesting an alteration in our law to comply with the *Rinner-Kühn* decision: *R* v *Secretary of State for Employment, ex parte Equal Opportunities Commission* [1993] 1 All ER 1022. It lost in the Court of Appeal on the technical ground that the EOC did not have the legal standing to bring such a claim. But on appeal its case was received more favourably. Here (reported at

[1994] IRLR 176) the House of Lords held that the *Rinner-Kühn* reasoning applied so that the 'hours qualification' threshold for redundancy payments entitlement contravened the Treaty of Rome and the Equal Pay Directive 75/117.

That was not the end of the story. This decision begged the question whether the same reasoning applied to unfair dismissal rights as well as to redundancy pay entitlements, because the terms 'pay' (in redundancy pay) and 'compensation' (for unfair dismissal) had previously been held by the ECJ to lead to different entitlements. Case law started to spring up in employment tribunals, and a reference was made to the ECJ. To pre-empt matters the Government was forced to introduce the Employment Protection (Part-time Employees) Regulations 1995, SI 31/1995, which abolished the 'hours qualification' completely.

This much-abbreviated account illustrates the practical complexities that can arise from a decision by the ECJ. Remember that the original *Rinner-Kühn* decision had nothing whatsoever to do with how UK employers dismiss their part-time employees.

10.4 The Effect of EC Law on the Drafting and Interpretation of UK Legislation

There are two key areas here:

- How is EC Legislation enforced?
- What *style* of statutory interpretation is employed?

10.4.1 How is EC Legislation Enforced?

The main classification of EC legislation into 'Treaties', 'Regulations', and 'Directives' carries with it important concepts which determine how these various rules are actually implemented within the EC by the Member States. Those concepts are:

- Direct Applicability,
- Direct Effect, and
- Indirect Effect.

Direct applicability

Because the Treaty obligations and Regulations of the EC are designed to have overriding and universal application across Member States they are given special status, termed *direct applicability*. This means that these rules *automatically* become part of the law of each domestic legal system without the need (in most cases) for confirmation of their legitimacy by formal enactment in the legislatures of the Member States. Thus you will not find these rules in any UK statute book; you must research the Treaty or Regulation itself. The idea of *direct applicability* is really aimed at the Member States; it tells them that they are not required to do anything to implement the relevant rule.

The importance of this concept of *direct applicability* is that each Member State is bound by the rules contained in these documents. *Direct applicability* is therefore reserved for rules which need to have immediate and Community-wide binding enforceability. The rules which meet these criteria are the provisions of Treaties and Regulations, as described above. Matters such as equal pay and the free movement of workers, for instance, appear in Treaty Articles such as Article 141 and Article 39, respectively. On the other hand, Common Agricultural Policy matters will generally surface in the form of Regulations. These are all directly applicable.

Directives, on the other hand, do not have direct applicability because they lay down a **result** to be achieved rather than fixed and universal rules. We noted above that Directives have no effect at all on the laws of a Member State until that state's legislature incorporates the goals set out in the Directive into its own law. In the UK this means that Parliament must have passed a statute. Each Member State is given a time limit to achieve this (often two or three years from the date of the Directive). Thus, the process for implementation is as set out in **Figure 10.2**.

Directives therefore seek only to harmonise the laws of Member States, to make them approximately the same while still taking into account the economic, political, social, and legal differences that exist in each state. Directives **cannot** have direct applicability because they are too general and vague in what it is they are trying to achieve. If we were to draw an analogy with the rules of soccer, the rules on the size of playing area set out maximum and minimum measurements only to allow for the varying size of stadia, and

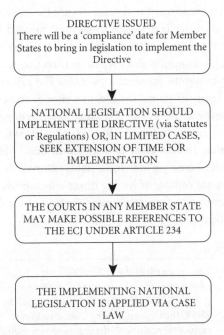

Figure 10.2 The Procedure for Implementing Directives

thus could be likened to the way Directives are often framed. Thus, as long as the football club does not infringe the maximum or minimum size, its ground measurements do not have to be identical to those of any other club.

In the end, though, the fact that Member States are bound to obey directly applicable rules only really tells us about their obligations as between themselves and as between them and the European Community. We are still left with the problem of how EC legislation can be enforced by individuals and companies within the EC. After all, the national courts of Member States are under a duty to interpret and apply EC law (Treaties, Regulations, and Directives alike) to any relevant matters arising in the national courts. They are also bound to interpret national laws to maintain consistency with EC law. Thus there has to be a system whereby EC legislation can be relied upon by citizens of the EC in suing other individuals or the state itself. This is achieved by courts across the EC using two devices—giving *direct effect* and *indirect effect* to EC legislation.

It is unfortunate that the terms 'Direct Applicability', 'Direct Effect', 'Indirect Effect', and even 'Directive' all sound so similar. They are often used, erroneously, as interchangeable terms, even by those who should know better. However, these are terms of major significance and one needs to be clear about the distinction and the interrelationship. We need, therefore, to examine what is meant by *direct* and *indirect* effect. We shall consider *direct effect* first.

Direct effect

The basic idea underlying direct effect is straightforward. *Direct effect* means that someone may cite a Directive as law without having to cite any domestic legislation which was meant to implement that Directive. It may seem strange that this is not done all the time. But remember that a Directive is designed to be implemented by the Member States rather than stand as national law in its own right. So what we are dealing with here is the situation (an increasingly common one) where a Directive is used as the governing source of law, thus bypassing the national legislation. The principle of *direct effect* was not established by the Treaty of Rome. Instead, in a famous and controversial judgment (Case 26/62 *NV Algemene Transport en Expeditie Onderneming Van Gend en Loos* v *Nederlandse Administratie der Belastingen* [1963] ECR 1; [1963] CMLR 224) the ECJ said that where EC legislation creates '**clear and unconditional**' obligations on Member States, these were capable of creating individual rights enforceable in domestic courts. All forms of EC legislation are *capable* of having direct effect, provided they meet certain conditions. There are normally four overlapping conditions for direct effect, and these are set out in the table below.

Conditions for Direct Effect

(a) The provision of EC law must be clear and unambiguous.	The approach of the ECJ to this issue is highly flexible; e.g. in the joined cases of Cases C–6/90, C–9/90 *Francovich and Bonifaci* v *Italy* [1992] IRLR 84 the Court recognised that the provisions of Directive 80/987/EEC, guaranteeing compensation to individuals for loss of employment through the insolvency of their employer, gave Member states a wide element of discretion (and so were not unambiguous).

Nevertheless, the ECJ felt that it could discern a sufficient 'minimum guarantee' to make the provision precise enough to be capable of direct effect. In Case C–91/92 *Faccini Dori* v *Recreb srl* [1995] ECR I–3325; [1995] All ER (EC) 1, the ECJ returned to this concept and indicated that the provisions of a Directive can be sufficiently precise if they enable a national court to determine upon whom, and for whose benefit, the obligations are imposed, i.e. is it possible to determine minimum rights from the provision in question?

(b) The provision must be unconditional.	For example, it must not be subject to conditions requiring implementation by Member States, or giving Member States substantive discretion in respect of the period for implementation.
(c) The provision must be capable of taking effect without further action by the EC or a Member State.	For example, the EC legislation should not be dependent upon further clarifying regulations being passed in each Member State. Again, this test is of crucial significance in respect of both Treaty obligations and Directives which are initially expressed to be conditional *but become unconditional with the passing of time* and thereby become directly effective.
(d) The provision must be capable of creating rights for individuals.	The provision in question must go beyond merely imposing obligations on Member States, e.g., in their relationship with other Member States or the EC as an entity. The provision must be drafted in such a way that an individual gains some enforceable right to sue the state or another individual.

The operation of the principle of direct effect has spawned an extensive body of case law, before both the ECJ and domestic courts. This has added greatly to the complexity of the principle, but the central idea is quite simple: a person in any Member State can refer to the wording of the Directive *as law*, no matter what the national statute says, if that Directive is clear enough in its aims to be so enforceable. At this stage in your studies, judging exactly when a Directive meets these conditions is not something you should worry about.

The next thing you do have to worry about, however, is the question: can all Directives which have direct effect be relied upon by anyone suing another person or being prosecuted by the state?

The answer to this question is, 'No', because there is a further complication. A distinction is made between Directives having *vertical* and *horizontal direct effect*:

- **'Vertical effect'**. The word 'vertical' refers to the relationship between the parties. Something is a *vertical* action where an individual (including a 'legal person' such as a company) is suing or being sued by the state (or, in Criminal Law, the individual is being prosecuted by the state). If a Directive has vertical direct effect it means that an individual may rely on the specific words set out in a Treaty, Directive (etc.) in any action against an organ of the state (see *Van Gend en Loos*) or against some other body having special powers to provide public services under the control of the state. Such bodies include, for example, a privatised industry under a statutory duty to provide a public utility—see Case C–188/89 *Foster* v *British Gas* [1990] ECR I–3313; [1991] 1 QB 405; [1990] 3 All ER 897 (ECJ); [1991] 2 AC 306; [1991] 2 All ER 705 (HL). The Court of Appeal has indicated that the definition of a 'public body' for these purposes should be a broad one: *National Union of Teachers* v *Governing Body of St Mary's Church of England (Aided) Junior School* [1997] 3 CMLR 630.

- **'Horizontal effect'.** The word 'horizontal' again refers to the relationship between the parties. This time, a case can be described as a *horizontal* action where an individual is suing someone of equivalent legal standing—unlike vertical actions where the state exists in a superior (and therefore vertical) relationship with the individual.

What distinctions are drawn between these two types of action in terms of relying on directly effective Directives?

The Key points on vertical and horizontal direct effect can be seen in the table below.

Vertical direct effect	Horizontal direct effect
It is now well-accepted by the ECJ that Directives may have a **vertical** direct effect, for to deny a vertical direct effect (i.e. an individual against an organ of the state) would thus enable a Member State to rely upon its own non-implementation of Community law to avoid liability.	Whether Directives can have a **horizontal** effect has been hotly debated for many years and we will return to this in discussing the legal method employed in the ECJ. For the moment, we should say that Directives do not have horizontal direct effect.

Indirect effect

Case 14/83 *Von Colson* v *Land Nordrhein-Westfalen* [1984] ECR 1891 is credited with creating a further principle, termed *indirect effect*. Indirect effect sidesteps some of the problems created by the vertical/horizontal direct effect distinction and allows for some very creative judicial reasoning.

If a Directive does not have horizontal direct effect it may be effective *indirectly* by means of domestic courts adopting an appropriately purposive form of interpretation for related national legislation. In other words, courts can read into the wording of the national legislation the *purpose* declared in the Directive. A court may thus give the citizen a right under domestic law where there would otherwise be none because the EC Directive lacks direct effect. The relationship between direct and indirect effect is a problematic feature of the European jurisprudence, and one to which we shall return in greater depth later in this chapter. In many ways, the idea of *indirect effect* is more important than direct effect as it means that, irrespective of who is suing whom, the courts can try to implement the spirit of the Directive in a wider range of cases.

Summary

- The idea of *direct applicability* is that the EC can instigate major and overriding legislation without having to rely on each Member State to implement it through its own parliamentary systems. Apart from matters such as Treaty obligations, this is not a common method of legislating.
- The idea of *direct effect* is to provide a mechanism whereby individuals can rely on the wording of EC legislation even when the Member State has implemented the Directive

incorrectly or not at all. For any EC legislation to have *direct effect* it must satisfy additional conditions of certainty and the time limit for implementation must have passed.

- Treaty obligations generally have *direct applicability*. In many cases this will mean that they also have *direct effect*, provided that they are certain and create rights for individuals (even some Treaty obligations are couched in terms of desirability rather than specific rules).

- Regulations also generally have *direct applicability*. In most cases this will mean that they also have *direct effect*, again provided that they are certain and create rights for individuals.

- Directives are not *directly applicable* and will have direct effect only in limited situations. The present position is that, even in these limited cases, they may have only *vertical direct effect*.

- The exact status of *indirect effect* cannot be stated with any clarity; it should be seen more as a tool of interpretation available to judges than as a fixed method of analysis.

Practical problem areas:

In reality, the case law reveals that there are three main areas where the problem of *direct* and *indirect effect* will arise, and they all relate to Directives:

(a) where the Member State implements the Directive but there is a conflict between the relevant statute and the wording of the Directive;

(b) where the Member State fails to implement the Directive at all;

(c) where the general laws of the Member State (e.g. precedents not based on statutes) seem to be in conflict with the Directive.

If a Directive is not implemented or is not implemented properly there is the question whether a UK citizen can nevertheless enforce the rights given under the Directive. We saw above that if the Directive satisfies the conditions of certainty and has vertical direct effect then the answer is generally 'Yes'; but if an individual wishes to sue another individual he/she must argue that the Directive has horizontal effect. This is more problematic. To give Directives horizontal direct effect, it is argued, equates them with Regulations—so what would be the distinction?

In one of the leading equal treatment cases, Case 152/84 *Marshall* v *Southampton and South West Hampshire AHA (Teaching)* [1986] ECR 723; [1986] 1 CMLR 688; [1986] 2 All ER 584 the ECJ denied the possibility of giving horizontal effect to Directives on the basis of the wording in the then Article 119 (now Article 141). Both the ECJ and the Advocate General agreed that the Directive could be relied upon only in actions against the state (i.e. having vertical effect). On the facts, Ms Marshall succeeded in her claim, as it was conceded that her employer (the health authority) was an emanation of the state. This analysis has now been affirmed by the ECJ in *Faccini Dori* v *Recreb*. Here, the ECJ confirmed that there could be no such thing as *horizontal direct effect*, and again in Case C–192/94 *El Corte Inglés SA* v *Blázquez Rivero* [1996] ECR I–1281; [1996] 2 CMLR 507.

Like most things involving EC law, that was not to be the final word. A series of cases in 1996 cast some doubt on this, e.g., Case C–94/94 *CIA Security* v *Signalson and Securitel* [1996] ECR I–2210; [1996] 2 CMLR 372, Case C–441/93 *Pafitis and Others* v *TKE and Others* [1996] ECR I–1347; [1996] 2 CMLR 551, Case C–129/94 *Ruiz Bernáldez* [1996] ECR I–1829; [1996] 2 CMLR 889, and Case C-168/95 *Arcaro* [1996] ECR I–4705; [1997] 1 CMLR 179. However, we are in some agreement with the editor of the *European Law Review* that these cases do not destroy the principle of the ineffectiveness of horizontal direct effect; indeed, *Arcaro* illustrates and confirms the point that a Member State which fails to comply with EC law cannot use that failure against an individual. *Arcaro* concerned criminal proceedings relating to pollution. Had the state been allowed to pursue an action against the individual based on Directives (i.e. a vertical action, but in reverse) when there was doubt whether the Italian criminal legislation conflicted with Community Directives, this would have allowed the state to benefit from its own failure.

As we have seen, the earlier case of *Von Colson* v *Land Nordrhein-Westfalen* is credited with creating a further principle of 'indirect effect'. *Indirect effect* enables a court to 'read in' to the statute the wording and even the aims of the original Directive. It is called indirect effect for this reason, since it gives an individual a right of action through national law, but based *indirectly* on the Directive. This takes us full circle because we are now back in the field of *how* the courts interpret statutes as seen above.

We have to say that the position is becoming more and more convoluted. The guidelines issued by the Court of Justice in *Von Colson* were less than clear. Courts in some Member States have taken the view that the rules of construction laid down in that case could not apply to national legislation enacted before the Directive. Thus, the United Kingdom and, to a lesser extent, France have argued that *Von Colson* creates no more than a rule against ambiguity for use in situations where the meaning of the domestic implementing legislation is unclear (see the discussion above on *Duke* and *Finnegan*; for the situation in France, see Galmot & Bonichot (1988)). In Case C–106/89 *Marleasing SA* v *La Commercial Internacional de Alimentación SA* [1990] ECR I–4135; [1992] 1 CMLR 305 the ECJ reaffirmed the views expressed in *Marshall* but introduced a further complication by adding that in cases where there is direct effect, national law (not just legislation) must comply with Community legislation, whether the Directive has been implemented, implemented improperly, or not implemented at all, once the time limit for implementation has passed. In coming to this conclusion, the ECJ has greatly extended the importance of indirect effect. Docksey and Fitzpatrick (1991:113) go so far as to suggest that indirect effect is now set to become the normal mechanism whereby individuals may enforce rights contained in Directives, though this view is not universally supported—see Snyder (1993:43). However, it is still open to debate whether, if domestic legislation is deemed clear and unambiguous, *Marleasing* should be taken to authorise domestic courts to go directly against national law.

English courts had to grasp this particular nettle in the case of *Webb* v *EMO Air Cargo (UK) Ltd* [1990] ICR 442 (EAT); [1992] ICR 445; [1992] 2 All ER 43 (CA); [1993] 1 CMLR 259 (HL), which posed the question whether the dismissal of an employee on grounds of pregnancy constituted sex discrimination when the dismissed employee had been engaged specifically to cover for another employee's absence. The Employment Appeal Tribunal and the Court of Appeal thought not (see Harrison, 1992). They said that a claim lies under the Sex Discrimination Act 1975 only where a pregnant woman is treated less favourably by her employer than a hypothetical man would be in 'comparable' circumstances; for example, where he is suffering from an illness of similar severity and duration. Ms Webb had argued that the dismissal was discriminatory, based on the fact that a man can never be in the same position as a pregnant woman.

However, there was contrary authority derived from the Equal Treatment Directive EC/76/207, as applied in Case 177/88 *Dekker* v *Stichting Vormings-centrum voor Jong Volwassen Plus* [1990] ECR I–3941; [1991] IRLR 27. Ms Webb's counsel argued that the Directive as interpreted in *Dekker* (although not having direct horizontal effect) should be applied according to *Marleasing* principles. The House of Lords in *Webb* indicated that, in its view, there was no discrimination here on a 'proper construction' of the 1975 Act. But their Lordships also stated that (*per* Lord Keith [1993] 1 CMLR 259 at 270):

> [I]t is for a United Kingdom court to construe domestic legislation so as to accord with the interpreta-
> tion of the directive as laid down by the European Court, if that can be done without distorting the
> meaning of the domestic legislation. . . . This is so whether the domestic legislation came after or, as in
> this case, preceded the directive: *Marleasing*. . . .

Their Lordships found that the *Dekker* case was not direct authority on the facts in *Webb* (and so implicitly not 'binding' upon them), and sought a preliminary ruling from the ECJ on the meaning of the Directive.

The ECJ (Case C–32/93 *Webb* v *EMO Air Cargo (UK) Ltd* [1994] ECR I–3567; [1994] ICR 770) ruled that under Articles 2(1) and 5(1) of Council Directive 76/207/EEC the 'dismissal of an employee who is recruited for an unlimited term with a view, initially, to replacing another employee during the latter's maternity leave and who cannot do so because, shortly after her recruitment, she is herself found to be pregnant' is precluded. In other words, there does not have to be a 'male comparator'; dismissal of a pregnant employee for that reason is discrimination. In turn the case came back to the House of Lords (*Webb* v *EMO Air Cargo (UK) Ltd (No. 2)* [1995] ICR 1021) where their Lordships held that the Sex Discrimination Act 1975 must be interpreted in a manner consistent with the ruling by the ECJ.

Thus the specific wording of the Sex Discrimination Act 1975 was subsumed within the broad principles enunciated by the ECJ so that this decision certainly complies with the idea of indirect effect. But, as the ECJ itself had noted and the House of Lords con-firmed, the decision related only to employees employed for an *indefinite term*; which means that we are still none the wiser if an employer does exactly the same again but em-ploys the replacement for a fixed term (of say one year).

10.4.2 State liability: the *Francovich* Priniciple

The final stage in this saga is to note the joined Cases C–6/90 and C–9/90 *Francovich and Bonifaci* v *Italy* [1991] ECR I–5357; [1992] IRLR 84, where the ECJ held that, under certain conditions, a Member State is liable to make good damage to individuals if loss is suffered because the state failed to implement a Community Directive.

The idea that the state should pay compensation to an individual or company because it has failed in its duty to implement an aspect of EC law seems perfectly sensible, but it did leave some outstanding questions such as: (i) should this apply to all EC law; and (ii) should the state be liable for faulty implementation of, say, a Directive, as well as non-implementation; and (iii) if the state should be liable for faulty implementation, should this cover those situations when that 'fault' only really becomes apparent from difficult case law; and (iv) how would the wronged individual actually enforce the right? Thus, in Case C–46/93 *Brasserie du Pêcheur SA* v *Federal Republic of Germany* and Case C–48/93 *R* v *Secretary of State for Transport, ex parte Factortame Ltd and Others* (both reported at [1996] ECR I–1029; [1996] 1 CMLR 889) the ECJ considered this area again. These two cases concerned, respectively, damages suffered by a French company based in Alsace, which had lost a substantial sum of money owing to German import laws regarding beer (held to be in breach of Community legislation), and our old friends, the Spanish fishermen.

The CJEC identified three main conditions governing state liability:

(a) The Community legislation must have been intended to confer rights on individuals.

(b) The breach by the Member State must be 'sufficiently serious'. This test involves a number of factors, e.g., whether the breach was intentional, whether there was an excusable error of law, and the clarity and precision of the rule itself (or relevant case law): see *R* v *Secretary of State, ex parte Factorame Ltd* [1999] 4 All ER 906.

(c) There must be established a causal link between the breach and the damage suffered.

Unfortunately, this is not as clear as it appears at first sight. Point (b) above is potentially explosive because, if too loose an interpretation is given to this, states could be held liable for their apparent failures even when their actions were excusable, e.g. where the wording of the Directive was not clear in the first place. In Case C–127/95 *Norbrook Laboratories* v *Ministry of Agriculture* [1998] ECR I–1531 the ECJ commented that, as regards point (b): 'first, that a breach is sufficiently serious where a Member State, in the exercise of its legislative powers, has manifestly and gravely disregarded the limits on its powers ... and, second, that where, at the time when it committed the infringement, the Member State in question was not called upon to make any legislative choice and had only considerably reduced, or even no, discretion, the mere infringement of Community law may be sufficient to establish the existence of a sufficiently serious breach ...'.

Point (c) is vague, not least because the obvious question to a lawyer is: what exactly are the aggrieved parties suing for? In many Member States there is no legal right to sue the government over domestic legislation. Now that the ECJ has decided that such an action is possible where breaches of Community Law are involved, how is the case to be framed (in lawyer's terms, *what is the cause of action*), and what are the practical effects such as the time limitations on bringing the claim? In *Norbrook* the ECJ stated that, as regards point (c): 'the State must make reparation for the consequences of the loss and damage caused, with the proviso that the conditions for reparation of loss and damage laid down by the national legislation must not be less favourable than those relating to similar domestic claims and must not be so framed as to make it in practice impossible or excessively difficult to obtain reparation.' And even on point (a), whereas the ECJ has applied the test very loosely in the past, we already have a much stricter approach from our own courts: *Three Rivers District Council* v *Bank of England* [1996] 3 All ER 558—where the Court held that the purpose of the directive in question was merely to harmonise banking systems; it had not been intended to confer rights on individuals.

10.4.3 Direct and Indirect Effect: a Working Example

Imagine that a new Council Directive has appeared—the Fairness in Life Assurance Contracts Directive. This seeks to impose a duty on insurance companies to identify and explain clearly all 'surrender value' clauses in their policies. You wish to stop payments on your life assurance and receive the surrender value of the policy. You are told by the company that the wording of their surrender value clause means that they do not have to pay anything. You claim that the company's clause does not comply with the Directive. Can you make use of the Directive?

To answer this you will need to take account of the following:

(a) Has the time passed when the Directive was meant to be implemented?	If not the Directive is, strictly, irrelevant.
(b) Assuming that the time period for implementation has passed, has the UK implemented the Directive?	(i) **If it has done so** then the primary source for establishing your rights will be the UK legislation and the Directive will be relevant only as an aid to interpretation (indirect effect).
	(ii) **If it has done so but there is a conflict** between the relevant UK legislation and the wording of the Directive (e.g. difference in wording or gaps in the UK Act), the wording of the Directive itself can be used if the Directive is certain enough to have direct effect (but this will only apply to cases of *vertical effect*, i.e. actions against the state).
	(iii) **If the UK has failed to implement the Directive at all**, the position is the same as in (ii) above. But, since our fictional case is a claim against an insurance company, vertical effect is of no use to you in (ii) or (iii) as the state is not a party to the action.
	(iv) As vertical direct effect is not relevant, and horizontal direct effect is not possible, the courts may invoke the principle of *indirect effect*.
(c) In any case, if the Government is at fault for not having implemented the Directive at all (or, more arguably, having implemented it incorrectly), the Government may be liable to individuals, companies' etc. under the *Francovich* principle.	**This applies whether the Directive does or does not have direct effect.** The Commission may also take action under Article 226 of the EC Treaty, but this is irrelevant to your particular claim.

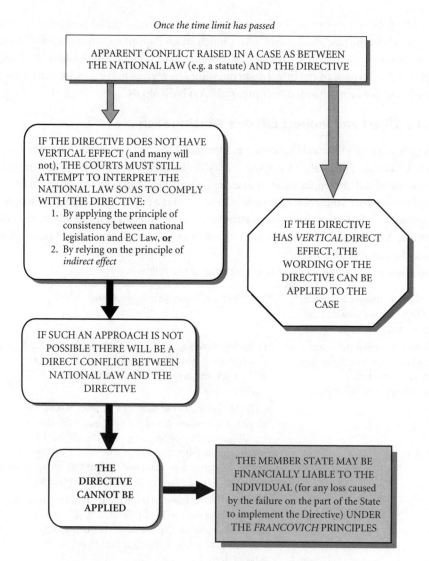

Once the time limit has passed

APPARENT CONFLICT RAISED IN A CASE AS BETWEEN
THE NATIONAL LAW (e.g. a statute) AND THE DIRECTIVE

IF THE DIRECTIVE DOES NOT HAVE
VERTICAL EFFECT (and many will
not), THE COURTS MUST STILL
ATTEMPT TO INTERPRET THE
NATIONAL LAW SO AS TO COMPLY
WITH THE DIRECTIVE:
  1. By applying the principle of
     consistency between national
     legislation and EC Law, **or**
  2. By relying on the principle of
     indirect effect

IF THE DIRECTIVE
HAS *VERTICAL* DIRECT
EFFECT, THE
WORDING OF THE
DIRECTIVE CAN BE
APPLIED TO THE
CASE

IF SUCH AN APPROACH IS NOT
POSSIBLE THERE WILL BE A
DIRECT CONFLICT BETWEEN
NATIONAL LAW AND THE
DIRECTIVE

THE
DIRECTIVE
CANNOT BE
APPLIED

THE MEMBER STATE MAY BE
FINANCIALLY LIABLE TO THE
INDIVIDUAL (for any loss caused
by the failure on the part of the State
to implement the Directive) UNDER
THE *FRANCOVICH* PRINCIPLES

Figure 10.3 Directive Improperly Implemented

We have sought to sum up this position in diagrammatic form (**Figures 10.3** and **10.4**).
We do not pretend that this level of uncertainty and complexity is justified.

10.4.4 The Style of Statutory Interpretation Employed

Historically, the Civil Law approach to statutory interpretation has been far more 'purposive' than that employed by the Common Law tradition. Civil Law legislation, and
therefore that of the EC also, is structured in a manner that is very different from English
Acts of Parliament. The *Civilian* tradition emphasises simplicity of drafting and a high

Once the time limit has passed

| INDIVIDUAL v. THE STATE *(a vertical action)* | INDIVIDUAL v. INDIVIDUAL *(a horizontal action)* |

THE DIRECTIVE HAS *VERTICAL* DIRECT EFFECT SO THE WORDING OF THE DIRECTIVE CAN BE RELIED UPON BY THE PARTIES

THE DIRECTIVE DOES NOT HAVE DIRECT EFFECT, SO THE WORDING OF THE DIRECTIVE CANNOT BE RELIED UPON BY THE PARTIES

THE COURT MAY ENFORCE THE PROVISIONS OF THE DIRECTIVE EVEN THOUGH THERE IS NO NATIONAL LEGISLATION

THE COURT WILL NOT ENFORCE THE DIRECTIVE

THE NATIONAL COURTS MUST STILL SEEK TO ACHIEVE THE PURPOSE OF THE DIRECTIVE (THROUGH THE USE OF THE CONCEPT OF 'INDIRECT EFFECT')

IF THIS IS NOT POSSIBLE

THE MEMBER STATE MAY BE FINANCIALLY LIABLE TO THE INDIVIDUAL (for any loss caused by the failure on the part of the State to implement the Directive) UNDER THE *FRANCOVICH* PRINCIPLES

Figure 10.4 Directive not Implemented at All

degree of abstraction; English Law statutes emphasise detail and comprehensiveness. What we saw in **Chapter 8**, however, is that the Common Law approach is changing inexorably, whether it is concerned with legislation derived from European sources or more 'home grown' material.

Although there has always been a battle between 'purposive' and 'literal' methods of interpretation in English law, it is undoubtedly true that a shift in balance occurred when English judges were called upon to apply Community legislation or to consider English statutes passed to fulfil an obligation under Community law. Throughout the 1970s the question of methods of interpretation arose in Court of Appeal cases such as *Bulmer* v *Bollinger* [1974] Ch 401; [1974] 2 All ER 1226, *Buchanan and Co. Ltd* v *Babco Forwarding and Shipping (UK) Ltd* [1977] 2 WLR 107; [1977] 1 All ER 518, and *Macarthys* v *Smith* [1979] 1 WLR 1189; [1979] 3 All ER 325.

The House of Lords has proved inconsistent in tackling this problem. Thus we find Lord Diplock advocating that *all* legislation passed since the UK's membership of the Community should be interpreted in the light of Community laws: see *Garland* v *British Rail* [1983] 2 AC 751; [1982] 2 All ER 402. Movement towards a more purposive approach (here, the use of Hansard) was seen in *Pickstone* v *Freemans* [1988] ICR 697; [1988] 2 All ER 803 and has been seen again in *Pepper* v *Hart*. But this more relaxed view was not reflected in the traditional approach evident in *Duke* v *GEC Reliance* [1988] AC 618; [1988] 1 All ER 626.

Again, the House of Lords completely (and openly) abandoned the literal approach in *Litster* v *Forth Dry Dock* [1990] AC 546; [1989] 1 All ER 1134 where the legislation in question (the Transfer of Undertakings (Protection of Employment) Regulations 1981) was derived from a Directive of the European Community. Instead of relying on a literal approach the Lords, particularly Lord Oliver, adopted a very wide purposive approach in line with European judges. However in *Finnegan* v *Clowney Youth Training Programme Ltd* [1990] 2 All ER 546, we have seen the House of Lords take an attitude which had all the hallmarks of 'We will fight them on the beaches...' written all over it. This was yet another addition to the long line of discrimination cases fought out between British and EC law.

The *Factortame* cases opened up a different angle of resistance. Here, the House of Lords originally deflected the arguments on interim protection by arguing (*per* Lord Bridge at [1990] 2 AC 85, 151) that the principles cited by the applicants were drawn, in effect, from *obiter* statements of the ECJ. Yet, as Gravells (1989:586) notes, 'the distinction between *ratio decidendi* and *obiter dicta* has no place in the jurisprudence of the European Court'. This view has been confirmed by the ECJ's reliance on the broad principles enunciated in those very cases when giving judgment both in the Article 234 proceedings in Case C–213/89 *R* v *Secretary of State for Transport, ex parte Factortame (No. 2)* [1991] 1 AC 603 and in the reference from the Divisional Court in the same matter—reported as Case C–221/89 *R* v *Secretary of State for Transport, ex parte Factortame (No. 3)* [1991] ECR I–3905; [1991] 3 CMLR 589; [1991] 3 All ER 769.

Most recently, however, the House of Lords in *Webb* v *EMO Air Cargo (UK) Ltd* [1993] 1 WLR 49 has sought to clarify the position. Lord Keith, in particular, recognised the fact that English courts must interpret domestic legislation in accordance with Community law as far as possible, provided that this can be achieved without distorting the meaning of the domestic legislation. Thus, it does not matter if the legislation in question is derived directly from European sources, and it does not matter whether the domestic legislation was adopted before or after any Community legislation. This pronouncement does not differ in many ways from that of Lord Templeman in *Duke* v *Reliance*, except that in *Webb* the House of Lords appears much more ready to give predominance to Community legislation and European styles of interpretation. This is partly because of the intervening 1990 ECJ decision in Case C–106/89 *Marleasing SA* v *La Comercial Internacional de Alimentación SA* [1990] ECR I–4135 (discussed below).

What are the other sources used by Civil lawyers to analyse legal problems?

Common to both traditions are sources such as legislation, case law, and custom. As we noted in **Chapter 8**, preparatory materials leading to legislation (*travaux préparatoires*) are given greater importance in statutory interpretation by the Civil system. Again in **Chapter 8** we noted the different approaches used by Civil Law lawyers and the Court of Justice, in contrast to Common Law lawyers, in interpreting legislation. We shall now explore these in greater detail under three headings.

(a) **Principles of interpretation**. In considering questions of interpretation Brown and Kennedy detail the options available to the court. They describe these as the literal, historical, contextual, comparative, and teleological methods. We shall briefly consider each of these in turn, but you are advised to refer to the fuller account in Brown and Kennedy (1994:302). It should be stressed that the ECJ is not bound to use only one approach; any one case may legitimately reflect a whole variety of judicial styles.

Like the English lawyer, the Civilian lawyers, too, recognise and make use of different styles of interpretation. First, there is the **literal** approach: it should come as no surprise that every court, not just English courts, turns first to the words of the text. But this is not the English law 'Literal Rule' in disguise. It is simply a common sense embarkation point which does not require the declaration of 'ambiguity' before it can be discarded. For a major difference between Common and Civil Law judges lies in the degree of willingness and freedom to move beyond the ordinary meaning of the words used.

In the Court of Justice, adherence to a literalist approach becomes even more difficult because, as we have already noted, texts have to be translated from one language to another: see, for instance Case C–372/88 *Milk Marketing Board* v *Cricket St Thomas Estate* [1990] ECR I–1345; [1990] 2 CMLR 800 on the meaning of 'pasteurised milk'. As Miers and Page note, however, there may also be a positive side to these linguistic differences: it may also be that 'the scope for doubt as to the meaning in one language may often be closed down by the language of the others' (1990:184).

Having at least noted the wording of the text, European judges have four methods at their disposal. The **historical** approach is described by David and Brierley as one 'clarifying present texts in the light of previous circumstances and taking into account the legislator's intention' (1985:125). Traditionally, European judges have been prepared to unearth the purpose behind legislation by examining what was actually intended by the legislature (i.e. by asking what was their 'subjective' intent). This has been achieved by turning to all manner of source documentation in the form of *travaux préparatoires*. Brown argues that the English mischief rule bears resemblance to this approach, though concentrating on a more limited and 'objective' assessment of legislative intent, as we saw in **Chapter 8**. There is an irony here. Whilst English lawyers are moving (slowly) towards admitting more in the way of *travaux préparatoires*, European lawyers have placed less reliance on such material.

The **contextual** approach, like the literal approach, concentrates upon the meaning of the words, except that it does not confine itself to investigating only the wording of *that* Act, but rather considers the whole legislative context. By this we mean that the court must consider the 'framework of Community law'—the interrelationship of all aspects of Community law: see Cases 90–91/63 *European Commission* v *Luxembourg and Belgium* [1964] ECR 625; Case 6/64 *Costa* v *ENEL* [1964] ECR 585. Brown and Kennedy regard this as one of the most important techniques used by the ECJ.

By **comparative** we mean that the judges of the ECJ are, by their very background, bound to draw upon their own experience as lawyers within the Member States. This means that inevitably the Court will seek to evaluate and maybe utilise solutions provided by the legal systems from which the judges are drawn, e.g., the adoption of the French Administrative law doctrine of *acte clair* to define when Article 234 reference is 'necessary': see Cases 28–30/62 *Da Costa en Schaake NV* [1963] ECR 31; *French Republic* v *Deroche, Cornet et Soc Promatex-France* [1967] CMLR 351. The term 'comparative' should not be taken as a euphemism for 'compromise'. The aim is to extract the appropriate principle, not to create some sort of mishmash.

Looking at the style of judicial pronouncements rather than any substantive law, it is also interesting that in recent years the influence of British judges has surfaced in ECJ decisions. Taking the case report as a whole, one can detect a greater tendency to explain decisions, analyse the points raised, and even consider previous cases in depth: a style of presentation more in keeping with Common Law than Civil Law: see, for instance, Case C–262/88 *Barber* v *Guardian Royal Exchange Assurance Group* [1990] ECR I–1889.

The last, but probably the most important, approach we need to consider is the **teleological** method (also known as the *schematic* approach). As we noted in **Chapter 8**, this may be defined as a broad 'purposive' approach which requires courts to place the legislation within the entire setting and spirit of Community law: see Case 106/77 *Amministrazione delle Finanze dello Stato* v *Simmenthal Spa* [1978] ECR 629. It is widely used by the ECJ, and increasingly employed by national courts in interpreting Community law. Thus, in *Murphy* v *An Bord Telecom Eireann* [1988] 2 CMLR 753, the Irish High Court held that where there was a right to 'equal pay for equal work' in accordance with Article 141, this must automatically include a right to equal pay for work of *greater* value. The Irish legislation stated only that equal pay was to be given for work 'equal in value'; and this had to be interpreted in keeping with the spirit of Article 139. As Keane J said, 'the literal construction . . . must give way in the present case to the teleological construction'.

(b) Doctrine. Legal writings (referred to as *doctrine*) hold a different place in the Civil system from that in the Common Law tradition. The status and influence of such writings are greater on the Continent than here. As we have seen, if one is seeking influence and authority as a writer on English law the general advice is to be ancient and dead. The continental academic lawyer is not required to make the same sacrifice. So, *doctrinal* writings hold a much more important place in the Civil system, though they are still not a formal source of law. The same is true of the American legal system, demonstrating that the relegation of legal writing is not a Common Law tradition, but an English law approach. Why this difference should exist is a question of history, prejudices, and attitude. The difference may be in the process of being eroded so that more heed will be paid to legal writers in English law.

(c) **General principles.** Finally, when all else fails—whether it is the analysis of a Code or the application of precedent—there is the ultimate fallback of 'general principles'. Some countries draw upon these unwritten rules because their Code allows them to do so, e.g. Spain and Italy. Others, such as France, discover them in the spirit and tradition of the law; often more assumed than debated. As Szladits and Germain point out (1985:44), it is in the systematising of these general principles that the role of *doctrine* can have its greatest effect. The Common Law too knows of 'general principles', though for the most part authority is still sought. Ultimately the Common Law lawyer will fall back on the notion that there exists an amorphous mass of laws termed 'The Common Law' from which the rules can be derived, or will refer to 'Equitable principles'.

The Court of Justice has developed its own sense of 'general principles' in the protection of fundamental human rights such as those found in the European Convention of Human Rights and Fundamental Freedoms. Thus we can discover principles of proportionality, equality, certainty, natural justice, and due process in the rulings of the Court of Justice (for a full discussion see Steiner and Woods (2001: chap. 6)).

10.5 CONCLUSION

There is a perceived difference between how the English lawyer and the continental lawyer approach their tasks. Much of the difference may, in the final analysis, be more to do with form than fundamentals. However, the difference is perceptible, and the reality is that it is the English lawyer who will have to change, more than his continental counterpart. Our system of precedent has been described as a system whereby 'we never clean our slates', or, more candidly, as an 'ungodly jumble'. It depends upon an immense network of narrow rules. It avoids working from general principles. It is only now, reluctantly, beginning to embrace purposiveness in interpretation. It rests on the sanctity of case law.

The contrast with Civil Law is obvious; perhaps the battle-lines are drawn. We may have to reassess the (perhaps apocryphal) headline in *The Times* early last century: 'Fog in the Channel—Europe Isolated'.

REFERENCES

*Bengoetxea, J. (1993), *The Legal Reasoning of the European Court of Justice* (Oxford: Clarendon Press).

Brown, L., and Kennedy, T. (1994), *The Court of Justice of the European Communities* (4th edn., London: Sweet & Maxwell).

Cohn, E. (1968), *Manual of German Law* (2 vols) (London: British Institute of International and Comparative Law).

Craig, P. (1997), 'Direct Effect, Indirect Effect and the Construction of National Legislation', 22 *European Law Review* 519.

*DAVID, R., and BRIERLEY, J. (1985), *Major Legal Systems in the World Today* (3rd edn., London: Stevens).

*DE BÚRCA, G. (1992), 'Giving Effect to European Community Directives', 55 *Modern Law Review* 215.

DOCKSEY, C., and FITZPATRICK, B. (1991), 'The Duty of National Courts to Interpret Provisions of National Law in Accordance with Community Law', 20 *Industrial Law Journal* 113.

GALMOT and BONICHOT (1988), 'La Cour de Justice des Communautés Européennes et la transposition des directives en droit national', 4 *Revue français de Droit administratif* 1.

GRAVELLS, N. (1989), 'Disapplying an Act of Parliament Pending a Preliminary Ruling: Constitutional Enormity or Community Law Right?', *Public Law* 568.

HARRIS, D., and TALLON, D. (1989), *Contract Law Today: Anglo-French Comparisons* (Oxford: Clarendon Press).

HARRISON, K. (1992), 'Pregnancy in the Court of Appeal', 142 *New Law Journal* 462.

*HORN, N., KÖTZ, H., and LESER, H. (1982), *German Private and Commercial Law: An Introduction* (Oxford: Clarendon Press).

KENNEDY, T. (1998), *Learning European Law* (London: Sweet & Maxwell).

LANGRISH, S. (1998), 'The Treaty of Amsterdam: Selected Highlights', 23 *European Law Review* 3.

LASOK, D., and BRIDGE, J.W. (1994), *Law and Institutions of the European Communities* (6th edn., London: Butterworths).

MARKESINIS, B. S. (1994), 'A Matter of Style', 110 *Law Quarterly Review* 607.

*MIERS, D., and PAGE, A. (1990), *Legislation* (2nd edn., London: Sweet & Maxwell).

NICHOLAS, B. (1992), *French Law of Contract* (2nd edn., London: Butterworths).

*SNYDER, F. (1993), 'The Effectiveness of European Community Law: Institutions, Processes, Tools and Techniques', 56 *Modern Law Review* 19.

*STEINER, J. (1993), 'From Direct Effect to *Francovich*: Shifting means of enforcement of Community Law', 18 *European Law Review* 3.

——. (1995) *Enforcing EC Law* (London: Blackstone Press).

*——, and Woods, L. (2000), *Textbook on EEC Law* (7th edn., London: Blackstone Press).

SZLADITS, C., and GERMAIN, C. (1985), *Guide to Foreign Legal Materials: French* (2nd edn., New York: Oceana Publishing).

WEATHERILL, S. (2000), *Cases & Materials on EEC Law* (5th edn., London: Blackstone Press).

11

Exploiting Legal Reasoning

In this chapter, we will consider explicitly the theories underpinning legal reasoning, and the way reasoning techniques are employed in legal contexts. In so doing we will examine, first, the logical foundations of legal reasoning, and then explore the extent to which legal reasoning requires us to consider criteria beyond those imposed by the strict necessity of logic (e.g. social values).

Law is often described as a system of 'practical reasoning'. We can see what this means when we think about what 'doing law' involves. Thus, a judge has to give judgment, lawyers have to advise their clients, legislators have to predict the impact of their laws. The key link between all these activities is that they are built upon some kind of reasoning process. The answers found by judges, lawyers, and legislators are not simply based upon some pre-existing knowledge of the law. Although the ability to find and use the various kinds of legal material is important, it is not enough, because your sources may not actually provide you with an answer. To be sure, there are some legal questions which can be resolved simply by looking the answer up in a book. If you wish to know what is the maximum compensation payable for, say, an unfair dismissal, you can find the answer in statute and statutory instrument, or in a textbook. But determining whether Jane Smith is likely to win her case, and what level of compensation she is likely to obtain cannot simply be looked up in a book. There is an important element of creativity, of working out an answer according to a whole range of supposedly rational criteria. In this and the following section, we are concerned with how lawyers must go beyond the legal texts, to *construct* their own answers to discrete legal problems. It is this that constitutes what we have already called the process of *legal argumentation* (see **Chapter 4** above).

Let's start by thinking about thinking itself. This is perhaps not something we are too used to doing, even in an educational setting. Obviously 'learning' is about acquiring new information—but don't forget that we have to be able to *use* that knowledge. Studying maths provides a good example. Mathematical skills reflect an ability to apply the appropriate formulae (knowledge) to a particular problem, e.g. calculating the sine of angle x in a triangle where the length of the sides are known. You might well know that the formula for that calculation is represented as:

$$\text{sine } x = \frac{opposite}{\text{hypotenuse}}$$

But that is not the end. You need to use that knowledge to produce a *specific* answer. That answer will of course vary according to the data you use. Similarly when structuring legal arguments we are working from a source of knowledge about law, and using that to construct an answer to a specific legal problem. It is the process of getting from knowledge to answer that involves our skills of practical reasoning. The aim of this chapter is to deepen our understanding of what this process involves.

11.1 Logic and Legal Reasoning

Legal argument is first based upon fundamental reasoning skills that are common to most disciplines. By 'reasoning', we mean, in essence, the process of deciding on a given course of action. It is important to distinguish 'reasoning' from the colloquial idea of 'having a reason'. Because we are rather careless in our use of language, it is easy, but wrong, to think of reasoning as simply a matter of cause and effect. It is not; reasoning reflects the ability to arrive at a rational, calculated decision.

Let us try to illustrate what we mean. If A hits B because B called him names, he has a reason. A is angry with B and has decided to hit him. Of course, since this is an emotional response, one could say it lacks rationality; in fact it is unlikely to be 'reasoned' at all in the true sense, since A's anger has probably prevented him from thinking through his actions. Would A have been so quick to hit B had he thought about it and realised that later B would come looking for him, with his brother, the champion boxer, seeking revenge? This emphasis upon rationality means that we are essentially grounding legal decisions in the mental process we call *logic*. This point is hardly new. Philip Leith (1991), for example, traces the contact between law and logic back through history to the Ancient Greeks, though, as his work shows, interest in the relationship has been given a modern boost by attempts to create computer models of legal decision-making. The link between law and logic has been frequently acknowledged by the judiciary, and notably by Lord Devlin in *Hedley Byrne* v *Heller & Partners* [1964] AC 465 at 516, where he said:

> The common law is tolerant of much illogicality, especially on the surface; but no system of law can be workable if it has not got logic at the root of it.

This is not to suggest that law is unusual; in much day-to-day life we are using basic logic without really knowing it. If I go out in the morning with only enough money for my bus fare back home, I have a simple choice: either I spend that money while out and walk home, or save it for the return bus ride. I know that I cannot do both. The conclusion that I have to choose is founded on a commonsense form of logic. Logic thus provides a commonplace basis for decision-making, by helping us plan our actions in a way that 'makes sense'. At this level, it is hardly surprising that logic is equally significant in helping us to make sense of legal argumentation; however, it is only fair to point out that the image of logic represented in this chapter is an extremely simplified one. Logic is a complex subject of academic concern in its own right, and, as Leith points out, the view that most individuals have of logic as clear and precise is erroneous; logicians are as prone to arguing about the merits of different theories and systems of logic as academics of other disciplines!

11.1.1 The Nature of Reasoning

Let us begin by formalising our notion of reasoning a little more clearly. We know that it reflects a particular kind of decision-making process, which, so far, we have described simply as 'rational'. By this, we mean that it is a structured form of discourse which involves passing from one proposition already known or assumed to be true, to another distinct from the first, but following from it. The classic example of the logical reasoning process is the 'syllogism', a verbal structure which draws a true conclusion from a major and minor premise, each of which is verifiable in its own right, thus:

> All men are mortal
> Socrates is a man
> Therefore Socrates is mortal

In this case the logic is impeccable. We know as a matter of fact that men are mortal; we also know that Socrates is a man. The conclusion of Socrates' mortality is therefore inescapable.

Now, in fact, this represents only one kind of logical reasoning. In logic conventionally we make a distinction between two different processes, called **inductive** and **deductive** reasoning. Robert M. Pirsig uses the example of locating a fault in a motor cycle to illustrate these logical modes in the process of scientific method. If the analogy seems rather out of place, persevere, because it is as applicable to lawyers as it is to scientists:

> Two kinds of logic are used, inductive and deductive. Inductive inferences start with observations of the machine and arrive at general conclusions. For example, if the cycle goes over a bump and the engine misfires, and then goes over another bump and the engine misfires..., and then goes over a long smooth stretch of road and there is no misfiring, and then goes over a fourth bump and the engine misfires again, one can logically conclude that the misfiring is caused by the bumps. That is induction: reasoning from particular experiences to general truths.
>
> Deductive inferences do the reverse. They start with general knowledge and predict a specific observation. For example, if from reading the hierarchy of facts about the machine, the mechanic knows the horn of the cycle is powered exclusively by electricity from the battery, then he can logically infer that if the battery is dead the horn will not work. That is deduction. (1974:107)

There is an important distinction between these modes of reasoning. The form of deductive reasoning is such that, so long as the major and minor premises are correctly constructed, the conclusion has to be true. Thus the syllogism we have just considered is a representation of the form of deductive reasoning. Inductive reasoning does not provide us with the same degree of certainty. We can reach an answer inductively on the basis of an assumption that our particular experience is of general application. In some cases, such as Pirsig's for example, our assumption is likely to be pretty accurate, and obviously the more information we have supporting our hypothesis, the more likely it is to stand up in the future. But, in terms of formal logic, we cannot say that our conclusion is conclusive. There is always the possibility that some other conclusion exists.

For example, Patrick Shaw (1981) tells of an experiment conducted in Birmingham some years ago. Drivers in the city were urged to use only dipped headlights at night.

During the experiment, it was shown that the number of road accidents had fallen sharply. The local papers immediately declared the experiment to have been a major success. However, it was subsequently found that there had been fewer vehicles on the road than usual during the experiment, so the press had not really got it right. There may have been some correlation between the dipped headlights and the reduction in accidents, but the connection was not as great as had been assumed. The relative inconclusiveness of inductive reasoning is a point to which we shall return shortly.

Lawyers use both inductive and deductive reasoning, and legal decision-making will usually involve *both* those modes, used in conjunction with each other to produce a reasoned conclusion. It is, however, helpful to distinguish between a number of processes. First, in reasoning about legal rules, as we have seen, we conventionally distinguish between two distinct contexts: the interpreting of statutes and the use of precedent through case law. Secondly, lawyers are also involved in reasoning about facts (what we shall call, following Alexy (1989), **empirical reasoning**). We will consider each of these in turn.

11.1.2 Reasoning and Precedent

Using precedent involves both deductive and inductive reasoning, but of these the inductive element is the most important.

Inductive reasoning in law can, in its simplest terms be described as follows:

> In case x, factors A, B and C existed. Judgment was given for the claimant.
> In case y, factors A, B and C existed. Judgment was given for the claimant.
> In case z, factors A, B and C exist. Judgment should, therefore, be given for the claimant.

It is thus a process of reasoning by example. It is a technique that we have all used. A child may well reason that it is safe to climb a tree in a friend's garden, because that friend has just done so without falling. That child has reasoned, inductively from the example of his or her friend.

Edward Levi (1949:2) developed this idea into what he called a 'three step process' of legal reasoning:

- *Step one* is where a judge sees a relevant factual similarity between an earlier case, or cases, and the present one.

- In *step two*, the judge identifies the rule of law on which the previous case(s) rested.

- Finally (*step three*) he or she applies that rule to the present case.

It is this final stage only, of applying the rule, that is deductive. As MacCormick (1978: 197) puts it, 'deduction comes in only after the interesting part of the argument, settling the ruling in law, has been carried through.' One of the clearest judicial examples to this effect comes from Lord Hailsham in *DPP* v *Morgan* [1976] AC 464 at 516. The case concerned the question whether an honest but unreasonable belief that the victim consented to sexual intercourse could negative the necessary intent on a charge of rape. His lordship identified the following legal propositions as being correct: *If*...the prohibited act in rape is non-consensual sexual intercourse *and* the guilty state of mind is an intention to commit' the prohibited act, *then*, he argued, an honest but mistaken belief as to consent must result in an acquittal (our emphasis, to highlight the deductive element of the argument). In effect, all he is saying is that the accused lacked the necessary intent, but the strength of the argument lies, in his lordship's view, in the fact that to convict would result in a logical absurdity. Up to this point in the reasoning, however, judges use an inductive process, often also called **reasoning by analogy** (though note, as a side issue, that there is a technical dispute between legal theorists about the nature of what is going on in this process and what we should call it—see **Figure 11.1**).

In practice, of course, the process of reasoning from cases is not quite as straightforward as the first example we gave. More often, it involves weighing up and balancing a whole variety of differences and similarities. It will be unusual for the analogy to be so clear, and what is more likely is that only a few of the common factors (for example, **A** and **B**, but not **C**) will be present in the later case, so the judge must weigh up the relative importance of **C** in deciding whether to apply the analogy. We have already given you an example of that kind of technique in **Chapter 6**. This reflects the fact that **inductive/ analogical reasoning cannot be conclusive**. Inductive/analogical reasoning is not about *proof* (unlike deductive reasoning); it is purely about *justification*. A case analogy justifies a later decision, it does not make it, logically, the only possible outcome. To use our earlier example, the child will not know conclusively that the climb will be safe. His or her friend may be lighter, stronger, or taller, all of which might make a difference to the outcome of the climb. It will be up to the child to weigh up the risks and decide whether the example is good enough to follow.

Equally, it follows that the inductive stages inevitably involve a degree of discretion. Levi's first step gives the judge freedom of action in deciding what similarities—and differences as well—are relevant. In step two, the judge again has some freedom in deciding what rules of law are discoverable from the earlier cases (this is part of what in **Chapter 4** we called the judge's freedom of justification). A judge is obliged to follow a precedent only once satisfied that *the precedent fits*. By this we mean that the judge must have first

---

Induction or Analogy: Is there a difference?

Some writers (e.g. Golding, 1984) seek to distinguish 'true' induction from a related process—which they believe is the one used by lawyers—called reasoning by analogy, whereas others (e.g. Levi, 1949; Brewer, 1996; Farrah, 1997) seem to treat inductive reasoning and reasoning by analogy as synonymous. To be sure, there is much that these writers agree on. Inductive reasoning/reasoning by analogy clearly involves a process of pattern-matching from previous examples. As Levi notes, finding cases with appropriate similarities is a critical first stage in the process. Where the theoretical dispute emerges is with respect to what follows this stage: having found the cases, how does the judge create his analogy? Thus, Brewer argues that the judge discovers (or constructs) a *general* rule that explains the examples—strictly an inductive process, while Golding favours the idea of an 'instance classification without generalisation', i.e., a genuine analogical process of reasoning by inference from *the specific to the specific*.

Philosophically, Golding undoubtedly has a point; analogy is a species of induction, but it is a sub-set that tends to be inferentially weaker. At the same time, we suggest that it is probably sensible to take the view that *both* the processes we have just described operate in Common Law systems—both reasoning by analogy from a specific set of facts and reasoning inductively from a set of cases, the latter arising where precedent has effectively hardened into an established Common Law principle.

Figure 11.1 Induction or Reasoning by Analogy?

accepted that the facts are, in material respects, sufficiently similar, and that the legal principle established in the earlier case(s) should apply.

This is also gives us a clue to the main means we have for countering an argument based on analogy or inductive reasoning, namely demonstrating that the analogy is not a good fit. In law, this is what we do when we seek to *distinguish* a case, e.g., by saying the similarities are insufficient or insufficiently important, or by proposing another, better, analogy. Of course, this is not the same as proving the analogy demonstrably and finally false; indeed, inductive reasoning cannot readily be refuted in that way.

11.1.3 Reasoning and Statutory Interpretation

Using Pirsig's analogy from section 11.1.1, consider the following question:

EXERCISE 19 **Zen and the art of legal reasoning?**

Statute requires that whosoever takes property belonging to another, with the intention of permanently depriving the other of it, shall be guilty of an offence.

X deliberately takes Y's bicycle and sells it to Z.

Has X committed the above offence?

This is, of course, a simple example—but in reaching the logical conclusion that X is guilty, were you using inductive or deductive reasoning?

The process you used is in fact deductive. Our starting point is a general rule, laid down in a statute, which we are then applying to a specific instance. We could convert this into a syllogism, thus:

> An individual who takes another's property
> with the intention permanently to deprive that
> other of it, shall be guilty of an offence.
> The accused X has committed the prohibited act
> Therefore X is guilty of the offence

A general way of looking at this would be to say that the legal syllogism involves the following elements:

(a) A rule of general application (*the major premise*);

(b) the particular fact(s) (*the minor premise(s)*);

(c) A legal outcome (*the conclusion*).

On the face of it, therefore, statutory interpretation seems to be chiefly a deductive process. However this is something of an oversimplification. 'Pure' deductive reasoning can be used only when applying clear rules to specific fact situations (MacCormick, 1978). Statutory interpretation, however, will often involve a significant element of inductive reasoning or analogy, notably where:

• the meaning of words used may be derived from analogous statutory provisions

• there are doubts about the scope of a statutory rule which have to be resolved on the basis of competing precedents.

Consequently it is a mistake to think of case law and statute as involving wholly separate reasoning processes. As our second point highlights, it is not unusual for cases which turn on a question of statutory interpretation to require the court to look at competing arguments about statutory meaning which have existing authority derived from case law. For example, in *R* v *Shivpuri* [1987] AC 1; [1986] 2 All ER 334, a case we have already considered, the essential problem was one of interpreting the scope of section 1 of the Criminal Attempts Act 1981. However, the House of Lords could not treat that simply as a question of interpreting the Act; it was required, by the rules of precedent, to consider the meaning given to the Act by an earlier House of Lords decision in the case of *Anderton* v *Ryan* [1985] AC 560; [1985] 2 All ER 355, and had to justify their decision accordingly.

Where a decision is based on deduction, how can it be challenged? As we have already noted, the difference between induction and deduction is primarily the difference between providing justification for and proof of an outcome. Consequently, where a decision is deductively correct, it cannot, logically, be gainsaid. It follows that the means of challenging deductive reasoning are limited. Nevertheless, they exist:

Denying the premise

If you can show the major (statement of the rule) or minor premise (statement of fact) is false, you can defeat the argument. For example:

> All cows eat grass
> Cows are mammals
> Therefore all mammals eat grass

In fact this syllogism is totally wrong. All we have are two independent statements: cows are mammals and they eat grass. Not only do the initial premises not establish a basis for saying that all mammals eat grass (there is no evidence here about the eating habits of other mammals, nor is there anything which predicates a sufficient similarity between cows and other mammals), the minor premise is flawed. If you think about it, it is really a rule (major premise) masquerading as a fact. Unsurprisingly, then, the conclusion as a matter of logic just does not follow.

By changing one or other of the premises to its 'correct' form we change the pathway through the problem, and hence the conclusion. So we could say:

> All cows eat grass
> Buttercup is a cow
> Therefore Buttercup eats grass

What this actually means in law is that you will attempt to challenge those elements of the reasoning that are more likely to have been arrived at inductively in the first place—the formulation of the rule, or the statement of fact.

Question the validity of the logic

Even where the major and minor premises are verifiable, they may not lead to the conclusion alleged; for example, consider the following syllogism:

> All MPs are elected
> The Mayor of London is elected
> Therefore the Mayor of London is an MP

The fallacy in the reasoning here can be exposed by reducing the syllogism to its basic logical structure. If we take the Buttercup syllogism as an example of one that works, it takes the form

> All As = B
> if C = A
> Then C = B

By contrast, the Mayor of London syllogism reduces to the form

> All As = B
> if C = B
> then C = A

and the fault in the reasoning becomes obvious. Judges are not likely to make this kind of mistake. Law students sometimes do. You have been warned!

11.1.4 Reasoning in Civil Law Systems

Before we move on, we shall consider, briefly, whether the Civilian tradition reflects a significantly different approach to legal reasoning.

Michel Villey makes the point that:

> Even today English law is the closest to the casuistic art of the classical Roman jurists. The law for the [English student] . . ., is above all a matter of science; or rather of case law; because the law is to be induced from nature, and by the study of each case. (1975:700)

So, do we assume from this that the role of induction, and hence of analogy, is of far less significance in continental European legal systems? Unfortunately it is not that simple. Legal theorists recognise that, in Civilian systems too, legal reasoning takes on a hybrid form which is neither wholly deductive nor inductive. There are, however, two distinctive features of Civilian systems which suggest some substantive differences from the Common Law lawyer's logic.

First, the codes are often said to provide an axiomatic basis for legal rules. By this we mean that they constitute often complete, self-contained principles of law. Secondly, as we have seen, precedent plays a lesser role in Civil Law systems, because of the interpretive traditions connected with codified law. Taken together these might indicate that deduction plays a larger role in Civil Law systems. However, the axiomatic basis of many of the codes only *reduces* (but does not obliterate) the need for the judges to reason from analogy.

The use of reasoning from analogy can certainly be traced back to the techniques used in Roman law and passed down to us through the Civilian tradition in the work of the mediaeval scholars we collectively term the 'Glossators' and (later) the 'Commentators' (see Robinson *et al.*, 1994). For them the distinction between *comprehensio legis* (the process of interpreting legislation) and *extensio legis* (the procedures for supplementing legislation) was already well understood. Within this tradition, two distinct analogical processes have been recognised (see, e.g., Zaccaria, 1991: 49–56; Esser, 1972).

First there is the notion of the *analogia legis*—the use of a single, statutory analogy (*Gesetzesanalogie* in German) to fill a gap in the legislation identified by a new or unforeseen situation. This operates by the court saying, in effect, 'the principle in Article 123 governs not only case A but also case B'. Cees Maris (1991:71) offers an example from Dutch Criminal Law which, interestingly, resonates in English law as well.

Under the Dutch Penal Code of 1881, the offence of theft required, *inter alia*, that the accused 'take away' property belonging to another. In 1920, a Dutch dentist was convicted of theft for 'milking' his electricity meter, i.e. extracting electricity by bypassing the meter. He argued that, as electricity was an intangible, it could not be 'taken away' since that term (in its Dutch linguistic context) referred only to tangible property. Unfortunately for the dentist, the Dutch Supreme Court disagreed; it felt that extracting electricity was sufficiently similar to a taking away of tangible property to be caught by the Code.

An interesting comparison can be made with England, where a similar problem has arisen both under the old Larceny Acts and under the Theft Act 1968 that replaced them. In *Low v Blease* [1975] Crim LR 513, the Divisional Court held that electricity was not 'appropriated' (the Theft Act alternative to 'taking away' used in the Larceny Act 1916) by switching on the current, nor, the court said, could electricity constitute 'property' within section 4 of the Theft Act. It may be that the Divisional Court was unduly influenced by the fact that a separate offence of abstracting electricity had been created by the Theft Act 1968, section 13, as a way of dealing with milking the meter and similar situtions (see *Boggeln v Williams* [1978] Crim LR 242), but its literalism was in stark contrast to the willingness of the Dutch court to reason, creatively, by analogy. As the commentary to *Low v Blease* points out, the decision does leave us with the rather bizarre situation where a 'trespasser who warms himself by lighting the gas fire is guilty of burglary while the trespasser who prefers the electric fire is not' ([1975] Crim LR 513). Clearly there are analogies and analogies.

Secondly, there is the *analogia juris*, which describes what German jurisprudence would call a legal analogy (*Rechtsanalogie*) as opposed to statutory analogy. This is where the judge reasons from outside the specific case or rule, usually by arguing that it is illustrative of a wider principle of law which can be applied to the new situation. Thus, for example, it is commonly accepted in the jurisprudence of many Civil systems that judges may need to take an approach to resolving cases based on a sense of 'justice' (in Germany, again, one finds direct reference to this as the *Rechtsgefühl*) rather than on statutory rules. In French private law, for example, the judges have developed a theory of abuse of rights (*l'abus des droits*). This is sometimes used, *inter alia*, in contractual disputes to impose obligations on the contracting parties in much the same way as the English courts have used the notion of 'implied terms'.

Today, the use of certain general principles has become so formalised that, in some cases, the courts no longer rely on the process of analogy for justification. Rather, these fundamental general principles have effectively hardened into a source of law in their own right. Indeed, in some countries, the right of recourse to general principles has become enshrined in the codified law: see, e.g., Article 6 of the Spanish Civil Code. Such general principles, including the principles of proportionality or reasonableness, meaning that state intervention must be restricted only to that which is necessary to achieve the aim of a particular law, operate in a number of domestic legal systems as well as in EC and European Human Rights law (as we saw in **Chapters 9** and **10**). Ultimately, therefore, we suggest that much of the supposed divergence between Civil and Common Law techniques involves drawing a distinction without a measurable difference.

11.1.5 Empirical Reasoning

Solving legal problems, we know, is not simply a question of reading the law. Legal arguments are not constructed in a vacuum, but arise out of real, human, situations. Legal rules are expressed only in very general terms. The application of a rule to a particular case is dependent ultimately on the court or tribunal deciding that the facts of that case fit the rule. This conceals what are in reality, as Ivainer (1988) notes, two distinct processes: the proving of alleged facts (see **Chapter 4**); and the subsequent interpretation of those same facts. The latter involves a reasoning process. It is up to the lawyers to construct a legal argument to the effect that the facts are x, y, and z, and that on those facts the rules should be applied in such-and-such a way. It is this aspect of the law–fact relationship that we shall concentrate upon for the remainder of this section, as the actual implications of finding that x is fact rather than law is best left to courses on the law of evidence, or on the particular area of substantive law concerned.

At the heart of empirical reasoning is what Ivainer (1988:22) defines as 'une démarche hermeneutiqué, i.e. a hermeneutic, or interpretive, process which seeks to draw a conclusion from the known facts in each case. This emphasis on interpretation is valuable in that it highlights again the extent to which the use of facts in the legal system involves a creative process, which we shall now examine.

From the perspective of the trial lawyer, as opposed to the judge, there are two discrete reasoning techniques that are central to the process of fact analysis. At the early stages of a case, the body of evidence relating to the case is likely to be incomplete; the first task of the lawyer is thus to establish what is sometimes called 'a theory of the case' (see Anderson & Twining, 1991; Maughan & Webb, 1995:chap. 3)—i.e. a plausible explanation of what may have happened and its legal consequences, which can then be used to assist further information-gathering. Developing a theory of the case itself involves two elements: the creation of both legal and factual theories. By *legal theory* we mean simply the creation of arguments for one or more potential causes of action, i.e. a claim for breach of contract, negligence, etc. Although a legal theory is triggered by the factual information you have available, it also underpins the process of fact analysis. A lawyer's legal theory is critical in determining how he or she organises and explains the facts of the case. As Paul Wangerin explains:

> Surprisingly, few lawyers and students seem to realize that creating a statement of facts must follow, rather than precede, creating the legal arguments. This chronology must be observed because the statement of facts plays two crucial roles for the advocate. The second role necessitates this order of preparation . . . [T]he statement of facts' first role is to generate psychological sympathy for the represented client. This role has nothing to do with the merits of any legal position . . . The statement of facts' second role is to prepare the reader for the legal arguments to follow. This is its key role, which explains why the legal theory must always be planned first. (1986:435–6)

Creating a *factual theory* involves what is termed abductive reasoning. Anderson and Twining define this as 'a creative process of using known data to generate hypotheses to be tested by further investigation' (1991:443). It is thus a style of reasoning that is essentially based on *inference*—on using your existing knowledge to infer potential facts and explanations. For example, assume that Lisa approaches you for advice. She tells you that her brother, Bart, was recently killed when his car ploughed through a motorway barrier and overturned. The road was quite wet when the accident happened, but no other car was involved in the accident. She cannot tell you whether there are any witness statements relating to the accident. She is convinced that there must be some explanation, other than Bart's own negligence. The accident occurred soon after he left home; he was not overtired, and he was an experienced and careful driver.

You know that, if you are to help your client, you need to establish that someone (other than Bart) was negligent or the vehicle was defective. So you would start by thinking about a legal theory of the case based either on negligence or, possibly, product liability. What factual theories might you develop? If no other car was involved, you might infer that you should rule out the negligence of another driver. So, alternatively, there is the possibility of a mechanical defect. You could hypothesise along the following lines—was the steering faulty; did a tyre burst, and, if so, was the burst due to a manufacturing defect or some other cause? And so on. Equally, you would have to consider the possibility of driver error: despite his sister's protestations, could Bart have fallen asleep at the wheel, for instance? To get an idea of abductive reasoning in action, see if you can construct a theory suggesting that there was negligence by another driver. (We pause here while you write.)

There are a number of possibilities. Perhaps a vehicle pulled into the lane too close to the front of Bart's car, causing him to brake hard and lose control on the wet road. Perhaps a vehicle in front temporarily lost control, because the driver fell asleep, or lost concentration, causing Bart to take avoiding action from which he was unable to recover, given the conditions. In both situations it is quite conceivable that the car causing the accident was not then caught up in it.

The key point to remember is that these are no more than hypotheses based on limited information. This means that, though akin to the inductive form of reasoning, the results of abductive reasoning are far more tentative, and would not be sufficient to persuade a court in your favour. To take the example above, it is pretty obvious that you would not get very far alleging that the accident was due to a burst tyre without evidence from a police accident report that a tyre had indeed burst, and expert evidence supporting your theory that the burst was due to defective manufacture. However, you must recognise that abductive reasoning techniques are necessary to establish the possibility that such an argument exists, before you can think about obtaining the evidence to change the possibility into a specific, supportable, theory at a later stage in the pre-trial process.

Once you have the evidence to establish a supportable theory, the reasoning process moves on to a second stage. Now your empirical reasoning falls firmly within the inductive sphere. Shakespeare, as usual, offers a suitably gory illustration (from *Henry VI*):

> Who finds the heifer dead and bleeding fresh,
> And sees fast bye a butcher with an axe;
> But will suspect twas he that made the slaughter.

Inductively, the conclusion that it was the butcher who did it is acceptable. It is not of course, in formal logic, the only possible answer, but it is *probable*. In any given case of induction the probability will vary by degrees from the slight to the overwhelming—as we have seen already, the law sets its own standards of probability in fact-finding. Deductive reasoning, because it requires that the formal conclusion is absolute, not merely probable, plays little part in empirical reasoning, because the facts are seldom conclusive. The process, therefore, is essentially one of mustering the information that you have, and using it to draw logical inferences regarding the guilt/innocence/liability of a particular person.

In seeking to resolve factual problems there are a number of useful techniques, though in the end much of this boils down to careful application of common sense.

First, think dialectically: essentially all this means is that you need to think through alternative explanations. Do not be afraid to challenge your own assumptions. It is not advisable to develop your own theory of why or how something happened, and ignore other possibilities. This applies as much to the student answering a problem question (where there will often be gaps in the facts waiting for you to construct alternative solutions) as it does to the practitioner preparing a case.

Secondly, be systematic. It is usually important to have an accurate picture of the nature and course of events in order to create a structure within which you can develop your argument.

Thirdly, and following from the above, proceed step by step in presenting the facts of a case. Proof is best built up in small stages. Making major quantum leaps from fact to conclusion may help in developing an initial strategy, but it is unlikely to build a convincing case. This too doubles as sound advice in dealing with problem questions as a student.

11.2 The Limits of Logic

In looking at the limits of logic, we shall again divide the issues into their two constituent areas of legal rules and facts.

11.2.1 Reasoning about Legal Rules

Under this heading there are two points to make. First, it follows from what we have already said that the form of logic in legal reasoning is qualitatively different in legal as opposed to scientific method. Secondly, the courts are willing to impose practical or policy-based limits on the extent to which they will apply logic. Let us consider each point in turn.

Earlier we suggested that reasoning is about discovering the truth. In law, we are not concerned with truth (or facts, if you prefer) in a scientific, i.e. verifiable, sense. The statement 'water is wet' is verifiable—no one would question the truth of that. Also in scientific method, logic enables prediction, so that it is possible to say that if conditions A and B are satisfied then C will follow as a matter of necessity. In law, we are dealing with rules which are—to use the technical jargon—**normative statements**. This means that they are based essentially upon a value judgement made by Parliament or a judge that a particular consequence *should* or *ought to* follow certain behaviour. The normative nature of law does not mean that we are stepping outside the realm of induction, but it does introduce the qualitative difference between legal and scientific method that was intimated. This was explained by the American jurist Karl Llewellyn (1960):

> in law your logical system refuses to remain on the level of description, of arranging existing observation. Backed by the fact and doctrine of precedent, your logical system shifts *its content* to the level of Ought (this does not affect the logic). Its remarks change in tone and substance. Now they run: '*If I am a correct description of the accepted doctrine*, the future cases *a* and *b* are to have the outcome *x*—they *should* have that outcome, and if the judge is on the job he will see to it that they do.'. . . No longer are these initial data statements *merely* of how courts have held on given facts. They have—thanks to the addition of precedent—become each one a statement simultaneously of how a court *has* held, and in addition how future courts *ought* to hold.

Let's look more closely at this statement in respect of two issues: first, the problem of defining accepted doctrine, and, secondly, the question of the relationship between prediction and what we shall call 'public policy'.

Defining legal doctrine

Llewellyn's 'if' in the above extract is crucial. As we have already seen from Levi's three-step process, the existence of competing analogies means that the arguments in law are not necessarily just about the logical deductions in step three, but about the premises upon which deduction is to be based. The difficult questions for law tend to be located at the point of defining 'accepted doctrine', and it is there that pure logic is often of little help. We can illustrate this by looking at two contrasting decisions of the Employment Appeal Tribunal (EAT) in the cases of *Kidd* v *DRG (UK) Ltd* [1985] ICR 405 and *Clarke* v *Eley (IMI) Kynoch Ltd* [1983] ICR 165. Both cases arose on very similar facts whereby the applicants had alleged that redundancy schemes operated by their respective employers were contrary to the Sex Discrimination Act 1975 in that, by selecting part-time workers for redundancy first, they indirectly discriminated against women, and married women in particular, who were disproportionately dependent upon part-time employment.

The legal basis of the women's claim, and the defence raised by the employers in each case, were also closely comparable. In *Clarke*, the EAT had found in favour of the women applicants, but in *Kidd* a differently constituted tribunal came to the opposite decision. How could this be? Had a strict analogy been applied, then *Kidd* should have followed *Clarke*. In departing from the latter, Waite J, giving the decision of the EAT in *Kidd*, recognised that their decision left the concept of indirect discrimination 'exposed to criticism by the orderly minded as lacking form or precision' (at 417). Clearly this did not unduly worry the tribunal; in fact, just the reverse, since they justified the refusal to apply *Clarke* on the ground that they wished to preserve flexibility in this area of law by avoiding drawing general principles from specific cases. In other words, the tribunal was really *rejecting* the need to define a precise legal doctrine in the first place!

Prediction and public policy

Llewellyn's reference to outcomes means that we are preserving the element of prediction based upon logical deduction, but the legal context changes the nature of that prediction from one of fact to one of value, or, if you prefer, from 'is' to 'ought'. This change is vital. We can see that there is a major qualitative difference between 'is' and 'ought' statements. A parent's comment that a naughty child *is* going to be smacked obviously has a very different meaning from an onlooker's observation that the child *ought* to be smacked.

Precedents in law are very much the second kind of statement. They show that there may be an answer which logic predicts should apply, but what if that runs contrary to the system of values held by the judge deciding a case which is analogous to the precedent? Is he bound to follow it? The answer is plainly no. The judicial ability to distinguish what are perceived to be 'awkward' precedents can often provide a judge who is sufficiently determined not to apply precedent strictly with the means of so doing. Similarly, in statutory interpretation, the element of choice between literal and purposive approaches also reduces predictability. In short, differences within accepted legal methods can justify different results.

The role of theoretical logic is thus limited by the fact that it may take the judge only as far as identifying a number of rational options. From there, the values that the legal system is seen to serve will play a significant part. This is often explicitly recognised in the legal process by reference to such terms as 'public policy' or 'public interest' (for a similar exposition in a Civil Law context, see Ghestin & Goubeaux, 1983:46–7). The idea of public policy has always played some part in the legal process. Many of the more recent innovative developments in the law have come about precisely because the judges have stopped to ask 'what is the best policy for the law to adopt'? Examples of this kind of reasoning have influenced developments in both the Common Law and the application of statute law. Thus, Lord Atkin's 'neighbour principle', developed in *Donoghue v Stevenson* [1932] AC 562, was clearly actuated by his lordship's belief that a generally applicable test for negligence was desirable. The case could have been resolved without the 'neighbour principle', as established criteria already existed which could have included the issue of manufacturer's liability raised by the facts of that case. Moreover, *Donoghue v Stevenson* would not have become a landmark case if other judges had chosen to interpret it restrictively rather than expansively (freedom of justification again!).

Similarly, questions of value cannot be excluded from the process of statutory interpretation. We cannot just sit down and logically analyse an Act of Parliament without taking any account of a whole variety of variables, including not least judicial attitudes to that legislation. In particular, any judicial claim to be adopting a broadly purposive approach to statutory interpretation is likely to disclose some element of policy analysis—as in the abortion law case of *Royal College of Nursing* v *DHSS* [1981] AC 800; [1981] 1 All ER 545. Historically, the extent to which judges depend upon policy arguments has not been openly acknowledged, for fear that the judges would be seen as adopting a 'political' law-making role as opposed to a 'legal' interpretive role (see Frank, 1947), however, this narrow view of judicial intervention has been largely rejected by academics and by increasing numbers of the judiciary in recent years.

Equally the judge may not be endorsing a specific public policy argument, but arguing from a more generalised sense of what is right. This is sometimes signalled in the courts by reference to concepts such as 'justice' or 'equity'. The meaning of such terms is, of course, virtually impossible to pin down with any degree of certainty—and indeed they have been the subject of debate among legal theorists for centuries! Nevertheless they provide a useful, but unpredictable, mechanism for a lawyer to favour one (more or less) rational answer over another. This can be illustrated by the case of *DPP* v *Majewski* [1977] AC 443. Like *Morgan*, this was a case dealing with the problem of *mens rea* in rape. However, here, the court refused to be swayed by the logical argument that if a person is incapable through drink of forming the requisite intent to commit the crime, he cannot be guilty of it. In finding that an intoxicated accused lacking intent could still be guilty of rape, certain members of the House of Lords recognised that they were departing from logic, but, in the words of Lord Salmon, to do so in this case accorded with 'justice, ethics and commonsense' (at 484).

The point is that pure logic does not necessarily give the desired answer, and may be, therefore, of limited value in predicting future decisions. To return to our original simile, the observer's prediction that the child ought to be smacked will be a pretty poor predictor if the parent is actually opposed to corporal punishment. Legal arguments and decisions are inevitably influenced by the values of the actors within the legal process, and there is thus no guarantee that what is formally logical will necessarily be 'right'.

In recognising this gap between logic and 'good law' (whatever that may be), we must recognise that the limiting of logic carries with it a definite cost. That is, that the introduction of policy or of notions of 'justice' creates greater uncertainty in legal reasoning. We might argue that it is worth the cost, because it enables the judges, and hence the law, to be responsive to changes in (say) social or economic conditions, or to cases which are taken to be exceptional. In responding to such changes, the judges are inevitably acting with a degree of subjectivity. This is not necessarily to imply political bias, but, given the homogeneity of the English judiciary, there is some recognition that the judiciary tends to speak with the voice of the 'Establishment'. As a senior judge admitted some years ago:

Impartiality is rather difficult to obtain in any system. I am not speaking of conscious impartiality, but the habits you are trained in, the people with whom you mix, lead to your having a certain class of ideas of such a nature that, when you have to deal with other ideas, you do not give as sound and accurate judgments as you would wish. (Scrutton LJ, 1923:8)

Whether, therefore, the judiciary is well placed to evaluate the demands of public inter-est or policy is a debatable question, though one that goes beyond the scope of this book. It is, however, worth noting that a number of academic critiques (notably Griffith, 1997) have suggested that it frequently fails in that evaluation. Ultimately, the significance of such value-based reasoning might also lead us to question whether there is, in reality, any truly deductive basis within legal reasoning as practised; though this too remains an issue over which legal theorists are themselves divided.

The growing recognition amongst philosophers that formal logic perhaps does not play as major a part in legal reasoning as we may have assumed has re-opened interest in a sister discipline called **Rhetoric** (see Goodrich, 1986:168–208). Put simply, rhetoric is the art of constructing an argument. Like logic, it recognises that a persuasive argument must be built upon certain rules. The father of what is now called the 'New Rhetoric', Professor Chaim Perelman, argued that:

> the domain of argumentation is that of the likely, the plausible, the probable, to the extent that the latter escapes mathematical certitude (1963:134).

In this way rhetoric has always recognised that truth is contingent, and the establishment of any version of 'the truth' is dependent upon argument. Historically this meant the religious, political, and legal emphasis on oral argument central to Ancient Greek and also Roman society; hence the colloquial understanding of rhetoric as oratory or 'speechifying'. Current legal interest in rhetoric has understandably centred upon this emphasis on argu-mentation and its opposition to formal reasoning processes. As an alternative view on the construction of legal arguments it has been significant in the development of elements of European Critical Legal Theory (Goodrich, 1986; cf. Alexy, 1989).

11.2.2 Reasoning about Facts

In empirical reasoning, the quality of our decisions on the facts of a case will be depend-ent upon the quality of the fact-finding process, and it is this relationship which probably constitutes the greatest limit on the role of logic in empirical reasoning. We have already considered, in **Chapter 4**, some of the problems of fact finding. Here, we intend to develop some of those issues in a more abstract and theoretical fashion.

Most cases that come before a court concern a dispute over the facts. *R v Wallace*, discussed in Chapter 4, is a prime example. The difficulties referred to by the Court of Criminal Appeal in that case did not concern tricky questions of law, but arose in trying to sort out what actually happened.

The first limitation we explore concerns the way in which lawyers perceive facts. In the classic type of problems set by law teachers, that issue normally does not arise. You will be given a set of 'facts' and asked to advise on the law. Though such exercises have practical value in developing problem-solving skills, they inevitably bypass this rather funda-mental issue.

Formal definitions of 'fact' in the abstract are, as we have shown, thin on the ground; though there are plenty of cases where the judges have to decide whether a particular issue is one of fact or law. This reflects the commonsense approach to facts, which says (to put it a little crudely): 'we all know what a fact is, don't we? Facts are things we know to be true. They just exist. So what's the problem?'. We argue that this level of certainty itself is a problem. Our sense of what is fact is largely based upon observation (what we perceive with one of our five senses) or else some more abstract form of knowledge (generally 'received wisdom', or, e.g., in a more specialised sense, a forensic scientist's, or other specialist's, expertise). The danger is of treating instances of 'observation' or 'knowledge' as absolute truths—a fallacy we first discussed in the context of **Chapter 4**. In law, fact-finding is not that simple. We know that one and one make two, but in the courts facts have to be established from a very unscientific source—us! Kohler's famous drawing of the goblet/faces is an example of the kind of difficulty we must deal with (see **Figure 11.2**).

If I tried to describe this I might simply say that I saw the profiled faces of two people, staring at each other from close to. That might be an accurate, and therefore 'true', description, because it might be all that I saw. If another person described accurately a drawing of a goblet she had been shown, would you necessarily realise that each of us was describing the same thing? Two individual perceptions of the same fact may thus be very different, because there may well be equally valid alternative forms of explanation.

This example does not take into account another variable, which is the quality of the observation. Considerable psychological research into skills of observation has emphasised human fallibility (Lloyd-Bostock, 1988:3–23). To put it bluntly; we are not particularly good at remembering what we have seen or heard or done. To make matters worse, the more time that passes between the event and the point of recall and the more stress we were under at the time the event happened, the less accurate our recollections are likely to be.

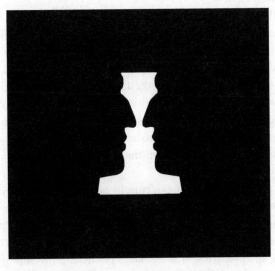

Figure 11.2 Kohler's Goblet/Faces

Stress or external factors may not be the only cause of unreliability. The internalised values of a particular witness may, consciously or unconsciously, influence testimony; personal expectations or prejudices may well play an important part. For example, Mr Brown lives in a wealthy suburb of town which has suffered a recent spate of burglaries. One day he sees two cars drive slowly down his road. The first is driven by Mrs Smith, the second by Mr Jones. He informs the police about Mr Jones, but does not mention Mrs Smith because he does not think it relevant. Why? Because Mr Brown may be influenced by his own value judgements of what is suspicious behaviour. He may assume that a woman is less likely to be engaged in criminal activity than a man; if Mrs Smith is well dressed and in a smart car, while Mr Jones is badly dressed and in a battered old car, he may be more likely to consider Mr Jones's behaviour deviant, and so on. In recent decades, some scientists and social scientists have come together to argue that we too easily disregard the extent to which what we call 'knowledge' is not wholly objective, but socially constructed. This is what Hanson means by his observation: 'seeing is a theory-laden undertaking' (1958:19). This applies not just to lay witnesses, but also to expert evidence.

Expert evidence is quite commonly used in court to establish technical evidence outside the competence of lawyers and ordinary witnesses—the cause of an accident, the handwriting on a letter, the ballistics of a particular gun are all likely subjects of expert testimony. Given the adversarial nature of proceedings, each side may have its own experts, whose opinions may well be diametrically opposed. This is because expert testimony, which may reflect on not only what has happened, but also a version of how or why, will depend heavily upon the individual's perspective on his or her subject. Courtrooms can often become a point at which different 'world views' meet head-on.

This is a tendency which is exacerbated by the manner in which such evidence is used in the trial process. To explain this, let us consider an example from a real, American, case which is of some notoriety.

On 30 March 1981, John Hinckley attempted to assassinate the US President, Ronald Reagan. The assassination attempt failed, though four people, including the President, received bullet wounds from Hinckley's gun. Hinckley was arrested on the spot and subsequently put on trial for attempted murder (see Low et al., 1986). His (successful) defence was one of insanity, and it was the facts that would be used to establish that defence which, even more than the celebrity of his intended victim, caught the public attention. It soon emerged that Hinckley was obsessed with the actress Jodie Foster, then a student at Yale University. He had written to her, phoned her, and followed her repeatedly, and, a fact that was to take on major significance in the trial, watched her in the film *Taxi Driver* over fifteen times.

Taxi Driver became a key piece of evidence in establishing Hinckley's insanity. It was alleged that Hinckley had been particularly influenced by a leading character in the film, the lonely and mentally unstable taxi driver Trevis Bickle, who was befriended by the young prostitute portrayed by Jodie Foster. Of critical importance was the fact that, in the film, Bickle was stalking and preparing to assassinate a politician who employed a woman with whom Bickle had unsuccessfully tried to form a relationship. Using *Taxi Driver* as evidence, the defence sought to show that Hinckley's behaviour was consistent with schizophrenia. It was argued that there were clear links between the actions of Bickle and the formulation of Hinckley's bizarre plan to assassinate Reagan and thereby 'rescue' Foster. In essence, it was argued that Hinckley had adopted the persona of Bickle, and turned the fantasy into his own 'reality'. Conversely, the prosecution sought to show that although he may have held certain false beliefs or delusions, this proved only that Hinckley was a 'dreamer'— an essentially ordinary man—and not that he was mentally ill. In an intriguing re-evaluation of the case, Rosanne Kennedy (1992) has focused on the ways in which expert explanations of Hinckley's behaviour and beliefs were polarised by the advocates into sets of binary images: rational/irrational; real/imaginary; mad/bad. As she concludes:

> Over and over, the trial lawyers force essentially indeterminate medical testimony into categories of truth or falsity, thereby masking the undecidability on which the insanity defence is based. (1992:21)

The role of the advocate in creating an image of the 'facts' of a case, therefore, should not be overlooked. It is worth thinking back to the quotation from Paul Wangerin, cited earlier in this chapter. What Wangerin is stressing is not just an analytical technique, but a *rhetorical* device. It is a creative use of fact whereby the statement of facts is constructed so as to support the legal argument and persuade an adjudicator of its correctness. Do not forget that this is a technique used not only by advocates. Judges may also use the statement of facts as a rhetorical device, as we have seen from Lord Denning's judgment in *Miller* v *Jackson* in **Chapter 4**.

This limited objectivity in fact-finding has important implications in the legal context. It means that there is often something to be said both supporting and denying the existence of a supposed fact, to the extent that it may be difficult to establish that one party's assertion constitutes fact at all. It is hardly surprising that many cases revolve around disputed testimony from witnesses about their observations. The uncertainties of fact-finding in law led some legal theorists to become what have been described as 'fact-sceptics'—theorists who have used the uncertainty of the fact-finding process to challenge the rationality of legal decision-making—the most famous of these was the American Jerome Frank, who once, succinctly if provocatively, argued that 'facts are guesses' (1949). Although such fact-scepticism may seem negative, it provides an important insight into the legal process. By recognising that 'truth' in the courtroom is established by the court arriving at an agreed view of events, rather than by discovering an absolute reality, we are recognising both the extent to which facts have to be created in court, and the extent to which that means that inferences drawn upon legally established facts may be based upon uncertain foundations. This much has been admitted extra-judicially by the Australian judge, Fox J when he said:

> When it is said that the rules of evidence tend to the ascertainment of truth, the most that can be meant is that by their application a particular piece of evidence may be more reliable, or may be the more correctly assessed by the tribunal. This may or may not be the effect in relation to a particular piece of evidence, but one cannot by any process of aggregation of those pieces have any assurance that what is seen as the resultant situation (the ultimate proposition, or finding on the issue) accords with the truth. (1982:152)

The extent to which facts are established according to rules of evidence and procedure may itself set a further limit on the value of logic to empirical reasoning. The point is that the application of such rules may not accord with strict logic, but with other values endorsed by the legal system. As Fox J points out, these rules frequently depend upon the demands of expediency, such as expense or delay to proceedings, or upon substantive claims of public policy (for example the assumption, only recently challenged, that the evidence of young children is inherently unreliable, and therefore insufficient by itself to ground a criminal conviction), rather than any devotion to the ascertainment of truth.

We thus concur with Professor Julius Stone in his description of the limits of logic:

> the outcomes of 'pure' logical procedures do not correspond to what necessarily is (or will become) law of any actual community. They may be invaluable for criticising existing legal propositions by reference to a hypothetical model of internal logical consistency or . . . to test the extent to which a legal system can be conceived as a logically consistent set of legal propositions . . . These are all legitimate outcomes of logical analysis; but they must always be carefully distinguished from erroneous uses of these outcomes. (1985:45–6)

The various forms of uncertainty we have discussed suggest that the best that *we* can try to achieve is to ensure that our arguments or decisions are essentially rational in the way they are structured, and that they take into account the considerations of legal principle and/or public policy that seem to apply. In this final section which follows, we suggest a practical technique for structuring legal decisions that you will be able to use.

11.3 The Decision Analysis Method

The technique we are about to describe is derived from techniques of decision analysis in business decision-making. The idea of decision analysis is a useful one. Keeney and Raiffa summarise its aims succinctly:

> The major role of formal analysis is 'to promote good decision-making' . . . As a process, it is intended to force hard thinking about the problem area: generation of alternatives, anticipation of future contingencies, examination of . . . effects, and so forth. (in Moore & Thomas, 1988:245)

Do not be put off by this; the model we have adopted is a much simplified version of the original, which has been adapted to fit the legal context more closely. It also builds on the basic techniques of problem solving that we have already discussed. The method involves six steps.

(i) *Structure the problem:* make sure you know who you are and for whom you are acting; in practice, begin to establish the parameters of your theory of the case (in a 'law school' problem, simply identify your relevant facts).

(ii) *Identify alternative courses of action:* e.g., do the facts disclose an action in contract and/or tort (e.g., the possibility of an action on the basis of both negligent misrepresentation and negligent misstatement); civil and/or criminal proceedings; multiple or alternative grounds for proceeding (e.g., theft and handling of stolen goods;

innocent or negligent misrepresentation); a court action or some alternative form of resolution (e.g., a common law action for wrongful dismissal and an unfair dismissal claim before an industrial tribunal)?

(iii) *Determine your objectives:* what does the 'client' want—compensation; some other remedy (e.g., injunction, specific performance) or just advice as to his or her liability?

(iv) *Assess the consequences:* will each of your alternative courses of action achieve the objectives you have identified? For example, it may be little consolation advising X that he might be able to sue Y for trespass (by Y stealing fruit from his orchard), if X is concerned at his own liability to Y for the injuries that Y suffered being chased off the land by X's Doberman dog! Discard any alternatives that are clearly incompatible with your objectives. By this stage you should have a clearer idea of the facts that will be material to your case.

(v) *Identify and account for uncertainty:* what are the main uncertainties you face— are there gaps in the facts, or alternative arguments that may be constructed from the same facts; contradictory precedents; ambiguous wording in the Act creating liability, etc. (in which case, can you create rational arguments supporting your case)? Are there strong policy arguments which might sway a court one way or another? Determine which of these uncertainties you can resolve and which you cannot.

(vi) *Evaluate your remaining alternatives:* taking into account the uncertainties you face, decide which alternative(s) come(s) closest to achieving your objective(s).

This technique is not foolproof—none is! Ultimately it can only be as good as your initial preparation. Do bear in mind that a decision-making technique such as this is dependent upon your doing sufficient thorough research into the issues first—it cannot make a poorly prepared argument look good!

REFERENCES

ALEXY, R. (1989), *A Theory of Legal Argumentation* (trans. R. Adler & N. MacCormick) (Oxford: Clarendon Press).

ANDERSON, T., and TWINING, W. (1991), *Analysis of Evidence* (London: Butterworths).

BREWER, S. (1996), 'Exemplary Reasoning: Semantics, Pragmatics and the Rational Force of Legal Argument by Analogy', 109 *Harvard Law Review* 923.

ESSER, J. (1972), *Vorverständnis und Methodenwahl in der Rechtsfindung* (Frankfurt: Athenäum).

FARRAR, J. (1997), 'Reasoning by Analogy in Law', 9 *Bond Law Review* 149.

FOX, MR JUSTICE R. (1982), 'Expediency and Truth-Finding in the Modern Law of Evidence' in Campbell & L. Waller (eds.), *Well and Truly Tried* (Sydney: Law Book Co).

*FRANK, J. (1947), 'Words and Music: Some Remarks on Statutory Interpretation', 47 *Columbia Law Review* 1267.

—— (1973), *Courts on Trial* (Princeton, NJ: Princeton University Press).

GHESTIN, J., and GOUBEAUX, G. (1983), *Traité de droit civil: introduction générale* (2nd edn., Paris: Librairie générale de droit et de jurisprudence).

GOLDING, M. (1984), *Legal Reasoning* (New York: Alfred Knopf).

*GOODRICH, P. (1986), *Reading the Law* (Oxford: Basil Blackwell).

GRIFFITH, J. (1997), *The Politics of the Judiciary* (5th edn., London: Fontana Press).

*HANSON, N. (1958), *Patterns of Discovery: an Inquiry into the Conceptual Foundations of Science* (Cambridge: Cambridge University Press).

IVAINER, T. (1988), *L'interprétation des faits en droit* (Paris: Librairie générale de droit et de jurisprudence).

KENNEDY, R. (1992), 'Spectacular Evidence: Discourses of Subjectivity in the Trial of John Hinckley', III(1) *Law and Critique* 3.

LEITH, P. (1991), *The Computerised Lawyer* (London: Springer-Verlag).

LEVI, E. (1949), *An Introduction to Legal Reasoning* (Chicago, Ill.: University of Chicago Press).

*LLEWELLYN, K. (1960), *The Bramble Bush* (New York: Oceana Pub).

*LLOYD-BOSTOCK, S. (1988), *Law in Practice* (London: British Psychological Society/Routledge).

LOW, P., *et al.* (1986), *The Trial of John W. Hinckley, Jr.: A Case Study in the Insanity Defence* (New York: The Foundation Press).

MACCORMICK, N. (1978), *Legal Reasoning and Legal Theory* (Oxford: Clarendon Press).

MARIS, C., (1991), 'Milking the Meter: On Analogy, Universalisability and World Views' in P. Nerhot (ed.), *Legal Knowledge and Analogy: Fragments of Legal Epistemology, Hermeneutics and Linguistics* (Dordrecht: Kluwer).

MAUGHAN, C., and WEBB, J. (1995), *Lawyering Skills and the Legal Process* (London: Butterworths).

MOORE, P., and THOMAS, H. (1988), *The Anatomy of Decisions* (2nd edn., London: Penguin Books).

PERELMAN, C. (1963), *The Idea of Justice and the Problem of Argument* (trans. J. Petrie) (London: Routledge & Kegan Paul).

*PIRSIG, R. (1974), *Zen and the Art of Motor Cycle Maintenance* (London: The Bodley Head).

ROBINSON, O., FERGUS, T., and GORDON, W. (1994), *European Legal History* (2nd edn., London: Butterworths).

SCRUTTON, LORD JUSTICE (1923), 'The Work of the Commercial Courts', 1 *Cambridge Law Journal* 6.

SHAW, P. (1981), *Logic and Its Limits* (London: Penguin).

STONE, J. (1985), *Precedent and Law: Dynamics of Common Law Growth* (Sydney: Butterworths).

VILLEY, M. (1975), *La formation de la pensée juridique moderne* (4th edn., Paris: Les Editions Montchretien).

WANGERIN, P. (1986), 'Skills Training in Legal Analysis: A Systematic Approach', 40 *University of Miami Law Review* 409.

ZACCARIA, G. (1991), 'Analogy as Legal Reasoning: The Hermeneutic Foundation of the Analogical Procedure' in P. Nerhot (ed.) *Legal Knowledge and Analogy: Fragments of Legal Epistemology, Hermeneutics and Linguistics* (Dordrecht: Kluwer).

Index